GO!

with Microsoft®

Excel 2007

Brief

Shelley Gaskin and Alicia Vargas

PEARSON

Prentice Hall

Upper Saddle River, New Jersey

This book is dedicated to my students, who inspire me every day, and to my husband, Fred Gaskin.
—Shelley Gaskin

This book is dedicated with all my love to my husband Vic, who makes everything possible;
and to my children Victor, Phil, and Emmy, who are an unending source of inspiration
and who make everything worthwhile.
—Alicia Vargas

Library of Congress Cataloging-in-Publication Data

Gaskin, Shelley.
  GO! with Excel 2007 brief / Shelley Gaskin and Alicia Vargas Pearson.
    p. cm.
  ISBN 0-13-513003-4
  1. Microsoft Excel (Computer file) 2. Business--Computer programs.
  3. Electronic spreadsheets. I. Vargas, Alicia. II. Title.
  HF5548.4.M523G374 2008
  005.54--dc22

2007011742

Vice President and Publisher: Natalie E. Anderson
Associate VP/Executive Acquisitions Editor,
  Print: Stephanie Wall
Executive Acquisitions Editor, Media: Richard Keaveny
Product Development Manager: Eileen Bien Calabro
Senior Editorial Project Manager: Laura Burgess
Development Editor: Ginny Munroe
Editorial Assistants: Becky Knauer, Lora Cimiluca
Executive Producer: Lisa Strite
Content Development Manager: Cathi Profitko
Senior Media Project Manager: Steve Gagliostro
Production Media Project Manager: Lorena Cerisano
Director of Marketing: Margaret Waples
Senior Marketing Manager: Jason Sakos
Marketing Assistants: Angela Frey, Kathryn Ferranti
Senior Sales Associate: Rebecca Scott

Managing Editor: Lynda J. Castillo
Manufacturing Production Project Manager:
  Wanda Rockwell
Production Editor: GGS Book Services
Photo Researcher: GGS Book Services
Manufacturing Buyer: Natacha Moore
Production/Editorial Assistant: Sandra K. Bernales
Design Director: Maria Lange
Art Director/Interior Design: Blair Brown
Cover Photo: Courtesy of Getty Images, Inc./Marvin
  Mattelson
Composition: GGS Book Services
Project Management: GGS Book Services
Cover Printer: Phoenix Color
Printer/Binder: RR Donnelley/Willard

Microsoft, Windows, Word, PowerPoint, Outlook, FrontPage, Visual Basic, MSN, The Microsoft Network, and/or other Microsoft products referenced herein are either trademarks or registered trademarks of Microsoft Corporation in the U.S.A. and other countries. Screen shots and icons reprinted with permission from the Microsoft Corporation. This book is not sponsored or endorsed by or affiliated with Microsoft Corporation.

Credits and acknowledgments borrowed from other sources and reproduced, with permission, in this textbook are as follows or on the appropriate page within the text.

    Pages 2, and 112: iStockphoto.com; and page 196: Dorling Kindersley Media Library.

10 9 8 7 6 5 4 3
ISBN 0-13-513003-4

Contents in Brief

Table of Contents

Letter from the Editor

Dear Instructors and Students,

The primary goal of the *GO!* Series is two-fold. The first goal is to help instructors teach the course they want in less time. The second goal is to provide students with the skills to solve business problems using the computer as a tool, for both themselves and the organization for which they might be employed.

The *GO!* Series was originally created by Series Editor Shelley Gaskin and published with the release of Microsoft Office 2003. Her ideas came from years of using textbooks that didn't meet all the needs of today's diverse classroom and that were too confusing for students. Shelley continues to enhance the series by ensuring we stay true to our vision of developing quality instruction and useful classroom tools.

But we also need your input and ideas.

Over time, the *GO!* Series has evolved based on direct feedback from instructors and students using the series. *We are the publisher that listens.* To publish a textbook that works for you, it's critical that we continue to listen to this feedback. It's important to me to talk with you and hear your stories about using *GO!* Your voice can make a difference.

My hope is that this letter will inspire you to write me an e-mail and share your thoughts on using the *GO!* Series.

Stephanie Wall
Executive Editor, *GO!* Series
stephanie_wall@prenhall.com

GO! System Contributors

We thank the following people for their hard work and support in making the *GO!* System all that it is!

Additional Author Support

Coyle, Diane	Montgomery County Community College
Fry, Susan	Boise State
Townsend, Kris	Spokane Falls Community College
Stroup, Tracey	Amgen Corporation

Instructor Resource Authors

Amer, Beverly	Northern Arizona University	Paterson, Jim	Paradise Valley Community College
Boito, Nancy	Harrisburg Area Community College	Prince, Lisa	Missouri State
Coyle, Diane	Montgomery County Community College	Rodgers, Gwen	Southern Nazarene University
Dawson, Tamara	Southern Nazarene University	Ruymann, Amy	Burlington Community College
Driskel, Loretta	Niagara County Community College	Ryan, Bob	Montgomery County Community College
Elliott, Melissa	Odessa College		
Fry, Susan	Boise State	Smith, Diane	Henry Ford Community College
Geoghan, Debra	Bucks County Community College	Spangler, Candice	Columbus State Community College
Hearn, Barbara	Community College of Philadelphia	Thompson, Joyce	Lehigh Carbon Community College
Jones, Stephanie	South Plains College	Tiffany, Janine	Reading Area Community College
Madsen, Donna	Kirkwood Community College	Watt, Adrienne	Douglas College
Meck, Kari	Harrisburg Area Community College	Weaver, Paul	Bossier Parish Community College
Miller, Cindy	Ivy Tech	Weber, Sandy	Gateway Technical College
Nowakowski, Tony	Buffalo State	Wood, Dawn	
Pace, Phyllis	Queensborough Community College	Weissman, Jonathan	Finger Lakes Community College

Super Reviewers

Brotherton, Cathy	Riverside Community College	Maurer, Trina	Odessa College
Cates, Wally	Central New Mexico Community College	Meck, Kari	Harrisburg Area Community College
		Miller, Cindy	Ivy Tech Community College
Cone, Bill	Northern Arizona University	Nielson, Phil	Salt Lake Community College
Coverdale, John	Riverside Community College	Rodgers, Gwen	Southern Nazarene University
Foster, Nancy	Baker College	Smolenski, Robert	Delaware Community College
Helfand, Terri	Chaffey College	Spangler, Candice	Columbus State Community College
Hibbert, Marilyn	Salt Lake Community College	Thompson, Joyce	Lehigh Carbon Community College
Holliday, Mardi	Community College of Philadelphia	Weber, Sandy	Gateway Technical College
Jerry, Gina	Santa Monica College	Wells, Lorna	Salt Lake Community College
Martin, Carol	Harrisburg Area Community College	Zaboski, Maureen	University of Scranton

Technical Editors

Janice Snyder
Joyce Nielsen
Colette Eisele
Janet Pickard
Mara Zebest
Lindsey Allen
William Daley

Student Reviewers

Allen, John	Asheville-Buncombe Tech Community College	Erickson, Mike	Ball State University
		Gadomski, Amanda	Northern Michigan University
Alexander, Steven	St. Johns River Community College	Gyselinck, Craig	Central Washington University
Alexander, Melissa	Tulsa Community College	Harrison, Margo	Central Washington University
Bolz, Stephanie	Northern Michigan University	Heacox, Kate	Central Washington University
Berner, Ashley	Central Washington University	Hill, Cheretta	Northwestern State University
Boomer, Michelle	Northern Michigan University	Innis, Tim	Tulsa Community College
Busse, Brennan	Northern Michigan University	Jarboe, Aaron	Central Washington University
Butkey, Maura	Central Washington University	Klein, Colleen	Northern Michigan University
Christensen, Kaylie	Northern Michigan University	Moeller, Jeffrey	Northern Michigan University
Connally, Brianna	Central Washington University	Nicholson, Regina	Athens Tech College
Davis, Brandon	Northern Michigan University	Niehaus, Kristina	Northern Michigan University
Davis, Christen	Central Washington University	Nisa, Zaibun	Santa Rosa Community College
Den Boer, Lance	Central Washington University	Nunez, Nohelia	Santa Rosa Community College
Dix, Jessica	Central Washington University	Oak, Samantha	Central Washington University
Moeller, Jeffrey	Northern Michigan University	Oertii, Monica	Central Washington University
Downs, Elizabeth	Central Washington University	Palenshus, Juliet	Central Washington University

Pohl, Amanda	Northern Michigan University	Shanahan, Megan	Northern Michigan University
Presnell, Randy	Central Washington University	Teska, Erika	Hawaii Pacific University
Ritner, April	Northern Michigan University	Traub, Amy	Northern Michigan University
Rodriguez, Flavia	Northwestern State University	Underwood, Katie	Central Washington University
Roberts, Corey	Tulsa Community College	Walters, Kim	Central Washington University
Rossi, Jessica Ann	Central Washington University	Wilson, Kelsie	Central Washington University
Shafapay, Natasha	Central Washington University	Wilson, Amanda	Green River Community College

Series Reviewers

Abraham, Reni	Houston Community College
Agatston, Ann	Agatston Consulting Technical College
Alexander, Melody	Ball Sate University
Alejandro, Manuel	Southwest Texas Junior College
Ali, Farha	Lander University
Amici, Penny	Harrisburg Area Community College
Anderson, Patty A.	Lake City Community College
Andrews, Wilma	Virginia Commonwealth College, Nebraska University
Anik, Mazhar	Tiffin University
Armstrong, Gary	Shippensburg University
Atkins, Bonnie	Delaware Technical Community College
Bachand, LaDonna	Santa Rosa Community College
Bagui, Sikha	University of West Florida
Beecroft, Anita	Kwantlen University College
Bell, Paula	Lock Haven College
Belton, Linda	Springfield Tech. Community College
Bennett, Judith	Sam Houston State University
Bhatia, Sai	Riverside Community College
Bishop, Frances	DeVry Institute—Alpharetta (ATL)
Blaszkiewicz, Holly	Ivy Tech Community College/Region 1
Branigan, Dave	DeVry University
Bray, Patricia	Allegany College of Maryland
Brotherton, Cathy	Riverside Community College
Buehler, Lesley	Ohlone College
Buell, C	Central Oregon Community College
Byars, Pat	Brookhaven College
Byrd, Lynn	Delta State University, Cleveland, Mississippi
Cacace, Richard N.	Pensacola Junior College
Cadenhead, Charles	Brookhaven College
Calhoun, Ric	Gordon College
Cameron, Eric	Passaic Community College
Carriker, Sandra	North Shore Community College
Cannamore, Madie	Kennedy King
Carreon, Cleda	Indiana University—Purdue University, Indianapolis
Chaffin, Catherine	Shawnee State University
Chauvin, Marg	Palm Beach Community College, Boca Raton
Challa, Chandrashekar	Virginia State University
Chamlou, Afsaneh	NOVA Alexandria
Chapman, Pam	Wabaunsee Community College
Christensen, Dan	Iowa Western Community College
Clay, Betty	Southeastern Oklahoma State University
Collins, Linda D.	Mesa Community College
Conroy-Link, Janet	Holy Family College
Cosgrove, Janet	Northwestern CT Community
Courtney, Kevin	Hillsborough Community College
Cox, Rollie	Madison Area Technical College
Crawford, Hiram	Olive Harvey College

Crawford, Thomasina	Miami-Dade College, Kendall Campus
Credico, Grace	Lethbridge Community College
Crenshaw, Richard	Miami Dade Community College, North
Crespo, Beverly	Mt. San Antonio College
Crossley, Connie	Cincinnati State Technical Community College
Curik, Mary	Central New Mexico Community College
De Arazoza, Ralph	Miami Dade Community College
Danno, John	DeVry University/Keller Graduate School
Davis, Phillip	Del Mar College
DeHerrera, Laurie	Pikes Peak Community College
Delk, Dr. K. Kay	Seminole Community College
Doroshow, Mike	Eastfield College
Douglas, Gretchen	SUNYCortland
Dove, Carol	Community College of Allegheny
Driskel, Loretta	Niagara Community College
Duckwiler, Carol	Wabaunsee Community College
Duncan, Mimi	University of Missouri-St. Louis
Duthie, Judy	Green River Community College
Duvall, Annette	Central New Mexico Community College
Ecklund, Paula	Duke University
Eng, Bernice	Brookdale Community College
Evans, Billie	Vance-Granville Community College
Feuerbach, Lisa	Ivy Tech East Chicago
Fisher, Fred	Florida State University
Foster, Penny L.	Anne Arundel Community College
Foszcz, Russ	McHenry County College
Fry, Susan	Boise State University
Fustos, Janos	Metro State
Gallup, Jeanette	Blinn College
Gelb, Janet	Grossmont College
Gentry, Barb	Parkland College
Gerace, Karin	St. Angela Merici School
Gerace, Tom	Tulane University
Ghajar, Homa	Oklahoma State University
Gifford, Steve	Northwest Iowa Community College
Glazer, Ellen	Broward Community College
Gordon, Robert	Hofstra University
Gramlich, Steven	Pasco-Hernando Community College
Graviett, Nancy M.	St. Charles Community College, St. Peters, Missouri
Greene, Rich	Community College of Allegheny County
Gregoryk, Kerry	Virginia Commonwealth State
Griggs, Debra	Bellevue Community College
Grimm, Carol	Palm Beach Community College
Hahn, Norm	Thomas Nelson Community College
Hammerschlag, Dr. Bill	Brookhaven College
Hansen, Michelle	Davenport University
Hayden, Nancy	Indiana University—Purdue University, Indianapolis

Hayes, Theresa	Broward Community College	Lord, Alexandria	Asheville Buncombe Tech
Helfand, Terri	Chaffey College	Lowe, Rita	Harold Washington College
Helms, Liz	Columbus State Community College	Low, Willy Hui	Joliet Junior College
Hernandez, Leticia	TCI College of Technology	Lucas, Vickie	Broward Community College
Hibbert, Marilyn	Salt Lake Community College	Lynam, Linda	Central Missouri State University
Hoffman, Joan	Milwaukee Area Technical College	Lyon, Lynne	Durham College
Hogan, Pat	Cape Fear Community College	Lyon, Pat Rajski	Tomball College
Holland, Susan	Southeast Community College	MacKinnon, Ruth	Georgia Southern University
Hopson, Bonnie	Athens Technical College	Macon, Lisa	Valencia Community College, West Campus
Horvath, Carrie	Albertus Magnus College		
Horwitz, Steve	Community College of Philadelphia	Machuca, Wayne	College of the Sequoias
Hotta, Barbara	Leeward Community College	Madison, Dana	Clarion University
Howard, Bunny	St. Johns River Community	Maguire, Trish	Eastern New Mexico University
Howard, Chris	DeVry University	Malkan, Rajiv	Montgomery College
Huckabay, Jamie	Austin Community College	Manning, David	Northern Kentucky University
Hudgins, Susan	East Central University	Marcus, Jacquie	Niagara Community College
Hulett, Michelle J.	Missouri State University	Marghitu, Daniela	Auburn University
Hunt, Darla A.	Morehead State University, Morehead, Kentucky	Marks, Suzanne	Bellevue Community College
		Marquez, Juanita	El Centro College
Hunt, Laura	Tulsa Community College	Marquez, Juan	Mesa Community College
Jacob, Sherry	Jefferson Community College	Martyn, Margie	Baldwin-Wallace College
Jacobs, Duane	Salt Lake Community College	Marucco, Toni	Lincoln Land Community College
Jauken, Barb	Southeastern Community	Mason, Lynn	Lubbock Christian University
Johnson, Kathy	Wright College	Matutis, Audrone	Houston Community College
Johnson, Mary	Kingwood College	Matkin, Marie	University of Lethbridge
Johnson, Mary	Mt. San Antonio College	McCain, Evelynn	Boise State University
Jones, Stacey	Benedict College	McCannon, Melinda	Gordon College
Jones, Warren	University of Alabama, Birmingham	McCarthy, Marguerite	Northwestern Business College
Jordan, Cheryl	San Juan College	McCaskill, Matt L.	Brevard Community College
Kapoor, Bhushan	California State University, Fullerton	McClellan, Carolyn	Tidewater Community College
Kasai, Susumu	Salt Lake Community College	McClure, Darlean	College of Sequoias
Kates, Hazel	Miami Dade Community College, Kendall	McCrory, Sue A.	Missouri State University
		McCue, Stacy	Harrisburg Area Community College
Keen, Debby	University of Kentucky	McEntire-Orbach, Teresa	Middlesex County College
Keeter, Sandy	Seminole Community College	McLeod, Todd	Fresno City College
Kern-Blystone, Dorothy Jean	Bowling Green State	McManus, Illyana	Grossmont College
		McPherson, Dori	Schoolcraft College
Keskin, Ilknur	The University of South Dakota	Meiklejohn, Nancy	Pikes Peak Community College
Kirk, Colleen	Mercy College	Menking, Rick	Hardin-Simmons University
Kleckner, Michelle	Elon University	Meredith, Mary	University of Louisiana at Lafayette
Kliston, Linda	Broward Community College, North Campus	Mermelstein, Lisa	Baruch College
		Metos, Linda	Salt Lake Community College
Kochis, Dennis	Suffolk County Community College	Meurer, Daniel	University of Cincinnati
Kramer, Ed	Northern Virginia Community College	Meyer, Marian	Central New Mexico Community College
Laird, Jeff	Northeast State Community College	Miller, Cindy	Ivy Tech Community College, Lafayette, Indiana
Lamoureaux, Jackie	Central New Mexico Community College		
		Mitchell, Susan	Davenport University
Lange, David	Grand Valley State	Mohle, Dennis	Fresno Community College
LaPointe, Deb	Central New Mexico Community College	Monk, Ellen	University of Delaware
		Moore, Rodney	Holland College
Larson, Donna	Louisville Technical Institute	Morris, Mike	Southeastern Oklahoma State University
Laspina, Kathy	Vance-Granville Community College		
Le Grand, Dr. Kate	Broward Community College	Morris, Nancy	Hudson Valley Community College
Lenhart, Sheryl	Terra Community College	Moseler, Dan	Harrisburg Area Community College
Letavec, Chris	University of Cincinnati	Nabors, Brent	Reedley College, Clovis Center
Liefert, Jane	Everett Community College	Nadas, Erika	Wright College
Lindaman, Linda	Black Hawk Community College	Nadelman, Cindi	New England College
Lindberg, Martha	Minnesota State University	Nademlynsky, Lisa	Johnson & Wales University
Lightner, Renee	Broward Community College	Ncube, Cathy	University of West Florida
Lindberg, Martha	Minnesota State University	Nagengast, Joseph	Florida Career College
Linge, Richard	Arizona Western College	Newsome, Eloise	Northern Virginia Community College Woodbridge
Logan, Mary G.	Delgado Community College		
Loizeaux, Barbara	Westchester Community College	Nicholls, Doreen	Mohawk Valley Community College
Lopez, Don	Clovis-State Center Community College District	Nunan, Karen	Northeast State Technical Community College

Odegard, Teri	Edmonds Community College
Ogle, Gregory	North Community College
Orr, Dr. Claudia	Northern Michigan University South
Otieno, Derek	DeVry University
Otton, Diana Hill	Chesapeake College
Oxendale, Lucia	West Virginia Institute of Technology
Paiano, Frank	Southwestern College
Patrick, Tanya	Clackamas Community College
Peairs, Deb	Clark State Community College
Prince, Lisa	Missouri State University-Springfield Campus
Proietti, Kathleen	Northern Essex Community College
Pusins, Delores	HCCC
Raghuraman, Ram	Joliet Junior College
Reasoner, Ted Allen	Indiana University—Purdue
Reeves, Karen	High Point University
Remillard, Debbie	New Hampshire Technical Institute
Rhue, Shelly	DeVry University
Richards, Karen	Maplewoods Community College
Richardson, Mary	Albany Technical College
Rodgers, Gwen	Southern Nazarene University
Roselli, Diane	Harrisburg Area Community College
Ross, Dianne	University of Louisiana in Lafayette
Rousseau, Mary	Broward Community College, South
Samson, Dolly	Hawaii Pacific University
Sams, Todd	University of Cincinnati
Sandoval, Everett	Reedley College
Sardone, Nancy	Seton Hall University
Scafide, Jean	Mississippi Gulf Coast Community College
Scheeren, Judy	Westmoreland County Community College
Schneider, Sol	Sam Houston State University
Scroggins, Michael	Southwest Missouri State University
Sever, Suzanne	Northwest Arkansas Community College
Sheridan, Rick	California State University-Chico
Silvers, Pamela	Asheville Buncombe Tech
Singer, Steven A.	University of Hawai'i, Kapi'olani Community College
Sinha, Atin	Albany State University
Skolnick, Martin	Florida Atlantic University
Smith, T. Michael	Austin Community College
Smith, Tammy	Tompkins Cortland Community Collge
Smolenski, Bob	Delaware County Community College
Spangler, Candice	Columbus State
Stedham, Vicki	St. Petersburg College, Clearwater
Stefanelli, Greg	Carroll Community College
Steiner, Ester	New Mexico State University
Stenlund, Neal	Northern Virginia Community College, Alexandria
St. John, Steve	Tulsa Community College
Sterling, Janet	Houston Community College
Stoughton, Catherine	Laramie County Community College
Sullivan, Angela	Joliet Junior College
Szurek, Joseph	University of Pittsburgh at Greensburg
Tarver, Mary Beth	Northwestern State University
Taylor, Michael	Seattle Central Community College
Thangiah, Sam	Slippery Rock University
Thompson-Sellers, Ingrid	Georgia Perimeter College
Tomasi, Erik	Baruch College
Toreson, Karen	Shoreline Community College
Trifiletti, John J.	Florida Community College at Jacksonville
Trivedi, Charulata	Quinsigamond Community College, Woodbridge
Tucker, William	Austin Community College
Turgeon, Cheryl	Asnuntuck Community College
Turpen, Linda	Central New Mexico Community College
Upshaw, Susan	Del Mar College
Unruh, Angela	Central Washington University
Vanderhoof, Dr. Glenna	Missouri State University-Springfield Campus
Vargas, Tony	El Paso Community College
Vicars, Mitzi	Hampton University
Villarreal, Kathleen	Fresno
Vitrano, Mary Ellen	Palm Beach Community College
Volker, Bonita	Tidewater Community College
Wahila, Lori (Mindy)	Tompkins Cortland Community College
Waswick, Kim	Southeast Community College, Nebraska
Wavle, Sharon	Tompkins Cortland Community College
Webb, Nancy	City College of San Francisco
Wells, Barbara E.	Central Carolina Technical College
Wells, Lorna	Salt Lake Community College
Welsh, Jean	Lansing Community College Nebraska
White, Bruce	Quinnipiac University
Willer, Ann	Solano Community College
Williams, Mark	Lane Community College
Wilson, Kit	Red River College
Wilson, Roger	Fairmont State University
Wimberly, Leanne	International Academy of Design and Technology
Worthington, Paula	Northern Virginia Community College
Yauney, Annette	Herkimer County Community College
Yip, Thomas	Passaic Community College
Zavala, Ben	Webster Tech
Zlotow, Mary Ann	College of DuPage
Zudeck, Steve	Broward Community College, North

About the Authors

Shelley Gaskin, Series Editor, is a professor of business and computer technology at Pasadena City College in Pasadena, California. She holds a master's degree in business education from Northern Illinois University and a doctorate in adult and community education from Ball State University. Dr. Gaskin has 15 years of experience in the computer industry with several Fortune 500 companies and has developed and written training materials for custom systems applications in both the public and private sector. She is also the author of books on Microsoft Outlook and word processing.

Alicia Vargas is a faculty member in Business Information Technology at Pasadena City College. She holds a master's and a bachelor's degree in business education from California State University, Los Angeles, and has authored several textbooks and training manuals on Microsoft Word, Microsoft Excel, and Microsoft PowerPoint.

Visual Walk-Through of the *GO!* System

The *GO!* System is designed for ease of implementation on the instructor side and ease of understanding on the student. It has been completely developed based on professor and student feedback.

The *GO!* System is divided into three categories that reflect how you might organize your course—**Prepare**, **Teach**, and **Assess**.

Prepare

GO!

Because the GO! System was designed and written by instructors like yourself, it includes the tools that allow you to Prepare, Teach, and Assess in your course. We have organized the GO! System into these three categories that match how you work through your course and thus, it's even easier for you to implement.

To help you get started, here is an outline of the first activities you may want to do in order to conduct your course.

There are several other tools not listed here that are available in the GO! System so please refer to your GO! Guide for a complete listing of all the tools.

Prepare
1. Prepare the course syllabus
2. Plan the course assignments
3. Organize the student resources

Teach
4. Conduct demonstrations and lectures

Assess
5. Assign and grade assignments, quizzes, tests, and assessments

PREPARE

1. Prepare the course syllabus
A syllabus template is provided on the IRCD in the **go07_syllabus_template** folder of the main directory. It includes a course calendar planner for 8-week, 12-week, and 16-week formats. Depending on your term (summer or regular semester) you can modify one of these according to your course plan, and then add information pertinent to your course and institution.

2. Plan course assignments
For each chapter, an Assignment Sheet listing every in-chapter and end-of-chapter project is located on the IRCD within the **go01_goloffice2007intro_instructor_resources_by_chapter** folder. From there, navigate to the specific chapter folder. These sheets are Word tables, so you can delete rows for the projects that you choose not to assign or add rows for your own assignments—if any. There is a column to add the number of points you want to assign to each project depending on your grading scheme. At the top of the sheet, you can fill in the course information.

Transitioning to GO! Office 2007 — Page 1 of 1

NEW

Transition Guide

New to *GO!*–We've made it quick and easy to plan the format and activities for your class.

Syllabus Template

Includes course calendar planner for 8-,12-, and 16-week formats.

GO! with Microsoft Office 2007 Introductory
SAMPLE SYLLABUS (16 weeks)

I. COURSE INFORMATION

Course No.:
Course Title:
Course Hours:

Semester:
Credits:

Instructor:
Office Hours:
Email:

Office:

Phone:

II. TEXT AND MATERIALS
Before starting the course, you will need the following:

> GO! with Microsoft Office 2007 Introductory by Shelley Gaskin, Robert L. Ferrett, Alicia Vargas, Suzanne Marks ©2007, published by Pearson Prentice Hall. ISBN 0-13-167990-6

> Storage device for saving files (any of the following: multiple diskettes, CD-RW, flash drive, etc.)

III. WHAT YOU WILL LEARN IN THIS COURSE
This is a hands-on course where you will learn to use a computer to practice the most commonly used Microsoft programs including the Windows operating system, Internet Explorer for navigating the Internet, Outlook for managing your personal information and the four most popular programs within the Microsoft Office Suite (Word, Excel, PowerPoint and Access). You will also practice the basics of using a computer, mouse and keyboard. You will learn to be an intermediate level user of the Microsoft Office Suite.

Within the Microsoft Office Suite, you will use Word, Excel, PowerPoint, and Access. Microsoft Word is a word processing program with which you can create common business and personal documents. Microsoft Excel is a spreadsheet program that organizes and calculates accounting-type information. Microsoft PowerPoint is a presentation graphics program with which you can develop slides to accompany an oral presentation. Finally, Microsoft Access is a database program that organizes large amounts of information in a useful manner.

Assignment Sheet

One per chapter. Lists all possible assignments; add to and delete from this simple Word table according to your course plan.

File Guide to the *GO!* Supplements

Tabular listing of all supplements and their file names.

NEW

Assignment Planning Guide

Description of *GO!* assignments with recommendations based on class size, delivery mode, and student needs. Includes examples from fellow instructors.

Student Data Files

Online Study Guide for Students
Interactive objective-style questions based on chapter content.

PowerPoint Slides

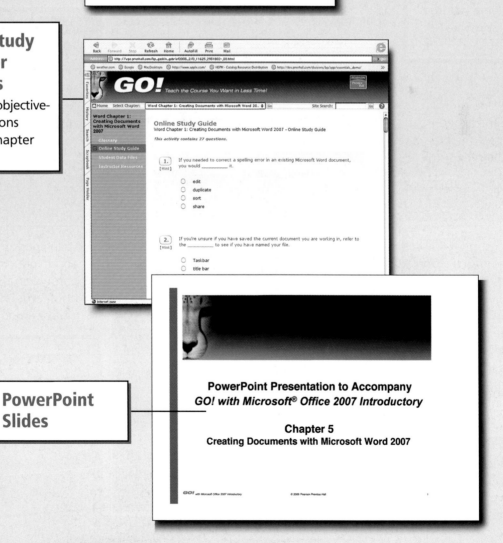

Teach

Student Textbook

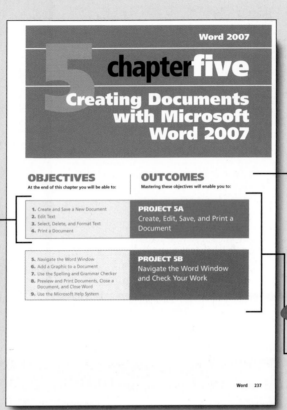

Learning Objectives and Student Outcomes

Objectives are clustered around projects that result in student outcomes. They help students learn how to solve problems, not just learn software features.

Project-Based Instruction

Students do not practice features of the application; they create real projects that they will need in the real world. Projects are color coded for easy reference and are named to reflect skills the students will be practicing.

A and B Projects

Each chapter contains two instructional projects—A and B.

Each chapter opens with a story that sets the stage for the projects the student will create; the instruction does not force the student to pretend to be someone or make up a scenario.

Each chapter has an introductory paragraph that briefs students on what is important.

Visual Summary

Shows students upfront what their projects will look like when they are done.

Objective

The skills the student will learn are clearly stated at the beginning of each project and color coded to match projects listed on the chapter opener page.

NEW

Screen Shots

Larger screen shots.

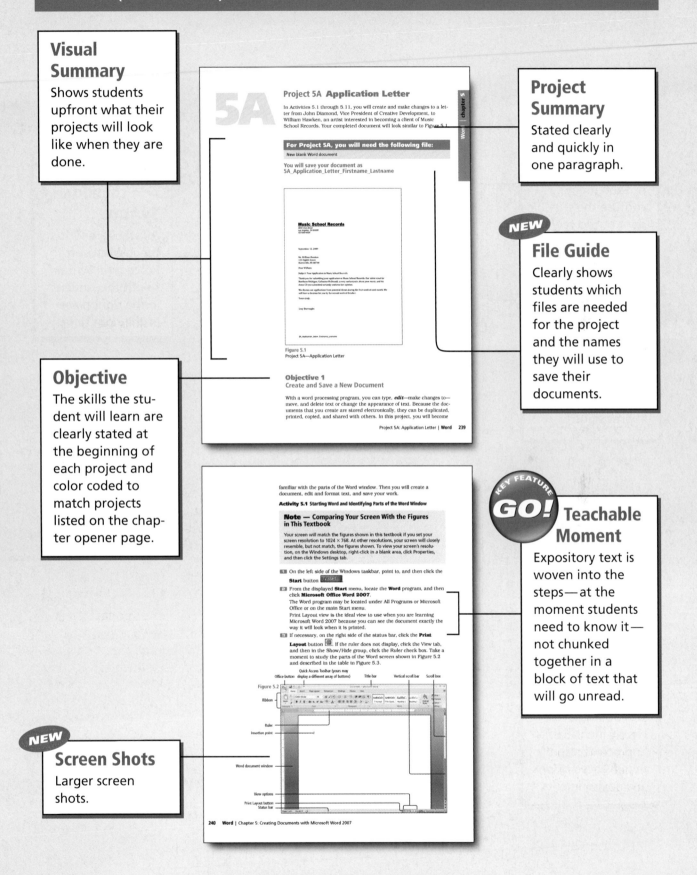

Project Summary

Stated clearly and quickly in one paragraph.

NEW

File Guide

Clearly shows students which files are needed for the project and the names they will use to save their documents.

KEY FEATURE

GO! Teachable Moment

Expository text is woven into the steps—at the moment students need to know it—not chunked together in a block of text that will go unread.

Steps

Color coded to the current project, easy to read, and not too many to confuse the student or too few to be meaningless.

Sequential Pagination

No more confusing letters and abbreviations.

Microsoft Procedural Syntax

All steps are written in Microsoft Procedural Syntax to put the student in the right place at the right time.

---

5 Press Enter two more times.

In a business letter, insert two blank lines between the date and the inside address, which is the same as the address you would use on an envelope.

6 Type **Mr. William Hawken** and then press Enter.

The wavy red line under the proper name *Hawken* indicates that the word has been flagged as misspelled because it is a word not contained in the Word dictionary.

7 On two lines, type the following address, but do not press Enter at the end of the second line:

123 Eighth Street
Harrisville, MI 48740

Note — Typing the Address

Include a comma after the city name in an inside address. However, for mailing addresses on envelopes, eliminate the comma after the city name.

8 On the **Home tab**, in the **Styles group**, click the **Normal** button.

The Normal style is applied to the text in the rest of the document. Recall that the Normal style adds extra space between paragraphs; it also adds slightly more space between lines in a paragraph.

9 Press Enter. Type **Dear William:** and then press Enter.

This salutation is the line that greets the person receiving the letter.

10 Type **Subject: Your Application to Music School Records** and press Enter. Notice the light dots between words, which indicate spaces and display when formatting marks are displayed. Also, notice the extra space after each paragraph, and then compare your screen with Figure 5.6.

The subject line is optional, but you should include a subject line in most letters to identify the topic. Depending on your Word settings, a wavy green line may display in the subject line, indicating a potential grammar error.

Note — Space Between Lines in Your Printed Document

The Cambria font, and many others, uses a slightly larger space between the lines than more traditional fonts like Times New Roman. As you progress in your study of Word, you will use many different fonts and also adjust the spacing between lines.

9 From the **Office** menu, click **Close**, saving any changes if prompted to do so. Leave Word open for the next project.

Another Way | **To Print a Document**

To Print a document:

- From the Office menu, click Print to display the Print dialog box (to be covered later), from which you can choose a variety of different options, such as printing multiple copies, printing on a different printer, and printing some but not all pages.
- Hold down Ctrl and then press P. This is an alternative to the Office menu command, and opens the Print dialog box.
- Hold down Alt, press F, and then press P. This opens the Print dialog box.

End You have completed Project 5A

End-of-Project Icon

All projects in the *GO! Series* have clearly identifiable end points, useful in self-paced or on-line environments.

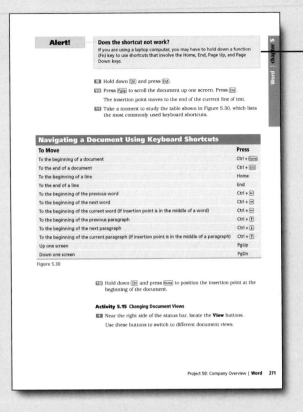

Alert box
Draws students' attention to make sure they aren't getting too far off course.

Another Way box
Shows students other ways of doing tasks.

More Knowledge box
Expands on a topic by going deeper into the material.

Note box
Points out important items to remember.

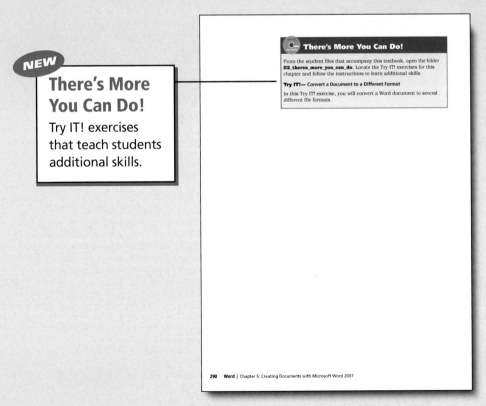

NEW

There's More You Can Do!
Try IT! exercises that teach students additional skills.

End-of-Chapter Material

Take your pick! Content-based or Outcomes-based projects to choose from. Below is a table outlining the various types of projects that fit into these two categories.

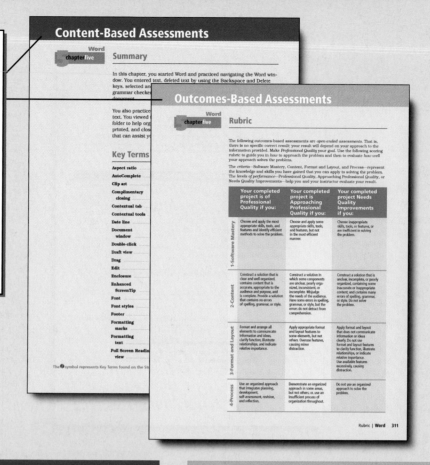

Content-Based Assessments

(Defined solutions with solution files provided for grading)

Project Letter	Name	Objectives Covered
N/A	Summary and Key Terms	
N/A	Multiple Choice	
N/A	Fill-in-the-blank	
C	Skills Review	Covers A Objectives
D	Skills Review	Covers B Objectives
E	Mastering Excel	Covers A Objectives
F	Mastering Excel	Covers B Objectives
G	Mastering Excel	Covers any combination of A and B Objectives
H	Mastering Excel	Covers any combination of A and B Objectives
I	Mastering Excel	Covers all A and B Objectives
J	Business Running Case	Covers all A and B Objectives

Outcomes-Based Assessments

(Open solutions that require a rubric for grading)

Project Letter	Name	Objectives Covered
N/A	Rubric	
K	Problem Solving	Covers as many Objectives from A and B as possible
L	Problem Solving	Covers as many Objectives from A and B as possible.
M	Problem Solving	Covers as many Objectives from A and B as possible.
N	Problem Solving	Covers as many Objectives from A and B as possible.
O	Problem Solving	Covers as many Objectives from A and B as possible.
P	You and GO!	Covers as many Objectives from A and B as possible
Q	GO! Help	Not tied to specific objectives
R	* Group Business Running Case	Covers A and B Objectives

* This project is provided only with the *GO! with Microsoft Office 2007 Introductory* book.

Objectives List

Most projects in the end-of-chapter section begin with a list of the objectives covered.

End of Each Project Clearly Marked

Clearly identified end points help separate the end-of-chapter projects.

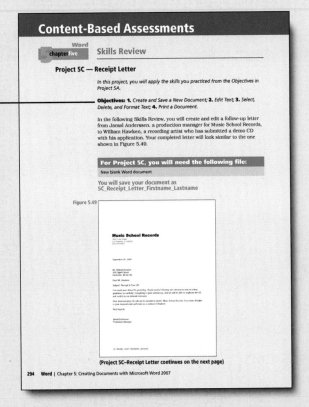

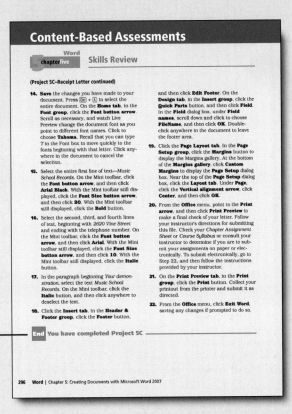

NEW

Rubric

A matrix that states the criteria and standards for grading student work. Used to grade open-ended assessments.

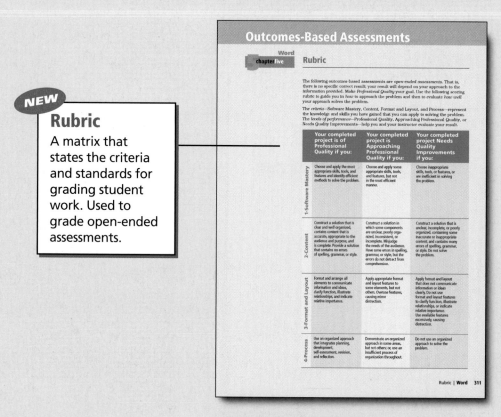

GO! with Help

Students practice using the Help feature of the Office application.

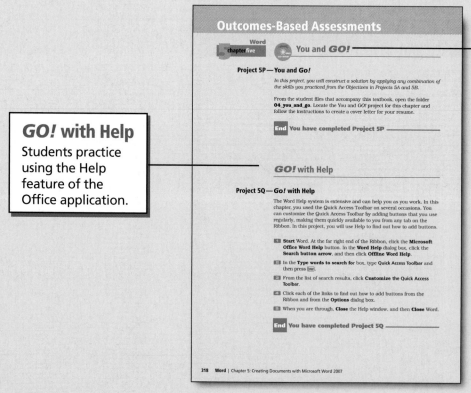

NEW

You and *GO!*

A project in which students use information from their own lives and apply the skills from the chapter to a personal task.

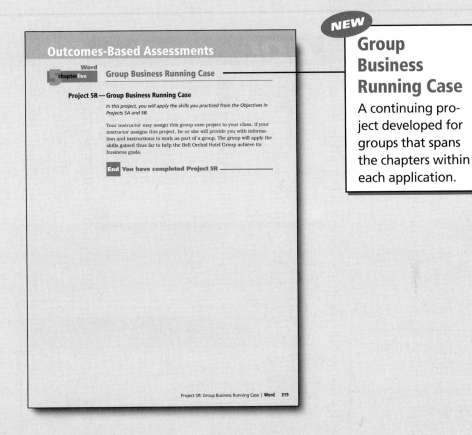

NEW

Group Business Running Case

A continuing project developed for groups that spans the chapters within each application.

Student CD includes:

- Student Data Files
- There's More You Can Do!
- Business Running Case
- You and GO!

Companion Web site

An interactive Web site to further student leaning.

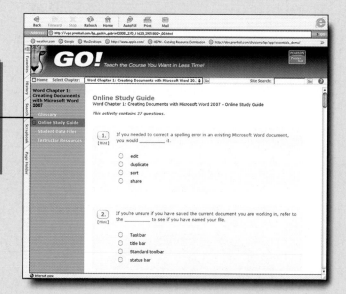

Online Study Guide

Interactive objective-style questions to help students study.

Annotated Instructor Edition

The Annotated Instructor Edition contains a full version of the student textbook that includes tips, supplement references, and pointers on teaching with the *GO!* instructional system.

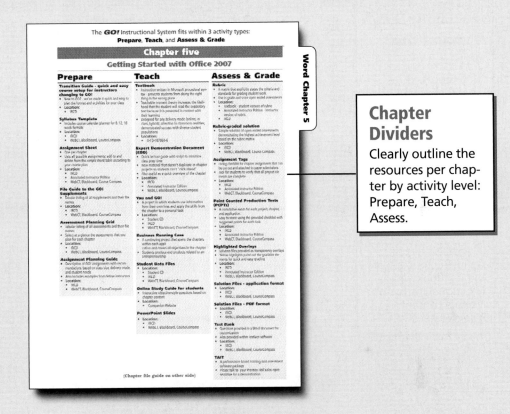

Chapter Dividers

Clearly outline the resources per chapter by activity level: Prepare, Teach, Assess.

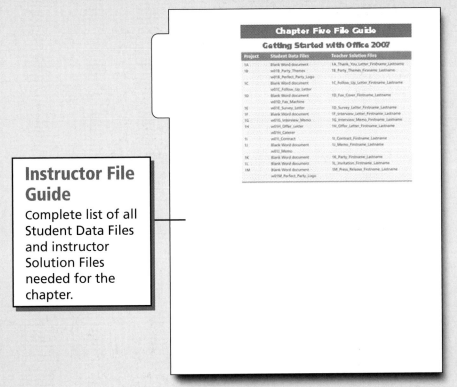

Instructor File Guide

Complete list of all Student Data Files and instructor Solution Files needed for the chapter.

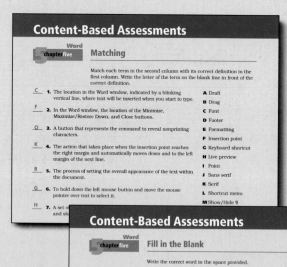

Helpful Hints, Teaching Tips, Expand the Project

References correspond to what is being taught in the student textbook.

NEW

Full-Size Textbook Pages

An instructor copy of the textbook with traditional Instructor Manual content incorporated.

End-of-Chapter Concepts Assessments contain the answers for quick reference.

NEW

Rubric

A matrix to guide the student on how they will be assessed is reprinted in the Annotated Instructor Edition with suggested weights for each of the criteria and levels of performance. Instructors can modify the weights to suit their needs.

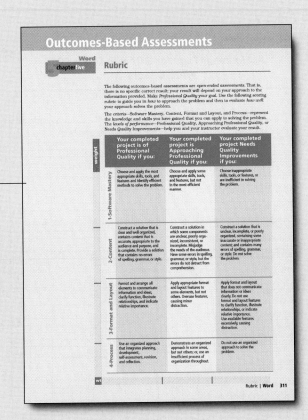

Assignment Tags

NEW

Scoring checklist for assignments. Now also available for Problem-Solving projects.

GO! with Microsoft® Office 2007

Assignment Tags for GO! with Office 2007
Word Chapter 5

| Name: | Project: | 5A |
| Professor: | Course: | |

Task	Points	Your Score
Center text vertically on page	2	
Delete the word "really"	1	
Delete the words "try to"	1	
Replace "last" with "first"	1	
Insert the word "potential"	1	
Replace "John W. Diamond" with "Lucy Burrows"	2	
Change entire document to the Cambria font	2	
Change the first line of text to Arial Black 20 pt. font	2	
Bold the first line of text	2	
Change the 2nd through 4th lines to Arial 10 pt.	2	
Italicize the 2nd through 4th lines of text	2	
Correct/Add footer as instructed	2	
Circled information is incorrect or formatted incorrectly		
Total Points	**20**	**0**

| Name: | Project: | 5B |
| Professor: | Course: | |

Task	Points	Your Score
Insert the file w05B_Music_School_Records	4	
Insert the Music Logo	4	
Remove duplicate "and"	2	
Change spelling and grammar errors (4)	8	
Correct/Add footer as instructed	2	
Circled information is incorrect or formatted incorrectly		
Total Points	**20**	**0**

| Name: | Project: | 5C |
| Professor: | Course: | |

Task	Points	Your Score
Add four line letterhead	2	
Insert today's date	1	
Add address block, subject line, and greeting	2	
Add two-paragraph body of letter	2	
Add closing, name, and title	2	
In subject line, capitalize "receipt"	1	
Change "standards" to "guidelines"	1	
Insert "quite"	1	
Insert "all"	1	
Change the first line of text to Arial Black 20 pt. font	2	
Bold the first line of text	1	
Change the 2nd through 4th lines to Arial 10 pt.	1	
Italicize the 2nd through 4th lines of text	1	
Correct/add footer as instructed	2	
Circled information is incorrect or formatted incorrectly		
Total Points	**20**	**0**

| Name: | Project: | 5D |
| Professor: | Course: | |

Task	Points	Your Score
Insert the file w05D_Marketing	4	
Bold the first two title lines	2	
Correct spelling of "Marketting"	2	
Correct spelling of "geners"	2	
Correct all misspellings of "allready"	2	
Correct grammar error "are" to "is"	2	
Insert the Piano image	4	
Correct/add footer as instructed	2	
Circled information is incorrect or formatted incorrectly		
Total Points	**20**	**0**

Highlighted Overlays

Solution files provided as transparency overlays. Yellow highlights point out the gradable elements for quick and easy grading.

Music School Records

← 20 point Arial Black, bold and underline

2620 Vine Street
Los Angeles, CA 90028 ← 10 point Arial, italic
323-555-0028

September 12, 2009

Mr. William Hawken
123 Eighth Street
Harrisville, MI 48740

Text vertically centered on page

Body of document changed to Cambria font, 11 point

Dear William:

Subject: Your Application to Music School Records

Thank you for submitting your application to Music School Records. Our talent scout for Northern Michigan, Catherine McDonald, is very enthusiastic about your music, and the demo CD you submitted certainly confirms her opinion.

Word "really" deleted

We discuss our applications from potential clients during the first week of each month. We will have a decision for you by the second week of October.

Words "try to" deleted

Yours Truly,

Lucy Burroughs

Point-Counted Production Tests (PCPTs)

A cumulative exam for each **project**, **chapter**, and **application**. Easy to score using the provided checklist with suggested points for each task.

GO! with Microsoft® Office 2007 Introductory

Point-Counted Production Test—Project for GO! with Microsoft® Office 2007 Introductory Project 5A

Instructor Name: _____
Course Information: _____

1. Start Word 2007 to begin a new blank document. Save your document as 5A_Cover_Letter_Firstname_Lastname Remember to save your file frequently as you work.

2. If necessary, display the formatting marks. With the insertion point blinking in the upper left corner of the document to the left of the default first paragraph mark, type the current date (you can use AutoComplete).

3. Press Enter three times and type the inside address:

    Music School Records
    2620 Vine Street
    Los Angeles, CA 90028

4. Press Enter three times, and type Dear Ms. Burroughs:

    Press Enter twice, and type Subject: Application to Music School Records

    Press Enter twice, and type the following text (skipping one line between paragraphs):

    I read about Music School Records in Con Brio magazine and I would like to inquire about the possibility of being represented by your company.

    I am very interested in a career in jazz and am planning to relocate to the Los Angeles area in the very near future. I would be interested in learning more about the company and about available opportunities.

    I was a member of my high school jazz band for three years. In addition, I have been playing in the local coffee shop for the last two years. My demo CD, which is enclosed, contains three of my most requested songs.

    I would appreciate the opportunity to speak with you. Thank you for your time and consideration. I look forward to speaking with you about this exciting opportunity.

5. Press Enter three times, and type the closing Sincerely, Press enter four times, and type your name.

6. Insert a footer that contains the file name.

7. Delete the first instance of the word *very* in the second body paragraph, and insert the word modern in front of *jazz*.

Copyright © 2008 Pearson Prentice Hall   Page 1 of 1

Test Bank

Available as TestGen Software or as a Word document for customization.

Chapter 5: Creating Documents with Microsoft Word 2007

Multiple Choice:

1. With word processing programs, how are documents stored?

    A. On a network

    B. On the computer

    C. Electronically

    D. On the floppy disk

    Answer: C   **Reference:** Objective 1: Create and Save a New Document   **Difficulty:** Moderate

2. Because you will see the document as it will print, _____ view is the ideal view to use when learning Microsoft Word 2007.

    A. Reading

    B. Normal

    C. Print Layout

    D. Outline

    Answer: C   **Reference:** Objective 1: Create and Save a New Document   **Difficulty:** Moderate

3. The blinking vertical line where text or graphics will be inserted is called the:

    A. cursor.

    B. insertion point.

    C. blinking line.

    D. I-beam.

    Answer: B   **Reference:** Objective 1: Create and Save a New Document   **Difficulty:** Easy

Solution Files– Application and PDF format

Music School Records

Music School Records discovers, launches, and develops the careers of young artists in classical, jazz, and contemporary music. Our philosophy is to not only shape, distribute, and sell a music product, but to help artists create a career that can last a lifetime. Too often in the music industry, artists are forced to fit their music to a trend that is short-lived. Music School Records does not just follow trends, we take a long-term view of the music industry and help our artists develop a style and repertoire that is fluid and flexible and that will appeal to audiences for years and even decades.

The music industry is constantly changing, but over the last decade, the changes have been enormous. New forms of entertainment such as DVDs, video games, and the Internet mean there is more competition for the leisure dollar in the market. New technologies give consumers more options for buying and listening to music, and they are demanding high quality recordings. Young consumers are comfortable with technology and want the music they love when and where they want it, no matter where they are or what they are doing.

Music School Records embraces new technologies and the sophisticated market of young music lovers. We believe that providing high quality recordings of truly talented artists make for more discerning listeners who will cherish the gift of music for the rest of their lives. The expertise of Music School Records includes:

- Insight into our target market and the ability to reach the desired audience
- The ability to access all current sources of music income
- A management team with years of experience in music commerce
- Innovative business strategies and artist development plans
- Investment in technology infrastructure for high quality recordings and business services

pagexxxix_top.docx

Online Assessment and Training

my**it**lab is Prentice Hall's new performance-based solution that allows you to easily deliver outcomes-based courses on Microsoft Office 2007, with customized training and defensible assessment. Key features of my**it**lab include:

A *true* "system" approach: my**it**lab content is the same as in your textbook.

Project-based *and* skills-based: Students complete real-life assignments.

Advanced reporting *and* gradebook: These include student click stream data.

***No* installation required:** my**it**lab is completely Web-based. You just need an Internet connection, small plug-in, and Adobe Flash Player.

Ask your Prentice Hall sales representative for a demonstration or visit:

www.prenhall.com/myitlab

1 chapterone

Creating a Worksheet and Charting Data

OBJECTIVES

At the end of this chapter you will be able to:

OUTCOMES

Mastering these objectives will enable you to:

1. Create, Save, and Navigate an Excel Workbook
2. Enter and Edit Data in a Worksheet
3. Construct and Copy Formulas, Use the Sum Function, and Edit Cells
4. Format Data, Cells, and Worksheets
5. Close and Reopen a Workbook
6. Chart Data
7. Use Page Layout View, Prepare a Worksheet for Printing, and Close Excel

PROJECT 1A
Create a Worksheet and Chart Data

8. Design a Worksheet
9. Construct Formulas for Mathematical Operations
10. Format Percentages and Move Formulas
11. Create a Pie Chart and a Chart Sheet
12. Use the Excel Help System

PROJECT 1B
Perform Calculations and Make Comparisons by Using a Pie Chart

Rio Rancho Auto Gallery

Rio Rancho Auto Gallery is a one-stop shop for car enthusiasts. The auto sales group sells a wide variety of manufacturer-certified pre-owned cars, cars that have passed rigorous inspection as determined by the manufacturers and that meet strict mileage and condition standards. The retail department sells automotive accessories such as custom wheels and performance parts, gadgets, gifts, books, magazines, and clothing, including branded items from major manufacturers. To complete the package, the company also offers auto financing and repairs and service.

Creating a Worksheet and Charting Data

With Microsoft Office Excel 2007, you can create and analyze data organized into columns and rows. After you have entered data in a worksheet, you can perform calculations, analyze the data to make logical decisions, and create a visual representation of the data in the form of a chart. In addition to its worksheet capability, Excel can manage your data, sort your data, and search for specific pieces of information.

In this chapter, you will create and modify Excel workbooks. You will practice the basics of worksheet design, create a footer, enter and edit data in a worksheet, and save, preview, and print your work. You will construct formulas to perform calculations, automatically complete text, use Excel's spelling tool, create a chart, and access Excel's Help feature.

Project 1A **Auto Sales**

In Activities 1.1 through 1.17, you will construct an Excel worksheet for Sandy Cizek, the Auto Sales Manager for Rio Rancho Auto Gallery. The worksheet will display the first quarter sales of vehicle types for the current year, and will include a chart to visually represent the worksheet. Your completed worksheet will look similar to Figure 1.1.

For Project 1A, you will need the following file:

New Excel workbook

You will save your workbook as
1A_Auto_Sales_Firstname_Lastname

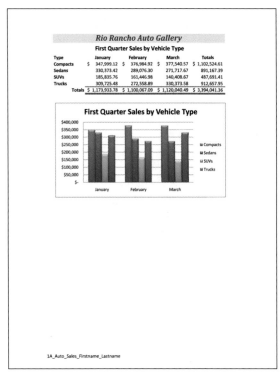

Figure 1.1
Project 1A—Auto Sales

Objective 1
Create, Save, and Navigate an Excel Workbook

When you start the Excel program, a new blank **workbook** displays. A workbook contains one or more pages called **worksheets**. A worksheet—also called a **spreadsheet**—is the primary document that you use in Excel to store and work with data.

A worksheet is formatted as a pattern of uniformly spaced horizontal and vertical lines. This grid pattern of the worksheet forms vertical columns and horizontal rows. The intersection of a column and a row forms a small rectangular box referred to as a **cell**. A worksheet is always stored in a workbook.

Activity 1.1 Starting Excel and Naming and Saving a Workbook

In this activity, you will start Excel and use the first worksheet in the workbook to prepare a report of quarterly auto sales for the current year.

> ### Note — Comparing Your Screen with the Figures in This Textbook
>
> Your screen will match the figures shown in this textbook if you set your screen resolution to 1024 x 768. At other resolutions, your screen will closely resemble, but not match, the figures shown. To view your screen's resolution, on the Windows desktop, right-click in a blank area, click Properties, and then click the Settings tab.

1 On the Windows taskbar, click the **Start** button `start`, determine where the Excel program is located, point to **Microsoft Office Excel 2007**, and then click to open the program. Take a moment to compare your screen with Figure 1.2 and study the parts of the Microsoft Excel window described in the table in Figure 1.3.

Figure 1.2

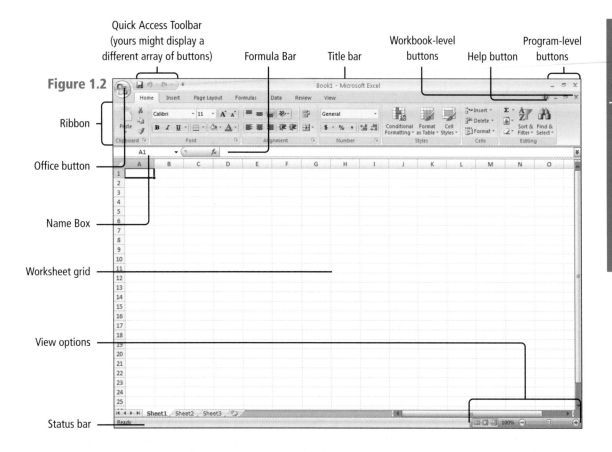

Quick Access Toolbar (yours might display a different array of buttons) · Formula Bar · Title bar · Workbook-level buttons · Help button · Program-level buttons

Ribbon · Office button · Name Box · Worksheet grid · View options · Status bar

Figure 1.3

Parts of the Excel Window

Screen Part	Description
Formula Bar	Displays the value or formula contained in the active cell; also permits entry or editing of values or formulas.
Help button	Displays the Help window.
Name Box	Displays the name of the selected cell, table, chart, or object.
Office button	Displays a list of commands related to things you can do *with* a workbook, such as opening, saving, printing, or sharing.
Program-level buttons	Minimizes, restores, or closes the Excel program.
Quick Access Toolbar	Displays buttons to perform frequently used commands with a single click. Frequently used commands in Excel include Save, Undo, and Redo. For commands that *you* use frequently, you can add additional buttons to the Quick Access Toolbar.
Ribbon	Groups the commands for performing related workbook tasks.
Status bar	Displays, on the left side, the current cell mode, page number, and worksheet information. On the right side, displays buttons to control how the window looks; when numerical data is selected, common calculations such as Sum and Average display.
Title bar	Indicates the name of the current workbook and the program name.
View options	Contain buttons for viewing the workbook in Normal view, Page Layout view, or Page Break Preview, and also displays controls for Zoom Out and Zoom In to increase or decrease the number of rows and columns displayed.
Workbook-level buttons	Minimizes or restores the displayed workbook.
Worksheet grid	Displays the columns and rows that intersect to form the worksheet's cells.

2 In the upper left corner of your screen, click the **Office** button 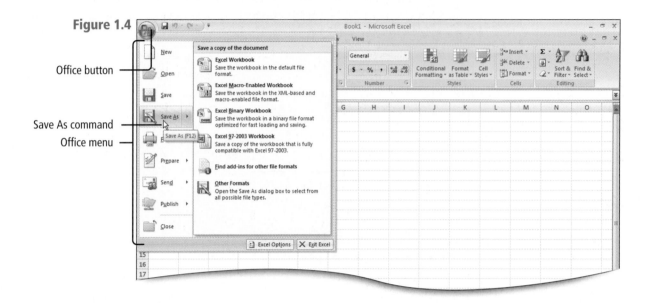, and then from the displayed menu, point to **Save As**. Compare your screen with Figure 1.4.

Figure 1.4

Office button

Save As command

Office menu

3 Click the **Save As** command. In the displayed **Save As** dialog box, click the **Save in arrow** to view a list of the drives available to you, and then navigate to the drive on which you will be storing your folders and workbooks for this textbook—for example, a USB flash drive such as the one shown in Figure 1.5.

Your disk or drive selected
(yours may indicate a different drive letter)

Save in arrow

Figure 1.5

Save As dialog box

Save As dialog box toolbar

Create New Folder button

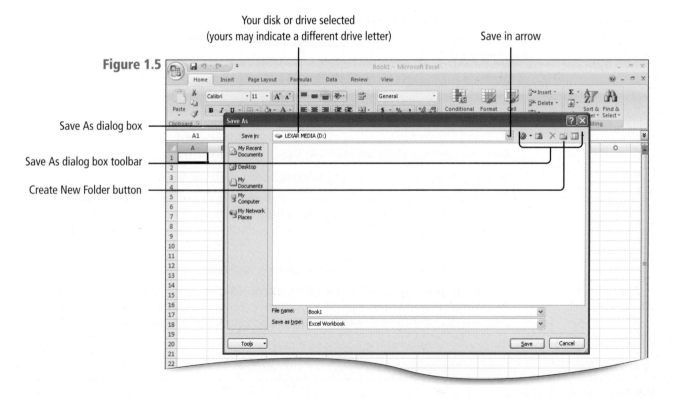

4 On the **Save As** dialog box toolbar, click the **Create New Folder** button. In the displayed **New Folder** dialog box, in the **Name** box, type **Excel Chapter 1** In the **New Folder** dialog box, click **OK**.

Windows creates the *Excel Chapter 1* folder and makes it the active folder in the Save As dialog box. At the bottom of the Save As dialog box, in the File name box, *Book1* displays as the default file name.

5 In the **File name** box, using your own first and last name, delete *Book1* and type **1A_Auto_Sales_Firstname_Lastname** being sure to include the underscore (⇧ Shift + -) instead of spaces between words. Compare your screen with Figure 1.6.

Windows recognizes file names that use spaces between words, but some electronic file transfer programs do not. In this text, you will use underscores instead of spaces between words for your file names.

Save in box indicates your new folder name

Figure 1.6

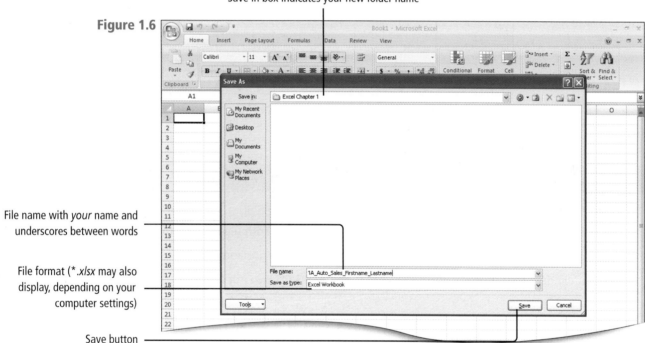

File name with *your* name and underscores between words

File format (*.xlsx* may also display, depending on your computer settings)

Save button

6 In the lower right corner of the **Save As** dialog box, click **Save** or press Enter.

The file is saved in the new folder with the new name. The workbook redisplays, and the new name displays in the title bar.

Activity 1.2 Navigating a Worksheet and a Workbook

1 Take a moment to study Figure 1.7 and the table in Figure 1.8 to become familiar with the Excel workbook window.

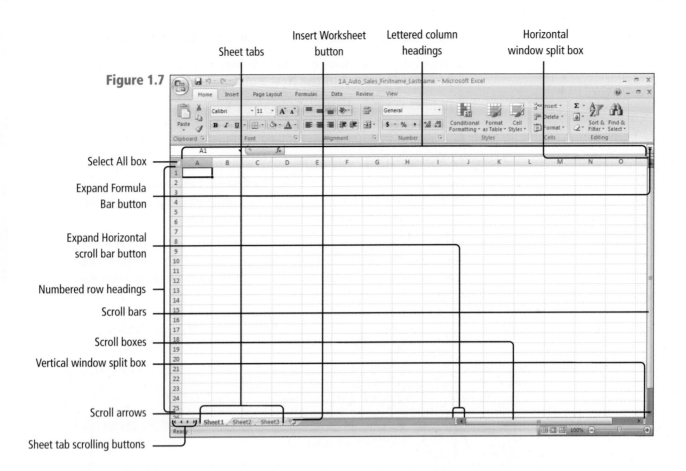

Figure 1.7

Labels (clockwise from top): Sheet tabs · Insert Worksheet button · Lettered column headings · Horizontal window split box

Labels (left side, top to bottom): Select All box · Expand Formula Bar button · Expand Horizontal scroll bar button · Numbered row headings · Scroll bars · Scroll boxes · Vertical window split box · Scroll arrows · Sheet tab scrolling buttons

Excel Workbook Window Elements

Workbook Window Element	Description
Expand Formula Bar button	Increases the height of the Formula Bar to display lengthy cell content.
Expand horizontal scroll bar button	Increases the width of the horizontal scroll bar.
Horizontal window split box	Splits the worksheet into two horizontal views of the same worksheet.
Insert Worksheet button	Inserts an additional worksheet into the workbook.
Lettered column headings	Indicate the column letter.
Numbered row headings	Indicate the row number.
Scroll arrows	Scroll one column or row at a time.
Scroll bars	Scroll the Excel window up and down or left and right.
Scroll boxes	Move the position of the window up and down or left and right.
Select All box	Selects all the cells in a worksheet.
Sheet tab scrolling buttons	Display sheet tabs that are not in view; used when there are more sheet tabs than will display in the space provided.
Sheet tabs	Identify the worksheets in a workbook.
Vertical window split box	Splits the worksheet into two vertical views of the same worksheet.

Figure 1.8

2 In the horizontal scroll bar, point to, and then click the **right scroll arrow**.

The workbook window shifts so that column A moves out of view. The number of times you click one of the arrows on the horizontal scroll bar determines the number of columns by which the window shifts—either to the left or to the right.

3 In the horizontal scroll bar, click the **right scroll arrow**, and then hold down the left mouse button until the columns begin to scroll rapidly to the right; release when you begin to see pairs of letters as the column headings.

The workbook window moves rapidly. This technique also works for the left scroll arrow and for the two vertical scroll arrows.

4 In the horizontal scroll bar, click the **left scroll arrow** to shift one column. Then, in the horizontal scroll bar, point to the **horizontal scroll box**. Hold down the left mouse button, *drag* the box to the left to display **column A**, and then notice that *ScreenTips* with the column letters display as you drag. Release the mouse button.

To drag is to move something from one location on the screen to another; the action of dragging includes releasing the mouse button at the desired time or location. ScreenTips display useful information when you perform various mouse actions such as pointing to screen elements or dragging.

Use the scroll boxes in this manner to move various parts of the worksheet into view. Scroll boxes change in size to indicate how the visible portion of the worksheet compares to the total amount of the worksheet in use.

5 Use the techniques you just practiced to scroll the worksheet to position **column Z** near the center of your screen.

Column headings to the right of column Z use two letters starting with AA, AB, AC, and so on. After that, columns begin with three letters beginning with AAA. This pattern is used to provide a total of 16,384 columns. The last column available is column XFD.

6 Near the lower left of the screen, point to, and then click the **Sheet2 tab**.

The second worksheet in the workbook displays and becomes the active worksheet. Column A displays at the left.

7 Click the **Sheet1 tab**.

The first worksheet in the workbook becomes the active worksheet. A workbook consists of one or more worksheets. By default, new workbooks contain three worksheets. When you save a workbook, the worksheets are contained within it and do not have separate file names.

8 In the vertical scroll bar, point to, and then click the **down scroll arrow** one time.

Row 1 moves out of view. The number of times you click the arrows on the vertical scroll bar determines the number of rows shifted either up or down. You can drag the vertical scroll box to scroll downward in a manner similar to the technique used in the horizontal scroll bar.

9 In the vertical scroll bar, point to, and then click the **up scroll arrow**.

Row 1 comes back into view. The maximum number of rows on a single Excel worksheet is 1,048,576.

10 Use the skills you just practiced to scroll horizontally to display **column A**.

Activity 1.3 Selecting Parts of a Worksheet

In the following activity, you will **select** both individual cells and groups of cells in the worksheet. Selecting refers to highlighting, by clicking or dragging with your mouse, one or more cells so that the selected cells can be edited, formatted, copied, or moved. Selected cells are indicated by a dark border, and Excel treats the selected **range**—two or more cells on a worksheet that are adjacent or nonadjacent—as a single unit; thus, you can make the same change, or combination of changes, to more than one cell at a time.

In Excel, text or numbers in a cell are referred to as **data**. Before you enter data into a worksheet, you must select the location in the worksheet where you want the data to display. After the data is in the worksheet, you can select one or more cells of data to which you can apply Excel's formatting, features, and functions.

1 In **Sheet1**, move the mouse pointer over—**point** to—the cell at the intersection of **column A** and **row 3**, and then click. Compare your screen with Figure 1.9.

A black border surrounds the cell, indicating that it is the **active cell**. The active cell in a worksheet is the cell ready to receive data or be affected by the next Excel command. A cell is identified by the intersecting column letter and row number, which forms the **cell reference**. A cell reference is also referred to as a **cell address**. The cell reference displays in the **Name Box**. Although either lowercase or uppercase letters can be used to indicate columns, uppercase letters are commonly used.

Figure 1.9

Cell A3 is selected

Cell address displays in the Name Box

Mouse pointer

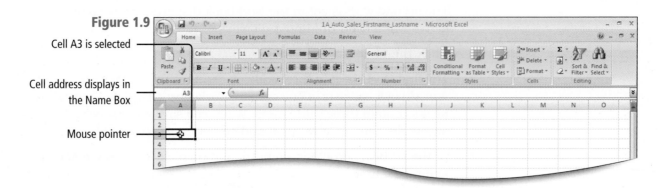

2 On the keyboard, press ⬇ three times, and then look at the cell address in the **Name Box**.

Cell A6 becomes the active cell. Pressing one of the four direction arrow keys relocates the active cell. The cell address of the active cell always displays in the Name Box.

3 Point to cell **B2**, hold down the left mouse button, drag downward to select cells **B2**, **B3**, **B4**, and **B5**, and then continue to drag across to cell **C5** and release the left mouse button. Alternatively, drag diagonally from cell B2 to C5. If you are not satisfied with your result, click anywhere and begin again. Compare your screen with Figure 1.10.

The eight cells, B2 through B5 and C2 through C5 are selected. This range of cells is referred to as *B2:C5*. When you see a colon (:) between two cell references, the range includes all the cells between the two cell references. The cell references used to indicate the range are the upper left cell and the lower right cell—in this instance, B2 and C5. When you select a range of cells, the cells are bordered by a thick black line, and the cells change color except for the first cell in the range, which displays in the Name Box.

Selected range B2:C5

Black border surrounds selected range

Figure 1.10

Name Box always indicates address of the first cell in range

First cell selected but not highlighted

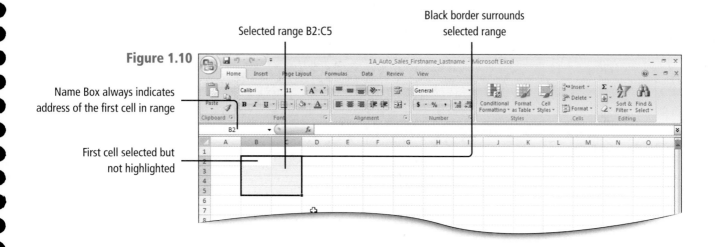

4 At the left edge of the worksheet, point to the number **3** to display the ➡ pointer, and then click the **row 3** heading.

Row 3 is selected. A *row* is a horizontal group of cells in a worksheet. Beginning with number 1, a unique number identifies each row—this is the *row heading*, located at the left side of the worksheet. All the cells in the row are selected, including those that are out of view.

5 In the upper left corner of **Sheet1**, point to the letter **A** to display the ⬇ pointer, and then click one time.

Column A is selected. A *column* is a vertical group of cells in a worksheet. Beginning with the first letter of the alphabet, A, a unique letter identifies each column—this is called the *column heading*. All the cells in the column are selected, including those that are out of view.

6 Click in the **Name Box** and notice that the cell reference *A1* moves to the left edge and is highlighted in blue. In any Windows program, text highlighted in blue in this manner will be replaced by your typing. Type **d4:f6** and then compare your screen with Figure 1.11.

Figure 1.11

Range typed in Name Box—
OK to type lowercase or
uppercase letters

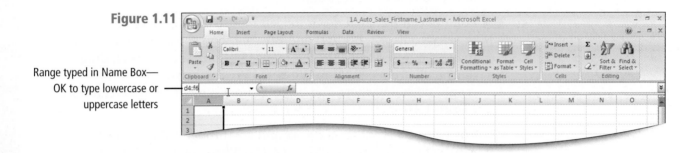

7 Press Enter to select the range. Then, click in the **Name Box**, type **b2:b8,e2:e8** press Enter, and then compare your screen with Figure 1.12.

Two ***nonadjacent***—not next to each other—ranges are selected. Ranges of cells that are not ***adjacent***—next to each other—can be selected by typing the ranges into the Name Box separated by a comma.

Figure 1.12

Name Box displays the first
cell in the second range

Selected ranges
B2:B8 and E2:E8

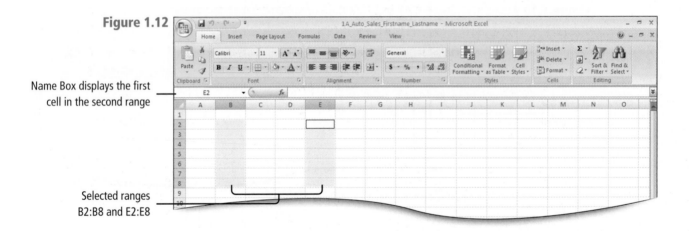

8 Select the range **C3:C5** and notice that the previously selected cells are deselected. Then, with the range selected, hold down Ctrl, and select the range **E3:E5**.

Use either technique to select cells that are nonadjacent (not next to one another). A range of cells can be adjacent or nonadjacent. Recall that a range of cells that is nonadjacent can be indicated by separating the ranges with a comma. In this instance, the selected ranges can be referred to as *c3:c5,e3:e5*.

9 At the upper left corner of your worksheet, locate, and then click the **Select All** box—the small box above **row heading 1** and to the left of **column heading A** to select all of the cells in the worksheet. Then, point to any cell on your worksheet and click to cancel the selection.

Objective 2
Enter and Edit Data in a Worksheet

Anything typed into a cell is referred to as **cell content**. Cell content can be one of two things—either a **constant value**—referred to simply as a **value**—or a **formula**. A value can be numbers, text, dates, or times of day that you type into a cell. A formula is an equation that performs mathematical calculations on values in your worksheet.

After you enter values into a cell, they can be **edited**—changed—or cleared from the cell. Words—text—typed in a worksheet usually provide information about numbers in other worksheet cells. For example, a title such as *Quarterly Auto Sales* gives the reader an indication that the data in the worksheet relates to information about sales of autos during a 3-month period.

Activity 1.4 Entering Text, Using AutoComplete, Filling a Series with Auto Fill, and Using Spelling Checker and Undo to Correct Typing Errors

To enter text into a cell, select the cell and type. In this activity, you will enter a title for the worksheet and titles for the rows and columns that will identify the types of vehicles purchased and the monthly sales amount for each vehicle type.

1 Click the **Sheet1 tab**, if necessary, so that Sheet 1 is the active sheet. Click cell **A1**, type **Rio Rancho Auto Gallery** and then press Enter.

After you type data into a cell, you must confirm the entry to store it in the cell. One way to do this is to press the Enter key, which typically moves the selection to the cell *below* to facilitate entry in a column of cells. You can also use other keyboard movements, such as Tab, or one of the arrow keys on your keyboard to make another cell active and confirm the entry.

2 Look at the text you typed in cell **A1**, and notice that the text does not fit into cell A1; the text spills over and displays in cells **B1** and **C1** to the right.

If text is too long for a cell and the cells to the right are empty, the text will display. If the cells to the right contain other data, only the text that will fit in the cell will display. Cell A2 is the active cell, as indicated by the black border surrounding it.

3 In cell **A2**, type **Monthly Sales by Vehicle Type** and then press Enter. In cell **A3**, type **Type** and then press Enter. Compare your screen with Figure 1.13.

Text too long for cell spills into adjacent
cells if the adjacent cells are empty

Figure 1.13

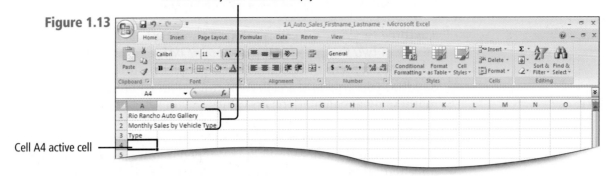

Cell A4 active cell

4 In cell **A4**, type **Sedans** and then press Enter.

The text is left aligned in the cell and the selection moves to cell A5. *Left alignment* —characters align at the left edge of the cell—is the default for text entries. Formatting information of this type is stored with the cell.

5 In cell **A5**, type **S** and notice the text from the previous cell displays.

Excel assists you in typing. If the first characters you type in a cell match an existing entry in the column, Excel fills in the remaining characters for you. This feature, called *AutoComplete*, speeds your typing. AutoComplete assists only with alphabetic values; it does not assist with numeric values.

6 Continue typing the remainder of the row title, **UVs** and press Enter.

As soon as the entry you are typing differs from the previous value, the AutoComplete suggestion is removed.

7 Without correcting the spelling error, in cell **A6**, type **Truks** and then press Enter. Then, in cell **A7**, type **Convertibles** and press Enter. In cell **A8**, type **Totals** and then press Enter.

8 Click cell **B3** to make it the active cell. Type **J** and notice that when you begin to type in a cell, on the **Formula Bar**, the **Cancel** and **Enter** buttons become active, as shown in Figure 1.14.

Enter button   Formula Bar

Figure 1.14

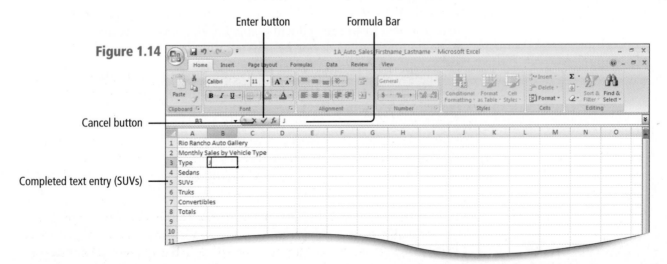

Cancel button

Completed text entry (SUVs)

9 Continue to type **anuary** and then on the **Formula Bar**, click the **Enter** button ☑ to keep cell **B3** the active cell.

Clicking the Enter button on the Formula Bar confirms the entry and maintains the current cell as the active cell. This is convenient if you want to take further action on the cell. If you mistakenly press Enter, reselect the cell.

10 With **B3** as the active cell, notice the small black square in the lower right corner of the selected cell.

You can drag the *fill handle*—the small black square in the lower right corner of a selected cell—to adjacent cells to fill the cells with values based on the first cell or cells in the series.

11 Point to the fill handle until the ➕ pointer displays, hold down the left mouse button, drag to the right to cell **F3**, and as you drag notice the ScreenTips *February*, *March*, *April* and *May*. Release the left mouse button, point to the **Auto Fill Options** button that displays, and then compare your screen with Figure 1.15.

Excel's *Auto Fill* feature can generate a *series* of values into adjacent cells, based on the value of other cells. A series is a group of things that come one after another in succession. For example, *January, February, March*, and so on, is a series. Likewise, *1st Qtr, 2nd Qtr, 3rd Qtr*, and *4th Qtr* form a series.

Auto Fill Options button

Figure 1.15

Series of months completed

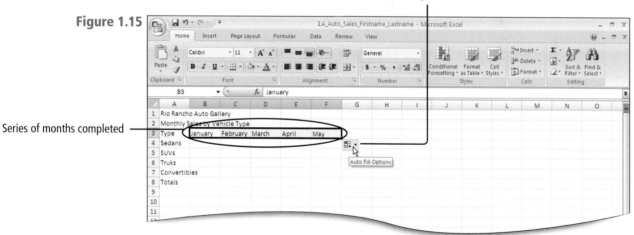

12 To the right of and below the filled data, point to, and then click the **Auto Fill Options** button.

The Auto Fill Options button displays just below a filled selection after you fill data in a worksheet. When you click the button, a list displays with options to fill the data. The list of options varies depending on the content you are filling, the program you are filling from, and the format of the data you are filling.

Fill Series is selected, indicating the action that was taken. Note that you can also fill only *Formatting*. Because the options are related to the current task, the button is referred to as being *context sensitive*.

13 Click in any cell to cancel the display of the Auto Fill Options list.

The list no longer displays; the button will display until some other screen action takes place.

14 Hold down $\boxed{\text{Ctrl}}$, and then press $\boxed{\text{Home}}$ to make cell **A1** the active cell—this is a ***keyboard shortcut***, which is an individual keystroke or a combination of keys pressed simultaneously that can either access an Excel command or move to another location on your screen.

15 Take a moment to study the table in Figure 1.16 to become familiar with additional keyboard shortcuts with which you can navigate the Excel worksheet.

Keyboard Shortcuts to Navigate the Excel Screen

To Move the Location of the Active Cell:	Press:
Up, down, right, or left one cell	$\boxed{\uparrow}$, $\boxed{\downarrow}$, $\boxed{\rightarrow}$, $\boxed{\leftarrow}$
Down one cell	$\boxed{\text{Enter}}$
Up one cell	$\boxed{\text{Shift}}$ + $\boxed{\text{Enter}}$
Up one full screen	$\boxed{\text{Page Up}}$
Down one full screen	$\boxed{\text{PgDn}}$
Left one full screen	$\boxed{\text{Alt}}$ + $\boxed{\text{Page Up}}$
Right one full screen	$\boxed{\text{Alt}}$ + $\boxed{\text{PgDn}}$
To column A of the current row	$\boxed{\text{Home}}$
To the last cell in the last column of the active area (the rectangle formed by all the rows and columns in a worksheet that contain entries)	$\boxed{\text{Ctrl}}$ + $\boxed{\text{End}}$
To cell A1	$\boxed{\text{Ctrl}}$ + $\boxed{\text{Home}}$
Right one cell	$\boxed{\text{Tab}}$
Left one cell	$\boxed{\text{Shift}}$ + $\boxed{\text{Tab}}$

Figure 1.16

16 With cell **A1** as the active cell, on the Ribbon, click the **Review tab**, and then in the **Proofing** group, click the **Spelling** button. Alternatively, press $\boxed{\text{F7}}$, which is the keyboard shortcut for the Spelling command. Compare your screen with Figure 1.17.

Spelling dialog box

Figure 1.17

Word indicated as
Not in Dictionary

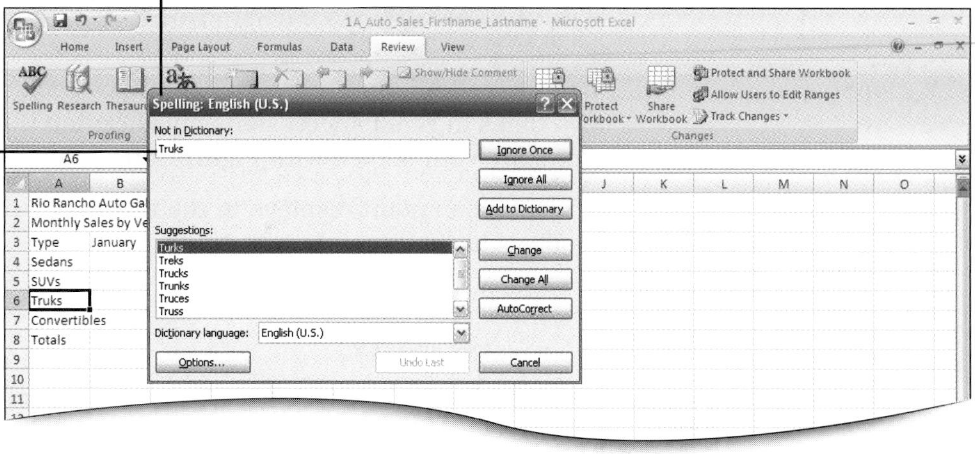

Alert!

Does a message display asking if you want to continue checking at the beginning of the sheet?

If a message displays asking if you want to continue checking at the beginning of the sheet, click Yes. The Spelling command begins its checking process with the currently selected cell and moves to the right and down. Thus, if your active cell was a cell after A6, this message may display.

17 In the displayed **Spelling** dialog box, under **Not in Dictionary**, notice the word *Truks*.

The spelling tool does not have this word in its dictionary. Under *Suggestions*, Excel provides a list of suggested spellings.

18 Under **Suggestions**, click **Trucks**, and then click the **Change** button.

Truks, which was a typing error, is changed to *Trucks*. A message box displays *The spelling check is complete for the entire sheet*. Because the spelling check begins its checking process starting with the currently selected cell, it is a good habit to return to cell A1 before starting the Spelling command.

Note — Words Not in the Dictionary Are Not Necessarily Misspelled

Many proper nouns or less commonly used words are not in the dictionary used by Excel. If Excel indicates a correct word as *Not in Dictionary*, you can choose to ignore this word or add it to the dictionary. You may want to add proper names that you expect to use often, such as your own last name, to the dictionary if you are permitted to do so.

19 Correct any other errors that you may have made. When the message displays, *The spelling check is complete for the entire sheet,* click **OK**.

20 Point to cell **A5**, and then ***double-click***—click the left mouse button two times in rapid succession while keeping the mouse still. Compare your screen with Figure 1.18.

The insertion point displays in the text in cell A5, and the text also displays in the Formula Bar.

Cell content displays
in the Formula Bar

Figure 1.18

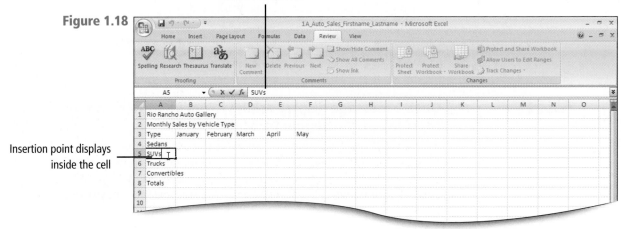

Insertion point displays
inside the cell

21 Move the mouse pointer away from the cell so that you have a clear view, and then using the arrow, [Del] or [←Bksp] keys as necessary, edit the text and change it to **Vans** Confirm the change by pressing [Enter].

22 On the **Quick Access Toolbar**, click the **Undo** button . Alternatively, you can press [Ctrl] + [Z] on the keyboard to reverse (undo) the last action.

SUVs is restored and *Vans* is deleted—your action was undone.

More Knowledge

AutoCorrect Also Assists in Your Typing

AutoCorrect assists in your typing by automatically correcting and formatting some text as you type. Excel compares your typing to a list of commonly mistyped words and when it finds a match, it substitutes the correct word. For example, if you type *monday*, Excel will automatically correct to *Monday*. To view the AutoCorrect options, display the Office menu. At the lower right, click Excel Options; on the left, click Proofing, and then click the AutoCorrect Options button.

Activity 1.5 Aligning Text and Adjusting the Size of Columns and Rows

Data typed into a cell can be aligned at the left, at the right, or centered. You can make columns wider or narrower and make rows taller or shorter. In this activity, you will adjust the size of columns and rows and right-align and center data in a cell.

1 In the **column heading area**, point to the vertical line between

column **A** and column **B** to display the ⊕ pointer, press and hold down the left mouse button, and then compare your screen with Figure 1.19.

A ScreenTip displays information about the width of the column.

ScreenTip

Figure 1.19

Pointer

Dotted line indicates
column divider is selected

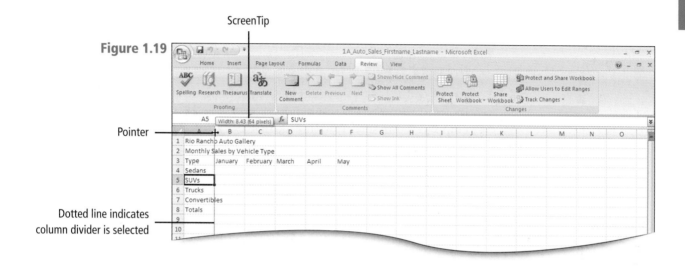

2 Drag to the right and release the mouse button when the number of pixels indicated in the ScreenTip reaches **90 pixels**, which is wide enough to display the longest row title in cells A4 through A7—the worksheet title in A1 will span more than one column and still does not fit in column A. If you are not satisfied with your result, click the Undo button and begin again.

The default width of a column is 64 *pixels*. A pixel, short for *picture element*, is a point of light measured in dots per square inch on a screen. Sixty-four pixels equals 8.43 characters, which is the average number of digits that will fit in a cell using the default *font*—a set of characters with the same design, size, and shape. The default font in Excel is Calibri, and the default *font size*—the size of characters in a font measured in *points*—is 11. There are 72 points in an inch, with 10 or 11 points being a typical font size in Excel. Point is usually abbreviated as *pt*.

3 Click cell **A8**. On the Ribbon click the **Home tab**, and then in the

Alignment group, click the **Align Text Right** button ▤.

The row title is aligned at the right side of the cell to distinguish it from the other row titles in the column. Text can be aligned at the center, left, or right of a cell. By default, text aligns at the left, but is easily changed as you have done here.

4 Select the range **B3:F3**, and then with your pointer positioned anywhere over the selected range, ***right-click***—click the right mouse button—to display a ***shortcut menu*** and a ***Mini toolbar***—both of which display commands most commonly used in the context of selected text of this type. On the Mini toolbar, click the **Center** button 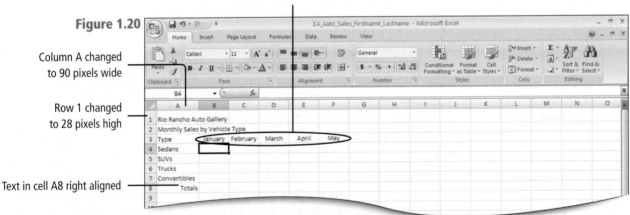 and notice that the shortcut menu no longer displays. Then, move the mouse slightly below the displayed Mini toolbar and notice that the Mini toolbar fades so that you can see the result of your formatting. Move the pointer back into the Mini toolbar, and then notice that it displays and once again becomes a functioning toolbar.

The column titles *January – May* align in the center of each cell. A shortcut menu offers the most commonly used commands relevant to the selected area and thus is context sensitive. You can also display a shortcut menu by pressing ⇧Shift + F10.

5 Click in any cell to cancel the selection and close the Mini toolbar. In the **row heading area**, point to the boundary between **row 1** and **row 2** until the ⊕ pointer displays. Drag downward, release the mouse button when the height of **row 1** is **28 pixels**, and then compare your screen with Figure 1.20.

The height of the row is increased. Row height is measured in points or in pixels. Points are the units in which font size is measured and pixels are units of screen display. The default height of a row is 15.00 points or 20 pixels.

Text centered within the cells

Figure 1.20

Column A changed to 90 pixels wide

Row 1 changed to 28 pixels high

Text in cell A8 right aligned

6 On the **Quick Access Toolbar**, click the **Save** button to save the changes you have made to your workbook; alternatively, press Ctrl + S.

Activity 1.6 Entering Numbers

When typing numbers in an Excel worksheet, you can use either the number keys across the top of your keyboard or the number keys and Enter key on the numeric keypad. Try to develop some proficiency in touch control of the numeric keypad. In this activity, you will enter the sales amounts for Rio Rancho Auto Gallery.

1 Click cell **B4**, type **330373.42** and then on the **Formula Bar**, click the **Enter** button ☑ to maintain cell **B4** as the active cell. Compare your screen with Figure 1.21.

By default, numbers align at the right edge of the cell. The default *number format*—a specific way in which Excel displays numbers—is the *general format*. The general format has no specific characteristics —whatever you type in the cell will display, with the exception that trailing zeros to the right of a decimal point will not display. For example, if you type *125.50* the cell will display *125.5* instead.

Numbers that are too long to fit in the cell do *not* spill over into the unoccupied cell to the right in the same manner as text. Rather, the number is rounded. However, the entire number still exists and displays in the Formula Bar. Data displayed in a cell is referred to as the *displayed value*. Data displayed in the Formula Bar is referred to as the *underlying value*. The number of digits or characters that display in a cell—the displayed value—depends on the width of the column.

Cell content, in full, displays in Formula Bar

Figure 1.21

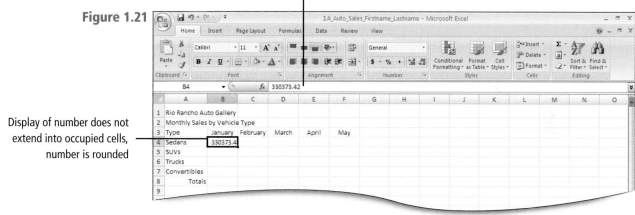

Display of number does not extend into occupied cells, number is rounded

2 Enter the remaining sales figures for *Sedans* and *SUVs* in the months of January through May, as shown in the following table. Press Tab to simultaneously confirm your entry and move across the row, and then press Enter at the end of a row to move to the next row. Notice that as you type, if the column is too narrow to display all of the decimal places in a number, the display of the number will be rounded to fit the available space. When finished, compare your screen with Figure 1.22.

Rounding is a procedure in which you determine which digit at the right of the number will be the last digit displayed and then increase it by one if the next digit to its right is 5, 6, 7, 8, or 9.

Recall that trailing zeros to the right of a decimal point will not display. So for example, if you type 289076.30, the cell will display 289076.3 and if you type 297467.00, the cell will display 297467.

Calculations performed on numbers in Excel will always be based on the underlying value, not the displayed value.

	January	February	March	April	May
Sedans	330373.42	**289076.30**	**271717.67**	**326243.00**	**297467.00**
SUVs	**185835.76**	**163446.98**	**140408.67**	**247780.87**	**189756.00**

Figure 1.22

Values entered for Sedans and SUVs

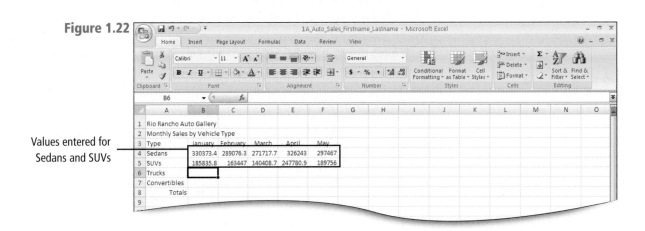

3 Click in the **Name Box**, type **b:f** and then press Enter. In the **column heading area**, point to the boundary between any two of the selected column headings to display the ⊞ pointer, drag to **50** pixels, and then notice that when a range of columns is selected in this manner, adjusting the width of one column adjusts the width of all. Release the mouse button, click cell **C5**, and then compare your screen with Figure 1.23.

In this example, as the columns become narrower and the decimal places cannot fit into the cell, the numbers are rounded further to fit the available space. The underlying value, however, is unchanged.

Cell content, in full, displays in Formula Bar; displays underlying value

Figure 1.23

Display of numbers does not extend into occupied cells; rounded to 163447

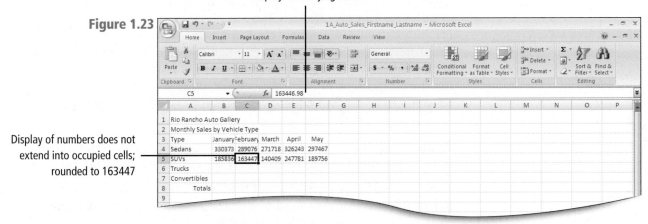

4 On the **Quick Access Toolbar**, click the **Undo** button 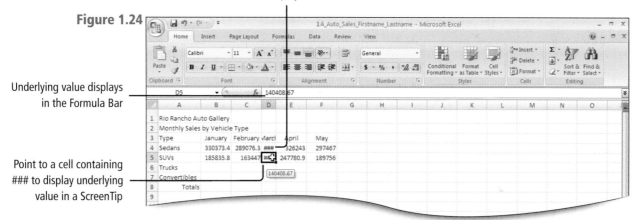 to restore the column widths to 64 pixels. Click in any cell to deselect the columns. In the **column heading area**, point to the right boundary of **column D**, and then drag the right column border to the left to set the width of **column D** to **30 pixels**. Then, click cell **D5** and compare your screen with Figure 1.24.

If a cell width is too narrow to display all of the number, Excel displays a series of pound signs instead; displaying only a portion of a whole number would be misleading. The underlying values remain unchanged and are displayed in the Formula Bar for the selected cell. The underlying value also displays in the ScreenTip if you point to a cell containing ###.

Pound signs indicate cell is too narrow to display the number

Figure 1.24

Underlying value displays in the Formula Bar

Point to a cell containing ### to display underlying value in a ScreenTip

5 On the **Quick Access Toolbar**, click the **Undo** button to restore **column D** to a width of 64 pixels. Select **columns B:F**. In the **column heading area**, point to the boundary between any two of the selected column headings to display the ⊞ pointer, and then drag to **85** pixels.

Recall that in the default general number format, trailing zeros to the right of a decimal point do not display regardless of the column width.

6 Click any cell to cancel the selection, and then **Save** your workbook.

Activity 1.7 Inserting and Deleting Rows and Columns, and Using the Insert Options Button

In this activity, you will insert a new row to record sales for the vehicle type *Compacts* and delete the *Convertibles* vehicle type.

1 Point to the **row 4** heading, and then right-click to simultaneously select the row and display the shortcut menu and the Mini toolbar. Compare your screen with Figure 1.25.

You can right-click row numbers or column headings to simultaneously select and display a context-sensitive shortcut menu and the Mini toolbar.

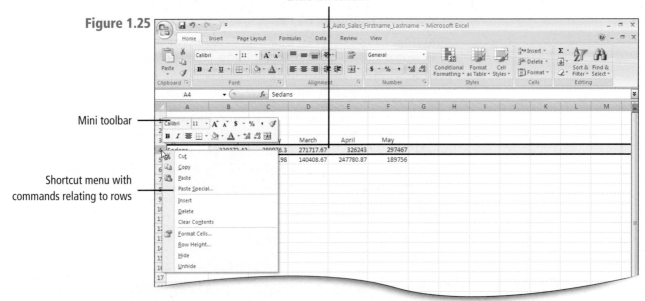

Entire row selected

Figure 1.25

Mini toolbar

Shortcut menu with commands relating to rows

2 From the displayed shortcut menu, click **Insert**.

A new row 4 is inserted above the selected row, and the existing rows shift down one row. Additionally, the Insert Options button displays.

Note — Insert Columns By Using the Same Shortcut Menu Technique

Use a similar technique to insert a new column in a worksheet. That is, from the column heading area, right-click to simultaneously select the column and display the context-sensitive shortcut menu. Click Insert to insert a new column and shift the remaining columns to the right. Alternatively, select the column, and then on the Ribbon, in the Cells group, click the Insert button or the Insert button arrow for additional options.

---

3 Point to the **Insert Options** button ![icon] to display its ScreenTip and its arrow, and then click the button to display a list of options.

From this menu, you can format the new row like the row above or the row below, or you can leave it unformatted. The default is *Format Same As Above*.

4 Click **Format Same As Below**.

The new row is formatted, using the format from the row of data *below* instead of the row of column titles above, which are centered. The Insert Options button remains visible until you perform another screen action.

5 Click cell **A4**, type **Compacts** and then press ⌷Tab⌷. Enter the values for *Compacts* for each month, as shown in the following table. Use ⌷Tab⌷ to confirm each entry and move the active cell across the row.

Type	January	February	March	April	May
Compacts	**326485.76**	**376984.92**	**367540.57**	**330373.58**	**345765.64**

6 From the **row heading area**, select **row 8**. On the Ribbon, in the **Cells group**, click the **Delete button arrow**, and then from the displayed menu, click **Delete Sheet Rows**. Alternatively, click the Delete button on the Ribbon; or, right-click the row 8 heading to simultaneously select the row and display a shortcut menu, and then from the displayed shortcut menu, click Delete.

7 Enter the remaining sales figures for *Trucks* as follows, and then compare your screen with Figure 1.26.

Type	January	February	March	April	May
Trucks	**309725.48**	**272558.89**	**330373.58**	**289076.55**	**319583.61**

Figure 1.26

Values entered for Compacts and Trucks

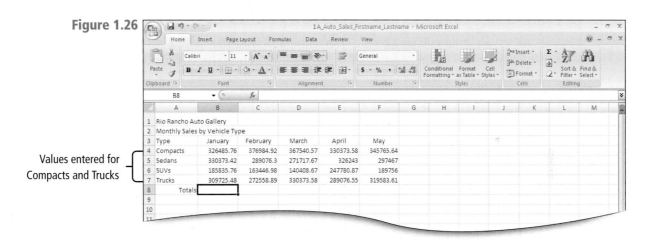

8 **Save** 💾 your workbook.

Objective 3
Construct and Copy Formulas, Use the Sum Function, and Edit Cells

Excel performs calculations on numbers; that is why you use Excel. If you make changes to the numbers, Excel automatically *re*-calculates. This is one of the most powerful and valuable features of Excel. You can arrange data in a format of columns and rows in other programs—in a word processing program, for example—and even perform simple calculations. Excel, however, performs complex calculations on numbers.

Recall that a cell contains either a constant value or a formula. Recall also that a formula is an equation that performs mathematical calculations on values in other cells, and then places the result in the cell containing the formula. You can create your own formulas, or you can use one of Excel's prewritten formulas called a ***function***. A function is a prewritten formula that takes one or more values, performs an operation, and then returns a value or values.

Activity 1.8 Constructing a Formula, Using the Sum Function, and Editing Numbers in Cells

In this activity, you will sum the sales of vehicles by month and by type and use various methods to edit numbers within a cell.

1 Click cell **B8** to make it the active cell and type **=**

The equal sign (=) displays in the cell with the insertion point blinking, ready to accept more data. All formulas begin with the = sign, which is the signal that directs Excel to begin a calculation. The Formula Bar displays the = sign, and the Formula Bar Cancel and Enter buttons display.

2 At the insertion point, type **b4** and then compare your screen with Figure 1.27.

A list of Excel functions that begin with the letter *B* may briefly display—as you progress in your study of Excel, you will use functions of this type. Cell B4 is surrounded by a blue border with small corner boxes. This indicates that the cell is part of an active formula. The color used in the box matches the color of the cell reference in the formula.

Your typing displays in Formula Bar

Figure 1.27

Cell outlined in the same color as the cell reference in the formula

Formula started in the active cell

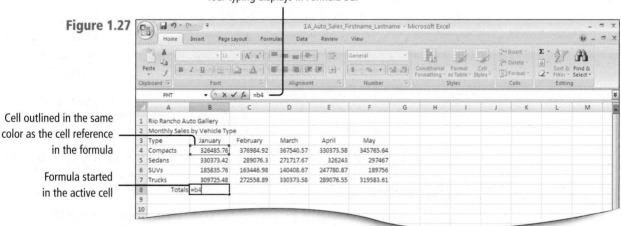

3 At the insertion point, type **+** and then type **b5** Alternatively, use the ⊕ key on your numeric keypad, which does not require the ⇧ Shift key.

A border of another color surrounds cell B5, and the color matches the color of the cell reference in the active formula. Recall that when typing cell references, it is not necessary to use uppercase letters.

4 At the insertion point, type **+b6+b7** and then press Enter.

The result of the formula calculation—*1152420.42*—displays in the cell.

5 Click cell **B8** again to make it the active cell, and then look at the **Formula Bar**. Compare your screen with Figure 1.28.

You created a formula that adds the values in cells B4 through B7, and the result of adding the values in those cells displays in cell B8. Although cell B8 displays the *result* of the formula, the formula itself is displayed in the Formula Bar. This is referred to as the ***underlying formula***. Always view the Formula Bar to be sure of the exact content of a cell—*a displayed number may actually be a formula.*

Figure 1.28

Underlying formula displays in the Formula Bar

Result of the formula displays in the active cell

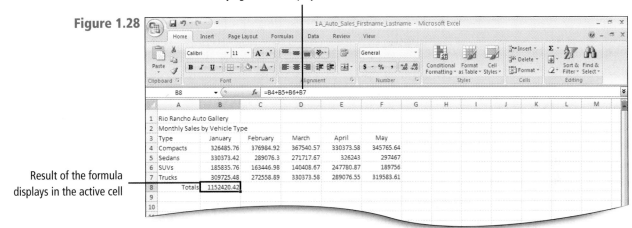

6 To change the value in cell B4, click cell **B4,** type **347999.12** and then watch cell **B8** as you press Enter.

Excel recalculates the formula and displays *1173933.78.* Recall that Excel formulas *recalculate* if you change values in a cell that is referenced in the formula. It is not necessary to delete the old value in a cell; selecting the cell and typing a new value replaces the old value with your new typing.

7 In cell **C8**, type **=** to signal the beginning of a formula. Then, point to cell **C4**, click once, and compare your screen with Figure 1.29.

The reference to the cell, C4, is added to the active formula. A moving border surrounds the referenced cell, and the border color and the color of the cell reference in the formula are color coded to match.

The cell referred to outlined with a moving border

Figure 1.29

Formula with cell reference created by pointing and clicking

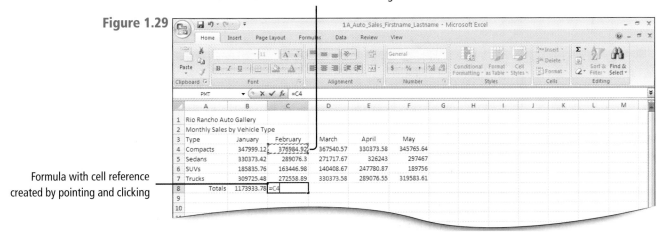

8 At the insertion point, type **+** and then click cell **C5**. Repeat this process to complete the formula to add cells **C4** through **C7**, and then press Enter.

The result of the formula calculation—*1102067.09*—displays in the cell. This method of constructing a formula is the ***point and click method***. Constructing a formula by using the point and click method is convenient when the referenced cells are not adjacent to one another.

9 Point to cell **C6**, and then double-click to place the insertion point within the cell. Use the arrow keys to move the insertion point to the left or right of *3*, and then use either Delete or ←Bksp to change *3* to **1** Watch cell **C8** as you press Enter, and then notice the recalculation of the formula.

10 Click cell **D8**. On the **Home tab**, in the **Editing group**, click the **Sum** button Σ ·. Alternatively, use the keyboard shortcut Alt + = or, on the Formulas tab, in the Function Library group, click the AutoSum button. Compare your screen with Figure 1.30.

Sum is an Excel function—a prewritten formula. Cells D4:D7 are surrounded by a moving border, and *=SUM(D4:D7)* displays in cell D8. The = sign signals the beginning of a formula, *SUM* indicates the type of calculation that will take place (addition), and *(D4:D7)* indicates the range of cells on which the sum operation will be performed. A ScreenTip provides additional information about the action.

ScreenTip with additional
information on the SUM function   Sum button on the Ribbon

Figure 1.30

Underlying formula displays
in Formula Bar

Moving border surrounds
the range selected by Sum

Formula generated by
the Sum function

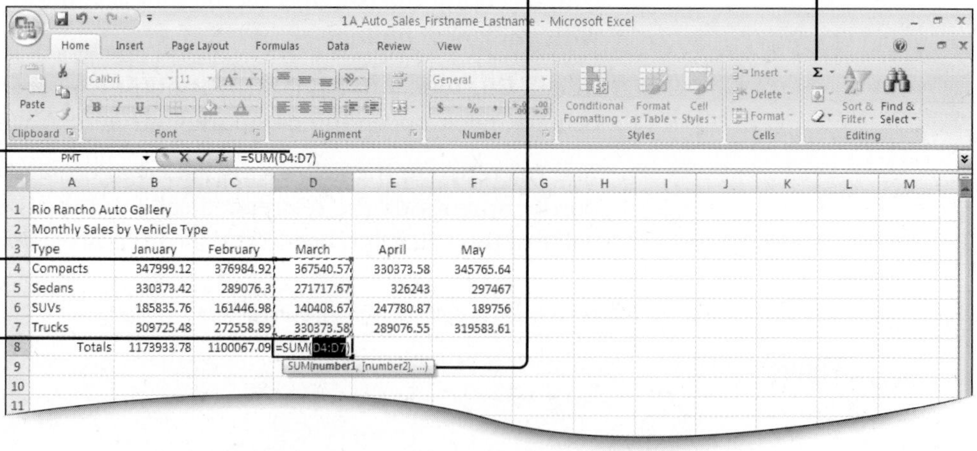

11 Look at the **Formula Bar**, and notice that the formula also displays there. Then, look again at the cells surrounded by the moving border.

When the Sum function is activated, Excel first looks *above* the active cell for a range of cells to sum. If no range is above the active cell, Excel will look to the *left* for a range of cells to sum. Regardless, Excel will propose a range of cells to sum, and if the proposed range is not what you had in mind, you can select a different group of cells.

12 Press Enter to view the sum of March sales—*1110040.49*—displayed in cell **D8**.

Because the Sum function is frequently used, it has its own button in the Editing group on the Ribbon. A larger version of the button also displays on the Formulas tab in the Function Library group. As you progress in your study of Excel, you will use additional Excel functions. This button is also referred to as ***AutoSum***.

13 Click cell **D4**, and then click in the **Formula Bar** to position the insertion point there. Change the number *6* to **7** so that the value is *377540.57*, and then press Enter to recalculate the formula.

The total for March is recalculated to *1120040.49*. You can edit cells in the Formula Bar or inside the cell itself.

14 Select the range **E4:F8**, look at the status bar at the lower right of your screen, and then compare your screen with Figure 1.31.

By selecting a range of cells and including the empty cells at the bottom of each column, you can apply the Sum function to sum several columns at once; the formula for adding each column will be placed in the empty cells at the bottom of each column.

Additionally, when you select a range of cells containing numbers, Excel displays the result of applying the Average, Count, or Sum functions in the status bar. You can see that if you averaged the numbers of the selected cells, the result would be 293255.7813; if you counted the cells in the selection that contain values (text or numbers), the result would be 8, and if you added the numbers in the selected cells, the total would be 2346046.25.

Selected range

Figure 1.31

Empty cells included in selected range

Status bar displays the result of the Average, Count, or Sum function

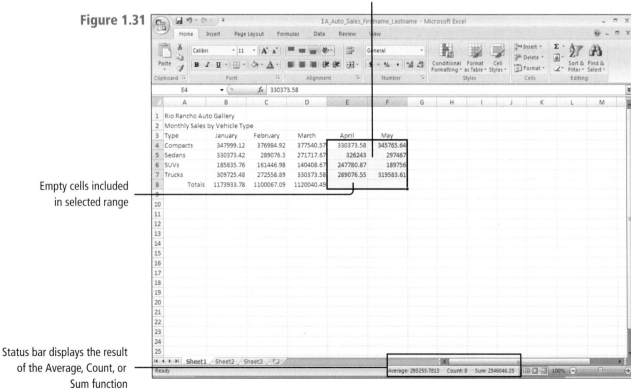

More Knowledge

Multiple Status Bar Calculations

When numerical data is selected, three calculations display in the status bar by default—Average, Count, and Sum. You can display a total of six of these calculations on the status bar by adding the Numerical Count (the number of cells within the selection that contain numbers), Minimum, and Maximum functions to the status bar. To add additional calculations, right-click the status bar and select the calculations you want to display.

15 In the **Editing group**, click the **Sum** button Σ ▾ or press Alt + =.

Excel places the Sum formula in cells E8 and F8 and a result displays in cells E8 and F8 indicating the sums *1193474* and *1152572.25*. Recall that in the General number format, trailing zeros do not display.

16 Click cell **E8**, and then notice the formula in the **Formula Bar**. Click cell **F8** to view the formula in the **Formula Bar**. Compare your screen with Figure 1.32.

The cells display the result of the calculated function, which is a formula that Excel has prewritten and named.

Formula indicated in Formula Bar

Figure 1.32

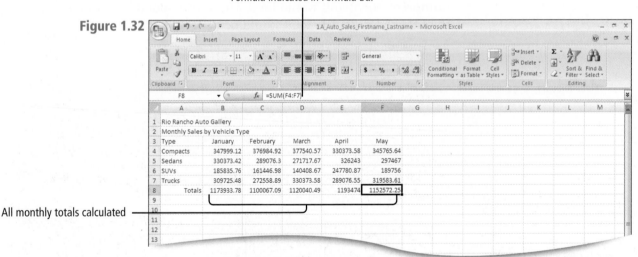

All monthly totals calculated

17 **Save** the changes you have made to your workbook.

Activity 1.9 Copying a Formula by Using the Fill Handle

Excel provides a quick method—called copying formulas—to create formulas without typing, pointing and clicking, or using a command from the Ribbon. When a formula is copied from one cell to another, Excel adjusts the cell references to fit the new location of the formula. In this activity, you will delete the columns that do not relate to the first quarter, and then copy formulas.

1 From the **column heading area**, select **columns E:F**. On the **Home tab**, in the **Cells group**, click the **Delete button arrow**, and then from the displayed list, click **Delete Sheet Columns**. Alternatively, click the Delete button; or, right-click over the selected columns to display the shortcut menu and click Delete.

Only the monthly sales for the first quarter of the year—January through March—display.

2 Click cell **E4**, hold down Alt, and then press =. Compare your screen with Figure 1.33.

Use this keyboard shortcut as the fastest way to apply the Sum function. Recall that when the Sum function is applied, Excel first looks above the selected cell for a proposed range of cells to sum, and if no data is detected, Excel then looks to the left and proposes a range of cells to sum.

Sum function applied with proposed range of cells to sum

Figure 1.33

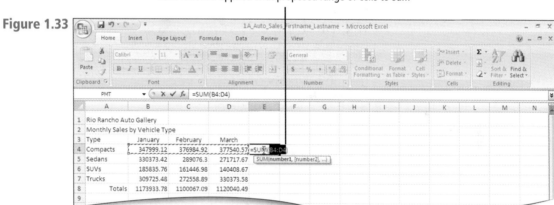

3 On the **Formula Bar**, click the **Enter** button ✓ so that cell **E4** remains the active cell.

The total dollar amount of *Compacts* sold in the quarter is *1102525*. You can see that in cells E5:E8, you need a formula similar to the one in E4, but one that refers to the cells in row 5, row 6, and so forth.

4 With cell **E4** selected, point to the fill handle in the lower right corner of the cell until the ➕ pointer displays. Then, drag downward through cell **E8**. Compare your screen with Figure 1.34.

Figure 1.34

Rows 4 – 8 summed   Auto Fill Options button

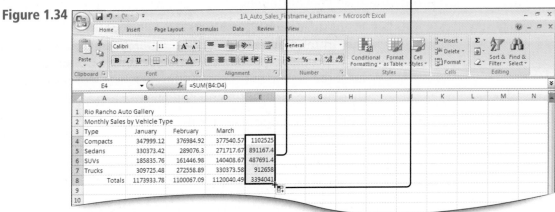

5 Click cell **E5**, look at the **Formula Bar**, and notice the formula =*SUM(B5:D5)*. Click cell **E6**, look at the **Formula Bar**, and then notice the formula =*SUM(B6:D6)*.

In each row, Excel copied the formula but adjusted the cell references *relative to* the row number. This is called a **relative cell reference**—a cell reference based on the relative position of the cell that contains the formula and the cells referred to. The calculation is the same, but it is performed on the cells in that particular row. Use this quick method to insert numerous formulas into spreadsheets.

6 **Save** 💾 your workbook.

Objective 4
Format Data, Cells, and Worksheets

Excel has many options for displaying numbers—think of percentages, fractions, or money. Recall that Excel refers to the various ways to write numbers as number formats. Some common number formats are those used for reporting financial information like monthly sales.

Formatting is the process of specifying the appearance of cells and the overall layout of a worksheet. Formatting is accomplished through various commands on the Ribbon, many of which are also available by using shortcut menus or keyboard shortcuts.

Activity 1.10 Formatting Financial Numbers, Using Column AutoFit, and Using Format Painter

The General format is the default format for a number that you type in a cell. Unless you apply a different number format to a cell, Excel will use the General format. The General format displays a number exactly as you type it—with three exceptions, as noted in the table in Figure 1.36.

1 Click cell **B4** so that a cell with numerical data is selected. On the **Home tab**, in the **Number group**, point to the **Dialog Box Launcher** button 🔲 in the lower right corner, as shown in Figure 1.35.

A ScreenTip displays what the result of clicking the icon will be. A **Dialog Box Launcher** displays in some groups on the Ribbon and opens a related dialog box providing additional options and commands related to that group.

Dialog Box Launcher button

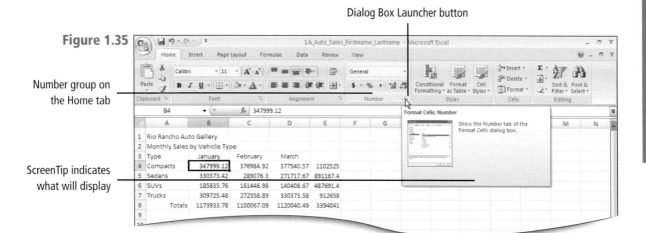

Figure 1.35

Number group on the Home tab

ScreenTip indicates what will display

2. Click the **Dialog Box Launcher** button, and then in the displayed **Format Cells** dialog box, on the **Number tab** under **Category**, click each category. As you do so, look at the **Sample** box to view the effect that each number format will have on the selected cell, and then take a moment to study the information about each Number format in the table in Figure 1.36.

Excel Number Formats

Number Format	Description
General	The General format is the default format for a number that you type in a cell. The General format displays a number exactly as you type it—with three exceptions: 1. Extremely long numbers may be abbreviated to a shorthand version of numbers called scientific notation; Excel will still use the underlying value in any calculations. 2. Trailing zeros will not display in the General format. 3. A decimal fraction entered without a number to the left of the decimal point will display with a zero.
Number	Number format is used for the general display of non-currency numbers. The default format has two decimal places, and you may choose to check the option for using a comma as a thousand separator. Negative numbers can display in red, be preceded by a minus sign, be enclosed in parentheses, or display both in red and in parentheses.
Currency	Currency format is used for general monetary values—the U.S. dollar sign is the default symbol.

(Continued)

(Continued)

Number Format	Description
Accounting	Accounting formats line up the currency symbols and decimal points in a column. It is similar to Currency format with two differences—the dollar sign (or other currency symbol) always displays at the left edge of the cell, rather than flush against the first number. Thus, both dollar signs and numbers are vertically aligned in the same column. Also, Accounting format adds a blank space equal to the width of a closing parenthesis on the right side of positive values to ensure that decimal points align if a column has both positive and negative numbers.
Date	Date format provides many common ways to display dates. The default format in the Format Cells dialog box is month, day, and year, separated by a slash. The year displays as four digits by default, but may be changed in the Control Panel to a two-digit display. Formats that begin with an asterisk are subject to change by regional date and time settings specified in the Control Panel.
Time	Time format provides many common ways to display time; formats are subject to change in the manner described above for dates.
Percentage	Percentage format multiplies the cell value by 100 and displays the result with a percent sign. The default is two decimal places.
Fraction	Fraction format displays fractional amounts as actual fractions rather than as decimal values.
Scientific	Scientific format displays numbers in scientific (exponential) notation. This is useful for extremely large numbers.
Text	Text format treats a number as if it were text. The number is left-aligned like text.
Special	Special formats used primarily with database functions such as postal codes, telephone numbers, and taxpayer ID numbers.
Custom	Custom format is used to create your own number format.

Figure 1.36

3 In the **Format Cells** dialog box, click **Cancel**. Hold down Ctrl, select the nonadjacent ranges **B4:E4** and **B8:E8**, and then on the Ribbon, in the **Number group**, click the **Accounting Number Format** button $ ▾. Compare your screen with Figure 1.37.

Columns B through D are not wide enough to accommodate the newly formatted numbers and thus display # signs. The *Accounting Number Format* button formats the number with the default Accounting format that uses the U.S. dollar sign. That is, it applies a thousand comma separator where appropriate, inserts a fixed U.S. dollar sign aligned at the left edge of the cell, applies two decimal places, and leaves a small amount of space at the right edge of the cell to accommodate a parenthesis for negative numbers.

Figure 1.37

Accounting Number Format applied to selected cells

Accounting Number Format button in Number group

Cells too narrow for newly formatted numbers display # signs

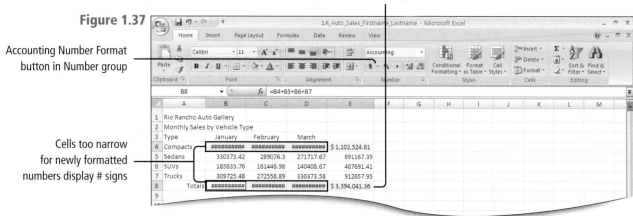

Note — Showing Fewer Decimal Places

Many financial documents do not display values with cents because either it is unnecessary to be completely precise or it not feasible to determine the exact number. To decrease the number of decimal places and round to the nearest whole dollar amount, select the cells, and then on the Home tab of the Ribbon, in the Number group, click the Decrease Decimal button two times to show a less precise value by showing fewer decimal places.

4 Select **column B**. On the Ribbon, in the **Cells group**, click the **Format button**, and then from the displayed menu, click **AutoFit Column Width**.

The width of the column is adjusted to accommodate the longest entry, which is the formatted total in cell B8.

5 Select **columns C:E**. In the **column heading area**, point to the right boundary of any of the selected columns to display the ⬌ pointer, and then double-click.

This is an alternative method to apply the AutoFit Column Width command. Each column width adjusts to accommodate the longest entry its column.

6 Select the range **B5:B7**, and then in the **Number group**, click the **Comma Style** button ⬚.

The **Comma Style** inserts thousand comma separators where appropriate and applies two decimal places. Comma Style also leaves space at the right to accommodate a parenthesis for negative numbers.

7 Click cell **B5**. On the Ribbon, in the **Clipboard group**, click the **Format Painter** button ⬚. With the ⬚ pointer, select the range **C5:E7**, and then compare your screen with Figure 1.38.

Use **Format Painter** to copy the *formatting* of one cell to other cells. You can see that there are numerous methods to apply formatting to cells.

When preparing worksheets with financial information, the first row of dollar amounts and the total rows of dollar amounts are formatted in the Accounting Number Format; that is, with thousand comma separators, dollar signs, two decimal places, and space at the right to accommodate a parenthesis for negative numbers, if any. Rows that are not the first row or the total row should be formatted with the Comma Style.

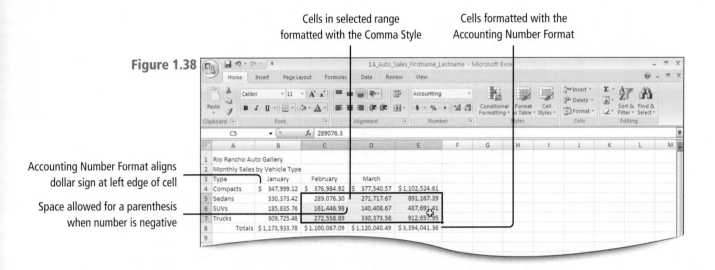

Figure 1.38

Cells in selected range formatted with the Comma Style

Cells formatted with the Accounting Number Format

Accounting Number Format aligns dollar sign at left edge of cell

Space allowed for a parenthesis when number is negative

Note — Double-Click Format Painter to Copy Formatting to Multiple Selections

Double-clicking the Format Painter button causes it to remain active until you click the button again to turn it off. Use this technique to copy cell formatting to two or more cells that are not adjacent.

8 Select the range **B8:E8**. In the **Font group**, click the **Borders button arrow** to display a *gallery* of commonly used border styles. Compare your screen with Figure 1.39.

A gallery displays a list of potential results. The Borders button displays the most recently used border style; clicking the button, rather than the arrow, applies the most recently used style as indicated by the button.

Borders arrow

Figure 1.39

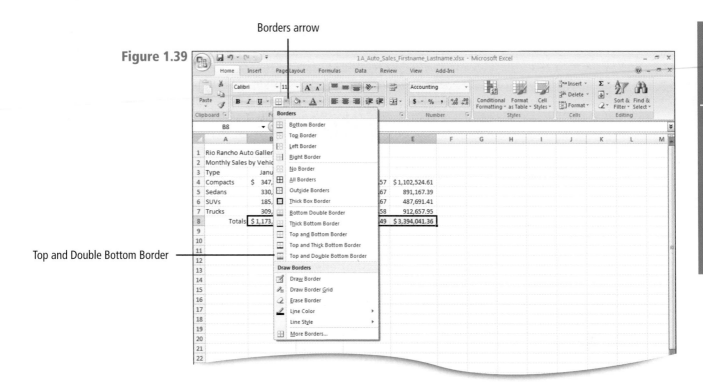

Top and Double Bottom Border

9 From the displayed list, click **Top and Double Bottom Border**. Click any empty cell to deselect the range, and then compare your screen with Figure 1.40.

This is a common way to apply borders to financial information. The single border indicates that calculations were performed on the numbers above, and the double border indicates that the information is complete.

Figure 1.40

Top border
Double bottom border

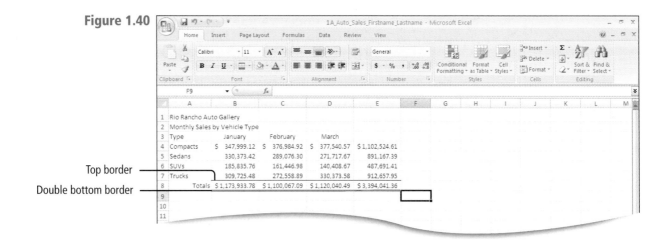

10 **Save** 💾 your workbook.

Note — Using Negative Numbers in a Worksheet

You can see a small amount of space to the right of each of the formatted number cells. The formats you applied allow this space in the event parentheses are needed to indicate negative numbers. If your worksheet contains negative numbers, display the Format Cells dialog box and select from among various formats to accommodate negative numbers. As you progress in your study of Excel, you will practice formatting negative numbers.

Activity 1.11 Formatting Text and Using Merge and Center

Use techniques similar to other Office programs to change fonts; you can add emphasis by using bold, italic, and underline, and align text in the center, or at the left or right edge of a cell. In this activity, you will format the worksheet's title and subtitle to increase their visibility and inform the reader of the worksheet's purpose.

1 Select the range **A1:E1**, and then in the **Alignment group**, click the **Merge and Center** button. Select the range **A2:E2**, right-click over the selection to display the shortcut menu and Mini toolbar, and then on the Mini toolbar, click the **Merge and Center** button.

The Merge and Center command joins the selected cells into one larger cell and centers the contents in the new cell; cells B1:E1 can no longer be selected individually because they are merged into cell A1. Access the Merge and Center command by using either method; this command works only on a single row at a time.

2 Click cell **A1**, which contains the merged and centered text *Rio Rancho Auto Gallery*. On the **Home tab**, in the **Font group**, click the **Font button arrow** Calibri.

3 At the top of the list, under **Theme Fonts**, point to **Cambria**, and notice *(Headings)* to the right.

A **theme** is a predefined set of colors, fonts, lines, and fill effects that look good together and that can be applied to your entire workbook or to specific items—for example, to a chart or table. As you progress in your study of Excel, you will use more theme features.

Cambria is a **serif** font—a font that includes small line extensions on the ends of the letters to guide the eye in reading from left to right. In the default theme, *Cambria* is the suggested font for headings, and *Calibri* is the suggested font for the body of the worksheet.

4 Click **Cambria** to apply the font. With cell **A1** still selected, in the **Font group**, click the **Font Size button arrow** 11, and then point to **14**, and then **16**, and then **18**, and notice how the text expands as you point to each size—this is **Live Preview**. Click **18**.

Live Preview is a technology that shows the results of applying an editing or formatting change as you move the pointer over the items presented in the gallery or list.

5 With cell **A1** selected, in the **Font group**, click the **Bold** button **B**.

The Bold *font style* is applied to your text. Font styles are used to emphasize text by using bold, italic, and underline.

6 With cell **A1** still selected, in the lower right corner of the **Font group**, click the **Dialog Box Launcher** button 🔲 to display the **Font tab** of the **Format Cells** dialog box. Notice that *Cambria* is selected and that a preview of the font is also displayed under **Preview**.

7 Under **Font style**, click **Bold Italic**, and then notice that the Preview changes to reflect your selection. Click the **Color arrow**. Under **Theme Colors**, point to the fourth box to display the ScreenTip *Dark Blue, Text 2*, and then in that column of colors, click the next to last color—**Dark Blue, Text 2, Darker 25%**—as shown in Figure 1.41.

From the Format Cells dialog box, you can apply multiple formats at one time in this manner.

Bold Italic indicated as Font style   18 indicated as Size

Figure 1.41

Cambria indicated as Font

Select this theme color

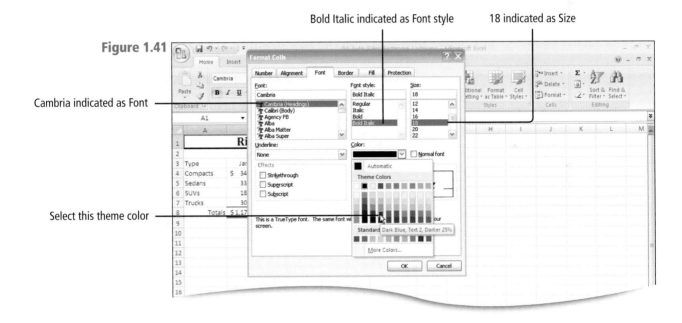

8 Click **OK**. With cell **A1** still selected, in the **Font group** click the **Underline** button 🔲.

From the Ribbon, you can apply some common formats such as this one. The **Underline** button places a single underline under the *contents* of a cell. The Bold, Italic, and Underline buttons on the Ribbon are *toggle buttons*, which means that you can click the button one time to turn the formatting on and click it again to turn it off.

9 With cell **A1** selected, in the **Font group** click the **Underline** button 🔲 again to turn off Underline.

The Underline font style is removed from the text, but the Bold and Italic font styles remain.

10 With cell **A1** selected, in the **Font group**, click the **Fill Color button arrow** . On the displayed color palette, under **Theme Colors**, in the fourth column, click the second color—**Dark Blue, Text 2, Lighter 80%**.

The background of the cell—its *fill color*—changes. If your printer does not print in color, the colors will print as shades of gray, so select light colors to provide better contrast. Colors are especially distinctive if your workbook will be viewed on a screen.

11 Point to cell **A2**, right-click, on the displayed Mini toolbar, click the **Increase Font Size** button A⁺ two times, and as you click, notice that the new Font Size number displays on both the Ribbon and the Mini toolbar. Then, on the Mini toolbar, click the **Bold** button B. Move the mouse pointer slightly away so that the Mini toolbar fades out, view your formatting, and then click any cell to cancel the selection and close the Mini toolbar.

12 Double-click cell **A2** and edit the word *Monthly* to change it to **First Quarter** Press Enter.

13 Select **row 2**, and in the **row heading area**, drag the lower border of **row 2** down to increase the row height to **35 pixels**. Select cell **A2**, and then in the **Alignment group**, click the **Middle Align** button ≡ to align the text vertically in the cell.

14 In cell **E3**, type **Totals** and then press Enter. Select the nonadjacent ranges **A3:E3** and **A4:A8** and apply **Bold** B emphasis. **Save** your workbook, click any cell, and then compare your screen with Figure 1.42.

The text in cell E3 is centered because the centered format continues from the adjacent cell. The same formatting will be applied to adjacent cells until two cells are left blank, and then the formatting is not continued.

Column title added

Figure 1.42

Formatting applied to worksheet title and subtitle

Column and row titles in bold

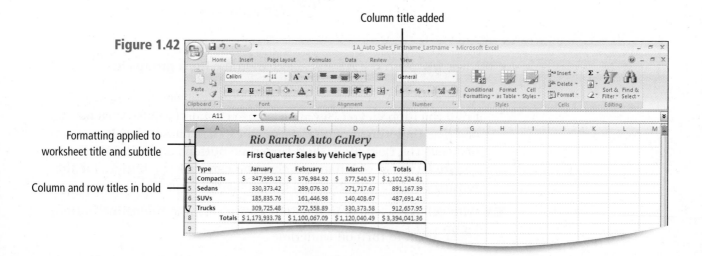

Objective 5
Close and Reopen a Workbook

You can save and close a workbook and then reopen it later to continue working. For example, at this point in this Project, you may want to close the workbook and continue working later.

Activity 1.12 Closing and Reopening an Existing Workbook

1 To close the workbook, from the **Office** menu, click **Close**—if there are changes to be saved, Excel will prompt you to save before closing. In the upper right corner of your screen, click the **Close** button

X to exit Excel. Alternatively, from the Office menu, click Exit Excel. Or, to simultaneously close your workbook and close the Excel program, from the Office menu in the lower right corner, click Exit Excel.

2 To reopen the workbook, **start** Excel, and then display the **Office** menu. From the list of **Recent Documents**, click your workbook name if it displays. Alternatively, click the Open button and navigate to your storage location, select your workbook, and then click Open.

Objective 6
Chart Data

A *chart* is a graphic representation of data in a worksheet. For the reader, data presented as a chart is usually easier to understand than a table of numbers.

Activity 1.13 Charting Data

In this activity, you will create a column chart showing the monthly sales of vehicles by type during the first quarter. The chart will allow Sandy Cizek, the Auto Sales Manager, to see a pattern of overall monthly sales and a pattern of monthly sales by vehicle type.

1 Select the range **A3:E8**. On the Ribbon, click the **Insert tab**, and then in the **Charts group**, click **Column** to display a gallery of Column *chart types*.

Various chart types are used to chart data in a way that is meaning-ful to the reader—common examples are column charts, pie charts, and line charts. A *column chart* is useful for illustrating compar-isons among related numbers.

2 From the displayed gallery of column chart types, under **2-D Column**, point to the first chart to display the ScreenTip *Clustered Column*, and then click to select it. Compare your screen with Figure 1.43.

A column chart displays in the worksheet, and the charted data is bordered by colored lines. Because the chart object is selected—surrounded by a border and displaying sizing handles—*contextual tools* named *Chart Tools* display and add **contextual tabs** next to the standard tabs on the Ribbon.

Contextual tools enable you to perform specific commands related to the selected object, and display one or more contextual tabs that contain related groups of commands that you will need when working with the type of object that is selected. Contextual tools display only when needed for a selected object; when you deselect the object, the contextual tools no longer display.

Cells outlined in blue represented in chart columns

Cells outlined in green represent the legend

Chart Tools indicates that tools for selected object added to the Ribbon

Chart Tools contextual tabs added to standard Ribbon tabs

Figure 1.43

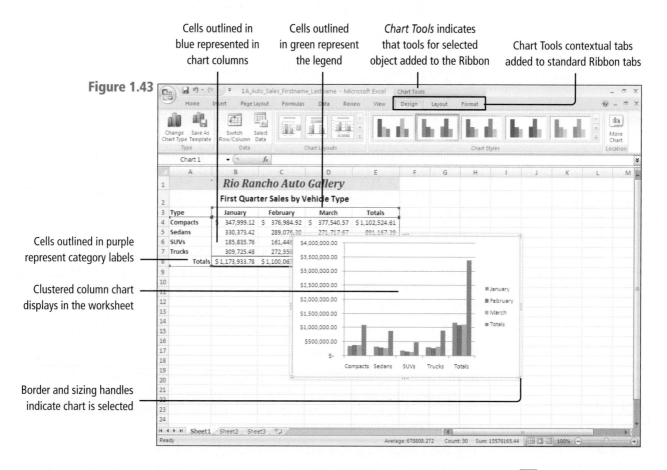

Cells outlined in purple represent category labels

Clustered column chart displays in the worksheet

Border and sizing handles indicate chart is selected

3 Point to the top border of the chart to display the ⬚ pointer, hold down the left mouse button, and then drag the upper left corner of the chart just inside the upper left corner of cell **A10**, approximately as shown in Figure 1.44.

Based on the data in your worksheet, Excel constructs a column chart and adds **category labels**—the labels that display along the bottom of the chart to identify the category of data. This area is referred to as the **category axis** or the **x-axis**. Excel uses the row titles as the category names.

On the left, Excel includes a numerical scale upon which the charted data is based; this is referred to as the **value axis** or the **y-axis**. On the right, a **legend**, which identifies the patterns or colors that are assigned to the categories in the chart, displays.

Figure 1.44

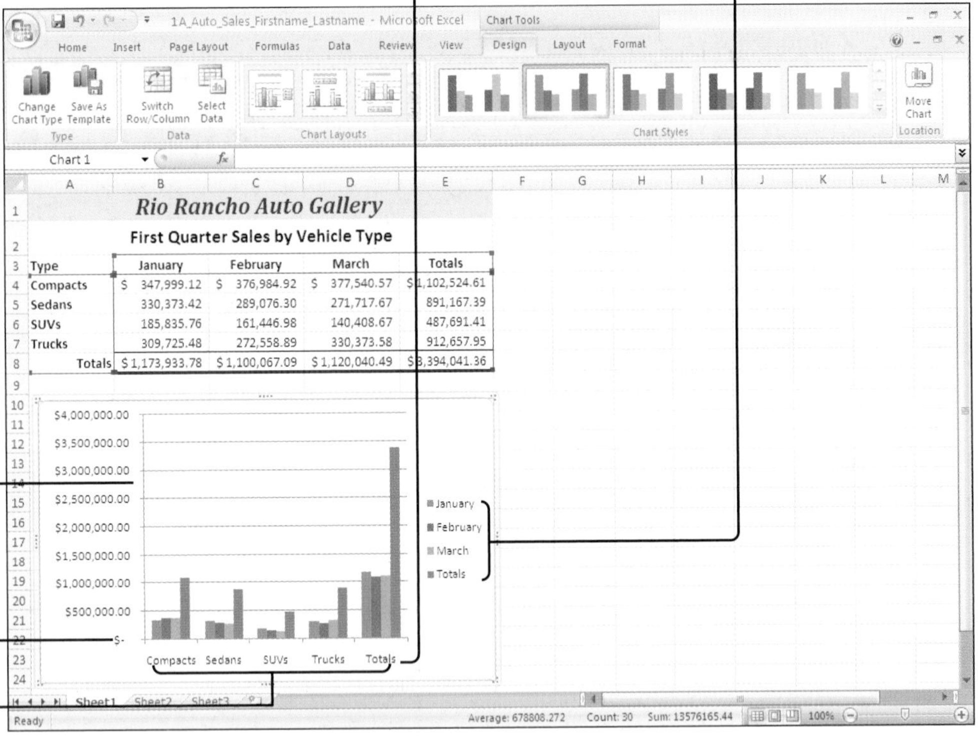

Totals included as a category

Legend

Value axis, also called y-axis (based on total quarterly sales)

Category axis, also called x-axis

Category labels

4️⃣ On the Ribbon, locate the three contextual tabs that are active under **Chart Tools—Design**, **Layout**, and **Format**.

When a chart is selected, Chart Tools become available and these three tabs—Design, Layout, and Format—provide commands for working with the chart. When the chart is not selected, the Chart Tools do not display.

5️⃣ Point to the lower right corner of cell **E8** to display the ⤡ pointer, and then notice that the blue border surrounding the group of charted cells becomes thicker and brighter in color. Compare your screen with Figure 1.45.

You can adjust the chart by selecting a different group of cells to chart. On this chart, Sandy Cizek, the Auto Sales Manager for Rio Rancho Auto Gallery, wants to see only the sales by month and not the total sales for the quarter.

When charting data, typically, you should not include totals—include only the comparable data.

Figure 1.45

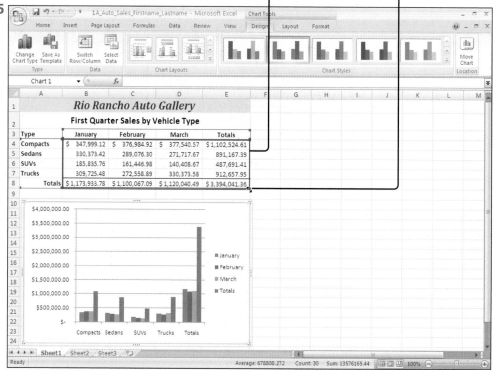

6 Drag the ⬉ pointer up and to the left until only the monthly dollar amounts in the range **B4:D7** are surrounded by the blue border. Release the left mouse button and notice the changes in your chart. Compare your screen with Figure 1.46.

Each of the twelve cells bordered in blue is referred to as a ***data point***—a value that originates in a worksheet cell. Each data point is represented in the chart by a ***data marker***—a column, bar, area, dot, pie slice, or other symbol in a chart that represents a single data point. Related data points form a ***data series***; for example, there is a data series for *January*, for *February*, and for *March*. Each data series has a unique color or pattern represented in the chart legend.

Only sales figures for January, February, and March display

Totals no longer included in the charted data

Color for each data series defined in legend

Figure 1.46

Each value in the selected range is a data point

Data markers (columns) represent each data point

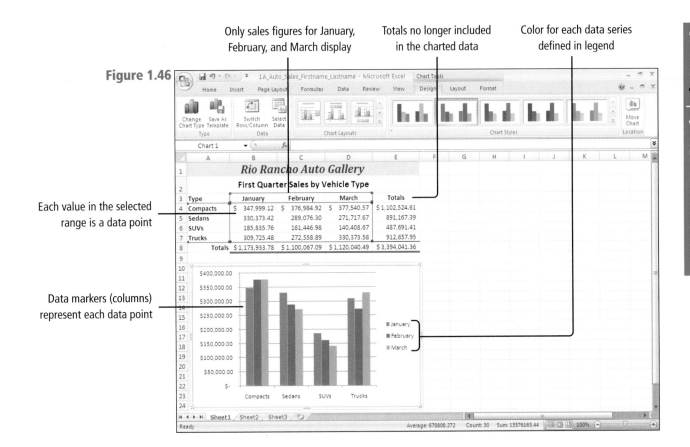

7 On the **Design tab** of the Ribbon, in the **Data group**, click the **Switch Row/Column** button, and then compare your chart with Figure 1.47.

In this manner, you can easily change the categories of data from the row titles, which is the default, to the column titles. Whether you use row or column titles as your category names depends on how you want to view your charted data. In this instance, the Sales Manager wants to see monthly sales and the breakdown of vehicle type within each month.

Figure 1.47

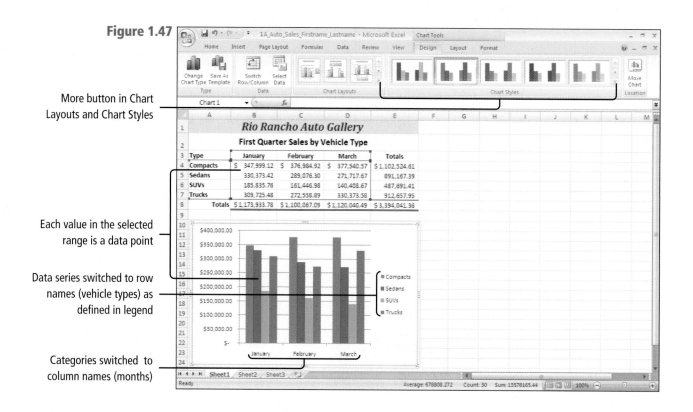

More button in Chart
Layouts and Chart Styles

Each value in the selected
range is a data point

Data series switched to row
names (vehicle types) as
defined in legend

Categories switched to
column names (months)

8 On the **Design tab** of the Ribbon, in the **Chart Layouts group**,
locate, and then click the **More** button ⬇️ , and then compare your
screen with Figure 1.48.

From the ***Chart Layouts gallery***, you can select a predesigned ***chart
layout***—the combination of chart elements you want to display, which
can include a title, legend, labels for the columns, and the table of
charted cells.

Chart Layouts gallery

Figure 1.48

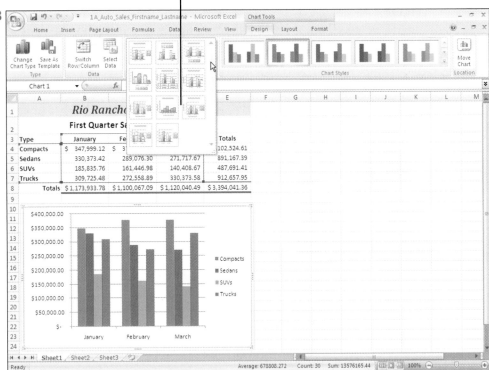

9 Click several different layouts to see the effect on your chart, and then using the ScreenTips as your guide, locate and click **Layout 1**.

10 In the chart, point to the text *Chart Title*, right-click, and then from the shortcut menu, click **Edit Text**. Alternatively, select the title and double-click. Delete the text, and then type **First Quarter Sales by Vehicle Type**

11 Click in a white area *inside* the chart to deselect the chart title, but leaving the chart itself selected. On the **Design tab**, in the **Chart Styles group**, point to, and then click the **More** button ⬇, and then compare your screen with Figure 1.49.

The **Chart Styles gallery** displays. Here you can select from among a large array of pre-defined **chart styles**—the overall visual look of the chart in terms of its graphic effects, colors, and backgrounds. For example, you can have flat or beveled columns, colors that are solid or transparent, and backgrounds that are dark or light.

Figure 1.49

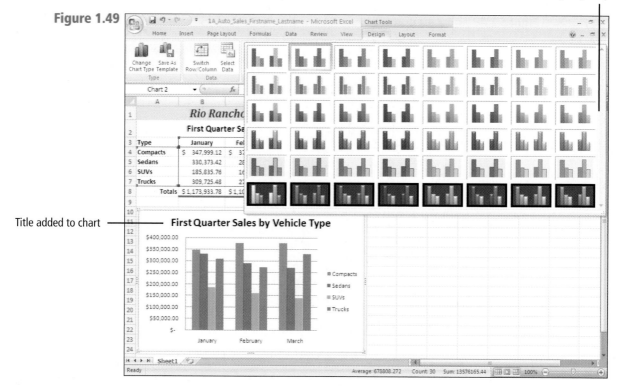

Title added to chart

First Quarter Sales by Vehicle Type

12 Click several different styles to see the effect on your chart, and then using the ScreenTips as your guide, locate and click **Style 26**.

This style uses a white background, formats the columns by using theme colors, and applies a slightly beveled effect to the columns.

With this clear visual representation of the data, Mr. Cizek can see that sales of compact cars have risen in each month of the quarter. He can also see that sales of sedans and SUVs have declined steadily in each month of the quarter. Finally, Mr. Cizek can see that truck sales declined slightly, and then rose again in March, possibly due to spring demand from local ranchers and farmers.

13 In your chart, notice that the values on the **value axis** include two decimal places. Then, on the Ribbon, click the **Layout tab**. In the **Axes group**, click the **Axes** button, point to **Primary Vertical Axis**, and then compare your screen with Figure 1.50.

More Primary Vertical
Axis Options

Layout tab

Figure 1.50

Axes button

Primary Vertical Axis gallery

Values on value axis
display two decimal points

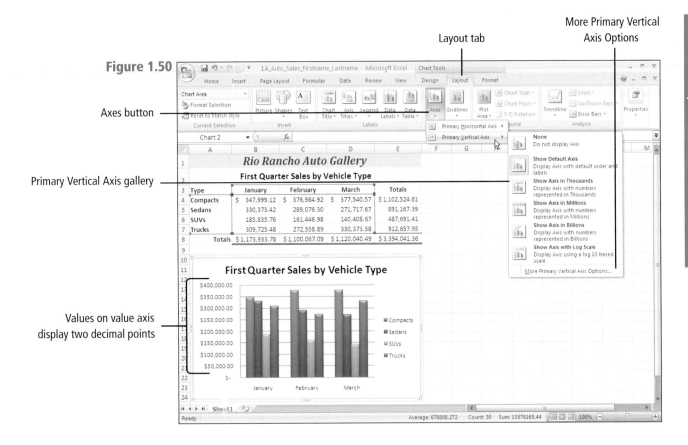

14 At the bottom of the gallery, click **More Primary Vertical Axis Options** to display the **Format Axis** dialog box. In the displayed dialog box, in the column at the left, click **Number**, and then in the **Decimal places** box, delete the existing number, type **0** and then click **Close**.

The decimal places are removed from the value axis, resulting in a less cluttered look, and the value axis area of the chart is selected.

15 Click any cell to deselect the chart, and notice that the *Chart Tools* no longer display in the Ribbon. Compare your screen with Figure 1.51.

Contextual tabs related to contextual tools in Office 2007 programs display when an object is selected, and then are removed from view when the object is deselected.

Figure 1.51

Chart Tools removed from view when chart not selected

Decimal points removed from value axis

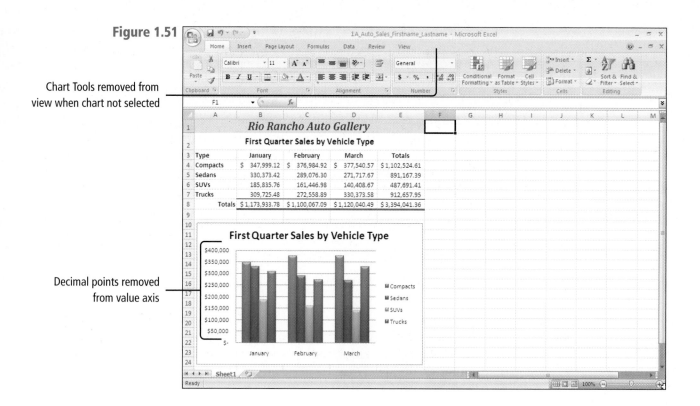

16 Save 💾 your workbook.

More Knowledge

A Chart Can Occupy a Separate Sheet in the Workbook

When a chart displays as an object within the worksheet, it is referred to as an *embedded chart*. On the Design tab of the Ribbon, the last button—Move Chart—creates a new workbook sheet and places the chart on a separate workbook sheet. An embedded chart is useful when you want to view or print a chart on the same page as its source data.

Objective 7
Use Page Layout View, Prepare a Worksheet for Printing, and Close Excel

Before you print a worksheet, use *Page Layout view* and the commands on the Page Layout tab to prepare your data for printing. In Page Layout view, you can use the rulers to measure the width and height of data, set margins for printing, hide or display the numbered row headings and the lettered column headings, and change the *page orientation*—the position of data on the paper.

In *portrait orientation*, the paper is taller than it is wide. In *landscape orientation*, the paper is wider than it is tall. In Page Layout view, you can also add *headers* or *footers* which are text, page numbers, graphics, and formatting that print at the top (header) or bottom (footer) of every page of a worksheet. Finally, you can see how the data and chart are centered on the page and if everything fits onto one page.

Activity 1.14 Changing Views, Creating a Footer, and Using Print Preview

For each of your projects in this textbook, you will create a footer containing your name and the project name. This will make it easy for you to identify your printed documents in a shared printer environment such as a lab or classroom, or if you or your instructor view your completed work electronically.

1 On the Ribbon, click the **Insert tab**, and then in the **Text group**, click **Header & Footer** to switch to **Page Layout view** and open the **Header area**. Compare your screen with Figure 1.52.

In this view you can see the edges of the paper of multiple pages, the margins, and the rulers. You can also insert a header or footer by typing in the areas indicated and using the Header & Footer Tools. Recall that contextual tools and tabs of this type become available when an object requiring the related commands is selected—in this instance the Header area object.

Edges of pages

Figure 1.52

Go to Footer button

Rulers

Header area open and selected

Margin

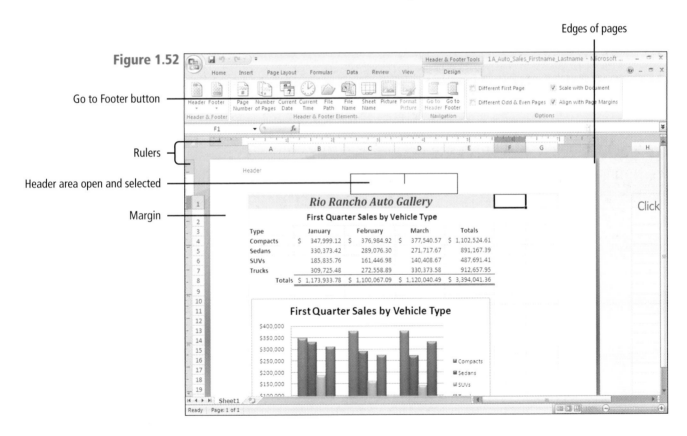

2 In the **Navigation group**, click the **Go to Footer** button to move to the bottom of the page and open the **Footer area**, and then click just above the word *Footer* to place the insertion point in the left section of the **Footer area**.

The Header and Footer areas have three distinct sections—left, center, and right.

3 On the Ribbon, in the **Header & Footer Elements group**, click the **File Name** button to add the name of your file to the footer—&[File] displays in the left section of the **Footer area**. Then, click in a cell just above the footer to exit the **Footer area** and view your file name.

The Header & Footer Tools are removed from view. In Page Layout View, you can also type a header or footer directly into the areas indicated, but use this technique to automatically insert the file name.

4 Scroll up to view your chart, click the upper right corner of the chart to select it, and then check to see if the chart is centered under the data in the cells. If necessary, point to the **right resize handle** to display the ↔ pointer, as shown in Figure 1.53.

Figure 1.53

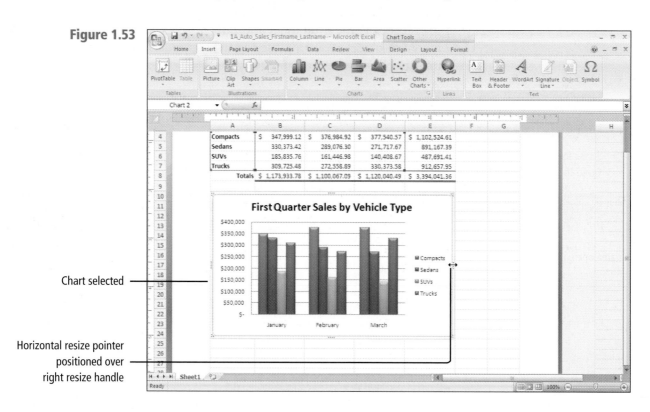

Chart selected

Horizontal resize pointer positioned over right resize handle

5 Drag the right border of the chart until it is almost even with the right border of **column E**, and then click any cell to deselect the chart. Be sure the left and right borders of the chart are just slightly inside the left border of **column A** and the right border of **column E**—adjust as necessary.

6 Click any cell to deselect the chart. Click the **Page Layout tab**, in the **Page Setup group**, click the **Margins** button, and then at the bottom of the **Margins gallery**, click **Custom Margins**. In the displayed **Page Setup** dialog box, under **Center on page**, select the **Horizontally** check box.

This action will center the data and chart horizontally on the page, as shown in the Preview area. Alternatively, you can display the Page Setup dialog box by clicking the Dialog Box Launcher in the Page Setup group, and then clicking the desired tab within the dialog box.

7 In the lower right corner of the **Page Setup** dialog box, click **OK**. In the upper left corner of your screen, click the **Office** button ⊞, from the displayed menu, point to the **Print button**, and then click **Print Preview**. Alternatively, press Ctrl + F2 to view the Print Preview. Compare your screen with Figure 1.54.

The Ribbon displays the Print Preview program tab, which replaces the standard set of tabs when you switch to Print Preview.

Figure 1.54

Print Preview tab

Close Print Preview button

Document displayed in Print Preview

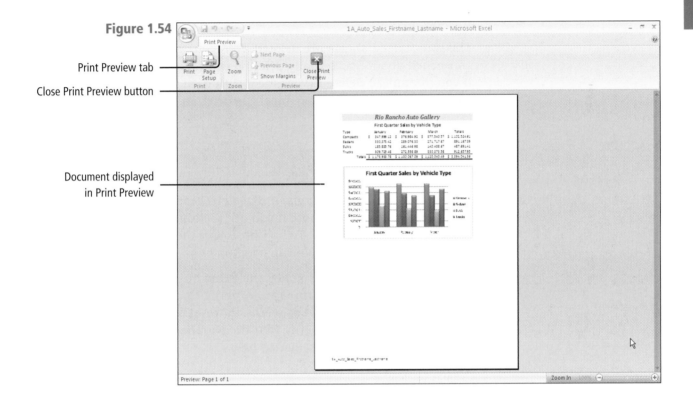

8 Note any adjustments that need to be made, and then on the Ribbon, click the **Close Print Preview** button. On the right side of the status bar, click the **Normal** button ⊞ to return to the Normal view, and then press Ctrl + Home to return to cell **A1**.

The ***Normal view*** maximizes the number of cells visible on your screen and keeps the column letters and row numbers closer. The vertical dotted line between columns indicates that as currently arranged, only the columns to the left of the dotted line will print on the first page. The exact position of the vertical line will depend on your default printer setting—yours may fall elsewhere.

9 **Save** 💾 your workbook.

Activity 1.15 Deleting Unused Sheets in a Workbook

By default, each new Excel workbook contains three blank worksheets. Although it is not necessary to delete unused sheets, doing so saves storage space and removes any doubt that additional information is in the workbook.

1 At the bottom of your worksheet, click the **Sheet2 tab** to display Sheet 2 and make it the active worksheet.

2 Hold down Ctrl, and then click the **Sheet3 tab**. With both sheets selected (tab background is white, not blue, on the selected sheets), display the **Home tab**. In the **Cells group**, click the **Delete button arrow**, and then click **Delete Sheet**. Alternatively, point to either of the selected sheet tabs, right-click, and then click Delete to delete the sheets.

The two unused sheets are deleted from your workbook. Do not be concerned about accidentally deleting worksheets that contain data. If you attempt to delete a worksheet with data, Excel will display a warning and permit you to cancel the deletion.

3 **Save** 💾 your workbook.

Activity 1.16 Printing a Worksheet

1 Check your *Chapter Assignment Sheet* or *Course Syllabus*, or consult your instructor, to determine if you are to submit your assignments on paper or electronically. To submit electronically, follow the instructions provided by your instructor.

2 From the **Office** menu 📄, click the **Print** button. In the displayed **Print** dialog box, under **Print range**, verify that the **All** option button is selected. Under **Print what**, verify that **Active sheet(s)** is selected, and then under **Copies**, verify that the **Number of copies** is **1**. Compare your screen with Figure 1.55.

Figure 1.55

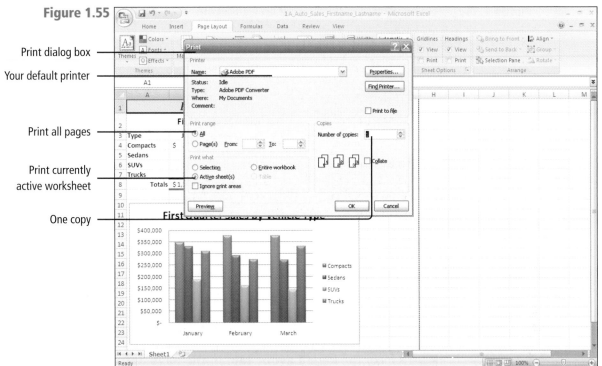

Print dialog box

Your default printer

Print all pages

Print currently active worksheet

One copy

---

3 Click **OK** to print your worksheet, and then **Save** your workbook.

Activity 1.17 Displaying, Printing, and Hiding Formulas

When you have a formula in a cell, the cell displays the results of the formula. Recall that this value is called the displayed value. You can view and print the underlying formulas in the cells. When you do so, a formula often takes more horizontal space to display than the result of the calculation. Thus, the landscape orientation is usually a better choice than portrait orientation to fit the formulas on one page. In this activity, you will print the formulas in Sheet1 in landscape orientation and then close the workbook without saving the changes.

1 Because you will make some temporary changes to your workbook,

on the **Quick Access Toolbar**, click the **Save** button to be sure that you have saved your work up to this point.

2 Hold down Ctrl, and then press ` (usually located below Esc), and then compare your screen with Figure 1.56. Alternatively, on the Formulas tab, in the Formula Auditing group, click the Show Formulas button.

Figure 1.56

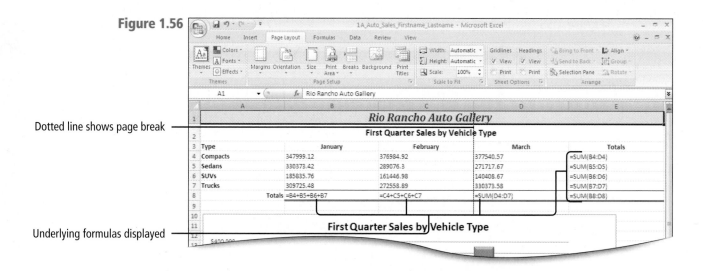

Dotted line shows page break

Underlying formulas displayed

3 From the **column heading area**, select columns **A:E**. Point to the column heading boundary between any two of the selected columns and double-click to AutoFit the selected columns.

4 Display the **Page Layout tab**. In the **Page Setup group**, click the **Orientation** button, and then click **Landscape**. In the **Scale to Fit group**, click the **Dialog Box Launcher** button 🔲 to display the **Page tab** of the **Page Setup** dialog box.

5 Under **Scaling**, click the **Fit to** option button, and then in the lower right corner, click the **Print Preview** button—this is another point from which you can display the Print Preview.

Scaling adjusts the size of the printed worksheet to fit on the page, and is convenient for printing formulas. Although it is not always the case, formulas frequently take up more space than the actual data.

6 Click **Close Print Preview**. Check your *Chapter Assignment Sheet* or *Course Syllabus*, or consult your instructor, to determine if you are to submit your printed formulas on paper or electronically. To submit electronically, follow the instructions provided by your instructor.

7 From the **Office** menu 🔲, click the **Print** button. In the displayed **Print** dialog box, under **Print range**, verify that the **All** option button is selected. Under **Print what**, verify that **Active sheet(s)** is selected, and then under **Copies**, verify that the **Number of copies** is **1**.

8 Click **OK** to print your worksheet. From the **Office** menu 🔲, click **Close**, and when prompted, click **No** so that you do *not* save the changes you made—displaying formulas, changing column widths and orientation, and scaling—to print your formulas.

9 In the upper right corner of your screen, click the **Close** button

🔲 to close Excel.

End You have completed Project 1A

Project 1B **Safety Shop**

In Activities 1.18 through 1.25, you will create a workbook for Arthur Potempa, the Retail Sales Manager for Rio Rancho Auto Gallery. One of the retail areas in the Auto Gallery carries an inventory of safety products. Mr. Potempa wants to calculate the retail value of the inventory of safety products and then, using a pie chart, display how each item's retail value contributes to the total retail value. Your completed worksheet and chart will look similar to Figure 1.57.

For Project 1B, you will need the following file:

New blank Excel workbook

You will save your workbook as
1B_Safety_Products_Firstname_Lastname

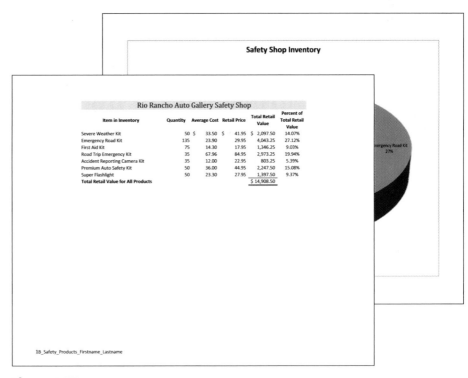

Figure 1.57
Project 1B—Safety Shop

Objective 8
Design a Worksheet

Good design techniques, which make your worksheet useful to the reader, include the following: generally it is best to use rows rather than columns for the most abundant data; if you will print the worksheet, consider how it will look on paper; and, arrange the data so that it is easily charted.

Activity 1.18 Setting Column Widths and Creating Row and Column Titles

The worksheet title is typically placed in the first row and centered above the columns of data.

1 With **Excel** open, from the **Office** menu [icon], click **New**. In the **New Workbook** dialog box, under **Blank and recent**, click **Blank Workbook**, and then in the lower right corner, click the **Create** button. Alternatively, press [Ctrl] + [N].

If the Excel program is already open, these are techniques you can use to begin a new workbook.

2 From the **Office** menu [icon], display the **Save As** dialog box, navigate to your **Excel Chapter 1 folder**, and then in the **File name** box, replace the existing text with **1B_Safety_Products_Firstname_Lastname** and then click **Save**.

3 Click cell **A2**, type **Item in Inventory** and then press [Tab]. In cell **B2**, type **Quantity** and then press [Tab]. In cell **C2**, type **Average Cost** and then press [Tab]. In cell **D2**, type **Retail Price** and then press [Tab]. In cell **E2**, type **Total Retail Value** and then press [Tab]. In cell **F2**, type **Percent of Total Retail Value** and then press [Enter].

4 In cell **A3**, type **Severe Weather Kit** and then press [Enter]. Type the remaining row titles in cells **A4:A9**, and then compare your screen with Figure 1.58.

Emergency Road Kit

First Aid Kit

Accident Reporting Camera Kit

Premium Auto Safety Kit

Super Flashlight

Total Retail Value for All Products

Figure 1.58

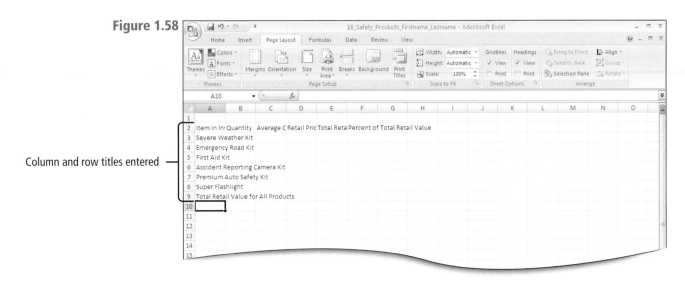

Column and row titles entered

5 Right-click cell **A9** and on the Mini toolbar, click **Bold** [B].

6 Select **columns A:F**, position the [✛] pointer over the right boundary of any of the selected column heading letters, and then double-click to apply **AutoFit Column Width**. Alternatively, click the Format button arrow, and then click AutoFit Column Width.

7 Click cell **A1** and type **Rio Rancho Auto Gallery Safety Shop** and then on the **Formula Bar**, click the **Enter** button [✓]. Select the range **A1:F1**, and then right-click over the selection.

On the Mini toolbar, click the **Merge and Center** button [▦▾], change the **Font** [Calibri ▾] to **Cambria**, and then change the **Font Size** [11 ▾] to **16**.

8 With cell **A1** still selected, click the **Fill Color arrow** [◇▾]. Under **Theme Colors**, in the first row, point to the seventh box to display the ScreenTip *Olive Green, Accent 3*, and then in that column of colors, click the third color—**Olive Green, Accent 3, Lighter 60%**.

Click anywhere to deselect cell **A1**, **Save** [💾] your workbook, and then compare your screen with Figure 1.59.

The worksheet title is formatted with a different font, font size, and fill color to distinguish it visually from the worksheet data.

Figure 1.59

Column widths adjusted

Worksheet title entered and formatted

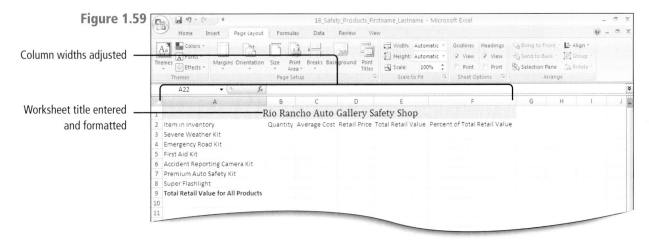

Activity 1.19 Entering Data by Range

In the following activity, you will enter data by first selecting a range of cells; this can be a time-saving technique. Use the numeric keypad on your keyboard to make this technique even faster.

1 Select the range **B3:D8**, type **50** and then press [Enter].

The first value is entered in cell B3 and cell B4 becomes the active cell.

2 Beginning in cell **B4** and pressing [Enter] after each entry, type the following, and then compare your screen with Figure 1.60:

135

75

35

50

50

After you enter the last value and press [Enter], the active cell moves to the top of the next column within the selected range. Selecting the range in this manner—before you enter data—saves time because it confines the movement of the active cell to the selected range.

Figure 1.60

Active cell moves to the next column

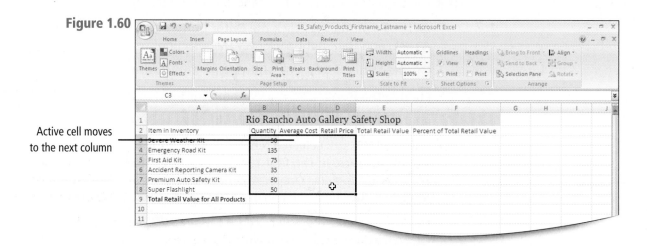

3 From the following table, beginning in cell **C3** and pressing [Enter] after each entry, enter the data for the **Average Cost** and **Retail Price** columns. Then compare your screen with Figure 1.61.

Average Cost	Retail Price
33.5	41.95
23.9	29.95
14.3	17.95
12	22.95
36	44.95
23.3	27.95

Recall that the default number format for cells is the *General* number format, in which numbers display exactly as you type them and trailing zeros do not display, even if you type them.

Figure 1.61

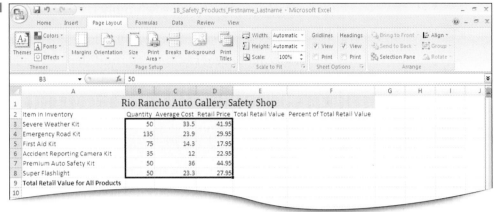

4 **Save** 💾 your workbook.

Objective 9
Construct Formulas for Mathematical Operations

Operators are symbols with which you can specify the type of calculation you want to perform in a formula.

Activity 1.20 Using Arithmetic Operators

1 In cell **E3**, type **=b3*d3** and press Enter.

The *Total Retail Value* of all *Severe Weather Kit* items in the shop—2097.5—equals the *Quantity* (50) times the *Retail Price* (selling price) of 41.95. In Excel, the asterisk (*) represents multiplication.

2 Take a moment to study the symbols you will use to perform basic mathematical operations in Excel, as shown in the table in Figure 1.62—these are referred to as ***arithmetic operators***.

Symbols Used in Excel for Arithmetic Operators

Operator Symbol	Operation
+	Addition
-	Subtraction (also negation)
*	Multiplication
/	Division
%	Percent
^	Exponentiation

Figure 1.62

3 Click cell **E3**.

You can see that in cells E4:E8, you need a formula similar to the one in E3, but one that refers to the cells in row 4, row 5, and so forth. Recall that you can copy formulas and the cell references will change *relative to* the row number.

4 With cell **E3** selected, position your pointer over the fill handle in the lower right corner of the cell until the ＋ pointer displays. Then, drag down through cell **E8** to copy the formula.

5 Select the range **C3:E3**, right-click over the selection, and then on the Mini toolbar, click the **Accounting Number Format** button `$ ▾`. Select the range **C4:E8**, right-click over the selection, and then on the Mini toolbar, click the **Comma Style** button `▾`. Click cell **E9**, in the **Editing group**, click the **Sum** button `Σ ▾`, and then press Enter. **Save** 🖫 your workbook, and then compare your screen with Figure 1.63.

Your result is *$11,935.25*. The Accounting Number Format is automatically applied to cell E9. The format of the cell containing the formula is the same as the format of the cells used in the formula. If the formula references a range of cells and those cells contain a mix of formats, the format from the cell in the upper left corner of the range is applied.

Retail Value calculated for
each row

Total Retail Value
calculated

Figure 1.63

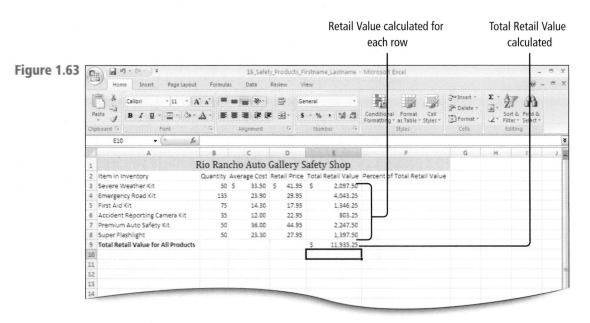

Activity 1.21 Copying Formulas Containing Absolute Cell References

You have seen that a relative cell reference refers to cells by their position in relation to the cell that contains the formula. *Absolute cell references*, on the other hand, refer to cells by their *fixed* position in the worksheet, for example, the total in cell E9.

A relative cell reference automatically adjusts when a formula is copied. An absolute cell reference does *not* adjust; rather, it remains the same when the formula is copied—and there are times when you will want to do this.

1 Click cell **F3**, type **=** and then click cell **E3**. Type **/** and then click cell **E9**.

The formula created, *=E3/E9*, indicates that the value in cell E3 will be divided by the value in cell E9. Why? Because Mr. Potempa wants to know the percentage by which each product's Total Retail Value makes up the Total Retail Value for All Products. Arithmetically, the percentage is computed by dividing the *Total Retail Value* for each product by the *Total Retail Value for All Products*. The result will be a percentage expressed as a decimal.

Workshop

Calculate a Percentage if You Know the Total and the Amount

Using the equation *amount/total = percentage*, you can calculate the percentage by which a part makes up a total—with the percentage formatted as a decimal.

For example, if on a quiz you score 42 points correctly out of 50, your percentage of correct answers is 42/50 = 0.84 or 84%.

2 Press Enter. Click cell **F3** and notice that the formula displays in the **Formula Bar**. Then, point to cell **F3** and double-click.

The formula, with the two referenced cells displayed in color and bordered with the same color, displays in the cell. This is the ***range finder***, and is useful for verifying formulas or quickly positioning the insertion point within the cell to perform editing directly in the cell.

3 Press Enter to redisplay the result of the calculation in the cell, and notice that approximately 17% of the total retail value of the inventory is made up of Severe Weather Kits. Then, click cell **F3** again, and drag the fill handle down through cell **F8**. Compare your screen with Figure 1.64.

Each cell displays an error message—*#DIV/0!* and a green triangle in the upper left corner of each cell indicates an error has been found. Like a grammar checker, Excel uses rules to check for formula errors and flags them in this manner. Additionally, the Auto Fill Options button displays, from which you can select formatting options for the copied cells.

Figure 1.64

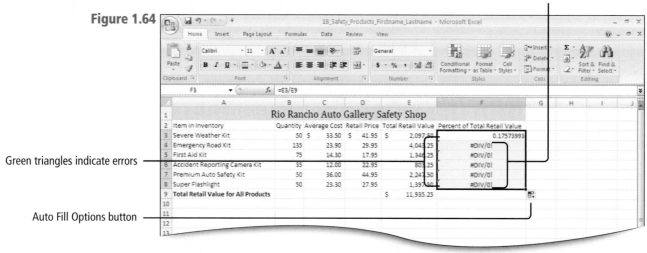

Error messages

Green triangles indicate errors

Auto Fill Options button

4 Click cell **F4**, and to the left of the cell, point to the displayed **Error Checking** button ⊕ to display its ScreenTip—*The formula or function used is dividing by zero or empty cells.*

In this manner, Excel suggests the cause of an error.

5 Look at the **Formula Bar** to examine the formula.

The formula is *=E4/E10*. The cell reference to *E4* is correct, but the cell reference following the division operator (/) is *E10*, and E10 is an *empty* cell.

6 Click cell **F5**, point to the **Error Checking** button ⊕, and in the **Formula Bar** examine the formula.

Because the cell references are relative, Excel attempts to build the formulas by increasing the row number for each equation. In this particular calculation, however, the divisor must always be the value in cell E9—the *Total Retail Value for All Products*.

7 Point to cell **F3**, and then double-click to have the range finder display the cell's formula and place the insertion point within the cell.

8 Within the cell, be sure the insertion point is blinking to the right of *E9*, and then press F4. Alternatively edit the formula so that it indicates **=E3/$E$9** Compare your screen with Figure 1.65.

To make a cell reference absolute, dollar signs are inserted into the cell reference. The use of the dollar sign to denote an absolute reference is not related in any way to whether or not the values you are working with are currency values. It is simply the symbol used by Excel to denote an absolute cell reference.

Edited formula with dollar signs denoting
an absolute cell reference

Figure 1.65

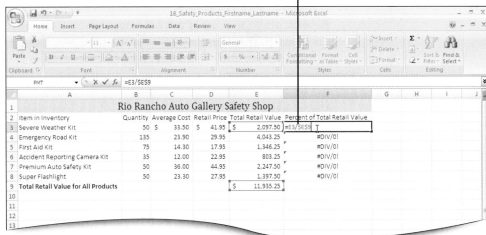

9 On the **Formula Bar**, click the **Enter** button ✓ so that **F3** is still the active cell. Then, drag the fill handle to copy the formula down through cell **F8**. Click cell **F4**, examine the formula in the **Formula Bar**, and then examine the formulas for cells **F5**, **F6**, **F7**, and **F8**. Compare your screen with Figure 1.66.

You can see that for each formula, the cell reference for the *Total Retail Value* of each product changed relative to its row; however, the value used as the divisor—*Total Retail Value for All Products* in cell E9—remained absolute. Thus, using either relative or absolute cell references, it is easy to duplicate formulas without typing them.

Absolute cell reference   Percentages calculated for each product

Figure 1.66

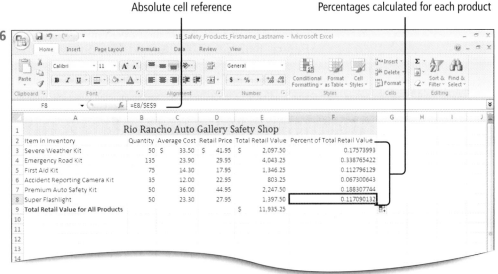

10 **Save** 💾 your workbook.

Objective 10
Format Percentages and Move Formulas

A percentage is part of a whole expressed in hundredths. For example, 75 cents is the same as 75 percent of one dollar. The Percent Style button formats the selected cell as a percentage rounded to the nearest hundredth.

If you move formulas by inserting additional rows or columns in your worksheet, Excel will adjust the formulas for you.

Activity 1.22 Formatting Cells with the Percent Style Button

1 Click cell **F3** and notice the number *0.17573993*. In the **Number group**, click the **Percent Style** button %.

Your result is 18%, which is *0.17573993* rounded up to the nearest hundredth and expressed as a percentage. Percent Style displays the value of a cell as a percentage.

2 Select the range **F3:F8**, right-click over the selection, and then on the Mini toolbar click the **Percent Style** button %, click the **Increase Decimal** button two times, and then click the **Center** button. Alternatively, click the commands in the appropriate groups on the Ribbon.

Percent Style may not offer a percentage precise enough to analyze important financial information—adding additional decimal places to a percentage makes data more precise. For example, with additional decimal places, Mr. Potempa can see a slight difference in the percentage of First Aid Kits and Super Flashlights.

3 Click any cell to cancel the selection, compare your screen with Figure 1.67, and then **Save** your workbook.

Figure 1.67

Percentages formatted

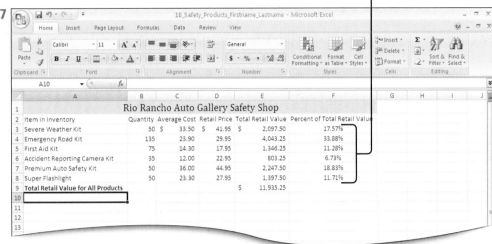

Activity 1.23 Inserting Rows in a Worksheet Containing Formulas and Wrapping Text in a Cell

You can edit formulas in the same manner as you edit text. In this activity, you will add a row for Road Trip Emergency Kits, which is another item carried by the Safety Shop, and wrap text.

1 Double-click cell **E9** and confirm that the range finder shows the formula to be the sum of cells *E3:E8*. Press Enter. Click cell **E6**. On the **Home tab**, in the **Cells group**, click the **Insert button arrow**, and then from the displayed list, click **Insert Sheet Rows**.

Another Way — **To Insert Rows**

Click the row heading and then in the Cells group, click the Insert button; or, right-click the cell, click Insert, and then click Entire row.

2 Click cell **E10**. On the **Formula Bar**, notice that the range was edited and changed to sum the newly expanded range **E3:E9**.

3 In the range **A6:D6**, type the following:

| Road Trip Emergency Kit | 35 | 67.96 | 84.95 |

4 Select the range **E5:F5** to select the two formulas above the new row, and then drag the fill handle to fill both formulas down to cells **E6** and **F6**.

5 Click cell **E10**. Move the pointer to the bottom edge of the cell until the ⬚ pointer displays, and then drag downward until cell **E11** is outlined, as shown in Figure 1.68.

Figure 1.68

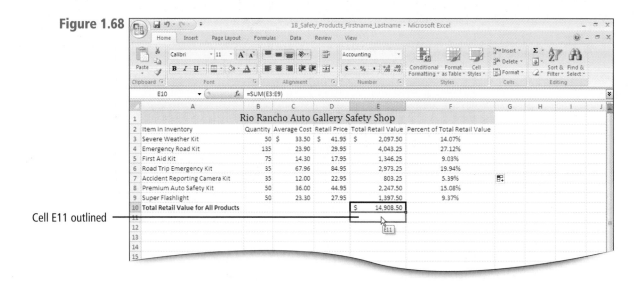

Cell E11 outlined

6 Release the mouse button, double-click cell **E11** to display the range finder, and then in cell **E11** and on the **Formula Bar**, notice that the range, **E3:E9**, did not change when you moved the formula.

If you move a formula to another cell, the cell references do not change.

7 Press `Esc` to cancel the range finder, and then on the **Quick Access Toolbar**, click **Undo** ↺ to return the formula to cell **E10**. **Save** 💾 your workbook.

8 In the **row heading area**, point to the lower boundary of **row 2** to display the ⊕ pointer, and then drag downward until the row is **60 pixels** high. Select **columns B:F**, and then from the **column heading area**, drag the right border of one of the selected columns to **80 pixels**.

9 Select the range **C2:F2**, and then in the **Alignment group**, click the **Wrap Text** button 📑.

Use the Wrap Text command to display text on multiple lines within a single cell when the column is not wide enough to display all of the cell's content.

10 Select the range **A2:F2**. In the **Font group**, click the **Bold** button **B** ; in the **Alignment group**, click the **Center** button ≡ and the **Middle Align** button ≡. Click cell **E10**. In the **Font** group, click the **Borders button arrow** ⊞ ▾, and then from the displayed list, click **Top and Double Bottom Border**. Click any cell to cancel the selection from cell E10. **Save** 💾 your workbook, and then compare your screen with Figure 1.69.

Figure 1.69

Percents formatted

Column widths adjusted

Text wrapped and centered
Row height increased

Border added

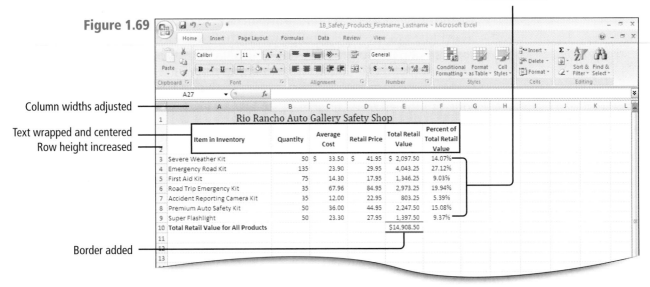

11 On the Ribbon, click the **Insert tab**, and then in the **Text group**, click **Header & Footer** to switch to **Page Layout view** and open the **Header area**. On the **Design tab**, in the **Navigation group**, click the **Go to Footer** button. Click just above the word *Footer* to place your insertion point in the left section of the **Footer area**, and then in the **Header & Footer Elements group**, click the **File Name** button. Click any cell above the footer to exit the **Footer area** and view your file name.

12 Press Ctrl + Home to move to cell **A1** and display the upper portion of your worksheet. Click the **Page Layout tab**. In the **Page Setup group**, click the **Orientation** button, and then click **Landscape**. Click the **Margins** button, and then at the bottom of the **Margins gallery**, click **Custom Margins**. In the displayed **Page Setup** dialog box, under **Center on page**, select the **Horizontally** check box. Click

OK, and then **Save** 🖫 the changes to your workbook.

Objective 11
Create a Pie Chart and a Chart Sheet

Pie charts show the relationship of each part to a whole. To create a pie chart, you must select two ranges. One range contains the labels for each slice of the pie chart, and the other range contains the values that add up to a total. The two ranges must have the same number of cells and the range with the values should *not* include the cell with the total. You can use a legend to identify the slices of the pie by using colors, but it is usually more effective to place the labels within or close to each pie slice.

Activity 1.24 Creating a Pie Chart and a Chart Sheet

The purpose of the inventory worksheet is to determine how each item contributes to the total retail value of the inventory. To display the relationship of parts to a whole, use a pie chart. In the 9B_Safety_Products worksheet, you calculated the percent of the total in column F. Alternatively, this percentage can be calculated by the Chart feature and added to the chart as a label.

1 In the lower right of your screen, on the status bar, click the **Normal** button ▦ to return to **Normal view**. Select the nonadjacent ranges **A3:A9** and **E3:E9** to select the item names and the total retail value of each item.

2 Click the **Insert tab**, and then in the **Charts group**, click **Pie**. Under **3-D Pie**, click the first chart—**Pie in 3-D**—to create the chart on your worksheet.

3 On the **Design tab**, in the **Location group**, click the **Move Chart** button. In the displayed **Move Chart** dialog box, click the **New sheet** option button. Replace the highlighted text *Chart1* by typing **Inventory Chart** and then click **OK**.

A *chart sheet* is created in your workbook, which is a workbook sheet that contains only a chart and is useful when you want to view a chart separately from the worksheet data. The sheet tab indicates *Inventory Chart*.

4 On the **Design tab**, in the **Chart Layouts group**, click the first layout—**Layout 1**. Right-click over the text *Chart Title*, click **Edit Text**, delete the existing text, and then type **Safety Shop Inventory**

In this layout, the legend is removed and the category labels and the percentages—calculated by the chart feature—display on the pie slices. Recall that *chart layout* refers to the combination of chart elements—title, legend, labels—that you want to display. If you plan to print a chart sheet on a printer that does not print in color, it is better to label each pie slice individually rather than use a legend.

5 In the **Chart Styles group**, click the **More** button ⯆ , and then click **Style 5**. Click anywhere in the white area of the chart to deselect the Chart Title, and then compare your screen with Figure 1.70.

To print on paper, the paler colors will display well. To present this chart in a PowerPoint presentation, you would likely pick one of the more vibrant styles with multiple colors.

Figure 1.70

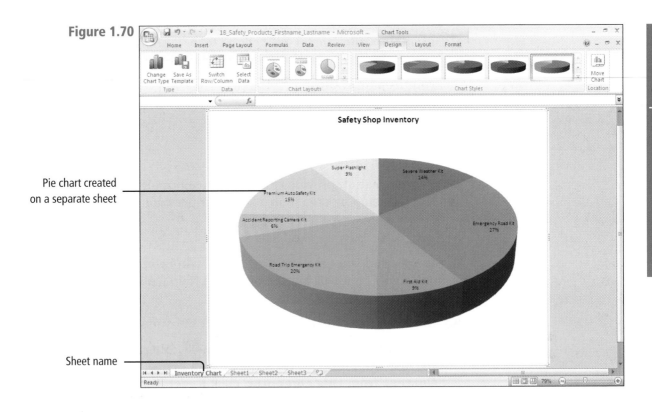

Pie chart created on a separate sheet

Sheet name

6 Click the **Insert tab**. In the **Text group**, click **Header & Footer**, and then in the **Page Setup** dialog box, click the **Custom Footer** button. With the insertion point positioned in the **Left section**, click the **Insert File Name** button, and then click **OK** two times.

Use the Page Setup dialog box in this manner to insert a footer on a chart sheet, which has no Page Layout view in which you can see the Header and Footer areas.

7 To delete the unused worksheets, click the **Sheet2 tab**, hold down Ctrl, and then click the **Sheet3 tab**. Right-click over one of the selected sheet tabs, and then from the shortcut menu, click **Delete**. Be sure **Sheet1** is the active sheet, and then press Ctrl + Home to cancel the selections and make cell **A1** the active cell.

8 **Save** your workbook. Check your *Chapter Assignment Sheet* or *Course Syllabus*, or consult your instructor, to determine if you are to submit your assignments on paper or electronically. To submit electronically, follow the instructions provided by your instructor.

9 To print, from the **Office** menu, click **Print**. In the displayed **Print** dialog box, under **Print what**, click the **Entire workbook** option button. In the lower left corner of the dialog box, click **Preview**, and notice in the status bar, *Preview: Page 1 of 2* displays.

10 Review the preview of your chart sheet, and then in the **Preview group**, click the **Next Page** button to preview the worksheet containing your data. In the **Print group**, click **Print** to print the two pages.

11 **Save** your workbook. If you are instructed to print your formulas on Sheet1, follow the instructions in Activity 1.17 to do so, and then redisplay the worksheet by pressing Ctrl + `.

12 From the **Office** menu ⊞, click **Close**. If prompted to save changes, click **No** so that you do not save the changes that you made to print your formulas. **Close** ☒ Excel.

Objective 12
Use the Excel Help System

Excel's Help feature provides information about all of Excel's features and displays step-by-step instructions for performing many tasks.

Activity 1.25 Using the Excel Help System

Workbooks that you create in Excel 2007 can be opened in Excel 2003. In this activity, you will use the Microsoft Help feature to learn more about this feature.

1 **Start** Excel. In the upper right corner of your screen, click the **Microsoft Office Excel Help** button ⊚. Alternatively, press F1. In the displayed window, click the **Search arrow**, and then under **Content from this computer**, click **Excel Help**. In the white box on the left, type **open an Excel 2007 workbook in Excel 2003.**

2 Click **Search** or press Enter. On the list of results, click **Open an Office Excel 2007 workbook in an earlier version of Excel**.

3 If you want to do so, click the **Print** button to print a copy of this information for your reference. Your name will not print.

4 On the title bar of the Excel Help window, click the **Close** button ☒. On the right side of the Microsoft Excel title bar, click the **Close** button ☒ to close Excel.

End **You have completed Project 1B** ——————————

There's More You Can Do!

From My Computer, navigate to the student files that accompany this textbook. In the folder **02_theres_more_you_can_do_pg1_36**, locate and open the folder for this chapter. Open and print the instructions for this project, which are provided to you in Adobe PDF format.

Try IT! 1—Change a Chart Type

In this Try IT! exercise, you will change the chart type of an existing chart from a column chart to a bar chart.

Content-Based Assessments

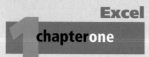

Summary

In this chapter, you used Microsoft Office Excel 2007 to create and analyze data organized into columns and rows and to chart and perform calculations on the data. By organizing your data with Excel, you will be able to make logical decisions and create visual representations of your data in the form of charts.

Key Terms

The 🔘 symbol represents Key Terms found on the Student CD in the 02_theres_more_you_can_do folder for this chapter.

Content-Based Assessments

Key Terms

Content-Based Assessments

Matching

Match each term in the second column with its correct definition in the first column by writing the letter of the term on the blank line in front of the correct definition.

N **1.** An Excel file that contains one or more worksheets.

O **2.** The primary document that you use in Excel to store and work with data, and which is formatted as a pattern of uniformly spaced horizontal and vertical lines.

B **3.** The intersection of a row and column in an Excel worksheet.

I **4.** An element in the Excel window that displays the value or formula contained in the active cell, and in which you can enter or edit values or formulas.

J **5.** The box to the left of the Formula Bar that identifies the selected cell, table, chart, or object.

L **6.** The user interface in Office 2007 that groups the commands for performing related tasks on tabs across the upper portion of the program window.

M **7.** Buttons on the right side of the status bar for viewing in Normal, Page Layout View, or Page Break Preview; also displays controls for zoom out and zoom in.

E **8.** The letters at the top of an Excel worksheet that designate the columns.

K **9.** Two or more selected cells on a worksheet that are adjacent or nonadjacent, and treated by Excel as a single unit for the purpose of editing.

A **10.** The cell, surrounded by a black border, ready to receive data or be affected by the next Excel command.

D **11.** The identification of a specific cell by its intersecting column letter and row number.

C **12.** Anything typed into a cell.

F **13.** Numbers, text, dates, or times of day that you type into a cell.

H **14.** An equation that performs mathematical calculations on values in a worksheet.

G **15.** The small black square in the lower right corner of a selected cell.

A Active cell

B Cell

C Cell content

D Cell reference

E Column headings

F Constant value

G Fill handle

H Formula

I Formula Bar

J Name Box

K Range

L Ribbon

M View options

N Workbook

O Worksheet

Fill in the Blank

Write the correct answer in the space provided.

1. A set of characters with the same design, size, and shape is called a
   Font.

2. A specific way in which Excel displays numbers in a cell is referred
   to as the ~~number format~~ _number format_.

3. The default format that Excel applies to numbers, which has no specific characteristics except that trailing zeros to the right of a decimal
   point will not display, is the _general_ format.

4. The data that displays in the Formula Bar is referred to as the
   underlying value.

5. A formula prewritten by Excel is a _function_.

6. In a formula, the address of a cell based on the relative position of
   the cell that contains the formula and the cell referred to is a
   relative cell reference.

7. The Excel number format that applies a thousand comma separator
   where appropriate, inserts a fixed U.S. dollar sign aligned at the left
   edge of the cell, applies two decimal places, and leaves a small
   amount of space at the right edge of the cell to accommodate a
   parenthesis for negative numbers is the _Accounting_
   number format.

8. The Excel number format that inserts thousand comma separators
   where appropriate, applies two decimal places, and leaves space at
   the right to accommodate a parenthesis for negative numbers is the
   Comma ~~format~~ _Style_

9. The area along the bottom of a chart that identifies the categories
   of data, and which is also referred to as the x-axis, is the
   Category axis.

10. A numerical scale on the left side of a chart that shows the range of
    numbers for the data points, and also referred to as the y-axis, is the
    Value axis.

11. In a chart, an explanation of the patterns or colors that are
    assigned to a data series that represents a category is called the
    legend.

(Fill in the Blank continues on the next page)

Fill in the Blank

12. Related data points represented by data markers in a chart, each of which has a unique color or pattern represented in the chart legend, are referred to as a <u>data series</u>.

13. The combination of chart elements that can be displayed in a chart such as a title, legend, labels for the columns, and the table of charted cells is referred to as the <u>chart layout</u>.

14. Symbols that specify addition, subtraction, multiplication, division, percentage, and exponentiation in an Excel formula are called <u>arithmetic operators</u>

15. A cell reference that refers to cells by their fixed position in a worksheet and which remain the same when the formula is copied is referred to as an <u>Absolute</u> cell reference.

Content-Based Assessments

Project 1C — Service

In this project, you will apply the skills you practiced from the Objectives in Project 1A.

Objectives: 1. *Create, Save, and Navigate an Excel Workbook;* **2.** *Enter and Edit Data in a Worksheet;* **3.** *Construct and Copy Formulas, Use the Sum Function, and Edit Cells;* **4.** *Format Data, Cells, and Worksheets;* **5.** *Close and Reopen a Workbook;* **6.** *Chart Data;* **7.** *Use Page Layout View, Prepare a Worksheet for Printing, and Close Excel.*

In the following Skills Review, you will create a worksheet for Ellie Rose, Service Manager at the Rio Rancho Auto Gallery, to track weekly service revenue. Your completed worksheet will look similar to the one shown in Figure 1.71.

For Project 1C, you will need the following file:

New blank Excel workbook

You will save your workbook as
1C_Service_Firstname_Lastname

Figure 1.71

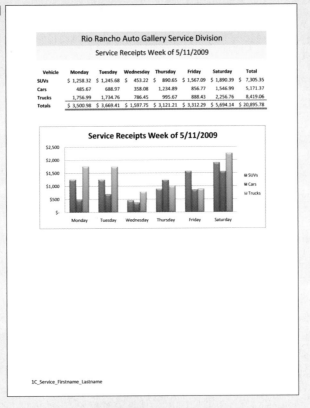

(Project 1C–Service continues on the next page)

Content-Based Assessments

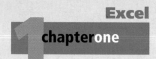

Skills Review

(Project 1C–Service continued)

1. **Start** Excel. In cell **A1**, type **Rio Rancho Auto Gallery Service Division** and then press Enter. In cell **A2**, type **Service Receipts Week of 5/11/2009** and then press Enter. Display the **Save As** dialog box, navigate to your **Excel Chapter 1** folder, and then using your own first and last name, **Save** the workbook as **1C_Service_Firstname_Lastname**

2. In cell **A3**, type **Vehicle** and then press Enter. Type **SUVs** and then press Enter. Type **Cars** and then press Enter. Type **Trucks** and then press Enter. In cell **A7**, type **Totals** and then press Enter.

3. In cell **B3**, type **Monday** and then press Enter. Click in cell **B3** again to make it the active cell. In the lower right corner of cell **B3**, point to the fill handle to display the ⊞ pointer, drag the fill handle to the right to cell **G3** so that the last ScreenTip that displays is *Saturday*, and then release the mouse button to fill the days of the week. In cell **H3**, type **Total** and then press Enter.

4. Press Ctrl + Home to move to cell **A1**, and then on the Ribbon, click the **Review tab**. In the **Proofing group**, click **Spelling**, and then correct any spelling errors that you may have made while typing. Beginning in cell **B4**, type the following data:

Vehicle	Monday	Tuesday	Wednesday	Thursday	Friday	Saturday
SUVs	1258.32	1245.68	453.22	890.65	1567.09	1890.39
Cars	485.67	688.97	358.08	1234.89	856.77	1546.99
Trucks	1756.99	1734.76	786.45	995.67	888.43	2256.76

5. From the **column heading area**, select **columns A:G**, and then point to the right boundary of any of the selected column letters to display the ↔ pointer. Drag to the right until the ScreenTip indicates **75 pixels**, and then release the mouse button to resize the selected columns.

6. Point to the **row 3** heading, and then right-click to simultaneously select the row and display the shortcut menu and the Mini toolbar. From the displayed shortcut menu, click **Insert** to insert a blank row—this will add some space between the worksheet titles and the column titles.

7. Click cell **H5**. On the **Home tab**, in the **Editing group**, click the **Sum** button, and then press Enter to enter the function—a prewritten formula. Your result is *7305.35*. Click cell **H5**, and then drag the fill handle down to cell **H7** to copy the formula. Recall that the cell references will adjust relative to their row.

8. Select the range **B5:H8**, which includes the columns to be totaled and the cells in which each total will display. Hold down Alt, and then press = to enter the Sum function in cells **B8:H8**. **Save** your workbook.

9. Select the range **A1:H1**, and then on the **Home tab**, in the **Alignment group**, click the **Merge and Center** button. Select the range **A2:H2**, right-click over the selection to display the short-cut menu and Mini toolbar, and then on the Mini toolbar, click the **Merge and Center** button. Both worksheet titles are centered over the worksheet.

(Project 1C–Service continues on the next page)

Content-Based Assessments

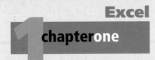

Excel
chapterone   **Skills Review**

(Project 1C–Service continued)

10. Right-click cell **A1** to display the shortcut menu and the Mini toolbar. On the Mini toolbar, click the **Font Size arrow**, and then click **18**. Then, click the **Fill Color button arrow**, and under **Theme Colors**, in the next to last column, click the third color—**Aqua, Accent 5, Lighter 60%**.

11. Right-click cell **A2**. On the Mini toolbar, change the **Font Size** to **16**. Click the **Fill Color button arrow**, and then under **Theme Colors**, in the next to last column, click the second color—**Aqua, Accent 5, Lighter 80%**.

12. Select **rows 1** and **2**. Position the ⊞ pointer over the lower border of either of the selected rows, and then drag downward to increase the row height of both rows to **40 pixels**. Then, in the **Alignment group**, click the **Middle Align** button to center the titles vertically in the cells. Select **rows 4:8**, and then increase the row height of all of the selected rows to **24 pixels**.

13. Select the range **A4:H4**. Then, hold down Ctrl, and select the nonadjacent range **A5:A8**, so that both the column and row titles are selected. On the **Home tab**, in the **Font group**, click the **Bold** button. Select the range **A4:H4**, and then in the **Alignment group**, click the **Center** button.

14. Select the range **B5:H5**. Then, hold down Ctrl and select the nonadjacent range **B8:H8**. In the **Number group**, click the **Accounting Number Format** button to apply the format to the selected ranges. Select the range **B6:H7**, and then in the **Number group**, click the **Comma Style** button. Select the range **B8:H8**. In the **Font group**, click the **Borders button arrow**, and then click **Top and Double Bottom Border**. **Save** your workbook.

15. To chart the week's receipts by day and vehicle type, select the range **A4:G7**. On the Ribbon, click the **Insert tab**, and then in the **Charts group**, click **Column**. Under **2-D Column**, click the first chart type—**Clustered Column**. Point to the top border of the chart to display the ⬚ pointer, and then drag to position the chart so that its upper left corner is positioned inside the upper left corner of cell **A11**.

16. On the **Design tab**, in the **Chart Layouts group**, click **Layout 1**. Click in the **Chart Title**, delete the existing text, and then type **Service Receipts Week of 5/11/2009** Click in a white area slightly *inside* the chart's border to deselect the chart title, but leave the chart itself selected. On the **Design tab**, in the **Chart Styles group**, click the **More** button to display the gallery of chart styles. Click **Style 26**.

17. Click the **Layout tab**, and then, in the **Axes group**, click the **Axes** button. Point to **Primary Vertical Axis**, and then click **More Primary Vertical Axis Options**. In the **Format Axis** dialog box, in the column at the left, click **Number**. In the **Decimal places** box, change the number to **0** and then click **Close**.

18. Click any cell to deselect the chart. Click the **Insert tab**, and then in the **Text group**, click the **Header & Footer** button to switch to **Page Layout view** and open the **Header area**. In the **Navigation group**, click the **Go to Footer** button, click just above the word *Footer*, and then in the **Header & Footer Elements group**, click the **File Name** button. Click in a cell just above the footer to exit the footer area and view your file name.

(Project 1C–Service continues on the next page)

(Project 1C–Service continued)

19. Scroll up to view your chart. Click the chart to select it, and notice that the chart is not centered under the data in the cells. Position the pointer over the **right resize handle**, which will display the pointer, and then drag to the right so that the right border of the chart is just inside the right border of **column H**. Release the mouse button to resize the chart.

20. Click any cell to deselect the chart. Click the **Page Layout tab**. In the **Page Setup group**, click the **Margins** button, and then at the bottom of the **Margins gallery**, click **Custom Margins**. In the displayed **Page Setup** dialog box, under **Center on page**, select the **Horizontally** check box. Click **OK** to close the dialog box, and then **Save** the changes to your workbook.

21. On the status bar, click the **Normal** button to return to **Normal view**, and then press Ctrl + Home to move to the top of your worksheet. At the lower edge of the window, click to select the **Sheet2 tab**, hold down Ctrl and click the **Sheet3 tab** to select the two unused sheets. On the **Home tab**, in the **Cells group**, click the **Delete button arrow**, and then from the displayed list, click **Delete Sheet**.

22. **Save** the changes you have made to your workbook. Check your *Chapter Assignment Sheet* or *Course Syllabus* or consult your instructor to determine if you are to submit your assignments on paper or electronically. To submit electronically, follow the instructions provided by your instructor.

23. From the **Office** menu, point to the **Print button**, and then click **Print Preview** to check the placement of your worksheet. In the **Print group**, click the **Print** button. In the displayed **Print** dialog box, under **Print range**, verify that the **All** option button is selected. Under **Print what**, verify that **Active sheet(s)** is selected, and then under **Copies**, verify that the **Number of copies** is **1**. Click **OK** to print your worksheet. If you are directed to submit printed formulas, refer to Activity 1.17 to do so.

24. If you printed your formulas, be sure to redisplay the worksheet by pressing Ctrl + `. From the **Office** menu, click **Close**. If the dialog box displays asking if you want to save changes, click **No** so that you do *not* save the changes you made for printing formulas. **Close** Excel.

End **You have completed Project 1C**

Content-Based Assessments

Skills Review

Project 1D — Tires

In this project, you will apply the skills you practiced from the Objectives in Project 1B.

Objectives: 8. *Design a Worksheet;* **9.** *Construct Formulas for Mathematical Operations;* **10.** *Format Percentages and Move Formulas;* **11.** *Create a Pie Chart and a Chart Sheet.*

In the following Skills Review, you will create a worksheet for Arthur Potempa, Retail Sales Manager of the Rio Rancho Auto Gallery, to track the sales of two different types of tires at the four subsidiary stores that sell only tires. Your completed worksheet will look similar to the one shown in Figure 1.72.

For Project 1D, you will need the following file:

New blank Excel workbook

You will save your workbook as
1D_Tires_Firstname_Lastname

Figure 1.72

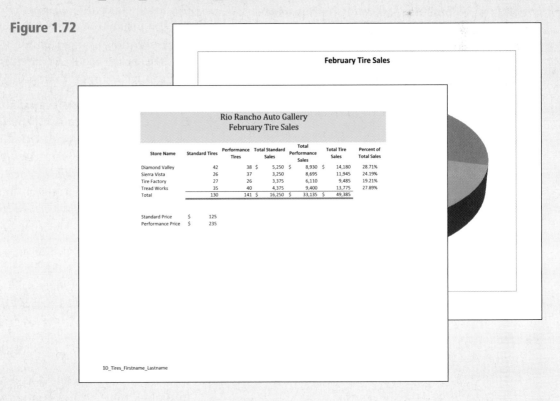

(Project 1D–Tires continues on the next page)

Content-Based Assessments

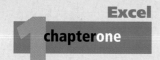

(Project 1D–Tires continued)

1. **Start** Excel so that a new blank workbook displays. In cell **A1**, type **Rio Rancho Auto Gallery** and then press Enter. In cell **A2**, type **February Tire Sales** and then press Enter. Select the range **A1:A2**. In the **Font group**, click the **Font arrow**, and then click **Cambria**. Click the **Font Size arrow**, and then click **18**. Display the **Save As** dialog box, navigate to your **Excel Chapter 1** folder, and then using your own first and last name, **Save** the workbook as **1D_Tires_Firstname_Lastname**

2. In cell **A3**, type **Store Name** and then press Tab. In cell **B3**, type **Standard Tires** and then press Tab. In cell **C3**, type **Performance Tires** and then press Tab. In cell **D3**, type **Total Standard Sales** and then press Tab. In cell **E3**, type **Total Performance Sales** and then press Tab. In **F3**, type **Total Tire Sales** and then press Tab. In cell **G3**, type **Percent of Total Sales** and then press Enter.

3. In the **column heading area**, point to the right boundary of **column A** to display the ⬌ pointer, and then drag to the right to widen the column to **120 pixels**. Select the range **A3:G3**, and then in the **Font group**, click the **Bold** button. In the **Alignment group**, click the **Wrap Text** button, click the **Center** button, and then click the **Middle Align** button. Select **columns B:G**. In the **column heading area**, point to the right boundary of any of the selected columns to display the ⬌ pointer, and then drag to the right to increase the column width to **90 pixels**.

4. Select the range **A4:C6**, and then type the following data, pressing Enter to move from cell to cell within the selected range.

Store Name	Standard Tires	Performance Tires
Diamond Valley	42	38
Sierra Vista	26	37
Tread Works	35	40

5. In the range **A10:B11** type the following:

Standard Price	125
Performance Price	235

6. Click cell **D4** and type = to begin a formula. Click cell **B4**, type * and then click cell **B10** to construct a formula that will multiply the number of Standard Tires sold at the Diamond Valley store by the Standard Price, which is 125. Then, press F4 to make the reference to cell **B10** absolute so that your formula indicates =B4*$B$10

   Because you will copy the formula down for the other two stores, the first cell reference should change relative to each row, but the price, located in cell B10, should remain the same for each formula.

7. Press Enter; your result is *5250*. Select cell **D4** again, and then drag the fill handle downward through cell **D6**. Check each formula to be sure that the first cell reference changed relative to the row and that the second cell reference remained absolute—in each formula referring to the price in cell **B10**.

8. In cell **E4**, construct a similar formula to calculate the total sales of Performance Tires at Diamond Valley, using the Performance Price in cell **B11**. Then, copy the formula down through cell **E6** to compute the sales of Performance Tires for the other locations.

9. In cell **F4**, type = and then use the point and click method to construct a formula to add the Total Standard Sales and the Total

(Project 1D– Tires continues on the next page)

Content-Based Assessments

Excel

chapterone   ## Skills Review

(Project 1D–Tires continued)

Performance Sales at the Diamond Valley store; your formula should indicate =D4+E4, and then click the **Enter** button on the **Formula Bar**. Your result is *14180*. With cell **F4** still selected, use the fill handle to copy the formula down to compute the Total Tire Sales for the Sierra Vista store and the Tread Works store.

10. In cell **A7**, type **Total** and then press Enter. Select the range **B4:F7**. On the **Home tab**, in the **Editing group**, click the **Sum** button to calculate totals for each column. Click any cell to deselect. Select the range **D4:F4**, and then hold down Ctrl and select the nonadjacent ranges **D7:F7** and **B10:B11**. On the **Home tab**, in the **Number group**, click **Accounting Number Format**, and then click the **Decrease Decimal** button two times to format the numbers with zero decimal places.

11. Select the range **D5:F6**, in the **Number group**, click **Comma Style**, and then click the **Decrease Decimal** button two times to format the numbers with comma separators and zero decimal places. Select the range **B7:F7**. In the **Font group**, click the **Borders button arrow**, and then from the displayed list, click **Top and Double Bottom Border**.

12. Point to the **row 6** heading and right-click to select the row and display the shortcut menu. Click **Insert** to insert a blank row, and as you type the following data in **A6:C6**, notice that the Total in cell **B8** and cell **C8** recalculates:

    Tire Factory   27   26

13. Select the range **D5:F5**, and then drag the fill handle down to fill the three formulas to the range **D6:F6**, which will calculate the sales for the Tire Factory store and recalculate the column totals.

14. Click in cell **G4**, type = click cell **F4**, type / click cell **F8**, and then press F4. Your formula *=F4/$F$8* will calculate the percentage by which Diamond Valley's sales contributes to the Rio Rancho Auto Gallery's total tire sales. Press Enter; your result is *0.28713172* or approximately 29 percent. Click cell **G4**, and then use the fill handle to copy the formula down through cell **G7**. In each formula, the first cell reference will change relative to its row, and the second cell reference will remain absolute—referring to the total in cell **F8**.

15. If necessary, select the range **G4:G7**. Right-click over the selection, on the Mini toolbar, click the **Percent Style** button, click the **Center** button, and then click the **Increase Decimal** button two times. Recall that for precise information, you can increase the decimal places in a percentage.

16. Select the range **A1:G1**, and then on the **Home tab**, in the **Alignment group**, click **Merge and Center**. Repeat this formatting for cells **A2:G2**. Select the range **A1:A2**, click the **Fill Color arrow**, and then under **Theme Colors**, in the last column, click **Orange, Accent 6, Lighter 40%**. Right-click the **row 3** heading and insert a blank row to create space between the worksheet titles and the column titles—recall that the formulas will be moved and adjusted accordingly. On the **Insert tab**, in the **Text group**, click the **Header & Footer** button. In the **Navigation group**, click the **Go to Footer** button. Click just above the word *Footer* in the left section of the **Footer area**, and then in the **Header & Footer Elements group**, click the **File Name** button. Click any cell just above the **Footer area** to deselect the footer and view your file name, and then press Ctrl + Home to move to the top of your worksheet.

(Project 1D Tires continues on the next page)

(Project 1D–Tires continued)

17. Click the **Page Layout tab**. In the **Page Setup group**, click the **Orientation** button, and then click **Landscape**. Click the **Margins** button, and then at the bottom of the **Margins gallery**, click **Custom Margins**. In the displayed **Page Setup** dialog box, under **Center on page**, select the **Horizontally** check box. Click **OK**.

18. **Save** the changes you have made. On the right edge of the status bar, click the **Normal** button to return to **Normal view**. Select the range **A4:A8**, hold down Ctrl, and then select the range **F4:F8**. Click the **Insert tab**. In the **Charts group**, click **Pie**, and then under **3-D Pie**, click the first chart—**Pie in 3-D**. On the **Design tab**, in the **Location group**, click the **Move Chart** button. In the **Move Chart** dialog box, click the **New sheet** option button and replace the highlighted text *Chart1* by typing **Tire Sales Chart** Click **OK** to move the pie chart to a separate chart sheet in the workbook.

19. On the **Design tab**, in the **Chart Layouts group**, click **Layout 1**. Click the text *Total Tire Sales*, and then edit to indicate **February Tire Sales** Click inside the white area of the chart to deselect the title. In the **Chart Styles group**, click the **More** button, and then click **Style 8**.

20. To create a footer on your chart sheet, click the **Insert tab**. In the **Text group**, click the **Header & Footer** button, and then in the displayed **Page Setup dialog box**, click the **Custom Footer** button. With the insertion point positioned in the

Left section, click the seventh button—**Insert File Name**, and then click **OK** two times.

21. Click the **Sheet1 tab** and press Ctrl + Home to cancel the selections. Click the **Sheet2** tab, hold down Ctrl and click the **Sheet3 tab**, right-click over the selected sheet tabs, and then click **Delete**.

22. **Save** your workbook. Check your *Chapter Assignment Sheet* or *Course Syllabus* or consult your instructor to determine if you are to submit your assignments on paper or electronically. To submit electronically, follow the instructions provided by your instructor.

23. To print, from the **Office** menu, click the **Print** button. In the displayed **Print** dialog box, under **Print what**, click the **Entire workbook** option button. In the lower left corner of the dialog box, click **Preview**, and notice in the status bar, *Preview: Page 1 of 2* displays. Check the preview, in the **Preview group**, click the **Next Page** button, and then in the **Print group**, click **Print** to print the two pages. If you are directed to submit printed formulas, refer to Activity 1.17 to do so.

24. If you printed your formulas, be sure to redisplay the worksheet by pressing Ctrl + `. From the **Office** menu, click **Close**. If the dialog box displays asking if you want to save changes, click **No** so that you do *not* save the changes you made for printing formulas. **Close** Excel.

End You have completed Project 1D

Excel

chapterone

Mastering Excel

Project 1E—Analysis

In this project, you will apply the skills you practiced from the Objectives in Project 1A.

Objectives: 1 *Create, Save, and Navigate an Excel Workbook;* **2.** *Enter and Edit Data in a Worksheet;* **3.** *Construct and Copy Formulas, Use the Sum Function, and Edit Cells;* **4.** *Format Data, Cells, and Worksheets;* **5.** *Close and Reopen a Workbook;* **6.** *Chart Data;* **7.** *Use Page Layout View, Prepare a Worksheet for Printing, and Close Excel.*

In the following Mastering Excel project, you will create a year-end sales analysis worksheet for Tony Konecki, President of Rio Rancho Auto Gallery, which will compare revenue from the organization's products and services. Your completed worksheet will look similar to Figure 1.73.

For Project 1E, you will need the following file:

New blank Excel workbook

You will save your workbook as
1E_Analysis_Firstname_Lastname

Figure 1.73

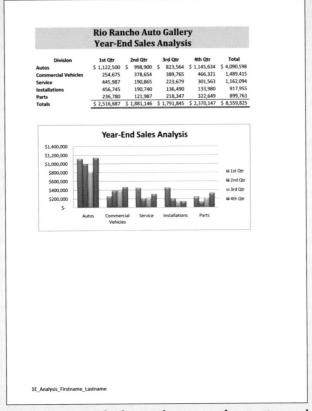

(Project 1E–Analysis continues on the next page)

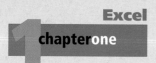
(Project 1E–Analysis continued)

1. **Start** Excel and display a new blank workbook. In cell **A1**, type **Rio Rancho Auto Gallery** and in cell **A2**, type **Year-End Sales Analysis** In cell **A3**, type **Division** In cell **B3**, type **1st Qtr** select the cell, and then use the fill handle to create a series in the range **B3:E3** so that *2nd Qtr* through *4th Qtr* displays in the cells. In cell **F3**, type **Total** and then in your **Excel Chapter 1** folder, **Save** the workbook as **1E_Analysis_Firstname_Lastname**

2. Select the range **A4:E8**, and then enter the following data, pressing [Enter] to move from cell to cell within the selected range.

Division	1st Qtr	2nd Qtr	3rd Qtr	4th Qtr
Autos	1122500	998900	823564	1145634
Commercial Vehicles	254675	378654	389765	466321
Service	445987	190865	223679	301563
Installations	456745	190740	136490	133980
Parts	236780	121987	218347	322649

3. Adjust the width of **column A** so that the row title *Commercial Vehicles* displays fully—approximately **140 pixels**. Use the **Sum** function to calculate the total for the Autos Division, and then copy the formula down for the remaining divisions. Then use the **Sum** function to total the columns—recall that you can select the range **B4:F9** and click the Sum button one time. In cell **A9**, type **Totals**

4. Insert a row above **row 3** to create space between the worksheet titles and the column titles—your formulas will move and adjust accordingly. Use the **Merge and Center** command to center the worksheet titles in cells **A1** and **A2** over the column titles. Select and format the two worksheet titles as follows: change the **Font** to **Cambria**, the **Font Size** to **18**, apply **Bold**, and then apply a **Fill Color**, using the **Theme Color Purple, Accent 4, Lighter 60%**.

5. Select the range **B6:F9**, apply **Comma Style**, and then **Decrease Decimal** to zero decimals. Select the nonadjacent ranges **B5:F5** and **B10:F10**, apply **Accounting Number Format**, and **Decrease Decimal** to zero decimals. Apply the appropriate **Top and Double Bottom Border** to the totals. **Center** the column titles in **Row 4**, apply **Bold** to the column titles and row titles, and then **AutoFit** columns **B:F**. Compare your formatting to Figure 1.73 if necessary.

6. Select the range **A4:E9**, and then **Insert** a **2-D Clustered Column chart**. Position the chart approximately two rows below the worksheet data slightly inside the left edge of **column A**. Be sure that the chart is selected so that the **Chart Tools** display. On the **Design tab**, in the **Chart Layouts group**, click **Layout 1**, and then in the **Chart Styles group**, click **Style 26**. Change the **Chart Title** to **Year-End Sales Analysis**

7. **Save** your workbook. Click any cell to deselect the chart. On the **Insert tab**, in the **Text group**, click the **Header & Footer** button to switch to **Page Layout view** and open the **Header area**. In the **Navigation group**, click the **Go to Footer** button, click just above the word *Footer*, and then in the **Header & Footer Elements group**, click the **File Name** button. Click in a cell just above the footer to deselect the **Footer area** and view your file name.

(Project 1E–Analysis continues on the next page)

(Project 1E–Analysis continued)

8. Scroll up to view your chart. Select the chart, and then drag the right sizing handle of the chart as necessary to widen the chart so that the right border of the chart is slightly inside the right border of **column F**. Deselect the chart. On the **Page Layout tab**, in the **Page Setup group**, click the **Margins** button, and then at the bottom of the **Margins gallery**, click **Custom Margins**. Under **Center on page**, select the **Horizontally** check box, click **OK**, and then **Save** the changes to your workbook. Return to **Normal view** and scroll up as necessary to view the top of your worksheet. Select and delete **Sheet2** and **Sheet3**.

9. **Save** the changes to your workbook. Check your *Chapter Assignment Sheet* or *Course Syllabus* or consult your instructor to determine if you are to submit your assignments on paper or electronically. To submit electronically, follow the instructions provided by your instructor.

10. From the **Office** menu, preview, and then print your worksheet. If you are directed to submit printed formulas, refer to Activity 1.17 to do so. If you printed your formulas, be sure to redisplay the worksheet by pressing Ctrl + `. From the **Office** menu click **Close**. If the dialog box displays asking if you want to save changes, click **No** so that you do *not* save the changes you made for printing formulas. **Close** Excel.

End **You have completed Project 1E** ————————————————

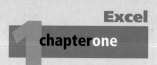

Project 1F—4th Quarter Sales

In this project, you will apply the skills you practiced from the Objectives in Project 1B.

Objectives: 8. *Design a Worksheet;* **9.** *Construct Formulas for Mathematical Operations;* **10.** *Format Percentages and Move Formulas;* **11.** *Create a Pie Chart and a Chart Sheet.*

In the following Mastering Excel project, you will create a worksheet and chart sheet for Sandy Cizek, the Auto Sales Manager for Rio Rancho Auto Gallery, to analyze fourth quarter vehicle sales. Your completed worksheet and chart will look similar to Figure 1.74.

For Project 1F, you will need the following file:

New blank Excel workbook

You will save your workbook as
1F_4th_Quarter_Sales_Firstname_Lastname

Figure 1.74

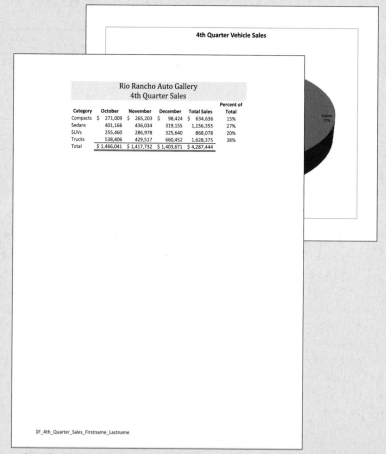

(Project 1F–4th Quarter Sales continues on the next page)

Content-Based Assessments

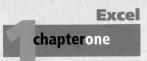

(Project 1F–4th Quarter Sales continued)

1. **Start** Excel and display a new blank workbook. In cell **A1**, type **Rio Rancho Auto Gallery** and in cell **A2**, type **4th Quarter Sales** In cell **A3**, type **Category** In cell **B3**, type **October** Select cell **B3**, and then use the fill handle to create a series in the range **C3:D3** so that *November* and *December* display in the cells. In cell **E3**, type **Total Sales** and in cell **F3**, type **Percent of Total** In your **Excel Chapter 1** folder, **Save** the workbook as **1F_4th_Quarter_Sales_Firstname_Lastname**

2. In the range **A4:D6**, type the following data; if you want to do so, select the range first and use Enter to confine the movement of the active cell within the range.

Category	October	November	December
Compacts	271009	265203	98424
Sedans	401166	436034	319155
Trucks	538406	429517	660452

3. Apply the **Wrap Text** command to cell **F3**, and then **Center** and **Bold** all the column titles in **row 3**. Adjust the width of **columns B:F** to **80 pixels**. **Merge and Center** the two worksheet titles over columns **A:F**, and then select and format the two titles by changing the **Font** to **Cambria**, the **Font Size** to **16**, and the **Fill Color** to **Blue, Accent 1, Lighter 80%**.

4. In cell **A7**, type **Total** In cell **E4**, **Sum** the three month's of sales for Compacts, and then copy the formula down for the remaining categories. **Sum** all of the columns in the range **B4:E7**. Apply the **Comma Style** to the range **B5:E6** and **Decrease Decimals** to zero decimals. (Hint: Recall that pound signs indicate that a cell is not wide enough to display the number without distortion; however after decreasing decimals, the cell width will accommodate the numbers.) Apply the **Accounting Number Format** to the ranges **B4:E4,B7:E7**, and then **Decrease Decimals** to zero decimals. Apply the appropriate border to the totals.

5. Insert a row above *Trucks* and enter the following data—recall that Excel will move and adjust formulas when rows are inserted. After you enter the data, use the fill handle to copy the formula from **E5** to **E6**.

SUVs	255460	286978	325640

6. In cell **F4**, type **=** and then construct a formula to calculate the percentage by which fourth quarter sales of Compacts makes up the Total Sales. (Hint: Divide the Total Sales of Compacts by the Total for all categories.) Use F4 to apply absolute cell referencing where necessary. To your result, apply **Percent Style** formatting with zero decimals, and then fill the formula down to cell **F7**. **Center** the percentages.

7. On the **Insert tab**, in the **Text group**, click **Header & Footer** to switch to **Page Layout View**. In the **Navigation group**, click the **Go to Footer** button, click just above the word *Footer*, and then in the **Header & Footer Elements group**, click the **File Name** button. Click a cell just above the footer to deselect the **Footer area** and view your file name. On the **Page Layout tab**, display the **Margins gallery**, click **Custom Margins**, and then under **Center on page**, select the **Horizontally** check box.

8. Switch to **Normal view** and press Ctrl + Home to move to the top of your worksheet. Select the vehicle categories in **A4:A7** and the Total Sales amounts in **E4:E7**. **Insert** a **Pie** chart, using the **Pie in 3-D** chart type. Move the chart to a new sheet and name the sheet **4th Quarter Chart**

(Project 1F–4th Quarter Sales continues on the next page)

(Project 1F—4th Quarter Sales continued)

Apply **Chart Layout 1**, **Chart Style 2**, and change the **Chart Title** to **4th Quarter Vehicle Sales** Deselect the chart title. To create a footer on the chart sheet, on the **Insert tab**, click the **Header & Footer** button, and then create a **Custom Footer** with the file name in the **Left section**.

9. Click the **Sheet1 tab** and press Ctrl + Home to cancel the selections. Select and delete **Sheet2** and **Sheet3**.

10. **Save** your workbook. Check your *Chapter Assignment Sheet* or *Course Syllabus* or consult your instructor to determine if you are to submit your assignments on paper or electronically. To submit electronically, follow the instructions provided by your instructor.

11. To print, from the **Office** menu, click the **Print** button. In the displayed **Print** dialog

box, under **Print what**, click the **Entire workbook** option button. In the lower left corner of the dialog box, click **Preview**, and notice in the status bar, *Preview: Page 1 of 2* displays. Check the preview, in the **Preview group**, click the **Next Page** button, and then in the **Print group**, click **Print** to print the two pages. If you are directed to submit printed formulas, refer to Activity 1.17 to do so.

12. If you printed your formulas, be sure to redisplay the worksheet by pressing Ctrl + `. From the **Office** menu, click **Close**. If the dialog box displays asking if you want to save changes, click **No** so that you do *not* save the changes you made for printing formulas. **Close** Excel.

End **You have completed Project 1F**

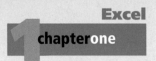
Project 1G — Compensation

In this project, you will apply the skills you practiced from the Objectives in Projects 1A and 1B.

Objectives: 1. *Create, Save, and Navigate an Excel Workbook;* **2.** *Enter and Edit Data in a Worksheet;* **3.** *Construct and Copy Formulas, Use the Sum Function, and Edit Cells;* **4.** *Format Data, Cells, and Worksheets;* **7.** *Use Page Layout View, Prepare a Worksheet for Printing, and Close Excel;* **9.** *Construct Formulas for Mathematical Operations;* **10.** *Format Percentages and Move Formulas.* **11.** *Create a Pie Chart and a Chart Sheet.*

In the following Mastering Excel project, you will create a worksheet for Clint Williams, Truck Sales Manager of Rio Rancho Auto Gallery. Members of the sales staff are paid a 5 percent commission on their total sales and also receive a small expense allowance to purchase promotional items like mugs, license plate holders, and key chains to give to customers. Your completed worksheet will look similar to Figure 1.75.

For Project 1G, you will need the following file:

New blank Excel workbook

You will save your workbook as
1G_Compensation_Firstname_Lastname

Figure 1.75

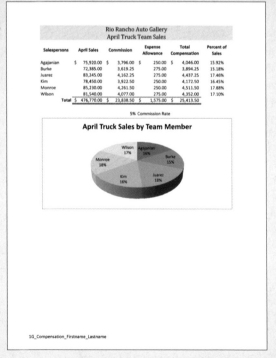

(Project 1G–Compensation continues on the next page)

(Project 1G–Compensation continued)

1. **Start** Excel and display a new blank workbook. In cell **A1**, type **Rio Rancho Auto Gallery** and in cell **A2**, type **April Truck Team Sales** In cell **A3**, type **Salespersons** and then press Tab. In cell **B3**, type **April Sales** In cell **C3**, type **Commission** In cell **D3**, type **Expense Allowance** In cell **E3**, type **Total Compensation** In cell **F3**, type **Percent of Sales** In your **Excel Chapter 1** folder, **Save** the workbook as **1G_Compensation_Firstname_Lastname**

2. Beginning in cell **A4**, enter the following data:

Salespersons	April Sales	Commission	Expense Allowance
Agajanian	75920		250
Burke	72385		275
Juarez	83245		275
Kim	78450		250
Monroe	85230		250
Wilson	81540		275

3. Apply the **Wrap Text** command to the range **D3:F3**. Widen all the columns to approximately **95 pixels**, and then select the column titles and apply **Bold**, **Center**, and **Middle Align**. **Merge and Center** cells **A1** and **A2**, over the column titles. Select the two worksheet titles and change the **Font** to **Cambria**, the **Font Size** to **14**, and apply a **Fill Color** of **Olive Green, Accent 3, Lighter 60%**.

4. In cell **C12**, type **5%** and in cell **D12**, type **Commission Rate** In cell **C4**, construct a formula to calculate the Commission for Agajanian—April Sales times the 5% rate in cell **C12**, using absolute cell references where necessary so that you can copy the formula down. Your result is *3796*. Copy the formula down for the remaining salespersons. In cell **E4**, construct a formula to calculate Agajanian's Total Compensation

by adding the Commission plus the Expense Allowance. Your result is *4046*. Copy the formula down for the remaining salespersons.

5. In cell **A10**, type **Total** Then, **Align Text Right** and apply **Bold**. Calculate totals for each of the four columns. Using financial formatting for the appropriate numbers, first apply **Comma Style**, next apply **Accounting Number Format**, and then apply a **Top and Double Bottom Border** to the total row.

6. In cell **F4**, construct a formula to calculate Agajanian's Percent of Sales by dividing Agajanian's April Sales in **B4** by Total April Sales in **B10**, using absolute cell references as necessary so that you copy the formula. Your result is *0.159238207*. Apply **Percent Style**, increase the decimal places to two, and then **Center** the percentage. Fill the formula down for the remaining salespersons.

7. Select the range of data containing the name of each salesperson and each salesperson's April Sales. **Insert** a **Pie** chart, using the **Pie in 3-D** chart type. Position the upper left corner of the chart just inside the upper left corner of cell **A13**. Apply **Chart Layout 1**, **Chart Style 5**, and as the **Chart Title** type **April Truck Sales by Team Member**

8. **Save** your workbook. Click any cell to deselect the chart. On the **Insert tab**, in the **Text group**, click **Header & Footer** to switch to **Page Layout view** and open the **Header area**. In the **Navigation group**, click the **Go to Footer** button, click just above the word *Footer*, and then in the **Header & Footer Elements group**, click the **File Name** button. Click in a cell just

(Project 1G–Compensation continues on the next page)

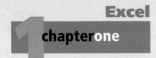

(Project 1G–Compensation continued)

above the footer to deselect the **Footer area** and view your file name.

9. Scroll up to view your chart. Select the chart, and then using the ↔ pointer, drag the right sizing handle of the chart as necessary to widen the chart so that the right border of the chart is just inside the right border of **column F**. Deselect the chart. On the **Page Layout tab**, in the **Page Setup group**, click the **Margins** button, and then at the bottom of the **Margins gallery**, click **Custom Margins**. Under **Center on page**, select the **Horizontally** check box, click **OK**, and then **Save** your workbook. Return to **Normal view** and scroll up as necessary to view the top of your worksheet. Select and delete **Sheet2**

and **Sheet3**.

10. **Save** the changes to your workbook. To submit electronically, follow the instructions provided by your instructor. To print on paper, from the **Office** menu, preview and then print your worksheet. If you are directed to submit printed formulas, refer to Activity 1.17 to do so. If you printed your formulas, be sure to redisplay the worksheet by pressing Ctrl + '. **Close** your workbook. If the dialog box displays asking if you want to save changes, click **No** so that you do *not* save the changes you made for printing formulas. **Close** Excel.

End You have completed Project 1G

Content-Based Assessments

Excel
chapterone   **Mastering Excel**

Project 1H—Warranties

In this project, you will apply the skills you practiced from the Objectives in Projects 1A and 1B.

Objectives: 1. *Create, Save, and Navigate an Excel Workbook;* **2.** *Enter and Edit Data in a Worksheet;* **3.** *Construct and Copy Formulas, Use the Sum Function, and Edit Cells;* **4.** *Format Data, Cells, and Worksheets;* **7.** *Use Page Layout View, Prepare a Worksheet for Printing, and Close Excel;* **8.** *Design a Worksheet;* **9.** *Construct Formulas for Mathematical Operations;* **11.** *Create a Pie Chart and a Chart Sheet.*

In the following Mastering Excel project, you will create a workbook for Sandy Cizek, the Auto Sales Manager, which summarizes both the sales of vehicle warranties and the commissions paid on the warranties that were sold. Your completed worksheets will look similar to Figure 1.76.

For Project 1H, you will need the following file:

New blank Excel workbook

**You will save your workbook as
1H_Warranties_Firstname_Lastname**

Figure 1.76

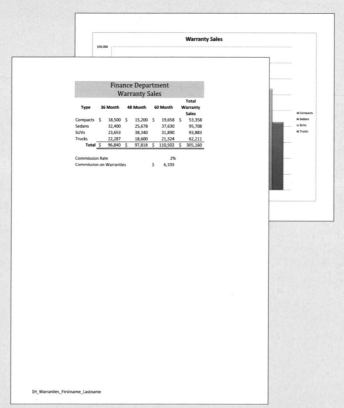

(Project 1H–Warranties continues on the next page)

Content-Based Assessments

(Project 1H–Warranties continued)

1. **Start** Excel and display a new blank work-book. In cell **A1**, type **Finance Department** and in cell **A2**, type **Warranty Sales** In cell **A3**, type **Type** and press Tab. In cell **B3**, type **36 Month** In cell **C3**, type **48 Month** In cell **D3**, type **60 Month** In cell **E3**, type **Total Warranty Sales** In your **Excel Chapter 1** folder, **Save** the workbook as **1H_Warranties_Firstname_Lastname**

2. In the range **A4:D7** type the following data; if you want to do so, select the range first and use Enter to confine the movement of the active cell within the range.

Type	36 Month	48 Month	60 Month
Compacts	18500	15200	19658
Sedans	32400	25678	37630
SUVs	23653	38340	31890
Trucks	22287	18600	21324

3. Apply the **Wrap Text** command to cell **E3**. Format all the column titles in **row 3** with **Center**, **Middle Align**, and **Bold**. Adjust the width of **columns B:E** to **80 pixels**. **Merge and Center** the two worksheet titles over columns **A:E**, and then select and for-mat the two titles by changing the **Font** to **Cambria**, the **Font Size** to **16**, and the **Fill Color** to **Red, Accent 2, Lighter 60%**.

4. In cell **E4**, **Sum** all the warranties sold for Compacts, and then copy the formula down for the remaining vehicle types. **Sum** the columns. In cell **A8**, type **Total** and apply **Bold** and **Align Text Right**. Using financial formatting for the appropriate numbers, first apply **Comma Style** with zero decimals, next apply **Accounting Number Format** with zero decimals, and then apply a **Top and Double Bottom Border** to the total row.

5. In cell **A10**, type **Commission Rate** and in cell **D10**, type **2%** In cell **A11**, type

Commission on Warranties In cell **D11**, construct a formula that multiplies the Total Warranty Sales in cell **E8** by the Commission Rate in **D10**, and then apply **Accounting Number Format** with zero decimals.

6. On the **Insert tab**, in the **Text group**, click **Header & Footer** to switch to **Page Layout view**. In the **Navigation group**, click the **Go to Footer** button, click just above the word *Footer*, and then in the **Header & Footer Elements group**, click the **File Name** button. Click a cell just above the footer to deselect the **Footer area** and view your file name. On the **Page Layout tab**, display the **Margins gallery**, click **Custom Margins**, and then under **Center on page**, select the **Horizontally** check box.

7. Switch to **Normal view** and scroll to the top of your worksheet. Select the range of data that represents the types of vehicles and the warranty sales for each of the three types, including the column titles. **Insert** a **Column** chart, using the **2-D Clustered Column** chart type. Move the chart to a new sheet and name the sheet **Warranty Sales Chart** On the **Design tab**, in the **Data group**, click the **Switch Row/Column** button to display the war-ranty periods as the categories. Apply **Chart Layout 1**, **Chart Style 26**, and change the **Chart Title** to **Warranty Sales** Deselect the chart by clicking in an area outside of the chart. To create a footer on the chart sheet, on the **Insert tab**, click the **Header & Footer** button, create a **Custom Footer** with the file name in the **Left section**.

(Project 1H–Warranties continues on the next page)

Excel
chapterone   Mastering Excel

(Project 1H–Warranties continued)

8. Click the **Sheet1 tab** and press Ctrl + Home to cancel the selections. Select and delete **Sheet2** and **Sheet3**.

9. **Save** your workbook. To submit electronically, follow the instructions provided by your instructor. To print, from the **Office** menu, click the **Print** button. In the displayed **Print** dialog box, under **Print what**, click the **Entire workbook** option button. In the lower left corner of the dialog box, click **Preview**, and notice in the status bar, *Preview: Page 1 of 2* displays. Check the preview, in the **Preview group**, click the **Next Page** button, and then in the **Print group**, click **Print** to print the two pages. If you are directed to submit printed formulas, refer to Activity 1.17 to do so.

10. If you printed your formulas, be sure to redisplay the worksheet by pressing Ctrl + `. From the **Office** menu, click **Close**. If the dialog box displays asking if you want to save changes, click **No** so that you do *not* save the changes you made for printing formulas. **Close** Excel.

End **You have completed Project 1H**

Content-Based Assessments

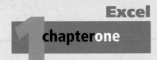
Mastering Excel

Project 1I — Team Comparison

In this project, you will apply the skills you practiced from all the Objectives in Projects 1A and 1B.

In the following Mastering Excel project, you will create a workbook for Sandy Cizek, Auto Sales Manager, which summarizes the monthly team sales for one of the three auto sales teams at Rio Rancho Auto Gallery. Your completed worksheet will look similar to Figure 1.77.

For Project 1I, you will need the following file:

New blank Excel workbook

You will save your workbook as
1I_Team_Comparison_Firstname_Lastname

Figure 1.77

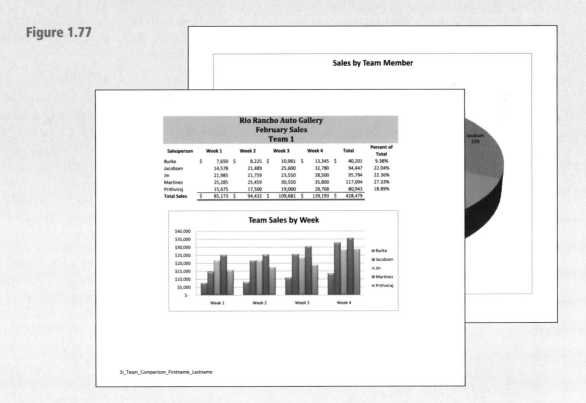

(Project 1I–Team Comparison continues on the next page)

Content-Based Assessments

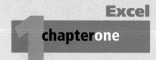

(Project 1I–Team Comparison continued)

1. **Start** Excel and display a new blank workbook. In cell **A1**, type **Rio Rancho Auto Gallery** In cell **A2**, type **February Sales** In cell **A3**, type **Team 1** In cell **A4**, type **Salesperson** and then press Tab. In cell **B4**, type **Week 1** Select cell **B4**, and then use the fill handle to create a series in the range **B4:E4** so that *Week 2* and *Week 3* and *Week 4* display in the cells. In cell **F4**, type **Total** and then in cell **G4**, type **Percent of Total** In your **Excel Chapter 1** folder, **Save** the workbook as 1I_Team_Comparison_Firstname_Lastname

2. In the range **A5:E8**, type the following data; if you want to do so, select the range first and use Enter to confine the movement of the active cell within the range.

Sales-person	Week 1	Week 2	Week 3	Week 4
Burke	7650	8225	10981	13345
Jacobsen	14578	21489	25600	32780
Jin	21985	21759	23550	28500
Prithviraj	15675	17500	19000	28768

3. Apply the **Wrap Text** command to cell **G4**. To all the column titles in **row 4**, apply the **Bold**, **Center**, and **Middle Align** commands. Adjust the width of **columns A:G** to **90 pixels**. **Merge and Center** the three worksheet titles over columns **A:G**, and then format the three titles by changing the **Font** to **Cambria**, the **Font Size** to **16**, the **Fill Color** to **Aqua, Accent 5, Lighter 40%** and applying **Bold**.

4. In cell **A9**, type **Total Sales** and format the cell with **Bold**. **Sum** the rows for each salesperson, and then **Sum** the columns for each week and for the Total. Insert a row above *Prithviraj* and enter the following data—recall that Excel will move and adjust formulas when rows are inserted.

After you enter the data, use the fill handle to copy the formula from **F7** to **F8**.

Martinez 25285 25459 30550 35800

5. Using financial formatting for the appropriate numbers, first apply **Comma Style** with zero decimals, next apply **Accounting Number Format** with zero decimals, and then apply a **Top and Double Bottom Border** to the total row.

6. In cell **G5**, construct a formula to calculate the percentage by which Burke's total sales makes up the Total in cell **F10**. Use F4 to apply absolute cell referencing where necessary. Apply **Percent Style** formatting with two decimals, and then fill the formula down to cell **G9**. **Center** the percentages.

7. Select the range of data that represents the names and each week's sales of each salesperson including the column titles. **Insert** a **2-D Clustered Column** chart, and then click the **Switch Row/Column** button so that the chart displays the weeks on the category axis and the salespersons as the data points. Position the upper left corner of the chart in the upper left corner of cell **A12**.

8. Click any cell to deselect the chart. On the **Insert tab**, click the **Header & Footer** button to switch to **Page Layout view**. Click the **Go to Footer** button, click just above the word *Footer*, and then click the **File Name** button. Click a cell just above the footer to deselect the **Footer area** and view your file name. On the **Page Layout tab**, change the **Orientation** to **Landscape**. Display the **Margins gallery**, click **Custom Margins**, and then under **Center on page**, select the **Horizontally** check box.

(Project 1I–Team Comparison continues on the next page)

Content-Based Assessments

(Project 1I–Team Comparison continued)

9. Scroll up, and then use the ↔ pointer to resize the chart so that its right edge is even with the right side of the data. Format the chart, using **Chart Layout 1**, **Chart Style 26** and then change the **Chart Title** to Team Sales by Week

10. **Save** your workbook, click any cell to deselect the chart, switch to **Normal view**, and then press Ctrl + Home to move to the top of your worksheet. Select the range of data that represents each salesperson's name and his or her Total for the month. **Insert** a **Pie** chart, using the **Pie in 3-D** chart type. Move the chart to a new sheet, and then name the sheet **Team Chart** Apply **Chart Layout 1**, **Chart Style 7**, and then change the **Chart Title** to Sales by Team Member Deselect the chart by clicking outside of the chart. To create a footer on the chart sheet, on the **Insert tab**, click the **Header & Footer** button, and then create a **Custom Footer** with the file name in the **Left section**.

11. Click the **Sheet1 tab**, and press Ctrl + Home to cancel the selections. Select and delete

Sheet2 and **Sheet3**. **Save** your workbook. Check your *Chapter Assignment Sheet* or *Course Syllabus* or consult your instructor to determine if you are to submit your assignments on paper or electronically. To submit electronically, follow the instructions provided by your instructor.

12. To print, from the **Office** menu, click the **Print** button. In the displayed **Print** dialog box, under **Print what**, click the **Entire workbook** option button. In the lower left corner of the dialog box, click **Preview**, and notice in the status bar, *Preview: Page 1 of 2* displays. Check the preview, in the **Preview group**, click the **Next Page** button, and then in the **Print group**, click **Print** to print the two pages. If you are directed to submit printed formulas, refer to Activity 1.17 to do so.

13. If you printed your formulas, be sure to redisplay the worksheet by pressing Ctrl + `. From the **Office** menu, click **Close**. If the dialog box displays asking if you want to save changes, click **No** so that you do *not* save the changes you made for printing formulas. **Close** Excel.

End You have completed Project 1I

Content-Based Assessments

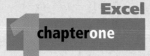

 Business Running Case

Project 1J — Business Running Case

In this project, you will apply the skills you practiced in Projects 1A and 1B.

From My Computer, navigate to the student files that accompany this textbook. In the folder **03_business_running_case_pg37_86**, locate and open the folder for this chapter. Open and print the instructions for this project, which are provided to you in Adobe PDF format. Follow the instructions and use the skills you have gained thus far to assist Jennifer Nelson in meeting the challenges of owning and running her business.

End **You have completed Project 1J** ———————

Outcomes-Based Assessments

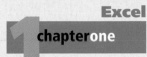
Rubric

The following outcomes-based assessments are *open-ended assessments*. That is, there is no specific correct result; your result will depend on your approach to the information provided. Make *Professional Quality* your goal. Use the following scoring rubric to guide you in *how* to approach the problem and then to evaluate *how well* your approach solves the problem.

The *criteria*—Software Mastery, Content, Format and Layout, and Process—represent the knowledge and skills you have gained that you can apply to solving the problem. The *levels of performance*—Professional Quality, Approaching Professional Quality, or Needs Quality Improvements—help you and your instructor evaluate your result.

	Your completed project is of Professional Quality if you:	Your completed project is Approaching Professional Quality if you:	Your completed project Needs Quality Improvements if you:
1-Software Mastery	Choose and apply the most appropriate skills, tools, and features and identify efficient methods to solve the problem.	Choose and apply some appropriate skills, tools, and features, but not in the most efficient manner.	Choose inappropriate skills, tools, or features, or are inefficient in solving the problem.
2-Content	Construct a solution that is clear and well organized, contains content that is accurate, appropriate to the audience and purpose, and is complete. Provide a solution that contains no errors of spelling, grammar, or style.	Construct a solution in which some components are unclear, poorly organized, inconsistent, or incomplete. Misjudge the needs of the audience. Have some errors in spelling, grammar, or style, but the errors do not detract from comprehension.	Construct a solution that is unclear, incomplete, or poorly organized, containing some inaccurate or inappropriate content; and contains many errors of spelling, grammar, or style. Do not solve the problem.
3-Format and Layout	Format and arrange all elements to communicate information and ideas, clarify function, illustrate relationships, and indicate relative importance.	Apply appropriate format and layout features to some elements, but not others. Overuse features, causing minor distraction.	Apply format and layout that does not communicate information or ideas clearly. Do not use format and layout features to clarify function, illustrate relationships, or indicate relative importance. Use available features excessively, causing distraction.
4-Process	Use an organized approach that integrates planning, development, self-assessment, revision, and reflection.	Demonstrate an organized approach in some areas, but not others; or, use an insufficient process of organization throughout.	Do not use an organized approach to solve the problem.

Outcomes-Based Assessments

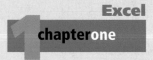
Problem Solving

Project 1K — Rims

In this project, you will construct a solution by applying any combination of the skills you practiced from the Objectives in Projects 1A and 1B.

For Project 1K, you will need the following file:

New blank Excel workbook

You will save your workbook as
1K_Rims_Firstname_Lastname

Rio Rancho Auto Gallery stocks one brand of tire rims and in January sold 10 16-inch rims priced at $150 each, 20 18-inch rims priced at $225 each, 32 20-inch rims priced at $375 each, and 16 22-inch rims priced at $500 each. The installation fee for all rims is $50 each.

Create a spreadsheet detailing this information and include a column that calculates the Installed Price for each rim size (Price + Installation Fee) and the Total Sales for each rim size (Installed Price times Number Sold). Total the columns to calculate the total number of rims sold and the Total Sales of all rims. Add an additional column in which you create a formula that calculates the Percent of Sales that each Rim Size is of the Total Sales of all rim sales. Create a 3-D pie chart that compares the Total Sales generated by each rim size. Position the pie chart below the worksheet.

Create a title that identifies the worksheet and apply appropriate formats to the data and the pie chart. Use borders, fill colors, and font styles and sizes to format a professional worksheet. Add a footer that includes the file name and center the worksheet on the page. Save the workbook as **1K_Rims_Firstname_Lastname** and submit it as directed.

 End **You have completed Project 1K** ———————————

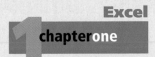

Excel
chapterone

Problem Solving

Project 1L—Finance

In this project, you will construct a solution by applying any combination of the skills you practiced from the Objectives in Projects 1A and 1B.

For Project 1L, you will need the following file:

New blank Excel workbook

You will save your workbook as
1L_Finance_Firstname_Lastname

In this project, you will create a worksheet for Tony Konecki, President of Rio Rancho Auto Gallery, which specifies, by quarter, the amount of credit extended to customers on vehicle purchases during the past fiscal year. The data is organized according to customer credit scores—overall, more credit was given to customers with higher credit scores. Create a worksheet with appropriate titles, and then enter the following data for Quarters 1 through 4.

Credit Score	Quarter 1	Quarter 2	Quarter 3	Quarter 4
750 or Above	350190	322489	368700	385644
700- 749	425654	496451	485200	501780
650- 699	328976	298560	316789	335679
600- 649	489561	462312	475232	490520
550- 599	182597	215600	202450	228600
Under 550	162487	175800	186532	188423

Calculate totals for each quarter and for each credit score, and then create a column chart that compares the amounts for each quarter by credit score. A chart layout that places the legend at the bottom of the chart will allow more space for the columns. Use formatting and editing techniques that you learned in this chapter so that the worksheet and chart are professional and accurate. Add the file name to the footer and save the workbook as **1L_Finance_Firstname_Lastname** Submit the project as directed.

End You have completed Project 1L ————————————

Outcomes-Based Assessments

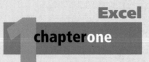

Excel
chapterone

Problem Solving

Project 1M—Labor

In this project, you will construct a solution by applying any combination of the skills you practiced from the Objectives in Projects 1A and 1B.

For Project 1M, you will need the following file:

New blank Excel workbook

You will save your workbook as
1M_Service_Firstname_Lastname

In this project, you will create a worksheet for the service department to analyze the labor costs associated with different types of repairs during the current month. Create an appropriate worksheet title and then enter the following data and column headings.

Service	Hours to Complete Service	Cost for Service at Standard Rate	Number Completed During June	Total Labor Cost
Valve replacement	8		13	
Head gasket	12		12	
Transmission	15		10	
Engine replacement	15		11	
Total Labor Cost				

Two rows below the Total Labor Cost row, in column A, type the **Standard Labor Rate** and in column B, type **35.75** In the Cost for Service at Standard Rate column, construct a formula to calculate the cost to compute each type of service at the standard rate. In the Total Labor Costs column, construct a formula to calculate the total labor cost for each of the services completed during the month.

Add a column to the worksheet with the column heading **Percent of Total Labor Costs** and calculate the percent that each service is of the Total Labor Costs. Create a pie chart on a separate chart sheet that compares the Total Labor Costs by Service. Add the file name to the footer in both sheets and check for spelling errors. Save the workbook as **1M_Service_Firstname_Lastname** and submit it as directed.

End You have completed Project 1M —————————

Outcomes-Based Assessments

Problem Solving

Project 1N—Incentives

In this project, you will construct a solution by applying any combination of the skills you practiced from the Objectives in Projects 1A and 1B.

> **For Project 1N, you will need the following file:**
>
> New blank Excel workbook

You will save your workbook as
1N_Incentives_Firstname_Lastname

In this project, you will create a worksheet for Ray Justham, the Finance Manager for Rio Rancho Auto Gallery, to track the cost of incentives offered to clients who purchase vehicles. Create an appropriate title for the worksheet and then enter the data below.

Vehicle Type	Dealer Rebates	Service Certificates	Complimentary Gas
New Cars	10500	8320	4380
New Trucks	12300	6350	3325
New SUVs	18650	13480	5825
Used Vehicles	11800	5650	1250

Sum the incentives by vehicle type and by incentive type. Then create a column chart comparing the data, switching rows and columns as necessary so that the vehicle types are the data series and placing the incentive type on the category axis. A chart layout that places the legend at the bottom of the chart will allow more space for the columns. Add the file name to the footer and check the workbook for spelling errors. Save the workbook as **1N_Incentives_Firstname_Lastname** and submit it as directed.

 End **You have completed Project 1N** ⎯⎯⎯⎯⎯⎯⎯

Outcomes-Based Assessments

Problem Solving

Project 10 — Rental

In this project, you will construct a solution by applying any combination of the skills you practiced from the Objectives found in Projects 1A and 1B.

For Project 10, you will need the following file:

New blank Excel workbook

**You will save your workbook as
10_Rental_Firstname_Lastname**

Rio Rancho Auto Gallery rents motorcycles, vans, SUVs, convertibles, pickup trucks, and motor scooters for short-term use by vacationers, tourists, and others who want to experience a different kind of drive. Create a workbook that Jane Gelson, Rental and Lease Manager for Rio Rancho Auto Gallery, can use to track the fees collected on the different types of vehicles rented by Rio Rancho customers in the month of August. Create an appropriate title for the worksheet and then enter the data below.

	Daily Rental Fee	Number of Days Rented	Rental Fees Collected
Motorcycle	35	22	
Van	45	30	
SUV	45	25	
Convertible	40	30	
Pickup truck	42	15	
Motor scooter	30	12	

Calculate the Rental Fees Collected by vehicle type and then total the Rental Fees Collected column. Create a 3-D pie chart to compare Rental Fees Collected by each vehicle. Add the file name to the footer and check the workbook for spelling errors. Save the workbook as **10_Rental_Firstname_Lastname** and submit it as directed.

End **You have completed Project 10** ———————

Outcomes-Based Assessments

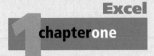
 You and **GO!**

Project 1P — You and *GO!*

In this project, you will construct a solution by applying any combination of the skills you practiced from the Objectives in Projects 1A and 1B.

From My Computer, navigate to the student files that accompany this textbook. In the folder **04_you_and_go_pg87_102**, locate and open the folder for this chapter. Open and print the instructions for this project, which are provided to you in Adobe PDF format. Follow the instructions to create a budget for yourself over a three month period.

End You have completed Project 1P ———————————

GO! with Help

Project 1Q — *GO!* with Help

The Excel Help system is extensive and can help you as you work. In this chapter, you used the Quick Access Toolbar on several occasions. You can customize the Quick Access Toolbar by adding buttons that you use regularly, making them quickly available to you from any tab on the Ribbon. In this exercise, you will use Help to find out how to add buttons.

1 **Start** Excel. At the far right end of the Ribbon, click the **Microsoft Office Excel Help** button . In the **Excel Help** dialog box, click the **Search button arrow**, and then, under **Content from this computer**, click **Excel Help**.

2 In the **Search** box, type **Quick Access Toolbar** and then press Enter. From the list of search results, click **Customize the Quick Access Toolbar**. Click each of the links to find out how to add buttons from the Ribbon and from the **Excel Options** dialog box.

3 When you are through, **Close** the Help window, and then **Close** Excel.

End You have completed Project 1Q ———————————

Outcomes-Based Assessments

Group Business Running Case

Project 1R — Group Business Running Case

In this project, you will apply the skills you practiced from the Objectives in Projects 1A and 1B.

Your instructor may assign this group case project to your class. If your instructor assigns this project, he or she will provide you with information and instructions to work as part of a group. The group will apply the skills gained thus far to help the Bell Orchid Hotel Group achieve its business goals.

End **You have completed Project 1R** _____

2 chaptertwo

Managing Workbooks and Analyzing Data

OBJECTIVES

At the end of this chapter you will be able to:

1. Create and Save a Workbook from an Existing Workbook
2. Navigate a Workbook and Rename Worksheets
3. Enter Dates, Clear Contents, and Clear Formats
4. Move, Copy, and Paste Cell Contents
5. Edit and Format Multiple Worksheets at the Same Time
6. Create a Summary Sheet
7. Format and Print Multiple Worksheets in a Workbook

8. Design a Worksheet for What-If Analysis
9. Perform What-If Analysis
10. Compare Data with a Line Chart

OUTCOMES

Mastering these objectives will enable you to:

PROJECT 2A
Create a Summary Sheet from Multiple Worksheets

PROJECT 2B
Make Projections Using What-If Analysis

The City of Golden Grove

Golden Grove is a California city located between Los Angeles and San Diego, about 20 miles from the Pacific shore. Ten years ago the population was just over 200,000; today it has grown to over 300,000. Community leaders focus on quality and economic development in decisions about housing, open space, education, and infrastructure, making the city a model for other communities its size. The city provides many recreational and cultural opportunities with a large park system and a thriving arts community.

Managing Workbooks and Analyzing Data

Organizations typically create workbooks that contain multiple worksheets. In such a workbook, the first worksheet usually summarizes the detailed information in the other worksheets. To make it easier to work with multiple worksheets, there are techniques to enter data into multiple worksheets simultaneously by grouping the worksheets. You can also copy, and then paste information from one worksheet to another. Additional techniques for managing workbooks with multiple worksheets include naming and color coding the sheet tabs so that you can quickly locate the detailed information you are looking for.

In Excel, you can explore options by recalculating formulas that depend on other formulas. For example, you can change the interest rate in a table of loan payments to determine the amount of monthly payments based on differing interest rates.

In this chapter, you will work with workbooks that contain multiple worksheets and analyze data by making projections of future growth.

Project 2A Ticket Sales

In Activities 2.1 through 2.10, you will edit an existing Excel workbook for Judith Amaya, the Director of Arts and Parks for Golden Grove. The annual Summer Fair and Arts Festival will be held during the last week in August. During the first week in August, the city is preselling tickets at three locations in the city. The four worksheets of your completed workbook will look similar to Figure 2.1.

For Project 2A, you will need the following file:

e2A_Ticket_Sales

You will save your workbook as
2A_Ticket_Sales_Firstname_Lastname

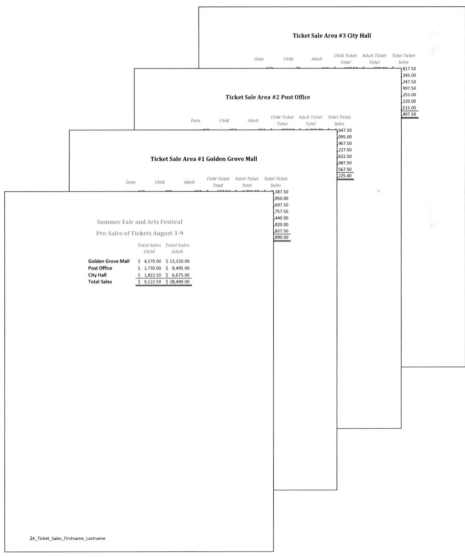

Figure 2.1
Project 2A—Ticket Sales

Objective 1
Create and Save a Workbook from an Existing Workbook

Within a workbook, individual worksheets may contain data for separate topics, locations, or periods of time related to the workbook's data. In such a workbook, it is common practice to have one worksheet that summarizes information from the other worksheets.

Activity 2.1 Creating and Saving a Workbook from an Existing Workbook

Judith has created a workbook with worksheets into which she can record the number of tickets sold at the three locations during the first week in August. In this activity, you will open the workbook and save it in your chapter folder with a different name.

1 **Start** Excel. From the **Office** menu 🔲, click **Open**. In the displayed **Open** dialog box, click the **Look in arrow**, navigate to the student files that accompany this textbook, click **e2A_Ticket_Sales**, and then in the lower right corner of the dialog box, click **Open**.

The workbook e2A_Ticket_Sales displays. Alternatively, you can double-click a file name to open it. Some information has already been entered into the worksheets. For example, on the first worksheet, the dates for the one-week period have been entered, along with information about the dates and ticket prices.

2 From the **Office** menu 🔲, click the **Save As** command. Navigate to the drive location where you will store your projects for this chapter. On the **Save As** dialog box toolbar, click the **Create New Folder** button 🔲. In the displayed **New Folder** dialog box, in the **Name** box, type **Excel Chapter 2** In the **New Folder** dialog box, click **OK**.

Windows creates the *Excel Chapter 2* folder and makes it the active folder in the Save As dialog box.

3 In the **File name** box, edit as necessary to indicate, using your own first and last name, **2A_Ticket_Sales_Firstname_Lastname** Be sure to include the underscore (⟮⇧ Shift⟯ + ⟮ - ⟯) instead of spaces between words.

4 In the lower right corner of the **Save As** dialog box, click **Save**.

Excel saves the file in your chapter folder with the new name. The workbook redisplays, and the new name displays in the title bar. In this manner, you can create a new workbook from an existing workbook.

Objective 2
Navigate a Workbook and Rename Worksheets

The default setting for the number of worksheets in a workbook is three. You can add additional worksheets or delete unused worksheets. Using multiple worksheets in a workbook is frequently a logical approach to arranging data.

Activity 2.2 Navigating Among Worksheets, Renaming Worksheets, and Changing the Tab Color of a Worksheet

When you have more than one worksheet in a workbook, you can **navigate** (move) among worksheets by clicking the **sheet tabs**. Sheet tabs identify each worksheet in a workbook and are located along the lower left edge of the workbook window. When you have more worksheets in the workbook than can be displayed in the sheet tab area, use the four sheet tab scrolling buttons to move sheet tabs into and out of view.

Excel names the first worksheet in a workbook *Sheet1* and each additional worksheet in order—*Sheet2*, *Sheet3*, and so on. Most Excel users rename the worksheets with names that are more meaningful. In this activity, you will navigate among three worksheets. You will also rename each worksheet and change the tab color of the sheet tabs.

1 Along the bottom of the Excel window, point to and then click the **Sheet2 tab**. Compare your screen with Figure 2.2.

The second worksheet in the workbook displays and becomes the active worksheet. *Sheet2* displays in bold.

Sheet tabs with *Sheet2* active sheet

Figure 2.2

Sheet tab scrolling buttons

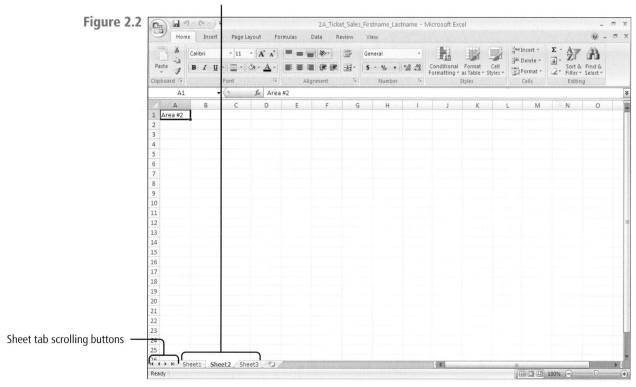

2 In cell **A1**, notice the text *Area #2*—this worksheet will contain data for Summer Fair tickets purchased at the Area #2 location. Click the **Sheet1 tab**.

The first worksheet in the workbook becomes the active worksheet, and cell A1, which is formatted with an orange background, displays *Area #1*.

3 Point to the **Sheet3 tab**, and then right-click. From the displayed shortcut menu, click **Rename**. With *Sheet3* selected, type **City Hall** and then press Enter.

4 Point to the **Sheet1 tab**, and then double-click to select its name. Type **Golden Grove Mall** and then press Enter. Using either of the two methods you just practiced, rename **Sheet2** as **Post Office**

5 Right-click the **Golden Grove Mall sheet tab**, and then from the displayed shortcut menu, point to **Tab Color** to display the colors associated with the workbook's theme. Under **Theme Colors**, locate and click **Purple, Accent 4, Lighter 40%**.

When the sheet is active, the tab color displays as an underline.

6 Click the **Post Office** sheet to make it the active sheet. On the Ribbon's **Home tab**, in the **Cells group**, click the **Format** button, and then from the displayed list, point to **Tab Color**. Under **Theme Colors**, click **Aqua, Accent 5, Lighter 40%**. Using either of the two techniques you have just practiced, change the **Tab Color** of the **City Hall** worksheet to **Orange, Accent 6, Lighter 40%**. Compare your screen with Figure 2.3.

Figure 2.3

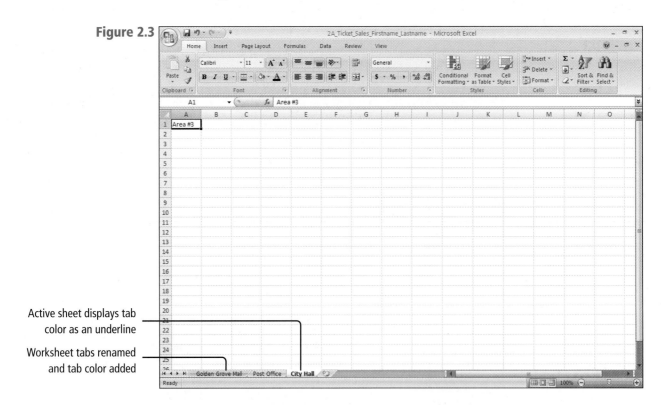

Active sheet displays tab color as an underline

Worksheet tabs renamed and tab color added

7 **Save** the changes you have made to your workbook.

Objective 3
Enter Dates, Clear Contents, and Clear Formats

Dates represent a type of value that you can enter in a cell. When you enter a date, Excel assigns a serial value—a number—to the date. This makes it possible to treat dates like other numbers. For example, if two cells contain dates, you can find the number of days between the two dates by subtracting the older date from the more recent date.

Activity 2.3 Entering and Formatting Dates

In this activity, you will examine the various ways that Excel can format a date that you type into a cell.

Date values entered in any of the following formats will be recognized by Excel as a date:

Format	Example
m/d/yy	7/4/09
d-mmm	4-Jul
d-mmm-yy	4-Jul-09
mmm-yy	Jul-09

On your keyboard, ⌐ (the hyphen key) and ⌐ (the forward slash key) function identically in any of these formats and can be used interchangeably. You can abbreviate the month name to three characters or spell it out. You can enter the year as two digits, four digits, or even leave it off. When left off, the current year is assumed but does not display in the cell.

A two-digit year value of 30 through 99 is interpreted by the Windows operating system as the four-digit years of 1930 through 1999. All other two-digit year values are assumed to be in the 21st century. If you always type year values as four digits, even though only two digits may display in the cell, you can be sure that Excel interprets the year value as you intended. See the table in Figure 2.4 for examples.

How Excel Interprets Dates

Date Typed As:	Completed by Excel As:
7/4/09	7/4/2009
7-4-98	7/4/1998
7/4	4-Jul (current year assumed)
7-4	4-Jul (current year assumed)
July 4	4-Jul (current year assumed)
Jul 4	4-Jul (current year assumed)
Jul/4	4-Jul (current year assumed)
Jul-4	4-Jul (current year assumed)
July 4, 1998	4-Jul-98
July 2009	Jul-09 (first day of month assumed)
July 1998	Jul-98 (first day of month assumed)

Figure 2.4

1 Click the **Golden Grove Mall sheet tab** to make it the active sheet. Click cell **A5** and notice that the cell indicates *8/3* (August 3). In the **Formula Bar**, notice that the full date of August 3, 2009 displays in the format *8/3/2009*.

2 With cell **A5** selected, on the Ribbon, in the **Number group**, click the **Number Format arrow**. From the bottom of the displayed menu, click **More Number Formats** to display the **Number tab** of the **Format Cells** dialog box. Compare your screen with Figure 2.5.

Under Category, *Date* is selected, and under Type, *3/14* is selected. All of the dates in Column A were formatted using this format type; that is, only the month and day display in the cell.

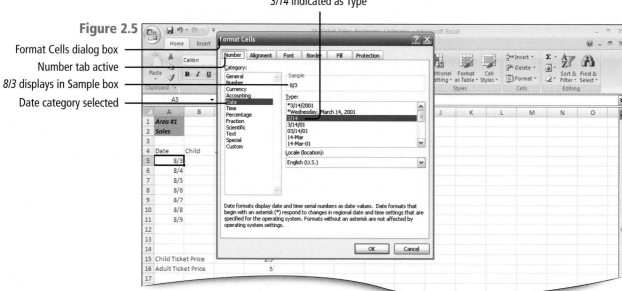

3/14 indicated as Type

Figure 2.5

Format Cells dialog box

Number tab active

8/3 displays in Sample box

Date category selected

3 In the displayed dialog box, under **Type**, click several other date types and watch the **Sample** area to see how applying the selected date format would format your cell. When you are finished, click the **3/14** type, and then at the bottom of the dialog box, click **OK**.

4 Click cell **A21**, type **8/10/2009** and then press Enter.

Cell A21 has no special date formatting applied, and thus displays in the default date format *8/10/2009*.

Alert

The Date Does Not Display as 8/10/2009

Settings in your Windows operating system determine the default format for dates. If your result is different, it is likely that the formatting of the default date was adjusted on the computer at which you are working.

5 Click cell **A21** again. Hold down `Ctrl` and press `;` (the semicolon key) on your keyboard. Press `Enter` to confirm the entry.

Excel enters the current date, obtained from your computer's internal calendar, into the selected cell using the default date format. `Ctrl` + `;` is a convenient keyboard shortcut for entering the current date.

6 Click cell **A21** again, type **8/10/09** and then press `Enter`.

Because the year *09* is less than 30, Excel assumes a 21st century date and changes *09* to *2009* to complete the four-digit year. Typing *98* would result in *1998*. For two-digit years that you type that are between 30 and 99, Excel assumes a 20th century date.

7 Click cell **A5**, and then on the **Home tab**, in the **Clipboard group**, click the **Format Painter** button. Click cell **A21**, and notice that the date format from cell **A5** is copied to cell **A21**. **Save** your workbook.

Activity 2.4 Clearing Cell Contents and Formats

A cell has contents—a value or a formula—and a cell may also have one or more formats applied, for example bold and italic font style, fill color, font color, and so on. You can choose to clear the contents of a cell, the formatting of a cell, or both. You can clear—delete—the contents of a selected cell in two ways: Press `Delete` or use the Clear Contents command available both from the Editing group on the Ribbon and from a shortcut menu.

Clearing the contents of a cell deletes the value or formula typed there, but it does *not* clear formatting applied to a cell. In this activity, you will clear the contents of a cell and then clear the formatting of a cell that contains a date to see its underlying content.

1 On the **Golden Grove Mall** worksheet, click cell **A1**. On the Ribbon, in the **Editing group**, click the **Clear** button. From the displayed list, click **Clear Contents**. Click cell **A2**, and then press `Delete`.

You can use either of these two methods to delete the *contents* of a cell. Deleting the contents does not, however, delete the formatting of the cell; you can see that the orange fill color format applied to the two cells still displays.

2 In cell **A1**, type **Area #1** and then on the **Formula Bar**, click the **Enter** button so that cell **A1** remains the active cell. In the **Editing group**, click the **Clear** button, and then from the displayed menu, click **Clear Formats**.

Clearing the Formats deletes formatting from the cell—the orange fill color and the bold and italic font styles—but does not delete the cell's contents.

3 Use the same technique to clear the orange fill color from cell **A2**.

4 Click cell **A5**, click the **Clear** button, and then click **Clear Formats**. In the **Number group**, notice that *General* displays as the number format of the cell.

The box at the top of the Number group indicates the current Number format of the selected cell. Clearing the date formatting from the cell displays the date's serial number. The date, August 3, 2009, is stored as a serial number that indicates the number of days since January 1, 1900. This date is the 40,028th day since the reference date of January 1, 1900.

5 On the **Quick Access Toolbar**, click the **Undo** button to restore the date format. **Save** your workbook, and then compare your screen with Figure 2.6.

Figure 2.6

Date indicated as the Number format

Date in Formula Bar

Orange fill color and bold italic font style cleared from cell A1

Contents of cell A2 deleted

A5 reformatted as a date

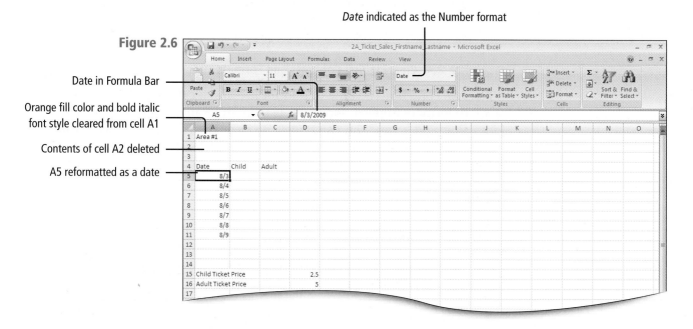

Objective 4
Move, Copy, and Paste Cell Contents

Data from individual cells and groups of cells can be copied to other cells in the same worksheet, to other sheets in the same workbook, or to sheets in another workbook. Likewise, data can be moved from one place to another. The action of placing cell contents that have been copied or moved to the Office Clipboard to another location is called *paste*.

Activity 2.5 Copying, Pasting, and Moving Cell Contents

The *Office Clipboard* is a temporary storage area maintained by your Windows operating system. When you select one or more cells, and then perform the Copy command or the Cut command, the selected data is placed on the Office Clipboard. From the Office Clipboard storage area, the data is available for pasting into other cells, other worksheets, other workbooks, and even into other Office programs.

1 On the **Golden Grove Mall** sheet, select the range **A20:A21**. Point to the upper edge of the black border surrounding the selected cells

until the ⬚ pointer displays. Drag upward until the ScreenTip displays *A18:A19*, as shown in Figure 2.7, and then release the mouse button to complete the move.

Using this technique, cell contents can be moved from one location to another; this is referred to as ***drag and drop***.

Figure 2.7

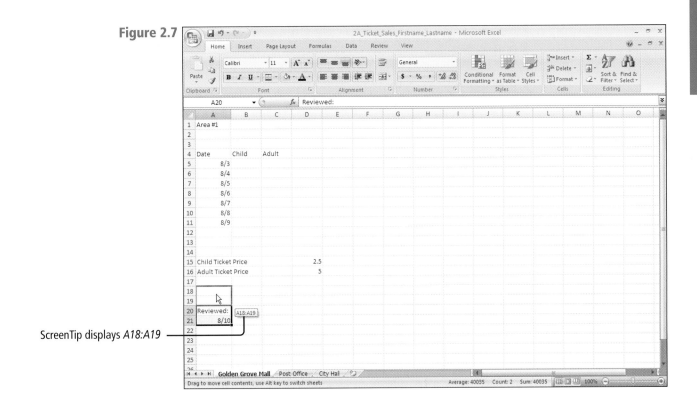

ScreenTip displays *A18:A19*

2 Select the range **A4:D16**.

A range of cells identical to this one is required for the *Post Office* worksheet and the *City Hall* worksheet.

3 On the **Home tab**, in the **Clipboard group**, click the **Copy** button to place a copy of the selected cells on the Office Clipboard. Alternatively, press Ctrl + C; or, right-click over the selected range, and then click Copy from the shortcut menu.

A moving border surrounds the selected range, and a message on the left side of the status bar indicates *Select destination and press ENTER or choose Paste*. These two results confirm that your selected range has been placed on the Office Clipboard.

4 At the bottom of the workbook window, click the **Post Office sheet tab** to make it the active worksheet. Click cell **A4**, and then on the **Home tab**, in the **Clipboard group**, click the **Paste** button. Alternatively, use the keyboard shortcut for Paste, which is Ctrl + V. Compare your screen with Figure 2.8.

The selected cells from the first worksheet are copied from the Office Clipboard to the second worksheet. When pasting a range of cells, you need only select the cell in the upper left corner of the **paste area**—the target destination for data that has been cut or copied using the Office Clipboard.

Figure 2.8

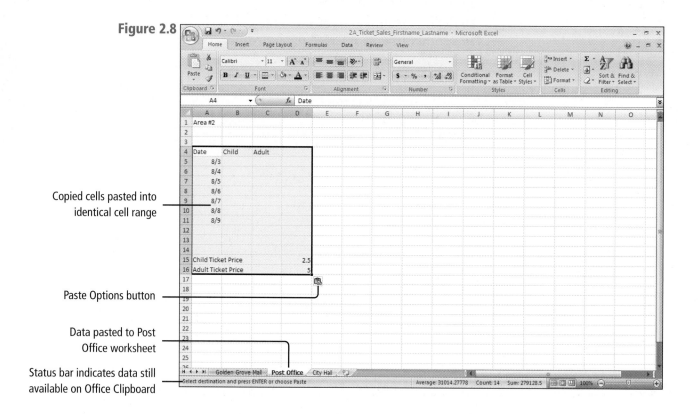

Copied cells pasted into identical cell range

Paste Options button

Data pasted to Post Office worksheet

Status bar indicates data still available on Office Clipboard

Note — Pressing Enter to Complete a Paste Action

Pressing Enter pastes the text and removes it from the Office Clipboard. Thus, if you want to paste the same text more than one time, click the Paste button so that the copied text remains available on the Office Clipboard.

5 In the lower right corner of the paste area, click the **Paste Options** button.

The **Paste Options button**, which displays just below your pasted selection after you perform the paste operation, displays a list of options that lets you determine how the information is pasted into your worksheet. The list varies depending on the type of content you are pasting and the program you are pasting from.

6 Click any cell to close the list and deselect the paste area. In the status bar, notice that the message still displays, indicating that your selected range remains on the Office Clipboard. Click the **City Hall sheet tab** to make it the active sheet, and then click cell **A4**. In the **Clipboard group**, click the **Paste** button.

7 On the **Home tab**, in the **Clipboard group**, click the **Clipboard Dialog Box Launcher** button ⬚, and then compare your screen with Figure 2.9.

The Clipboard task pane displays, and you can view your selection on the Clipboard. Here you can clear your selection from the Clipboard, although it is not necessary to do so.

Figure 2.9

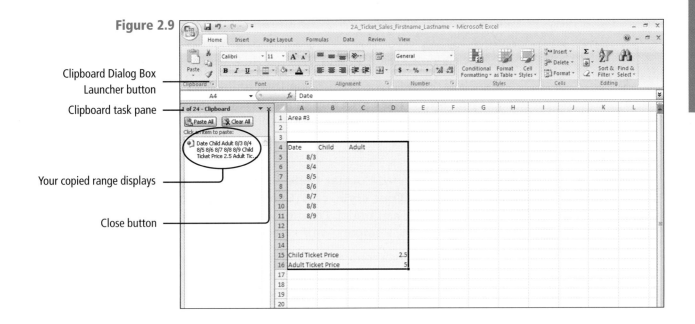

Clipboard Dialog Box Launcher button

Clipboard task pane

Your copied range displays

Close button

8 In the upper right corner of the **Office Clipboard task pane**, click the **Close** button ☒. Display the **Golden Grove Mall** sheet. Press ⎋Esc to cancel the moving border.

The status bar no longer displays the message.

9 **Save** 🖫 your changes.

Objective 5
Edit and Format Multiple Worksheets at the Same Time

You can enter or edit data on several worksheets at the same time by selecting and grouping multiple worksheets. Data that you enter or edit on the active sheet is reflected in all selected sheets. If you apply color to the sheet tabs, the name of the sheet tab will be underlined in the color you selected. If the sheet tab displays with a background color, the sheet has not been selected.

Activity 2.6 Wrapping Text in a Cell in Several Worksheets at the Same Time

If you want text to appear on multiple lines within a single cell, you can format the cell so that the text wraps automatically, or you can enter a manual line break. In this activity, you will group the worksheets for the three ticket sales locations, and then format additional column titles with wrapped text on all the worksheets at the same time.

1 With the **Golden Grove Mall** worksheet as the active sheet, press ⌃Ctrl + ⌂Home to make cell **A1** the active cell. Point to the sheet tab, right-click, and then from the displayed menu, click **Select All Sheets**. At the top of your screen, look at the title bar and notice that *[Group]* displays.

All the worksheets are selected, as indicated by *[Group]* in the title bar and the sheet tab names underlined in the selected tab color. Data that you enter or edit on the active sheet will also be entered or edited in the same manner on all the selected sheets in the same cells.

2 Select **columns A:F**, and then set their width to **83 pixels**.

3 Click cell **D4**, type **Child Ticket Total** and then press ⇥Tab. In cell **E4**, type **Adult Ticket Total** and then press ⇥Tab. In cell **F4** type **Total Ticket Sales** and then press ⏎Enter. Select the range **A4:F4**, right-click over the selection, and then from the displayed shortcut menu, click **Format Cells**.

4 In the displayed **Format Cells** dialog box, click the **Font tab**, and then under **Font style**, click **Bold Italic**. Under **Color**, click the arrow, and then under **Theme Colors**, click **Orange, Accent 6, Darker 25%**. Compare your screen with Figure 2.10.

Recall that commonly used Font formats are also available from the Font group on the Ribbon. However, when applying multiple formats to selected cells, it is efficient to do so from the Format Cells dialog box.

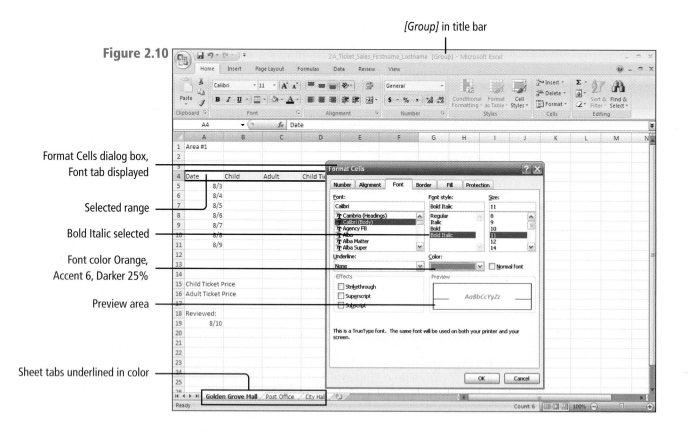

Figure 2.10

[Group] in title bar

Format Cells dialog box, Font tab displayed

Selected range

Bold Italic selected

Font color Orange, Accent 6, Darker 25%

Preview area

Sheet tabs underlined in color

5 In the **Format Cells** dialog box, click the **Alignment tab**.

Here you can change the alignment of text in the selected range.

6 Under **Text alignment**, click the **Horizontal arrow**, and then from the displayed list, click **Center**. Click the **Vertical arrow**, and then from the displayed list, click **Center**. Under **Text control**, click to select—place a check mark in—the **Wrap text** check box.

Data in the cell will wrap to fit the column width; a change in column width will automatically adjust the wrapping of the text.

Another Way — **To Wrap Text in a Cell**

To wrap text in a cell or range of cells, select the specific cells, and then in the Alignment group, click the Wrap Text button.

To start a new line of text at a specific point in a cell, regardless of column width, double-click the cell, click the location where you want to break the line in the cell, and then press [Alt] + [Enter] to insert a line break.

---

7 At the bottom of the dialog box, click **OK**, and then compare your screen with Figure 2.11.

All the formats that you selected in the Format Cells dialog box are applied to the selected range of cells. Those formats that have buttons on the Ribbon are shown as being selected.

Wrap Text button selected

Figure 2.11
Center and Middle
Align buttons selected

Bold and Italic buttons selected

Dialog Box Launcher button

All formats selected in
Format Cells dialog box
applied to range

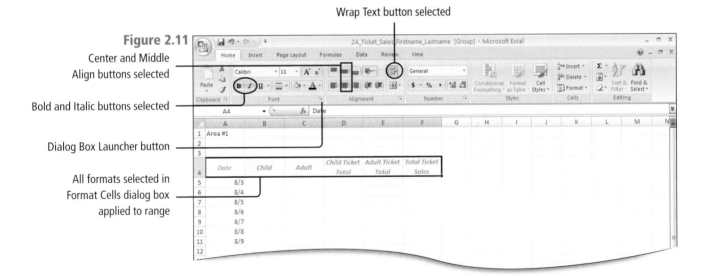

8 In the **Font group**, click the **Dialog Box Launcher** button.

The Font tab of the Format Cells dialog box displays. The most commonly used settings from this tab are displayed as buttons on the Ribbon.

9 Click **Cancel** to close the dialog box. On the Ribbon, in the **Alignment group**, click the **Dialog Box Launcher** button ⌐.

The Alignment tab of the Format Cells dialog box displays. The most commonly used settings from the Alignment tab are displayed as buttons in the Alignment group on the Ribbon. In this manner, Excel makes frequently used commands quickly available to you on the Ribbon. To perform multiple commands, use either the Ribbon buttons or the Format Cells dialog box. To use commands that are not commonly used and thus not displayed on the Ribbon, use the Format Cells dialog box.

10 Click **Cancel** to close the dialog box. Display the **Post Office** worksheet.

As soon as you select a single sheet, the grouping of the sheets is canceled and *[Group]* no longer displays in the title bar. Because the sheets were grouped, the same new text and formatting was applied to all of the selected sheets. In this manner, you can make the same changes to all the sheets in a workbook at one time.

11 Display the **City Hall** worksheet, and then verify that the changes have also been made to this worksheet. **Save** 🖫 your workbook.

Activity 2.7 Entering Data and Constructing Formulas on Multiple Worksheets

Recall that formulas are equations that perform calculations on values in your worksheet, and that a formula starts with an equal sign (=). Operators are the symbols with which you specify the type of calculation that you want to perform on the elements of a formula. In this activity, you will enter the number of Child and Adult tickets purchased at each of the three locations during the week of August 3, and then calculate the total sales.

1 Display the **Golden Grove Mall** worksheet as the active sheet. Verify that the sheets are not grouped—*[Group]* does *not* display in the title bar. Click cell **A1**, type **Ticket Sale Area #1 Golden Grove Mall** and then click the **Enter** button ✓ on the **Formula Bar**. With cell **A1** as the active cell, change the **Font** Calibri ▾ to **Cambria**, the **Font Size** 11 ▾ to **14**, and then apply **Bold** **B**.

Your new typing replaces the contents of the cell.

2 Select the range **A1:F1**, and then in the **Alignment group**, click the **Merge and Center** button 🔲 ▾.

3 Select the range **B5:C11**, type **255** and then press Enter Type **350** and then press Enter.

Although it is not required that you do so, recall that selecting a range in this manner lets you enter columns of data by pressing Enter after each entry, and keeps the entries within the defined range of cells. After you type in the last selected cell in column B, which is B11, pressing Enter will make cell C5 the active cell.

4 Type the remaining number of tickets sold as shown in the following table, pressing ⎡Enter⎤ after each entry, and then compare your screen with Figure 2.12.

	Child	**Adult**
8/3	255	350
8/4	350	415
8/5	295	392
8/6	115	294
8/7	214	381
8/8	304	412
8/9	295	420

Number of tickets sold
at this location entered

Figure 2.12

Worksheet title formatted

Typing and pressing Enter keeps
data within selected range

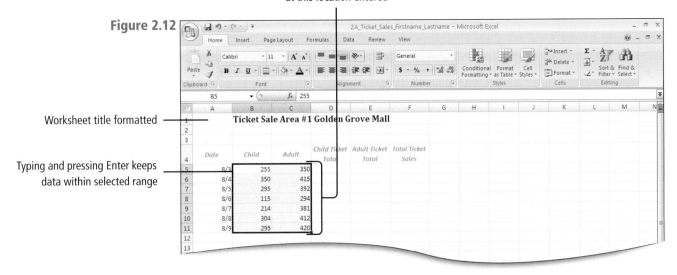

5 Click cell **A1**, and then in the **Clipboard group**, click the **Format Painter** button. Click the **Post Office sheet tab**, and then click cell **A1** in the active sheet to apply the formatting. In cell **A1**, replace *Area #2* by typing **Ticket Sale Area #2 Post Office** and then pressing ⎡Enter⎤.

6 Select the range **B5:C11**, enter the number of tickets purchased at this location as shown in the following table, and then compare your screen with Figure 2.13.

	Child	**Adult**
8/3	155	252
8/4	210	314
8/5	195	296
8/6	95	198
8/7	87	283
8/8	195	320
8/9	55	36

Figure 2.13

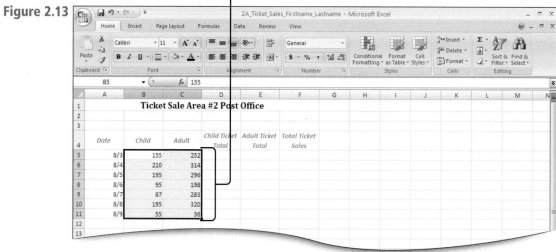

Ticket Sale Area #2 Post Office

Date	Child	Adult	Child Ticket Total	Adult Ticket Total	Total Ticket Sales
8/3	155	252			
8/4	210	314			
8/5	195	296			
8/6	95	198			
8/7	87	283			
8/8	195	320			
8/9	55	36			

7 Click cell **A1**, right-click, on the displayed Mini toolbar, click the

Format Painter button [icon], display the **City Hall** worksheet, and then click cell **A1** to copy the format. In cell **A1**, replace *Area #3* by typing **Ticket Sale Area #3 City Hall** and then pressing Enter. Enter the number of tickets sold at this location by selecting the appropriate data range, and then entering the information in the following table. Compare your screen with Figure 2.14.

	Child	**Adult**
8/3	75	126
8/4	110	214
8/5	105	197
8/6	85	157
8/7	92	205
8/8	104	212
8/9	158	224

Figure 2.14

Number of tickets sold
at this location entered

Ticket Sale Area #3 City Hall

Date	Child	Adult	Child Ticket Total	Adult Ticket Total	Total Ticket Sales
8/3	75	126			
8/4	110	214			
8/5	105	197			
8/6	85	157			
8/7	92	205			
8/8	104	212			
8/9	158	224			

8 **Save** 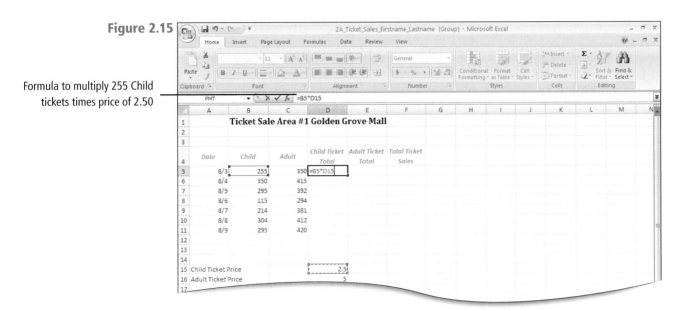 your changes. Right-click the **Golden Grove Mall sheet tab**, and then from the displayed shortcut menu, click **Select All Sheets**.

The first worksheet becomes the active sheet, and the worksheets are grouped. *[Group]* displays in the title bar, and the sheet tabs are underlined in the tab color to indicate they are selected as part of the group. Recall that when grouped, any editing or data entry that you perform on the active worksheet is *also* performed on the other selected worksheets.

9 Click cell **D5** and type **=** to begin a formula. Click cell **B5**, type ***** click cell **D15**, and then compare your screen with Figure 2.15.

Recall that the symbols + and − and * and / are used in formulas to perform addition, subtraction, multiplication, and division. This formula will calculate the total amount from the sale of Child tickets on August 3 at the Golden Grove Mall location.

Recall that in the General number format, trailing zeroes do not display.

Figure 2.15

Formula to multiply 255 Child tickets times price of 2.50

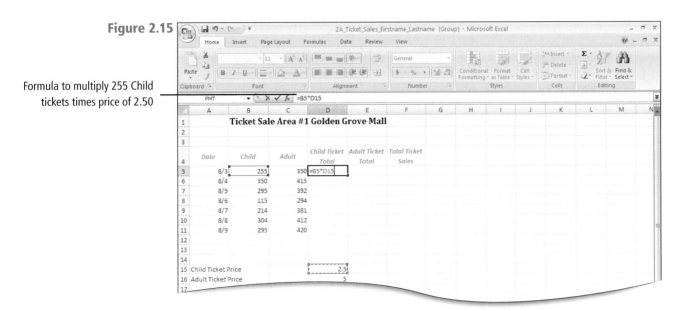

10 Press F4 to make the reference to **Child Ticket Price** in cell **D15** absolute.

Recall that when you copy formulas down to other cells in a column, the cell references change relative to the row number, and for the reference to each date in column A, that is the desired result. For the cell reference to the ticket price in cell D15, the cell reference should remain the same for each date.

11 On the **Formula Bar**, click the **Enter** button ✓ to display the formula result of *637.5* and then use the fill handle to copy the formula down for the remaining dates. Compare your screen with Figure 2.16.

Figure 2.16

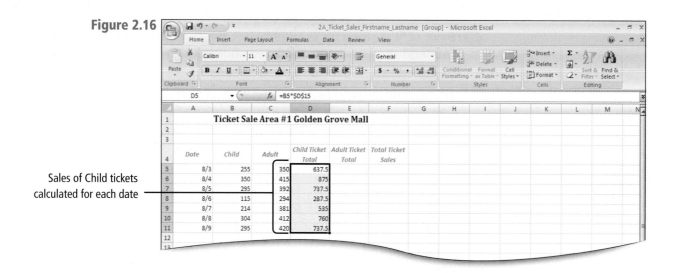

Sales of Child tickets
calculated for each date

12 In cell **E5**, construct a similar formula to multiply the number of **Adult** tickets sold on August 3 times the **Adult Ticket Price** in cell **D16**. Make the reference to cell **D16** absolute so that each day's sales are multiplied by the **Adult Ticket Price** in cell **D16**. Copy the formula down for the remaining dates, and then compare your screen with Figure 2.17.

Figure 2.17

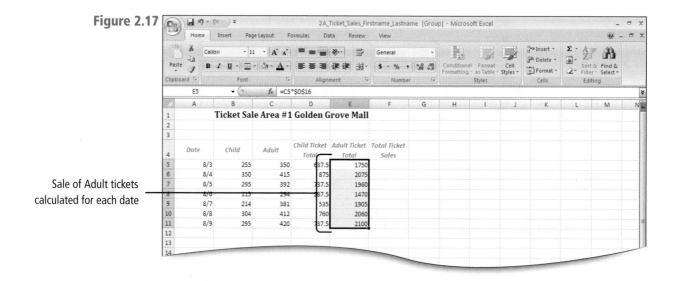

Sale of Adult tickets
calculated for each date

13 Click cell **F5**, and then in the **Editing group**, click the **Sum** button

. Notice that Excel selects all the numeric values—but not the date values—in the row. To Sum only the values in **D5** and **E5**—the **Child Total** and the **Adult Total**—with your mouse, select the range **D5:E5**, and then compare your screen with Figure 2.18.

Recall that the Sum function first looks above the selected cell for a range of numbers to sum. If no values display above the selected cell, Excel looks to the left for a range of numbers to sum. You can change the range to which you want to apply the Sum function by simply selecting the desired range.

Figure 2.18

New range selected
for the SUM function

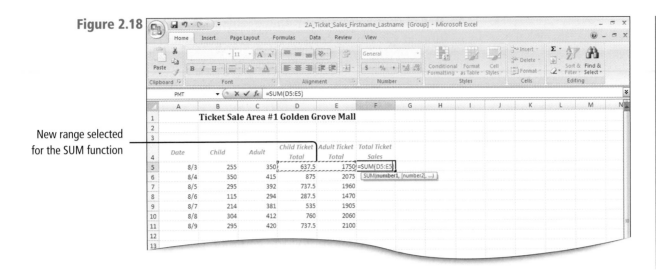

14 On the **Formula Bar**, click the **Enter** button ☑, and then copy the formula down for the remaining dates. Compare your screen with Figure 2.19.

Recall that because your worksheets are grouped, the calculations on the first worksheet are also being performed on the other two worksheets.

Daily totals for Child
and Adult tickets sold

Figure 2.19

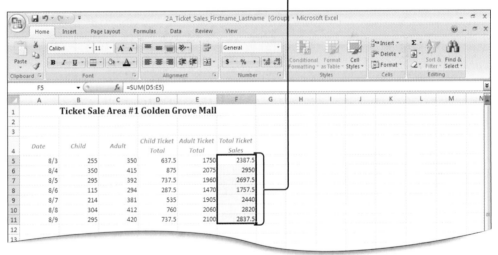

15 Click cell **F12**, and then in the **Editing group**, click the **Sum** button ☒. Be sure the range **F5:F11** is selected, and then press Enter.

Excel looks above the selected cell and proposes a range to sum. Your result is *17890*.

16 In cell **A12** type **Totals** and then on the **Formula Bar**, click the **Enter** button ☑ to confirm the entry and keep **A12** as the active cell. Then apply the **Align Text Right** ☰ format and **Bold** **B** to the cell.

17 Select the range **B5:E12**, and then in the **Editing group**, click the **Sum** button to apply the Sum function to the range.

Recall that selecting a range in this manner will place the Sum function in the empty cells at the bottom of each column.

18 Apply appropriate number and financial formatting as follows: Select the range **B5:C12**, click the **Comma Style** button [,], and then click **Decrease Decimal** [.00→.0] two times. Select the range **D6:F11** and apply **Comma Style** [,]—leave the two decimal places displayed in these currency amounts. Select the nonadjacent ranges **D5:F5** and **D12:F12**, and then click the **Accounting Number Format** button [$ ▾]. Select the range **B12:F12**, in the **Font group** click the **Borders button arrow** [▦ ▾], and then click **Top and Double Bottom Border** to apply the common format for financial numbers. Click any blank cell to deselect, and then compare your screen with Figure 2.20.

Accounting Number Format applied

Figure 2.20

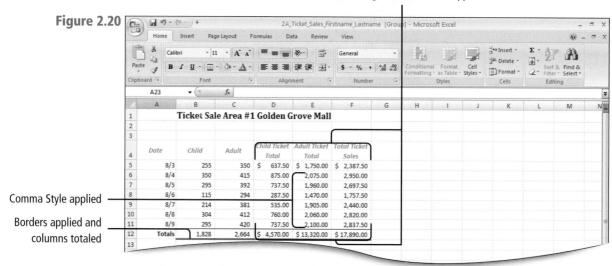

Comma Style applied

Borders applied and columns totaled

Note — Apply Comma Style first

When combining both the Comma Style and the Accounting Number Format to different ranges within a contiguous group of cells, apply Comma Style first.

19 Select the range **D15:D16**, right-click over the selection, and then on the Mini toolbar, click the **Accounting Number Format** [$ ▾] button.

20 Display the **Post Office** worksheet to examine the totals, and then compare your screen with Figure 2.21.

Recall that because your worksheets were grouped while making the calculations, all the calculations and formatting on the first worksheet were also being performed on the other two worksheets.

As soon as you select an individual sheet, as you have done here, the grouping is canceled. *[Group]* no longer displays in the title bar.

Figure 2.21

[Group] no longer displays
(sheets are ungrouped)

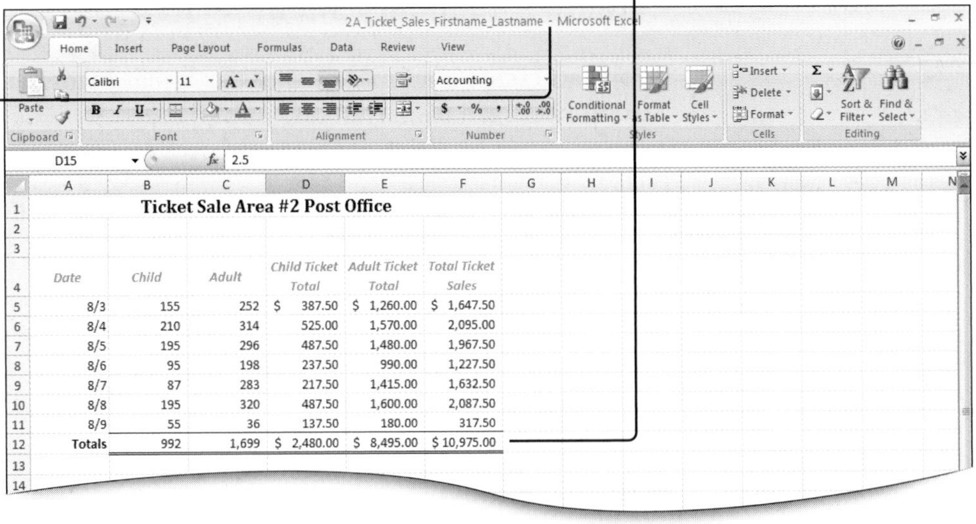

Totals calculated for Area #2

21 Display the **City Hall** worksheet to examine the totals, and then compare your screen with Figure 2.22.

You can see that by grouping sheets and copying formulas, it is easy to make multiple calculations in Excel without typing formulas multiple times.

Totals calculated for Area #3

Figure 2.22

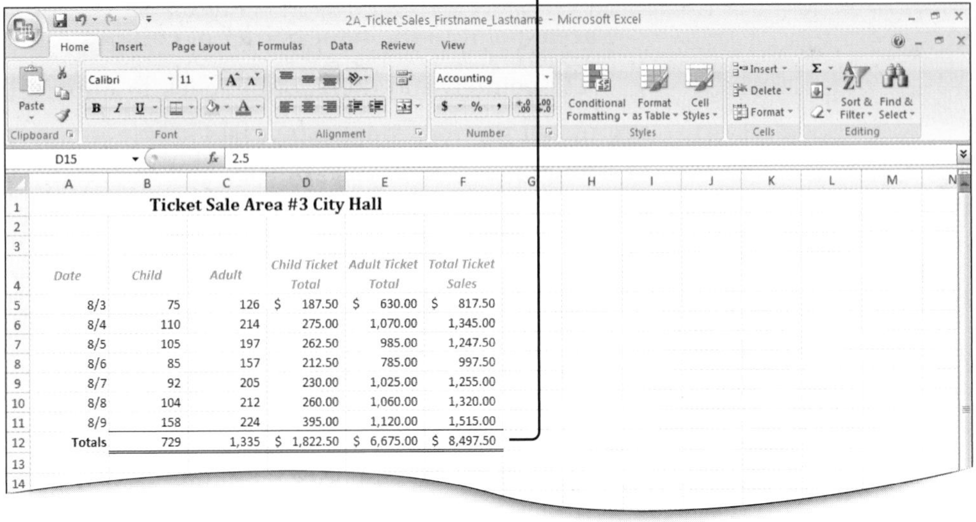

22 **Save** the changes you have made to your workbook.

Objective 6
Create a Summary Sheet

You can create a summary sheet as a place where totals from other worksheets are displayed and summarized.

Activity 2.8 Constructing Formulas That Refer to Cells in Another Worksheet

In this activity, you will insert a new worksheet in which you will place the totals from each ticket sale location's worksheet. You will construct formulas in the Summary worksheet to display the total revenue for each of the two types of tickets—Child and Adult—that will update the Summary worksheet whenever changes are made to the other worksheet totals.

1 To the right of the **City Hall** worksheet tab, click the **Insert Worksheet** button ⬚.

A new worksheet displays with the name *Sheet1* or *Sheet2* or some other number, depending on whether the other worksheets have been renamed and how many times a new worksheet has been inserted.

2 Rename the new worksheet **Summary** and then change the **Tab Color** to **Olive Green, Accent 3, Lighter 40%**. In cell **A4**, type **Golden Grove Mall** In cell **A5**, type **Post Office** and then in cell **A6**, type **City Hall** Select the range **A4:A6**, right-click, and then on the Mini toolbar, change the **Font Size** 11 ▾ to **12** and apply **Bold** B. In the **column heading area**, point to the right border of **column A** to display the ↔ pointer, and then double-click to AutoFit the column.

3 In cell **B3**, type **Total Sales Child** and then in cell **C3**, type **Total Sales Adult** Select the range **B3:C3**, and then right-click over the selection to display the Mini toolbar. Click **Bold** B, click **Italic** I, change the **Font** Calibri ▾ to **Cambria**, and then change the **Font Color** A▾ to **Orange, Accent 6, Darker 25%**. With the two cells still selected, in the **Alignment group**, click the **Wrap Text** button ⬚, the **Center** button ≡, and then click the **Middle Align** ≡ button.

Recall that you can apply common formats from the buttons on the Ribbon or you can use the Mini toolbar. The same formats can also be applied from the Format Cells dialog box. Additionally, the Format Cells dialog box contains some formatting commands that are not commonly used enough to warrant a button on the Ribbon or Mini toolbar.

4 Click cell **B4**. Type **=** and then click the **Golden Grove Mall sheet tab**. On the **Golden Grove Mall** worksheet, click cell **D12**, and then press Enter to redisplay the **Summary** worksheet.

5 Click cell **B4** to select it again. Look at the **Formula Bar** and notice that instead of a value, the cell contains a formula that is equal to the value in another cell in another worksheet. Compare your screen with Figure 2.23.

The value in this cell is equal to the value in cell D12 of the *Golden Grove Mall* worksheet. The Accounting Number Format applied to the referenced cell is carried over. By using a formula of this type, changes in cell D12 on the *Golden Grove Mall* worksheet will be automatically updated in this *Summary* worksheet.

Cell value equal to cell D12 in
the Golden Grove Mall worksheet

Figure 2.23

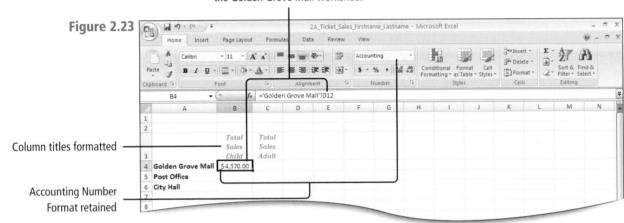

Column titles formatted

Accounting Number
Format retained

6 Click cell **C4**. Type **=** and then click the **Golden Grove Mall sheet tab**. Click cell **E12**, and then press **Enter**. Then, use the technique you just practiced to copy the week's total for **Child** and **Adult** ticket sales for the **Post Office worksheet** and the **City Hall worksheet**. Compare your screen with Figure 2.24.

The formulas in cells B4:C6 display the totals from the other three worksheets. Changes made to any of the other three worksheets—sometimes referred to as a ***detail worksheet*** because the details of the information are contained there—that affect their totals will display on this Summary worksheet. In this manner, the summary worksheet accurately displays the current totals from the other worksheets.

Total Child and Adult sales from each location

Figure 2.24

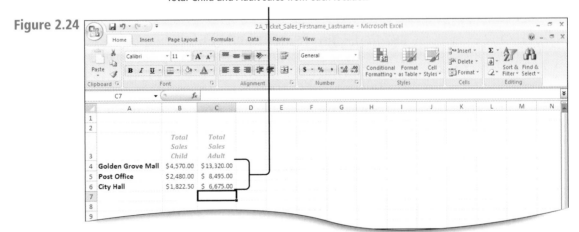

7 In cell **A1** type **Summer Fair and Arts Festival** and then **Merge and Center** ⊞▾ the text over the range **A1:C1**. In cell **A2** type **Pre-Sales of Tickets August 3-9** and then **Merge and Center** ⊞▾ the text over the range **A2:C2**. Select the two worksheet titles and change the Font [Calibri ▾] to **Cambria**, change the **Font Color** [A▾] to **Orange, Accent 6, Darker 25%**, change the **Font Size** [11 ▾] to **14**, and apply **Bold** [B].

8 Select **rows 1:2**. From the **row heading area**, point to the lower boundary of either selected row to display the ✛ pointer, increase the row height to **35 pixels**, and then click the **Middle Align** button ≡. Select **columns B:C**, and then set the column width to **80 pixels**.

9 In cell **A7**, type **Total Sales** press Enter, and then notice that the formatting from the cell above is carried down to the new cell. Select the range **B4:C7**, and then use the **Sum** button [Σ▾] to total the two columns. Compare your screen with Figure 2.25.

Recall that cell formatting carries over to adjacent cells unless two cells are left blank.

Worksheet titles formatted

Figure 2.25

Totals calculated for each type of ticket

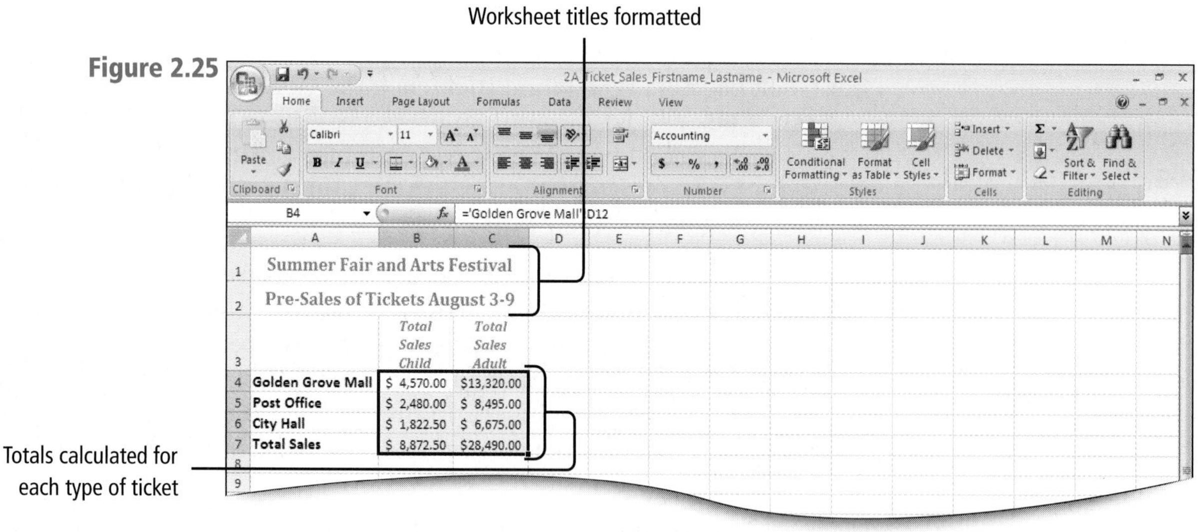

10 In the **Total Sales Child column**, notice the total for the *Post Office* location is *$2,480.00* and the *Total Sales* is *$8,872.50*. Display the **Post Office** worksheet, click cell **B11**, type **155** and then press Enter. Notice that the formulas in the worksheet recalculate. Display the **Summary** worksheet, and notice that in the **Total Sales Child column**, both the total for the *Post Office* location and the *Total Sales* also recalculated. Compare your screen with Figure 2.26.

In this manner, a Summary sheet recalculates any changes made in the other worksheets.

Figure 2.26

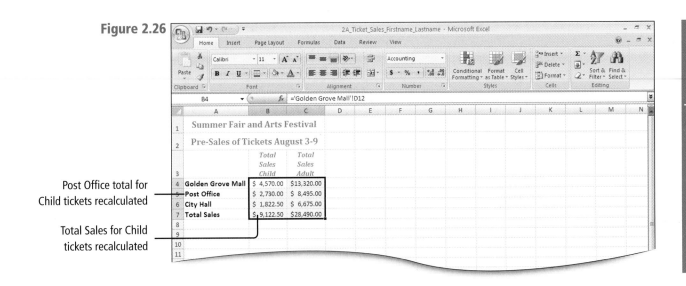

Post Office total for Child tickets recalculated

Total Sales for Child tickets recalculated

11 Select the range **B7:C7**, and then apply a **Top and Double Bottom** border.

12 **Save** 💾 your workbook.

Objective 7
Format and Print Multiple Worksheets in a Workbook

Each worksheet within a workbook can have different formatting, for example different headers or footers. If all the worksheets in the workbook will have the same header or footer, you can select all the worksheets and apply formatting common to all of the worksheets; for example, you can set the same footer in all of the worksheets.

Activity 2.9 Moving and Formatting Worksheets in a Workbook

In this activity, you will move the Summary sheet to become the first worksheet in the workbook. Then you will format and prepare your workbook for printing. The four worksheets containing data can be formatted simultaneously.

1 Point to the **Summary sheet tab**, hold down the left mouse button to display a small black triangle—a caret—and then notice that a small paper icon attaches to the mouse pointer. Drag to the left until the caret and mouse pointer are to the left of the **Golden Grove Mall sheet tab**, as shown in Figure 2.27, and then release the left mouse button.

Use this technique to rearrange the order of worksheets within a workbook.

Figure 2.27

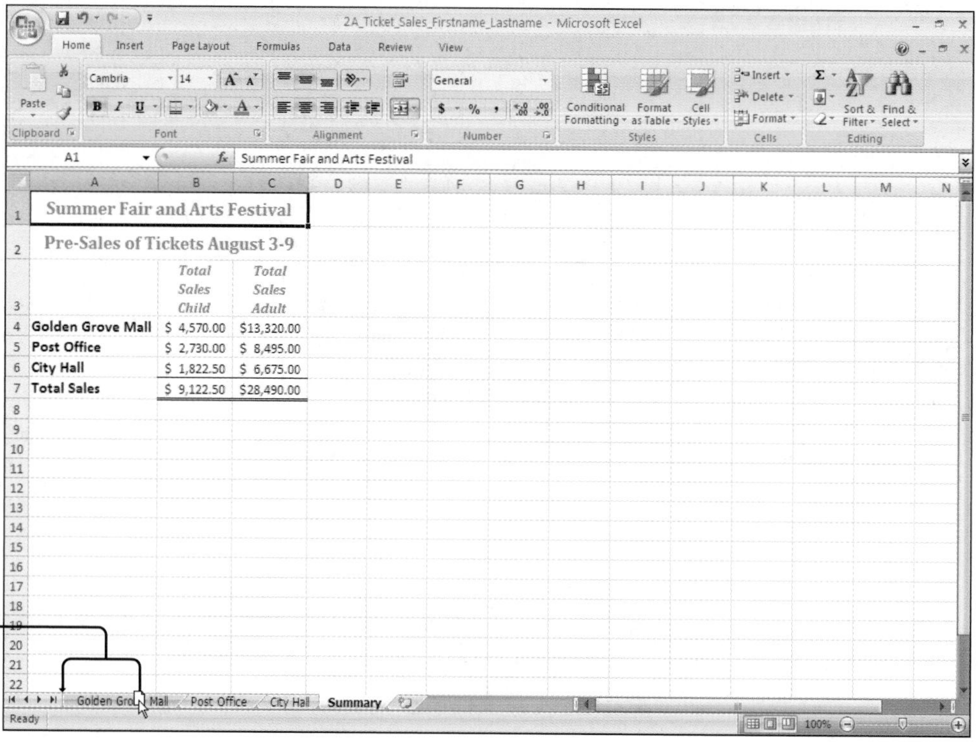

Caret moved to the left; mouse pointer with paper icon attached

2 Be sure the **Summary** worksheet is the active sheet. Then point to its sheet tab, right-click, and then click **Select All Sheets** to display *[Group]* in the title bar. Click the **Insert tab**, and then in the **Text group**, click the **Header & Footer** button. In the **Navigation group**, click the **Go to Footer** button, click in the **left section** above the word *Footer*, and then in the **Header & Footer Elements group**, click the **File Name** button.

3 Click in a cell above the footer to deselect the **Footer area** and view your file name. Click the **Page Layout tab**. In the **Page Setup group**, click the **Margins** button, and then at the bottom of the **Margins gallery**, click **Custom Margins**. In the displayed **Page Setup** dialog box, under **Center on page**, select the **Horizontally** check box. Click

OK, and then on the status bar, click the **Normal** button 🔳 to return to Normal view.

After displaying worksheets in Page Layout View, dotted lines display to indicate the page breaks when you return to Normal view.

4 Press Ctrl + Home to move to the top of the worksheet. Verify that *[Group]* still displays in the title bar.

Recall that by selecting all sheets, you can apply the same formatting to all the worksheets at the same time.

5 **Save** 🔳 your changes. From the **Office** menu 🔘, point to the **Print** button, and then from the displayed menu, click **Print Preview**. Alternatively, press Ctrl + F2 to display the Print Preview. Compare your screen with Figure 2.28.

With all the sheets grouped, you can view all of the sheets in Print Preview. If you do not see *Page 1 of 4* in the status bar, close the Preview, select all the sheets again, and then redisplay Print Preview.

Figure 2.28

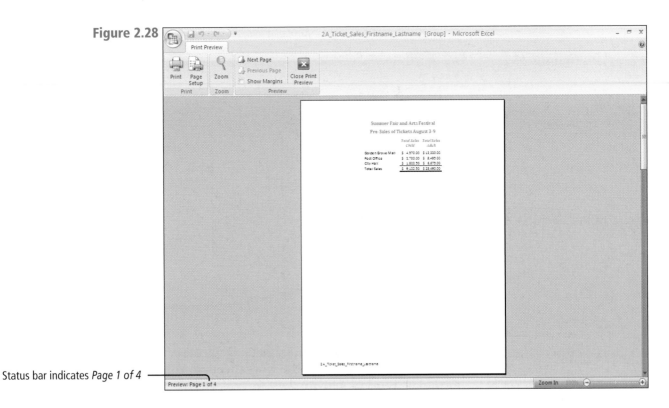

Status bar indicates *Page 1 of 4*

6 On the Ribbon, in the **Preview group**, click the **Next Page** button as necessary and take a moment to view each page of your workbook. After viewing all the worksheets, click the **Close Print Preview** button.

Activity 2.10 Printing All the Worksheets in a Workbook

1 **Save** 🖫 your workbook before printing. Check your *Chapter Assignment Sheet* or *Course Syllabus*, or consult your instructor, to determine if you are to submit your assignments on paper or electronically. To submit electronically, follow the instructions provided by your instructor.

2 Verify that the worksheets in your workbook are still grouped—

[Group] displays in the title bar. From the **Office** menu 🔘, click the **Print** button. In the displayed **Print** dialog box, under **Print range**, verify that the **All** option button is selected. Under **Print what**, verify that **Active sheet(s)** is selected. Alternatively, if your worksheets are not grouped, you can click Entire workbook in this dialog box to print all the worksheets in the workbook. Under **Copies**, verify that the **Number of copies** is **1**. Compare your screen with Figure 2.29.

Figure 2.29

Your default printer

One copy

Active sheets(s) selected

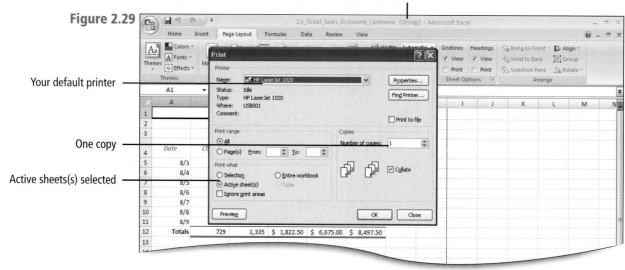

3 Click **OK** to print your worksheets. Determine if you are to print formulas for any or all of the worksheets in this workbook. To print formulas, refer to Activity 2.17 in Project 2A.

4 If you printed your formulas, be sure to redisplay the worksheet by pressing Ctrl + '. From the **Office** menu, click **Close**. If you are prompted to save changes, click **No** so that you do not save the changes to the Print layout that you used for printing formulas. **Close** Excel.

End **You have completed Project 2A**

Project 2B Growth Projection

In Activities 2.11 through 2.15, you will assist Mervyn Aghazarian, the City Planner for Golden Grove, in creating a workbook to estimate future population growth based on three different growth rates. Your resulting worksheet and chart will look similar to Figure 2.30.

For Project 2B, you will need the following file:

New blank Excel workbook

You will save your workbook as
2B_Growth_Projection_Firstname_Lastname

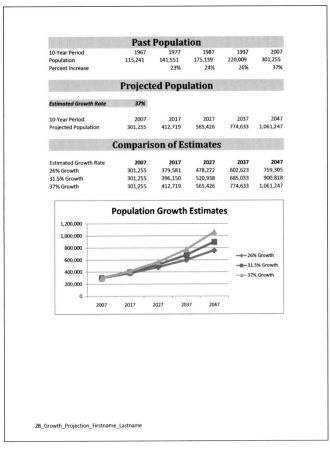

Figure 2.30
Project 2B—Growth Projection

Objective 8
Design a Worksheet for What-If Analysis

Excel recalculates; if you change the value in a cell referenced in a formula, the result of the formula is automatically recalculated. Thus, you can change cell values to see *what* would happen *if* you tried different values. This process of changing the values in cells to see how those changes affect the outcome of formulas in your worksheet is called **what-if analysis**.

Activity 2.11 Using Parentheses in a Formula

Mr. Aghazarian has the city's population figures for the past five 10-year periods. In each 10-year period, the population has increased. In this activity, you will construct a formula to calculate the **percentage rate of increase**—the percent by which one number increases over another number—for each 10-year period over the past 40 years. From this information, future population growth can be estimated.

1 **Start** Excel and display a new workbook. From the **Office** menu, click **Save As**. Navigate to your Excel Chapter 10 folder, in the **File name** box, name the file **2B_Growth_Projection_Firstname_Lastname** and then click **Save** or press Enter.

2 In cell **A3**, type **Population** and press Enter. In cell **A4**, type **Percent Increase** and press Enter. Point to the right boundary of **column A** to display the ⊕ pointer, and then double-click to AutoFit the column to accommodate its longest entry. Alternatively, on the Home tab, in the Cells group, click the Format button, and then click AutoFit Column Width.

3 In cell **A2**, type **10-Year Period** and then press Tab. In cell **B2**, type **1967** and then press Tab. In cell **C2**, type **1977** and then press Tab. Select the range **B2:C2**, drag the fill handle to the right through cell **F2**, and then compare your screen with Figure 2.31.

By establishing a pattern of 10-year intervals with the first two cells, you can use the fill handle to continue the series. The Auto Fill fea-

Figure 2.31

Pattern used to fill 10-year periods to create column titles

Row titles entered

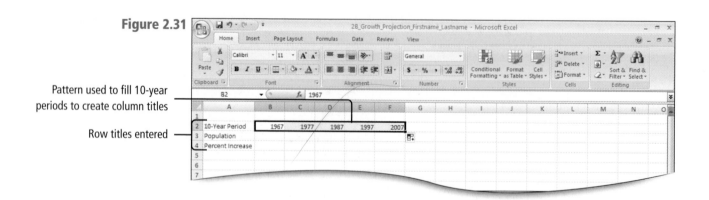

ture will do this for any pattern that you establish with two or more cells.

4 Click cell **A1**. Type **Past Population** and press Enter. Select the range **A1:F1**, and then right-click to display the Mini toolbar. Click the **Merge and Center** button [⊞ ▾], apply **Bold** [**B**], change the **Font** [Calibri ▾] to **Cambria**, and then change the **Font Size** [11 ▾] to **18**.

5 Beginning in cell **B3**, and then pressing Tab to move across the row, enter the following values for the population in the years listed:

1967	1977	1987	1997	2007
115241	**141551**	**175139**	**220009**	**301255**

6 Select the range **B3:F3**, right-click, on the Mini toolbar, click **Comma Style** [’], and then **Decrease Decimal** [.00→.0] two times.

7 Click cell **C4**. Being sure to include the parentheses, type **=(c3-b3)/b3** and then press Enter. Click cell **C4**. In the **Number group**, click the **Percent Style** button [%], and then examine the formula in the **Formula Bar**.

The mathematical formula to calculate the percentage rate of population increase from 1967 to 1977 is ***rate = amount of increase/base***.

The first step is to determine the *amount of increase*. This is accomplished by subtracting the ***base***—the starting point represented by the 1967 population—from the 1977 population. Thus, the *amount of increase* = 141,551 – 115,241 or 26,310. Between 1967 and 1977, the population increased by 26,310 people. In the formula, this calculation is represented by *c3-b3*.

The second step is to calculate the *rate*—what the amount of increase (26,310) represents as a percentage of the base (1967's population of 115,241). Determine this by dividing the amount of increase (26,310) by the base (115,241). Thus, 26,310 divided by 115,241 is equal to 0.22830416 or, when rounded to a percent—23%.

8 In the **Formula Bar**, locate the parentheses enclosing *C3-B3*.

Excel follows a set of mathematical rules called the ***order of operations***, which has four basic parts:

- Expressions within parentheses are processed first.

- Exponentiation, if present, is performed before multiplication and division.

- Multiplication and division are performed before addition and subtraction.

- Consecutive operators with the same level of precedence are calculated from left to right.

9 Click cell **D4**, type **=** and then by typing, or using a combination of typing and clicking cells to reference them, construct a formula similar to the one in cell **C4** to calculate the rate of increase in population from 1977 to 1987. Compare your screen with Figure 2.32.

Recall that the first step is to determine the *amount of increase*—1987 population minus 1977 population—and then to write the calculation so that Excel performs this operation first; that is, place it in parentheses.

The second step is to divide the result of the calculation in parentheses by the *base*—the population for 1977.

Figure 2.32

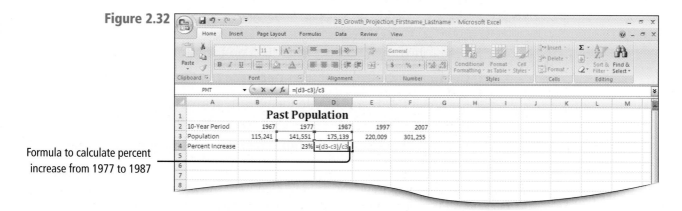

Formula to calculate percent increase from 1977 to 1987

10 Press Enter, and then format cell **D4** with the **Percent Style** %.

Your result is *24%*.

11 With cell **D4** selected, drag the fill handle to the right through cell **F4**. Click any empty cell to cancel the selection, **Save** your workbook, and then compare your screen with Figure 2.33.

Because this formula uses relative cell references—that is, for each year, the formula is the same but the values used are relative to the formula's location—you can copy the formula in this manner. For example, the result for 1987 uses 1977 as the base, the result for 1997 uses 1987 as the base, and the result for 2007 uses 1997 as the base.

The formula results show the percent of increase for each 10-year period between 1967 and 2007. You can see that in each 10-year period, the population has grown as much as 37%—between 1997 and 2007—and as little as 23%—between 1967 and 1977.

Percent increase calculated for the past 40 years

Figure 2.33

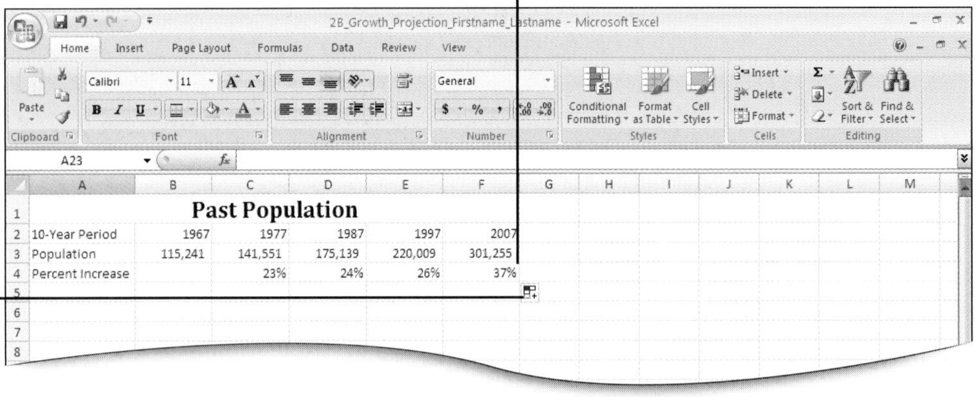

Auto Fill Options
button displays

Workshop

Use of Parentheses in a Formula

When writing a formula in Excel, use parentheses to communicate the order in which the operations should occur. For example, to average three test scores of 100, 50, and 90 that you scored on three different tests in a class, you would add the test scores and then divide by the number of test scores in the list. If you write this formula as =100+50+90/3, the result would be 180, because Excel would first divide 90 by 3 and then add 100+50+30. Excel would do so because the order of operations states that multiplication and division are calculated *before* addition and subtraction.

The correct way to write this formula is =(100+50+90)/3. Excel will add the three values, and then divide the result by 3, or 240/3 resulting in a correct average of 80. Parentheses play an important role in assuring that you get the correct result in your formulas.

Activity 2.12 Formatting as You Type

You can format numbers as you type them. When you type numbers in a format that Excel recognizes, Excel automatically applies that format to the cell. Recall that once applied, cell formats remain with the cell, even if the cell contents are deleted. In this activity, you will format cells by typing the numbers with percent signs and use the Format Painter to copy text (non-numeric) formats.

1 In cell **A6**, type **Projected Population** and then press Enter. Click cell **A1**. On the **Home tab**, in the **Clipboard group**, click the **Format Painter** button ![icon], and then click cell **A6**.

The format of cell A1 is *painted* or applied to cell A6, including the merging and centering of the text across cells A6:F6.

2 In cell **A8**, type **Estimated Growth Rate** and then press Enter. AutoFit **column A** to accommodate the new longer entry.

3 In cell **A10**, type **10-Year Period** and then in cell **A11**, type **Projected Population** In cell **B10**, type **2007** and then press Tab. In cell **C10**, type **2017** and then press Enter. Select the range **B10:C10**, and then drag the fill handle through cell **F10** to extend the pattern of years to *2047*. Compare your screen with Figure 2.34.

Figure 2.34

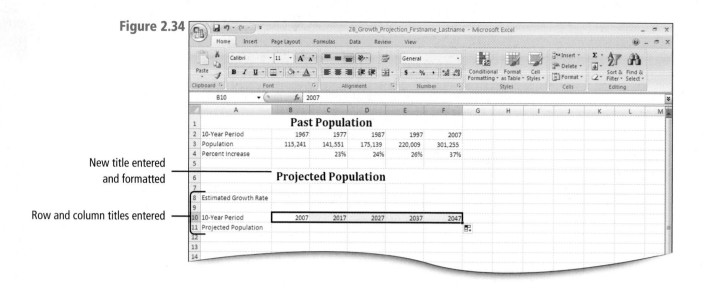

New title entered and formatted

Row and column titles entered

4 Click cell **B11**, and then in the **Number group**, notice that the format indicates *General.* Including the comma, type **301,255** On the **Formula Bar**, click the **Enter** button ✓ to keep the cell active, and then in the **Number group**, notice that the format changed to *Number.* Then, press [Delete], and in the **Number group**, notice that the *Number* format is still indicated.

Recall that deleting the contents of a cell does not delete the cell's formatting.

5 *Without* typing a comma, in cell **B11** type **301255** and then press [Enter].

The comma is inserted even though you did not type it. When you type a number and include a formatting symbol such as a comma, dollar sign, or percent sign, Excel applies the format to the cell. Thus, if you delete the contents of the cell and type in the cell again, the format you established remains applied to the cell. This if referred to as *format as you type*.

6 Examine the format of the value in cell **B11**, and then compare it to the format in cell **B3** where you used the Comma Style button to format the cell. Notice that the number in cell **B11** is flush with the right edge of the cell, but the number in cell **B3** leaves a small space on the right edge.

When you type commas as you enter numbers, Excel applies the *Number* format, which does *not* leave a space at the right of the number for a closing parenthesis in the event of a negative number. This is different from the format that is applied when you use the *Comma Style* button on the Ribbon or Mini toolbar, as you did for the numbers entered in row 3. Recall that the Comma Style format applied from either the Ribbon or the Mini toolbar leaves space on the right for a closing parenthesis in the event of a negative number.

7 In cell **B8**, type **26%** and then on the **Formula Bar**, click **Enter** ✓. Then, press [Delete] and *without* typing a percent sign, type **26** and then press [Enter].

The percent sign is inserted even though you did not type it—another example of the *format as you type* feature.

8 Select the range **A8:B8**, and then apply **Bold** [B] and **Italic** [I].

9 **Save** [💾] your workbook.

More Knowledge

Percentage Calculations

When you type a percentage into a cell—for example *26%*—the percentage format, without decimal points, displays in both the cell and the Formula Bar. Excel will, however, use the decimal value of *0.26* for actual calculations.

Activity 2.13 Calculating a Value After an Increase

A growing population results in increased use of streets, schools, and other city services. Thus, city planners in Golden Grove must estimate how much the population will increase in the future. The calculations you made in the previous activity show that the population has increased at varying rates during each 10-year period, ranging from a low of 23% to a high of 37% per 10-year period.

Population data from the state and surrounding areas suggests that future growth will trend closer to that of the recent past. To plan for the future, Mr. Aghazarian wants to prepare three forecasts of the city's population based on the percentage increases in 1997, in 2007, and for a percentage increase halfway between the two, that is, for 26%, 31.5%, and 37%. In this activity, you will calculate the population that would result from a 26% increase.

1 Click cell **C11**. Type **=b11*(100%+b8)** and then on the **Formula Bar**, click the **Enter** [✓] button. Compare your screen with Figure 2.35.

This formula calculates what the population will be in the year 2017 assuming an increase of 26% over 2007's population. The mathematical formula to calculate a value after an increase is **value after increase = base x percent for new value**.

The first step is to establish the *percent for new value*. The **percent for new value = base percent + percent of increase**. The *base percent* of 100% represents the base population and the *percent of increase* in this instance is 26%. Thus, the population will equal 100% of the base year plus 26% of the base year. This can be expressed as 126% or 1.26. In this formula, you will use 100% + the rate in cell B8, which is 26%, to equal 126%.

The second step is to enter a reference to the cell that contains the *base*—the population in 2007. The base value resides in cell B11—301,255.

The third step is to calculate the *value after increase*. Because in each future 10-year period the increase will be based on 26%—an absolute value located in cell B8—this cell reference can be formatted as absolute with the use of dollar signs.

Figure 2.35

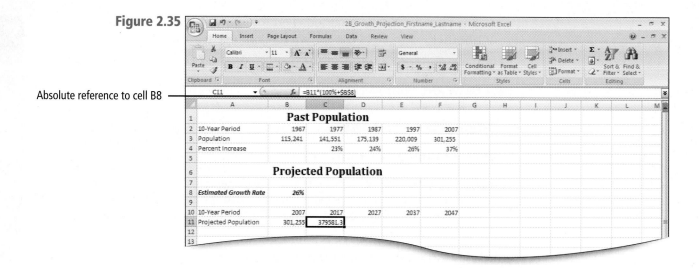

Absolute reference to cell B8 — =B11*(100%+$B$8)

2 With cell **C11** as the active cell, drag the fill handle to copy the formula to the range **D11:F11**. Click cell **B11**, click the **Format Painter** button, and then select the range **C11:F11**. Click an empty cell to cancel the selection, and then compare your screen with Figure 2.36.

This formula uses a relative cell address—B11—for the *base*; the population in the previous 10-year period is used in each of the formulas in cells D11:F11 as the *base* value. Because the reference to the *percent of increase* in cell B8 is an absolute reference, each *value after increase* is calculated with the value from cell B8.

The population projected for 2017—*379,581*—is an increase of 26% over the population in 2007. The projected population in 2027—*478,272*—is an increase of 26% over the population in 2017 and so on.

Figure 2.36

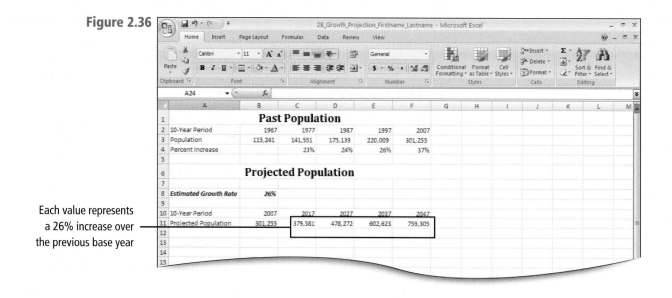

Each value represents a 26% increase over the previous base year

3 **Save** your workbook.

Workshop

Calculating Percent Increase or Decrease

The basic formula for calculating an increase or decrease can be done in two parts. First determine the percent by which the base value will be increased or decreased, and then add or subtract the results to the base. The formula can be simplified by using (1+amount of increase) or (1–amount of decrease), where 1 represents the whole, rather than 100%. Thus, the formula used in Step 1 of Activity 2.13 could also be written =b11*(1+b8), or =(b11*b8)+b11.

Objective 9
Perform What-If Analysis

If a formula depends on the value in a cell, you can see what effect it will have if you change the value in that cell. Then, you can copy the value computed by the formula and paste it into another part of the worksheet where it can be compared and charted. This can be done for multiple formulas.

Activity 2.14 Performing What-If Analysis and Using Paste Special

Mr. Aghazarian can see that a growth rate of 26% in each 10-year period will result in a population of almost 760,000 people by 2047. The city planners will likely ask him what the population might be if population grows at the highest rate (37%) or at a rate that is halfway between the 1997 and 2007 rates (31.5%). Because the formulas are constructed to use the growth rate displayed in cell B8, Mr. Aghazarian can answer these questions quickly by entering different percentages into that cell. To keep the results of each set of calculations so they can be compared, you will paste the results of each what-if analysis into another area of the worksheet.

1 In cell **A13**, type **Comparison of Estimates** and then press Enter. Click cell **A6**, click **Format Painter** ![icon], and then click cell **A13**. Select the range **A8:B8**, right-click to display the Mini toolbar, click the **Fill Color button arrow** ![icon], and then under **Theme Colors**, apply **Olive Green, Accent 3, Lighter 40%**. Click cell **A1**, hold down Ctrl, and then click cells **A6** and **A13**. In the **Font group**, click the **Fill Color** button ![icon] to apply the same fill color to these titles.

Recall that the Fill Color button retains its most recent color.

2 In the range **A15:A18** type the following row titles:

Estimated Growth Rate
26% Growth
31.5% Growth
37% Growth

3 Select the range **B10:F10**. On the **Home tab**, in the **Clipboard group**, click the **Copy** ![icon] button, click cell **B15**, and then in the **Clipboard group**, click the **Paste** button.

Recall that when pasting a group of copied cells to a target range, you need only select the first cell of the range.

4 Select the range **B11:F11**, click **Copy** 📋, click cell **B16**, and then click the **Paste** button. Click cell **C16**, and notice on the **Formula Bar** that the *formula* was pasted into the cell. Compare your screen with Figure 2.37.

This is *not* the desired result. The actual *calculated values*—not the formulas—are needed in the range B16:F16.

Column headings copied

Figure 2.37

Undo button

Formula Bar indicates copied formula

Fill color applied to cells

Row titles entered

Formulas copied

Status bar indicates copied cells on Office Clipboard

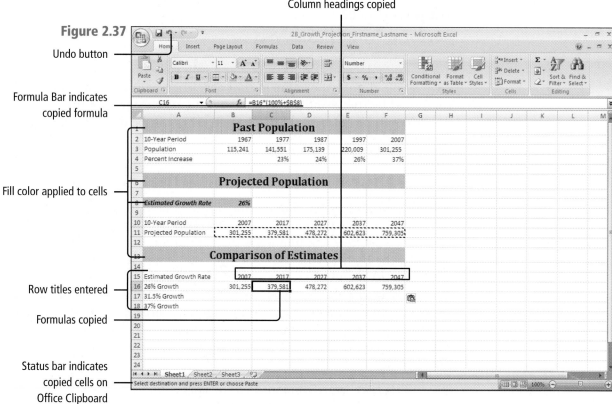

5 On the **Quick Access Toolbar**, click the **Undo** button 🔄. With the range **B11:F11** still copied to the Clipboard—as indicated by the message in the status bar and the moving border—in the **Clipboard group**, click the **Paste button arrow**. From the displayed menu, click **Paste Special**. In the displayed **Paste Special** dialog box, under **Paste**, click the **Values and number formats** option button.

The ***Paste Special*** dialog box offers various options for the manner in which you can paste the contents of the Office Clipboard. The *Values and number formats* command pastes the *calculated values* that result from the calculation of formulas into other cells—along with the formatting applied to the copied cells.

6 In the displayed **Paste Special** dialog box, click **OK**. Click cell **C16**. Notice on the **Formula Bar** that the cell contains a value, not a formula. Press [Esc] to cancel the moving border and then compare your screen with Figure 2.38.

The calculated estimates based on a 26% growth rate are pasted along with their formatting.

Figure 2.38

Formula Bar indicates the value

Calculated value pasted

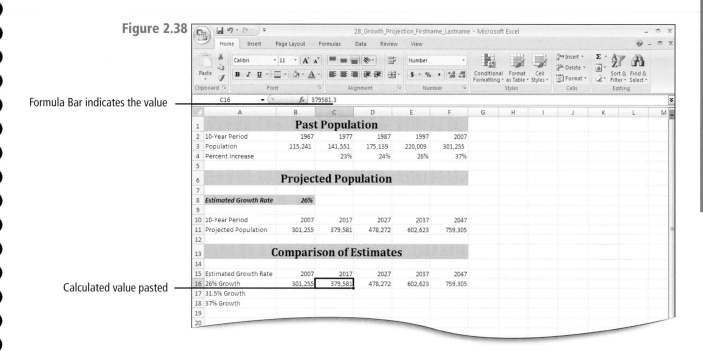

7 Click cell **B8**. Type **31.5** and then watch the values in **C11:F11** recalculate as, on the **Formula Bar**, you click the **Enter** button ☑ .

The value *31.5%* is halfway between 26% and 37%—the growth rates from the two most recent 10-year periods. Although the cell may display 32%, you can see that the underlying value is 31.5%.

8 Select the range **B11:F11**, and then press Ctrl + C, which is the keyboard shortcut for the Copy command. Click cell **B17**. In the **Clipboard group**, click the **Paste button arrow**, and then click **Paste Special**. In the **Paste Special** dialog box, click the **Values and number formats** option button, and then click **OK**.

9 In cell **B8**, type **37** and then press Enter. Notice that the projected values in **C11:F11** are recalculated.

10 Using the skills you just practiced, copy the range **B11:F11**, and then paste the **values and number formats** of the copied range to the range **B18:F18**.

11 Press Esc to cancel the moving border, and then click an empty cell to cancel the selection. In **rows 15:18**, notice that the data and titles are arranged in simple rows and columns in adjacent cells for convenient charting. Compare your screen with Figure 2.39.

With this information, Mr. Aghazarian can answer several what-if questions about the future population of the city and provide a range of population estimates based on the rates of growth over the past 10-year periods.

Values copied for each what-if analysis

Figure 2.39

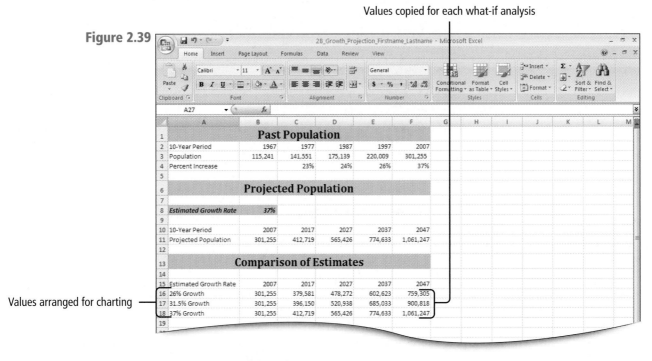

Values arranged for charting

12 Save 💾 your workbook.

Another Way

To Display the Paste Special Dialog Box

Right-click over the target area, and then from the shortcut menu, click Paste Special. In many instances, using this method shortens the distance your mouse must travel in order to select an option from this dialog box.

Objective 10
Compare Data with a Line Chart

A *line chart* displays trends over time. Time is displayed along the bottom axis and the data point values are connected with a line. If you want to compare more than one set of values, each group is connected by a different line. The curves and directions of the lines make trends obvious to the reader.

Activity 2.15 Creating a Line Chart

In this activity, you will chart the values that represent the three different possible rates of population growth for Golden Grove. The 10-year periods will form the categories of time along the bottom of the chart and each set of values corresponding to a different growth rate will be represented by a line.

1 Select the range **B15:F15** and apply **Bold** 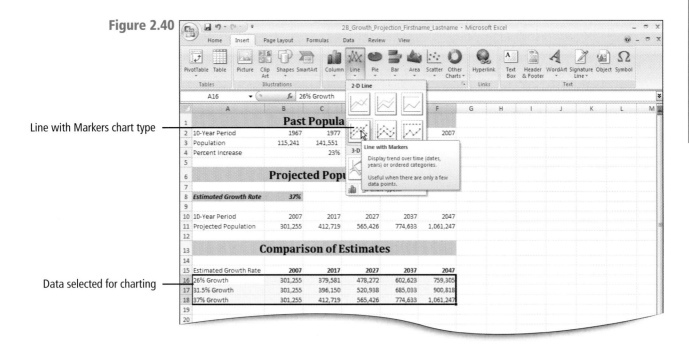B.

2 Select the range **A16:F18**. On the **Insert tab**, in the **Charts group**, click the **Line** button. From the displayed gallery of line charts, in the second row, point to the first chart type to display the ScreenTip *Line with Markers* as shown in Figure 2.40.

Figure 2.40

Line with Markers chart type

Data selected for charting

3 Click the **Line with Markers** chart type to create the chart as an embedded chart in the worksheet. Use the pointer to move the upper left corner of the chart just inside the upper left corner of cell **A20**. Then, scroll down so that you can view both the data and the chart on your screen. Compare your screen with Figure 2.41.

The chart still requires appropriate time labels along the category axis.

Line representing each growth rate

Figure 2.41

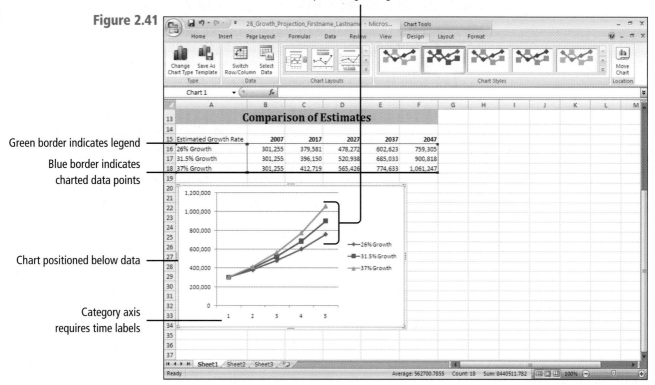

Green border indicates legend

Blue border indicates charted data points

Chart positioned below data

Category axis requires time labels

4 Be sure the chart is still selected. In the lower left corner of the chart, point to where the vertical and horizontal axis lines intersect near the *0* until the ScreenTip *Horizontal (Category) Axis* displays. Then, right-click, and from the displayed shortcut menu, click **Select Data**.

5 On the right side of the displayed **Select Data Source** dialog box, under **Horizontal (Category) Axis Labels**, locate the **Edit** button, as shown in Figure 2.42.

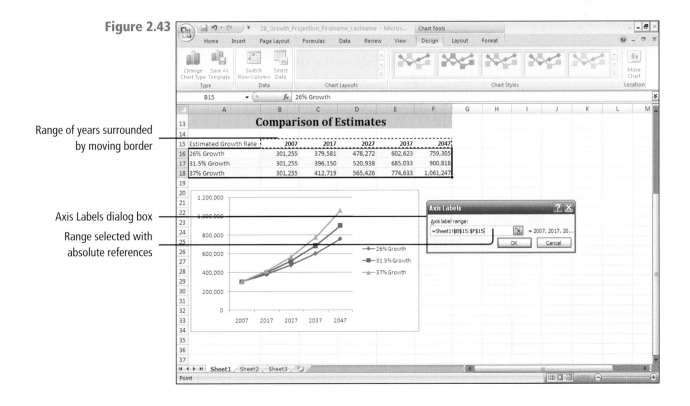

Figure 2.42

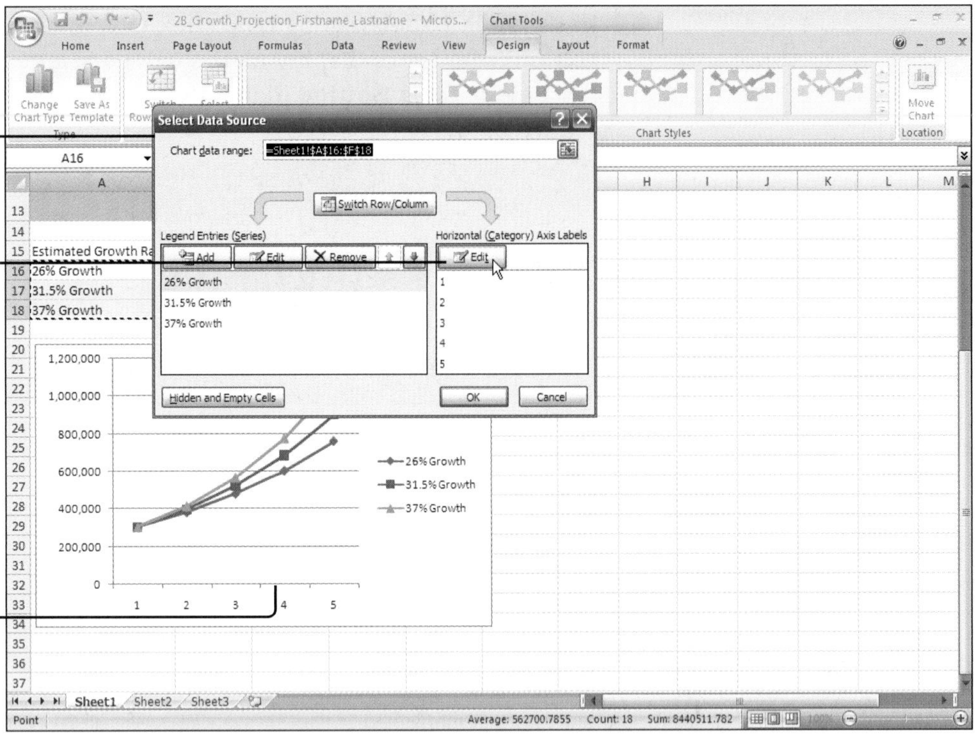

Select Data Source dialog box

Edit button to edit labels on the category axis

Category (X) axis requires labels to identify each 10-year period

6 In the right column, click the **Edit** button. Drag the title bar of the **Axis Labels** dialog box to the right of the chart as necessary so that it is not blocking your view of the data, and then select the range **B15:F15**. Compare your screen with Figure 2.43.

Figure 2.43

Range of years surrounded by moving border

Axis Labels dialog box

Range selected with absolute references

7 In the **Axis Labels** dialog box, click **OK**, and notice that in the right column, the years display as the category labels. Click **OK** to close the **Select Data Source** dialog box. Compare your screen with Figure 2.44.

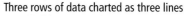
Three rows of data charted as three lines

Figure 2.44

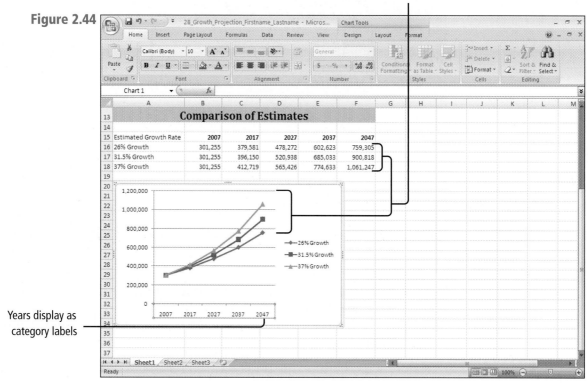

Years display as category labels

8 On the **Design tab**, in the **Chart Styles group**, click the **More** button , and then click **Style 10**. Click the **Layout tab**. In the **Labels group**, click the **Chart Title** button, and then click **Above Chart**.

9 Delete the text *Chart Title*, and then type **Population Growth Estimates** as the chart title. Compare your screen with Figure 2.45.

Based on the chart, city planners can see that the population will probably double between now and 2037 and could more than triple between now and 2047.

Figure 2.45

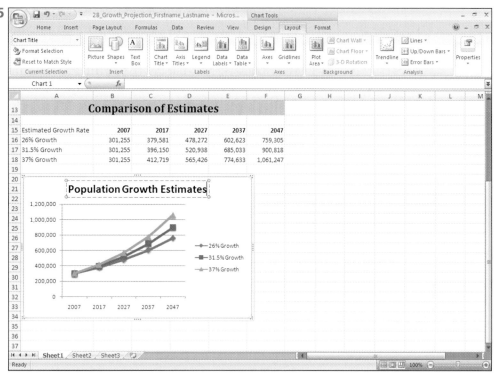

10 Click any cell to deselect the chart. Click the **Insert tab**, and then in the **Text group**, click **Header & Footer** to switch to **Page Layout View** and open the **Header area**. In the **Navigation group**, click the **Go to Footer** button, click just above the word *Footer*, and then in the **Header & Footer Elements group**, click the **File Name** button. Click in a cell just above the footer to exit the **Footer area** and view your file name.

11 Scroll up and to the left as necessary to view your chart. Click the chart to select it, and notice that the chart is not centered under the data in the cells. Position the pointer over the **right resize handle** to display the ↔ pointer, and then drag to the right so that the right border of the chart is just inside the right border of **column F**. Release the mouse button to resize the chart.

12 Click any cell to deselect the chart. Click the **Page Layout tab**. In the **Page Setup group**, click the **Margins** button, and then at the bottom of the **Margins gallery**, click **Custom Margins**. In the displayed **Page Setup** dialog box, under **Center on page**, select the **Horizontally** check box. Click **OK** to close the dialog box, and then **Save** the changes to your workbook.

13 On the status bar, click the **Normal** button to return to Normal view, and then press Ctrl + Home to move to the top of your worksheet. At the lower edge of the window, click to select the **Sheet2 tab**, hold down Ctrl, and then click the **Sheet3 tab** to select the two unused sheets. Right-click over the selected sheet tabs, and then on the displayed shortcut menu, click **Delete**.

14 **Save** 🖫 the changes you have made to your workbook. Check your *Chapter Assignment Sheet* or *Course Syllabus* or consult your instructor to determine if you are to submit your assignments on paper or electronically. To submit electronically, follow the instructions provided by your instructor.

15 Press Ctrl + F2 to display the **Print Preview** to check the placement of your worksheet. In the **Print group**, click the **Print** button. In the displayed **Print** dialog box, click **OK** to print your worksheet. If you are directed to submit printed formulas, refer to Activity 9.17 to do so.

16 If you printed your formulas, be sure to redisplay the worksheet by pressing Ctrl + `. From the **Office** menu 🗔, click **Close**. If the dialog box displays asking if you want to save changes, click **No** so that you do *not* save the changes you made for printing formulas. **Close** Excel.

End **You have completed Project 2B** ————————————

There's More You Can Do!

From My Computer, navigate to the student files that accompany this textbook. In the folder **02_theres_more_you_can_do_pg1_36**, locate and open the folder for this chapter. Open and print the instructions for this project, which are provided to you in Adobe PDF format.

Try IT! 1—Change the Office Theme in an Excel Workbook

In this Try IT! exercise, you will change an Office theme in an Excel workbook.

Content-Based Assessments

Excel
chaptertwo

Summary

In this chapter, you created and saved a workbook from an existing workbook, renamed worksheets, and color-coded worksheet tabs. You examined and practiced the various ways that Excel formats numbers in a worksheet. You moved, copied, and pasted cell contents using the Office Clipboard. Workbooks frequently contain multiple worksheets, and when they do, a Summary sheet is often included to summarize the data on the individual worksheets. You practiced grouping worksheets to enter and format data simultaneously on multiple worksheets, and then created a summary worksheet to summarize the data.

What-if analysis is used to determine what would happen to one value if another value changes. In this chapter, you used a what-if analysis process to project future trends, and then created a line chart to visually represent those trends.

Key Terms

The 🌐 symbol represents Key Terms found on the Student CD in the 02_theres_more_you_can_do folder for this chapter.

Content-Based Assessments

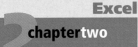

Excel

chaptertwo

Matching

Match each term in the second column with its correct definition in the first column. Write the letter of the term on the blank line to the left of the correct definition.

_E_ **1.** To move within a document or workbook.

_M_ **2.** The labels along the lower border of the worksheet window that identify each worksheet.

_H_ **3.** The action of placing cell contents that have been copied or moved to the Office Clipboard to another location.

_F_ **4.** A temporary storage area maintained by your Windows operating system.

_C_ **5.** A method of moving or copying the content of selected cells in which you point to the selection and then drag it to a new location.

_I_ **6.** The target destination for data that has been cut or copied using the Office Clipboard.

_J_ **7.** A button that displays in the lower right corner of a pasted selection and that displays a list of options that lets you determine how the information is pasted into your worksheet.

_B_ **8.** Within a workbook of multiple worksheets, a worksheet that contains the details of information summarized on a summary worksheet.

_O_ **9.** The process of changing the values in cells to see how those changes affect the outcome of formulas in your worksheet.

_K_ **10.** The percent by which one number increases over another.

_L_ **11.** The mathematical formula to calculate a rate of increase.

_A_ **12.** The starting point when you divide the amount of increase by it to calculate the rate of increase.

_G_ **13.** The mathematical rules for performing multiple calculations within a formula.

_D_ **14.** The Excel feature by which a cell takes on the formatting of the number typed into the cell.

_N_ **15.** The formula for calculating the value after an increase by multiplying the original value—the base—by the percent for new value.

A Base

B Detail worksheet

C Drag and drop

D Format as you type

E Navigate

F Office Clipboard

G Order of operations

H Paste

I Paste area

J Paste Options

K Percent rate of increase

L Rate = amount of increase/base

M Sheet tabs

N Value after increase = base X percent for new value

O What-if analysis

Fill in the Blank

Write the correct answers in the space provided.

1. When a worksheet is active, its tab color displays as an
   Underline .

2. When you enter a date, Excel assigns a *Serial* value to the
   date, which makes it possible to treat dates like other numbers for
   the purpose of calculating the number of days between two dates.

3. A two-digit year value of 30 through 99 is interpreted by the
   Windows operating system as the four-digit years 1930 through
   1999 .

4. The keyboard shortcut Ctrl + ; enters the *Current
   date* , which is obtained from your computer's internal
   calendar.

5. Clearing the contents of a cell does not clear the *formatting* of a
   cell—for example fill color applied to the cell.

6. You can view selections stored on the Office Clipboard by displaying
   its *task Pane* from the Dialog Box Launcher in the
   Clipboard group.

7. According to the order of operations for formulas, the first expressions calculated are those within *Parentheses*

8. According to the order of operations, *Multiplication* and division are
   performed before addition and subtraction.

9. According to the order of operations, consecutive operators with the
   same level of *Precedence* are calculated from left to right.

10. The symbol used to indicate the multiplication operation is the
    asterisk symbol.

11. In the formula *percent for new value = base percent + percent of
    increase*, the base percent is usually *100* %.

12. When pasting a group of copied cells to a target range, you need only
    select the *First* cell of the target range.

13. The chart type that displays trends over time and that connects data
    point values with a line is called a *Line* chart.

14. In the formula *=(B3-C4)*D3* the mathematical operation that is per-
    formed first is *(B3-C4)* .

15. When copying the formula *=(B3-B4)*$A$2* to the right, the formula in
    column C would be _____ .

Content-Based Assessments

Project 2C — Permit Sales

In this project, you will apply the skills you practiced from the Objectives in Project 2A.

Objectives: 1. *Create and Save a Workbook from an Existing Workbook;* **2.** *Navigate a Workbook and Rename Worksheets;* **3.** *Enter Dates, Clear Contents, and Clear Formats;* **4.** *Move, Copy, and Paste Cell Contents;* **5.** *Edit and Format Multiple Worksheets at the Same Time;* **6.** *Create a Summary Sheet;* **7.** *Format and Print Multiple Worksheets in a Workbook.*

In the following Skills Review, you will edit a workbook for the Golden Grove Parks and Recreation Director to summarize the sales of weekly and daily campground permits for the three city campgrounds in the month of June. The four worksheets of your completed workbook will look similar to those shown in Figure 2.46.

For Project 2C, you will need the following file:

e2C_Permit_Sales

**You will save your workbook as
2C_Permit_Sales_Firstname_Lastname**

Figure 2.46

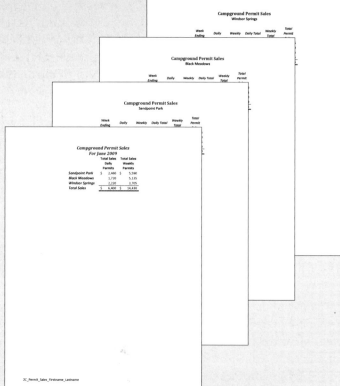

(Project 2C–Permit Sales continues on the next page)

Content-Based Assessments

(Project 2C–Permit Sales continued)

1. **Start** Excel. From the **Office** menu, click **Open**, and then navigate to the student files that accompany this textbook. Locate, select, and then open the file **e2C_Permit_Sales**. **Save** the file in your Excel Chapter 2 folder as **2C_Permit_Sales_Firstname_Lastname** Take a moment to examine the data in each of the three worksheets.

2. Point to the **Sheet1 tab**, and then double-click to select its name. Type **Sandpoint Park** and then press Enter to rename the sheet. Right-click the **Sandpoint Park sheet tab**, and then from the displayed shortcut menu, point to **Tab Color** to display the colors associated with the workbook's theme. Under **Theme Colors**, click **Purple, Accent 4, Lighter 40%**.

3. Point to the **Sheet2 tab**, right-click to display the shortcut menu, and then click **Rename**. Type **Black Meadows** and then press Enter to rename the sheet. On the **Home tab**, in the **Cells group**, click the **Format** button, and then from the displayed list, point to **Tab Color**. Under **Theme Colors**, click **Aqua, Accent 5, Lighter 40%**.

4. Using either of the two techniques you just practiced, change the name of the **Sheet3 tab** to **Windsor Springs** and then change the **Tab Color** to **Orange, Accent 6, Lighter 40%**.

5. Display the **Sandpoint Park** worksheet, and then select the range **A13:D14**. On the **Home tab**, in the **Clipboard group**, click the **Copy** button to place a copy of the selected cells on the Office Clipboard.

6. Click the **Black Meadows sheet tab** to make it the active worksheet. Click cell **A13**, and then on the **Home tab**, in the **Clipboard group**, click the **Paste** button. Click the **Windsor Springs sheet tab** to

make it the active worksheet, and then click cell **A13**. In the **Clipboard group**, click the **Paste** button. Click the **Sandpoint Park sheet tab** to make it the active worksheet, and then press Esc to cancel the moving border.

7. Right-click the **Sandpoint Park sheet tab**, and then from the displayed shortcut menu, click **Select All Sheets** to group the sheets—*[Group]* displays in the title bar. Select the range **A5:A8**. On the **Home tab**, in the **Number group**, click the **Number Format arrow**, at the bottom click **More Number Formats**, under **Category**, click **Date**, and then under **Type**, click **3/14** and click **OK**. The date format for the selected range of cells is changed for all three worksheets.

8. With the worksheets still grouped, click cell **D4**, type **Daily Total** and then press Tab. In cell **E4**, type **Weekly Total** and then press Tab. In cell **F4**, type **Total Permit Sales** and then press Enter. Select the range **A4:F4**, right-click over the selection, and then from the displayed shortcut menu, click **Format Cells**. Click the **Font tab**, and then under **Font style**, click **Bold Italic**. Click the **Alignment tab**. Under **Text alignment**, click the **Horizontal arrow**, and then from the displayed list, click **Center**. Click the **Vertical arrow**, and then from the displayed list, click **Center**. Under **Text control**, select the **Wrap text** check box. Click **OK**.

9. With the worksheets still grouped, select the range **A1:F1**, and then in the **Alignment group**, click the **Merge and Center** button. Change the **Font** to **Cambria**, the **Font Size** to **14**, and then apply **Bold**. Select the range **A2:F2**, right-click over the selection, and then on the Mini toolbar, click the **Merge and Center** button, change the **Font Size** to **12**, and then apply **Bold**.

(Project 2C–Permit Sales continues on the next page)

Content-Based Assessments

(Project 2C–Permit Sales continued)

10. With the worksheets still grouped, click cell **D5** and construct a formula to calculate the total sales of *Daily* permits for the week ending June 6 as follows: type = to begin a formula, click cell **B5**, type * click cell **D13**, and then press F4 to make the reference to cell **D13** absolute. On the **Formula Bar**, click the **Enter** button. Your result is *340*. Use the fill handle to copy the formula down for the remaining dates.

11. In cell **E5**, construct a similar formula to multiply the number of *Weekly* permits sold during the week of June 6 in cell **C5** times the *Weekly Permit Price* in cell **D14**. Make the reference to cell **D14** absolute so that each week's sales are multiplied by the *Weekly Permit Price* in cell **D14**. Your result is *585*. Copy the formula down for the remaining dates.

12. Click cell **A9**, and then apply **Align Text Right** and **Bold**. Select the range **B5:E9**, and then in the **Editing group**, click the **Sum** button to sum each column.

13. With the worksheets still grouped, select the range **D5:F9**, and then in the **Editing group**, click the **Sum** button to sum the rows for *Total Permit Sales* for each week.

14. With the worksheets still grouped, select the nonadjacent ranges **B5:C9** and **D6:F8**, and then apply the **Comma Style** with **zero decimal places**. Select the nonadjacent ranges **D5:F5** and **D9:F9**, and then apply **Accounting Number Format** with **zero decimal places**. Select the range **B9:F9**, in the **Font group**, click the **Borders button arrow**, and then click **Top and Double Bottom Border**. Select **columns B:F**, and then set the width to **70 pixels**.

15. Click the **Black Meadows sheet tab**, and then verify that the formulas and format-

ting that you applied in Steps 7–14 were applied to the worksheet—recall that selecting an individual worksheet ungroups the sheets. Click the **Windsor Springs sheet tab,** and then verify that the formulas and formatting that you applied in Steps 7–14 were applied.

16. **Save** your workbook. To the right of the **Windsor Springs** worksheet tab, click the **Insert Worksheet** button. Rename the new worksheet **Summary** and then change the **Tab Color** to **Olive Green, Accent 3, Lighter 40%**. In cell **A4** type **Sandpoint Park** In cell **A5** type **Black Meadows** In cell **A6** type **Windsor Springs** In cell **A7** type **Total Sales** Select the range **A4:A7**, change the **Font Size** to **12**, and then apply **Bold** and **Italic**. **AutoFit column A**.

17. In cell **B3**, type **Total Sales Daily Permits** and then in cell **C3**, type **Total Sales Weekly Permits** Select the two cells, and then in the **Alignment group**, click the **Wrap Text** button and the **Center** button. In the **Font group**, click **Bold**.

18. Click cell **B4**. Type = and then click the **Sandpoint Park sheet tab**. On the **Sandpoint Park** worksheet, click cell **D9**, and then press Enter to create a formula that references the *Daily Total Sales* for *Sandpoint Park*.

19. Click cell **C4**. Type = and then click the **Sandpoint Park sheet tab**. Click cell **E9** and then press Enter to create a formula that references the *Weekly Total Sales* for *Sandpoint Park*. Then, use the same technique to copy the totals for *Daily* and *Weekly* permit sales for the **Black Meadows worksheet** and the **Windsor Springs worksheet**.

20. In cell **A1**, type **Campground Permit Sales** and then **Merge and Center** the text over

(Project 2C–Permit Sales continues on the next page)

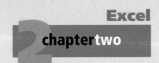

Excel

chaptertwo

Skills Review

(Project 2C–Permit Sales continued)

the range **A1:C1**. Change the **Font** to **Cambria**, the **Font Size** to **14**, and apply **Bold** and **Italic**. In cell **A2**, type **For June 2009** and then use the **Format Painter** to apply the format from cell **A1**.

21. Select the range **B4:C7**, click the **Sum** button to total the two columns. Format the range **B5:C6** with **Comma Style** and **zero decimal places**. Format the nonadjacent ranges **B4:C4** and **B7:C7** with the **Accounting Number Format** and **zero decimal places**. Apply a **Top and Double Bottom** border to the range **B7:C7**.

22. Point to the **Summary sheet tab**, hold down the left mouse button to display a small black caret symbol, and then drag to the left until the caret is positioned to the left of the **Sandpoint Park sheet tab**; release the left mouse button to make the Summary sheet the first sheet in the workbook.

23. Be sure the **Summary** worksheet is the active sheet. Then point to its sheet tab, right-click, and click **Select All Sheets** to display *[Group]* in the title bar. Click the **Insert tab**, and then in the **Text group**, click the **Header & Footer** button. In the **Navigation group**, click the **Go to Footer** button, click in the **left section** above the word *Footer*, and then in the **Header & Footer Elements group**, click the **File Name** button.

24. Click in a cell above the footer to deselect the **Footer area** and view your file name. Click the **Page Layout tab**. In the **Page Setup group**, click the **Margins** button, and then at the bottom of the **Margins**

gallery, click **Custom Margins**. In the displayed **Page Setup** dialog box, under **Center on page**, select the **Horizontally** check box. Click **OK**, and then on the status bar, click the **Normal** button. Press Ctrl + Home to move to the top of the worksheet. Verify that *[Group]* still displays in the title bar.

25. **Save** your workbook. Check your *Chapter Assignment Sheet* or *Course Syllabus*, or consult your instructor, to determine if you are to submit your assignments on paper or electronically. To submit electronically, follow the instructions provided by your instructor.

26. From the **Office** menu, point to the **Print arrow**, and then from the displayed menu, click **Print Preview**. At the top of the screen, click the **Next Page** button as necessary to view and check each page of your workbook.

27. Click the **Print** button. Under **Print range**, verify that the **All** option button is selected. Under **Print what**, click **Active sheet(s)** (assuming your worksheets are still grouped) and then under **Copies**, verify that the **Number of copies** is **1**. Click **OK** to print your workbook. Determine if you are to print formulas for any or all of the worksheets in this workbook. To print formulas, refer to Activity 1.17 in Project 1A.

28. If you printed your formulas, be sure to redisplay the worksheet by pressing Ctrl + `. From the **Office** menu, click **Close**. If you are prompted to save changes, click **No**. **Close** Excel.

End You have completed Project 2C

Content-Based Assessments

Skills Review

Project 2D—Property Tax

In this project, you will apply the skills you practiced from the Objectives in Project 2B.

Objectives: 8. *Design a Worksheet for What-If Analysis;* **9.** *Perform What-If Analysis;* **10.** *Compare Data with a Line Chart.*

In the following Skills Review, you will create a worksheet for the Controller of Golden Grove to forecast property tax revenue for the next 10 years. Your completed worksheet will look similar to the one shown in Figure 2.47.

For Project 2D, you will need the following file:

New blank Excel workbook

You will save your workbook as
2D_Property_Tax_Firstname_Lastname

Figure 2.47

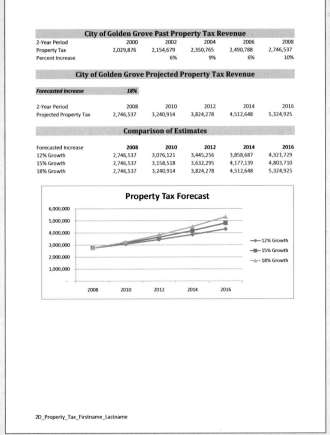

2D_Property_Tax_Firstname_Lastname

(Project 2D–Property Tax continues on the next page)

Content-Based Assessments

(Project 2D–Property Tax continued)

1. **Start** Excel and display a new workbook. In cell **A1**, type **City of Golden Grove Past Property Tax Revenue** and then press Enter. Adjust the width of **column A** to **155 pixels**. Select the range **A1:F1**, right-click over the selection, and then on the Mini toolbar, apply **Bold**, change the **Font** to **Cambria**, change the **Font Size** to **14**, and then click the **Merge and Center** button. From the **Office** menu, click **Save As**, navigate to your Excel Chapter 2 folder, in the **File name** box, name the file **2D_Property_Tax_Firstname_Lastname** and then click **Save**.

2. In cell **A2**, type **2-Year Period** In cell **B2**, type **2000** and then press Tab. In cell **C2**, type **2002** and then press Tab. Select the range **B2:C2**, and then drag the fill handle to the right through cell **F2** to enter years through *2008*.

3. In cell **A3**, type **Property Tax** and then press Enter. In cell **A4**, type **Percent Increase** and then press Enter. Beginning in cell **B3** and pressing Tab to move across the row, enter the following values for property tax revenue in the years listed:

2000	2002	2004	2006	2008
2029876	**2154679**	**2350765**	**2490788**	**2746537**

4. Select the range **B3:F3**, and then right-click over the selection. On the Mini toolbar, apply the **Comma Style**, and then click **Decrease Decimal** two times to apply **zero decimal places**.

5. Click cell **C4**. Type **=(c3-b3)/b3** and then press Enter to calculate the *Percent Increase* from the year 2000 to the year 2002. Point to cell **C4** and right-click, and then on the Mini toolbar, click the **Percent Style** button. Your result is *6%*.

6. Click cell **D4**, type **=** and then by either typing, or using a combination of typing

and clicking cells to reference them, construct a formula similar to the one in cell **C4** to calculate the rate of increase in property tax from 2002 to 2004. Press Enter, and then format cell **D4** with the **Percent Style**. With cell **D4** selected, drag the fill handle to the right through cell **F4** to calculate the property tax *Percent Increase* for each 2-year period.

7. In cell **A6**, type **City of Golden Grove Projected Property Tax Revenue** and then press Enter. Click cell **A1**. On the **Home tab**, in the **Clipboard group**, click the **Format Painter** button, and then click cell **A6**.

8. In cell **A8**, type **Forecasted Increase** and then press Enter. In cell **A10**, type **2-Year Period** and then in cell **A11**, type **Projected Property Tax** In cell **B10**, type **2008** and then press Tab. In cell **C10**, type **2010** and then press Enter. Select the range **B10:C10**, and then drag the fill handle through cell **F10** to extend the pattern of years to **2016**.

9. **Save** the changes you have made to your workbook thus far. In cell **B8**, type **12%** and then press Enter. Select the range **A8:B8**, right-click, and then on the Mini toolbar, click **Bold** and **Italic**.

10. In cell **B11**, type **=** click cell **F3**, and then press Enter to create a formula that references the 2008 Property Tax collected by the city.

11. Click cell **C11**. Type **=b11*(100%+b8)** and then on the **Formula Bar**, click the **Enter** button to create a formula that calculates the city's projected property tax revenue based on a forecasted increase of 12%. With cell **C11** as the active cell, drag the fill handle to copy the formula to **D11:F11**. Click cell **B11**, click the **Format Painter** button, and then select the range **C11:F11** to copy the formatting.

(Project 2D–Property Tax continues on the next page)

Content-Based Assessments

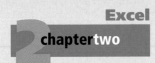
(Project 2D–Property Tax continued)

12. In cell **A13**, type **Comparison of Estimates** and then press Enter. Click **A6**, click the **Format Painter** button, and then click cell **A13**. Select the range **A8:B8**, right-click to display the Mini toolbar, click the **Fill Color button arrow**, and then under **Theme Colors**, click **Aqua, Accent 5, Lighter 40%**. Click cell **A1**, and then hold down Ctrl and click **A6** and **A13**. In the **Font group**, click the **Fill Color** button to apply the same fill color to these titles.

13. In cells **A15:A18**, type the following row titles:

    Forecasted Increase
    12% Growth
    15% Growth
    18% Growth

14. Select the range **B10:F10**. On the **Home tab**, in the **Clipboard group**, click the **Copy** button, click cell **B15**, and then in the **Clipboard group**, click the **Paste** button.

15. Select the range **B11:F11**, and then click **Copy**. Click cell **B16**, and then in the **Clipboard group**, click the **Paste button arrow**. From the displayed menu, click **Paste Special**. In the displayed **Paste Special** dialog box, under **Paste**, click the **Values and number formats** option button. Click **OK** to paste the values in the cells rather than the formulas.

16. Press Esc to cancel the moving border. Click cell **B8**. Type **15** and then press Enter to recalculate the values in cells **C11:F11** for a 15% increase.

17. Select the range **B11:F11**, and then press Ctrl + C to copy the selection. Click cell **B17**. In the **Clipboard group**, click the **Paste button arrow**, and then click **Paste**

Special. In the **Paste Special** dialog box, click the **Values and number formats** option button, and then click **OK**.

18. In cell **B8**, change the **Forecasted Increase** to **18** and press Enter. Using the skills you just practiced, copy the values and number formats in the range **B11:F11** to the range **B18:F18**. Press Esc to cancel the moving border.

19. **Save** your changes thus far. Select the range **B15:F15** and apply **Bold**.

20. Select the range **A16:F18**. On the **Insert tab**, in the **Charts group**, click the **Line** button. Click the **Line with Markers** chart type to create the chart as an embedded chart in the worksheet. Drag to position the upper left corner of the chart slightly inside the upper left corner of cell **A20**.

21. Along the lower portion of the chart, point to any of the category axis numbers such as *1* or *2* to display the ScreenTip *Horizontal (Category) Axis* displays. Then, right-click, and from the displayed shortcut menu, click **Select Data**. On the right side of the displayed **Select Data Source** dialog box, under **Horizontal (Category) Axis Labels**, click the **Edit** button. Drag the title bar of the **Axis Labels** dialog box to the right of the chart as necessary so that it is not blocking your view of the data, and then select the range **B15:F15**. Click **OK** two times so that the years display on the horizontal axis.

22. On the **Design tab**, in the **Chart Styles group**, click the **More** button, and then click **Style 2**. Click the **Layout tab**. In the **Labels group**, click the **Chart Title** button, and then click **Above Chart**. Delete the text *Chart Title*, and then type **Property Tax Forecast**

(Project 2D–Property Tax continues on the next page)

(Project 2D–Property Tax continued)

23. Click any cell to deselect the chart. Click the **Insert tab**, and then in the **Text group**, click **Header & Footer**. In the **Navigation group**, click the **Go to Footer** button, click just above the word *Footer*, and then in the **Header & Footer Elements group**, click the **File Name** button. Click in a cell just above the footer to exit the **Footer area** and view your file name.

24. Scroll up to view your chart, click an edge of the chart to select it, position the pointer over the right resize handle to display the ⟷ pointer, and then drag to the right so that the right border of the chart is just inside the right border of **column F**.

25. Click any cell to deselect the chart. Click the **Page Layout tab**. In the **Page Setup group**, click the **Margins** button, and then at the bottom of the **Margins gallery**, click **Custom Margins**. In the displayed **Page Setup** dialog box, under **Center on page**, select the **Horizontally** check box. Click **OK** to close the dialog box.

26. On the status bar, click the **Normal** button to return to Normal view, and then press [Ctrl] + [Home] to move to the top of your worksheet. At the lower edge of the window, click to select the **Sheet2 tab**, hold down [Ctrl], and then click the **Sheet3 tab** to select the two unused sheets. Right-click, and then click **Delete** to delete the unused sheets.

27. **Save** the changes you have made to your workbook. Check your *Chapter Assignment Sheet* or *Course Syllabus* or consult your instructor to determine if you are to submit your assignments on paper or electronically. To submit electronically, follow the instructions provided by your instructor.

28. From the **Office** menu, point to the **Print button arrow**, and then click **Print Preview** to check the placement of your worksheet. In the **Print group**, click the **Print** button. In the displayed **Print** dialog box, click **OK** to print your worksheet. If you are directed to submit printed formulas, refer to Activity 1.17 to do so.

29. If you printed your formulas, be sure to redisplay the worksheet by pressing [Ctrl] + [`]. From the **Office** menu, click **Close**. If the dialog box displays asking if you want to save changes, click **No** so that you do *not* save the changes you made for printing formulas. **Close** Excel.

End **You have completed Project 2D**

Content-Based Assessments

Mastering Excel

Project 2E — Summer Camp

In this project, you will apply the skills you practiced from the Objectives in Project 2A.

Objectives: 1. *Create and Save a Workbook from an Existing Workbook;* **2.** *Navigate a Workbook and Rename Worksheets;* **3.** *Enter Dates, Clear Contents, and Clear Formats;* **4.** *Move, Copy, and Paste Cell Contents;* **5.** *Edit and Format Multiple Worksheets at the Same Time;* **6.** *Create a Summary Sheet;* **7.** *Format and Print Multiple Worksheets in a Workbook.*

The city of Golden Grove offers summer camp for children at three different parks. Children are enrolled on a daily or a weekly basis. In the following Mastering Excel assessment, you will edit a workbook that summarizes the enrollments and fees at the three summer camp locations. Your completed worksheets will look similar to Figure 2.48.

For Project 2E, you will need the following file:

e2E_Summer_Camp

You will save your workbook as
2E_Summer_Camp_Firstname_Lastname

Figure 2.48

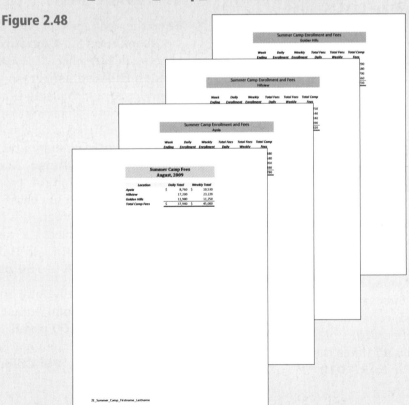

(Project 2E–Summer Camp continues on the next page)

(Project 2E–Summer Camp continued)

1. **Start** Excel and from your student files, open **e2E_Summer_Camp**. **Save** the workbook in your Excel Chapter 2 folder as **2E_Summer_Camp_Firstname_Lastname** Take a moment to examine the data in the three worksheets.

2. Rename the **Sheet1 tab** as **Ayala** and then change its **Tab Color** to **Blue, Accent 1, Lighter 40%**. Rename **Sheet2** as **Hillview** and then change its **Tab Color** to **Red, Accent 2, Lighter 40%**. Rename **Sheet3** as **Golden Hills** and then change its **Tab Color** to **Olive Green, Accent 3, Lighter 40%**.

3. Right-click the **Ayala sheet tab**, and then click **Select All Sheets** so that the three sheets are grouped. In cell **D4**, type **Total Fees Daily** in cell **E4**, type **Total Fees Weekly** and in cell **F4**, type **Total Camp Fees** Select the range **A4:F4**, and then apply the following formats: **Wrap Text**, **Center**, **Middle Align**, **Bold**, and **Italic**. Widen **columns A:F** to **75 pixels**.

4. With the worksheets still grouped, select the dates in the range **A5:A8**, display the **Format Cells** dialog box, and then on the **Number tab**, apply the third **Date** format—**3/14**. Right-click a sheet tab and click **Ungroup Sheets**. In the **Ayala sheet**, select, and then **Copy** the range **A12:D13**. Paste the selected range in the same location in both the **Hillview sheet** and the **Golden Hills sheet**. Make the **Ayala** sheet active, and then press [Esc] to cancel the moving border.

5. Right-click the **Ayala sheet tab**, and then click **Select All Sheets** to group the three sheets. In cell **D5**, construct a formula to multiply the *Daily Enrollment* for the week ending *8/7* in cell **B5** times the *Daily Summer Camp Fee* in cell **D12**. Be sure to

make the reference to cell **D12** absolute. Copy the formula down for the remaining weeks. In cell **E5**, construct a similar formula to multiply the *Weekly Enrollment* during the week of *8/7* in cell **C5** times the *Weekly Summer Camp Fee* in cell **D13**. Make the reference to cell **D13** absolute. **Copy** the formula down for the remaining dates.

6. With the worksheets still grouped, **Sum** the columns. Then, in each row, **Sum** the Daily and Weekly fees. Apply appropriate financial formatting to the range **D5:F9**, applying **Comma Style** first, using **zero decimal places**, and then applying a **Top and Double Bottom Border** to all appropriate cells. With the worksheets still grouped, **Merge and Center** the titles in **row 1** and **row 2** across columns **A:F**. To the two worksheet titles, apply a **Fill Color** using **Purple, Accent 4, Lighter 40%**.

7. **Save** the changes you have made to your workbook thus far. **Ungroup** the worksheets, and then view the **Hillview** and **Golden Hills** worksheets to verify that the formulas and formatting that you applied in the previous steps were applied to both worksheets. Insert a new worksheet, name the worksheet **Summary** and then change its **Tab Color** to **Orange, Accent 6, Lighter 40%**. In cell **A4**, type **Location** In cell **A5**, type **Ayala** In cell **A6**, type **Hillview** In cell **A7**, type **Golden Hills** In cell **A8**, type **Total Camp Fees** Select the range **A5:A8**, and then apply **Bold** and **Italic**. Adjust the width of **column A** to **150 pixels**.

8. In cell **B4**, type **Daily Total** and then in cell **C4**, type **Weekly Total** Adjust the width of **columns B:C** to **100 pixels**. Select the range **A4:C4**, and then apply **Center**, **Bold**, **Italic**, and a **Fill Color** of **Orange,**

(Project 2E–Summer Camp continues on the next page)

Content-Based Assessments

chapter**two**

Mastering Excel

(Project 2E–Summer Camp continued)

Accent 6, Lighter 80%. Beginning in cell **B5** and using the techniques you have practiced to create a summary sheet, create a formula to reference the *Total Fees Daily* in **row 9** from the **Ayala** worksheet. In cell **C5**, create a similar formula to reference the *Total Fees Weekly* in **row 9** of the **Ayala** worksheet. In the range **B6:C7**, create similar formulas to reference the appropriate cells in the **Hillview** and **Golden Hills** worksheets.

9. Calculate the *Total Camp Fees* for both *Daily* and *Weekly* enrollments, and then apply appropriate financial formatting to the numbers and the totals; first apply **Comma Style** and decrease to **zero decimal places**. In cell **A1**, type **Summer Camp Fees** and then **Merge and Center** the text over the range **A1:C1**. Change the **Font** to **Cambria**, the **Font Size** to **14**, and then apply **Bold**. In cell **A2**, type **August, 2009** and then use **Format Painter** to copy the format from cell **A1** to cell **A2**. Select both cells, and then apply a **Fill Color** of **Orange, Accent 6, Lighter 40%**.

10. Move the **Summary sheet** so that it is the first worksheet in the workbook. Group the worksheets again, insert a footer on

the left side with the **File Name**, and then center the worksheets **Horizontally**. Return to **Normal** view and display the top of the worksheet.

11. **Save** your workbook, and then view the worksheets in **Print Preview**. Check your *Chapter Assignment Sheet* or *Course Syllabus*, or consult your instructor, to determine if you are to submit your assignments on paper or electronically. To submit electronically, follow the instructions provided by your instructor.

12. **Print** the entire workbook, either by grouping the sheets or by clicking **Entire workbook** in the **Print** dialog box. Determine if you are to print formulas for any or all of the worksheets in this workbook. To print formulas, refer to Activity 1.17 in Project 1A.

13. If you printed your formulas, be sure to redisplay the worksheet by pressing Ctrl + `. From the **Office** menu, click **Close**. If you are prompted to save changes, click **No**. **Close** Excel.

End **You have completed Project 2E**

Project 2F—Gardens

In this project, you will apply the skills you practiced from the Objectives in Project 2B.

Objectives: 8. *Design a Worksheet for What-If Analysis;* **9.** *Perform What-If Analysis;* **10.** *Compare Data with a Line Chart.*

The city of Golden Grove is home to the Golden Botanical Gardens—a tourist attraction that draws visitors from around the world. The Board of Directors for the Gardens is considering an expansion plan for this popular attraction and wants to examine past attendance data and an estimate of future attendance. In the following Mastering Excel Assessment, you will create a worksheet with a line chart that projects future attendance based on varying estimates. Your completed worksheet will look similar to Figure 2.49.

For Project 2F, you will need the following file:

New blank Excel workbook

You will save your workbook as
2F_Gardens_Firstname_Lastname

Figure 2.49

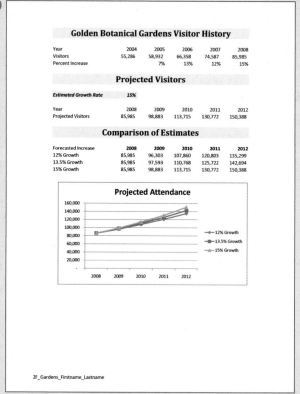

(Project 2F– Gardens continues on the next page)

Content-Based Assessments

(Project 2F–Gardens continued)

1. **Start** Excel and display a new workbook. Adjust the width of **column A** to **155 pixels**. In cell **A1**, type Golden Botanical Gardens Visitor History and then **Merge and Center** the title over **A1:F1**. Apply **Bold**, change the **Font** to **Cambria**, change the **Font Size** to **18**, and then apply a **Fill Color** of **Orange, Accent 6, Lighter 80%**. **Save** the file in your Excel Chapter 10 folder as **2F_Gardens_Firstname_Lastname**

2. In cell **A3**, type Year In cell **B3**, type **2004** and in cell **C3** type **2005** Select the range **B3:C3**, and then fill the years through *2008* in cell **F3**. In cell **A4**, type **Visitors** and then in cell **A5**, type **Percent Increase**

3. Enter the following attendance data in the range **B4:F4**, and then apply **Comma Style** with **zero decimal places** to the data.

2004	2005	2006	2007	2008
55286	58932	66358	74587	85985

4. In cell **C5**, construct a formula to calculate the *Percent Increase* in attendance from 2004 to 2005. Recall that you must first calculate the difference between 2005 and 2004 attendance figures by placing the expression in parentheses, and then divide the result by the base year attendance of 2004. Your result is *0.065948*. Apply **Percent Style** for a result of *7%*, and then fill the formula through cell **F5** to calculate the *Percent Increase* for the remaining years.

5. In cell **A7**, type **Projected Visitors** and then use **Format Painter** to copy the format from cell **A1** to cell **A7**. In cell **A9**, type **Estimated Growth Rate** In cell **A11**, type **Year** and then in cell **A12**, type **Projected Visitors** In cell **B11**, type **2008** and in cell **C11** type **2009** and then extend the pattern of years to *2012*. In cell **B12**, type **=f4** to create a reference to the attendance in year 2008.

6. **Save** the changes you have made to your workbook thus far. In cell **B9**, type **12%** Select the range **A9:B9**, and then apply **Bold**, **Italic**, and a **Fill Color** of **Orange, Accent 6, Lighter 80%**. The first projection will be based on an estimated growth in attendance of 12%.

7. In cell **C12**, construct a formula to calculate the 2009 estimated attendance based on an increase of 12% over the 2008 attendance—a value after an increase—as follows: multiply the base value in cell **B12** times 100% plus the value in cell **B9**. Place the second expression in parentheses so that addition is performed first, and make the reference to the value in **B9** absolute so you can copy the formula. Your result is *96303.2*. Copy the formula for the remaining years, and then use the **Format Painter** to apply the format of cell **B12** to the range **C12:F12**.

8. In cell **A14** type **Comparison of Estimates** and then use **Format Painter** to copy the formatting from **A7** to cell **A14**. **Copy** the dates in the range **B11:F11**, and then paste them in the range **B16:F16**. Apply **Bold** to the pasted range.

9. Board members want to look at estimates in visitor growth between 12% and 15% (the rates for the past two years) and the rate halfway between those two rates, which is 13.5%. In the range **A16:A19**, type the following row titles.

Forecasted Increase
12% Growth
13.5% Growth
15% Growth

(Project 2F–Gardens continues on the next page)

Excel

chapter two

Mastering Excel

(Project 2F–Gardens continued)

10. Copy the first set of projections in the range **B12:F12**, point to cell **B17** and right-click, from the shortcut menu click **Paste Special**, and then from the **Paste Special** dialog box, paste the **Values and number formats**—rather than the formulas—to the range **B17:F17**.

11. In cell **B9**, change the projected rate to **13.5** to recalculate the values in the range **C12:F12**. Copy the values and number formats in the range **B12:F12** to the range **B18:F18**. In cell **B9**, change the rate to **15** Copy the values and formats in the range **B12:F12** to the range **B19:F19**. Press Esc to cancel the moving border.

12. Using the data in the range **A17:F19**, insert a line chart using the **Line with Markers** chart type, and then position the upper left corner of the chart inside the upper left corner of cell **A21**. Right-click one of the numbers along the **Horizontal (Category) Axis**, and then click **Select Data**. From the **Select Data Source** dialog box, **Edit** the **Horizontal (Category) Axis Labels** by selecting the years in the range **B16:F16** as the category labels.

13. Apply **Chart Style 2**, and then click the **Layout tab**. In the **Labels group**, click the **Chart Title** button, and then click **Above Chart**. As the chart title, type **Projected**

Attendance Click any cell to deselect the chart, and then **Insert** a footer in the left section with the **File Name**. Scroll up to view the chart, and then widen the chart to display attractively below the data. Deselect the chart, and then center the worksheet **Horizontally** on the page. Switch to **Normal** view, **Delete** the extra worksheets in the workbook, and then press Ctrl + Home to display the top of the worksheet.

14. Save the changes you have made to your workbook. Check your *Chapter Assignment Sheet* or *Course Syllabus* or consult your instructor to determine if you are to submit your assignments on paper or electronically. To submit electronically, follow the instructions provided by your instructor.

15. Display your worksheet in **Print Preview**, and then **Print**. If you are directed to submit printed formulas, refer to Activity 9.17 to do so. If you printed your formulas, be sure to redisplay the worksheet by pressing Ctrl + `. From the **Office** menu, click **Close**. If the dialog box displays asking if you want to save changes, click **No** so that you do *not* save the changes you made for printing formulas. **Close** Excel.

End **You have completed Project 2F**

Content-Based Assessments

Mastering Excel

Project 2G—Operations Costs

In this project, you will apply the skills you practiced from the Objectives in Projects 2A and 2B.

Objectives: 1. *Create and Save a Workbook from an Existing Workbook;* **2.** *Navigate a Workbook and Rename Worksheets;* **3.** *Enter Dates, Clear Contents, and Clear Formats;* **4.** *Move, Copy, and Paste Cell Contents;* **5.** *Edit and Format Multiple Worksheets at the Same Time;* **6.** *Create a Summary Sheet;* **7.** *Format and Print Multiple Worksheets in a Workbook.* **10.** *Compare Data with a Line Chart.*

In the following Mastering Excel assessment, you will edit a workbook that summarizes and charts the operations costs of Golden Grove's Public Works Department. The department's three divisions are Engineering, Contract Administration, and Street Services. Your completed worksheet will look similar to Figure 2.50.

For Project 2G, you will need the following file:

e2G_Operations_Costs

You will save your workbook as
2G_Operations_Costs_Firstname_Lastname

Figure 2.50

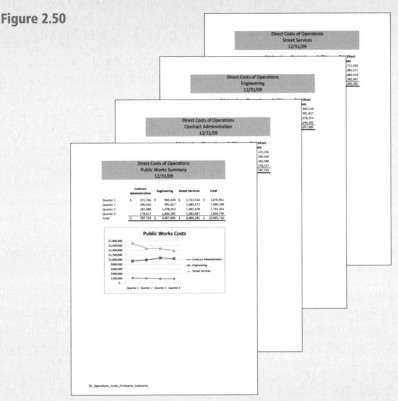

(Project 2G–Operations Costs continues on the next page)

(Project 2G–Operations Costs continued)

1. **Start** Excel and from your student files, open **e2G_Operations_Costs**. **Save** the workbook in your Excel Chapter 2 folder as **2G_Operations_Costs_Firstname_Lastname**

2. Rename the **Sheet1 tab** as **Contract Administration** and then change its **Tab Color** to **Purple, Accent 4, Lighter 40%**. Rename **Sheet2** as **Engineering** and then change its **Tab Color** to **Aqua, Accent 5, Lighter 40%**. Rename **Sheet3** as **Street Services** and then change its **Tab Color** to **Orange, Accent 6, Lighter 40%**.

3. Point to the **Contract Administration** sheet tab, right-click, and then select all of the sheets so that they are grouped. **Merge and Center** the titles in **A1** and **A2** over **columns A:E**. In cell **A3**, type **12/31/2009** and then apply the **03/14/01** date format to the cell. **Merge and Center** cell **A3** over **columns A:E**, and then change the **Font Size** to **16**. Select the range **A1:A3**, and then apply a **Fill Color** of **Red, Accent 2, Lighter 40%**.

4. With the worksheets still grouped, in **row 5**, apply **Wrap Text** formatting to the column titles, and then apply **Bold** and **Italic**. **Center** the column titles.

5. With the worksheets still grouped, sum the columns and then sum the rows. Beginning with **Comma Style**, apply appropriate financial formatting using **zero decimal places**, and then change the width of **column A** to **110 pixels**. Select cell **A10** and **Clear Formats** so that the text is aligned at the left and not bold.

6. Ungroup the worksheets and verify that the formulas and formatting applied in Steps 3 through 5 were applied to the **Engineering** and **Street Services** sheets. Insert a new worksheet and **Rename** it

Summary Change the **Tab Color** to **Olive Green, Accent 3, Lighter 40%**.

7. Display the **Contract Administration** worksheet. Select and **Copy** the range **A1:A3**, and then **Paste** the selection to the **Summary** worksheet in cell **A1**. In the **Summary** worksheet, click cell **A2**, and then type **Public Works Summary**

8. Display the **Contract Administration** worksheet. **Copy** the range **A6:A9**, **Paste** the selection to the **Summary** worksheet in cell **A6**, and then in the **Summary** worksheet, adjust the width of **column A** to **110 pixels** and the width of **columns B:E** to **100 pixels**. In cell **A10**, type **Total**—italic emphasis will carry forward from the cell above.

9. In cell **B5**, type **Contract Administration** In cell **C5**, type **Engineering** In cell **D5**, type **Street Services** In cell **E5**, type **Total Center** and apply **Wrap Text** formatting to the column titles in **row 5**, apply **Bold**, and then apply **Middle Align**.

10. **Save** the changes you have made to your workbook thus far. In the **Summary** worksheet in cell **B6**, create a formula that references the **Contract Administration** worksheet *Quarter 1 Total Direct Costs* in cell **E6**. Fill the formula down through **B9** to create formulas that reference the remaining quarter's *Total Direct Costs*. Create similar formulas for the **Engineering** and **Street Services** quarterly *Total Direct Costs*. Sum the columns and then sum the rows. Beginning with **Comma Style**, apply appropriate financial formatting using **zero decimal places**.

11. Select the range **A5:D9**, and then insert a line chart using the **Line with Markers** chart type. Position the upper left corner

(Project 2G–Operations Costs continues on the next page)

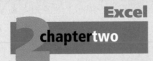
(Project 2G–Operations Costs continued)

of the chart inside the upper left corner of cell **A12**. Apply **Chart Style 10**, and then add a **Chart Title**—Public Works Costs in the **Above Chart** position. From the status bar, click the **Page Layout View** button, widen the chart to display attractively below the data, and then click any cell to deselect the chart. **Move** the **Summary** worksheet so that it is the first sheet in the workbook.

12. Group the worksheets, insert a footer with the **File Name** on the left, and then center the worksheets **Horizontally**. Return to **Normal** view and display the upper portion of the worksheet.

13. **Save** your workbook, and then examine your grouped worksheets in **Print Preview**. Print or submit electronically as directed. If the worksheets are grouped, all the worksheets will print. If the worksheets are not grouped, click Entire workbook to print all the sheets. Determine if you are to print formulas for any or all of the worksheets in this workbook. To print formulas, refer to Activity 9.17 in Project 9A.

14. If you printed your formulas, be sure to redisplay the worksheet by pressing Ctrl + `. From the **Office** menu, click **Close**. If you are prompted to save changes, click **No**. **Close** Excel.

 End **You have completed Project 2G**

Mastering Excel

Project 2H—Venue Revenue

In this project, you will apply the skills you practiced from the Objectives in Projects 2A and 2B.

Objectives: 3. *Enter Dates, Clear Contents, and Clear Formats;* **8.** *Design a Worksheet for What-If Analysis;* **9.** *Perform What-If Analysis;* **10.** *Compare Data with a Line Chart.*

In the following Mastering Excel assessment, you will complete a workbook for the Director of Conventions, Culture, and Leisure, which shows revenue estimates for city-owned venues for conventions, cultural events, and leisure activities and their associated parking structures. Your resulting worksheet and chart will look similar to Figure 2.51.

For Project 2H, you will need the following file:

New blank Excel workbook

You will save your workbook as
2H_Venue_Revenue_Firstname_Lastname

Figure 2.51

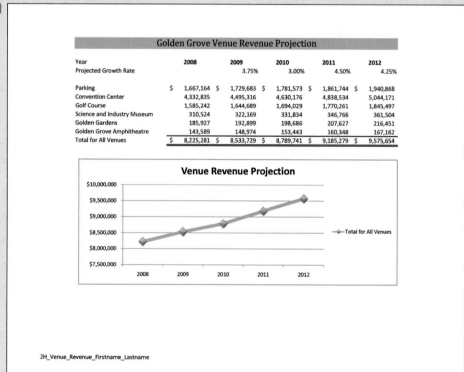

(Project 2H–Venue Revenue continues on the next page)

(Project 2H–Venue Revenue continued)

1. **Start** Excel and display a new blank workbook. **Save** the workbook in your Excel Chapter 2 folder as **2H_Venue_Revenue_ Firstname_Lastname**

2. In cell **A1**, type **Golden Grove Venue Revenue Projection** and then **Merge and Center** the title across cells **A1:F1**. Change the **Font** to **Cambria**, the **Font Size** to **16**, and then apply the **Olive Green, Accent 3 Fill Color**. In cell **A3**, type **Year** In the range **B3:F3**, create a pattern of years from 2008 through 2012. Format the years with **Bold** and **Center**.

3. In cell **A4**, type **Projected Growth Rate** In the range **C4:F4**, type the following percentages: **3.75% 3.0% 4.5% 4.25%**

4. Widen **column A** to **200 pixels** and widen columns **B:F** to **100 pixels**. In the range **A6:B11**, enter the following data:

Parking	1667164
Convention Center	4332835
Golf Course	1585242
Science and Industry Museum	310524
Golden Gardens	185927
Golden Grove Amphitheatre	143589

5. In cell **C6**, construct a formula that calculates the year *2009* revenue for *Parking* assuming an increase of 3.75% (the rate in cell C4) over the previous year. That is, multiply the base value in cell **B6** times 100% plus the value in cell **C4**. Place the second expression in parentheses so that addition is performed first, and make the reference to the value in **C4** absolute so that you can copy this formula down column C. In cell **D6**, for the year *2010*, construct a similar formula using the previous year's revenue and the rate in cell **D4**. Construct similar formulas for the years

2011 and *2012* using the previous year's revenue and the projected growth rate for the year indicated. **Copy** the formulas in **row 6** down through **row 11**.

6. In cell **A12**, type **Total for All Venues** and then in **row 12**, sum the values in **columns B:F**. Beginning with **Comma Style**, apply appropriate financial formatting with **zero decimal places**.

7. **Save** the changes you have made to your workbook thus far. Using the data in the range **A12:F12**, insert a line chart using the **Line with Markers** chart type, and then apply **Chart Style 29**. Edit the data source so that the **Horizontal (Category) Axis** uses the years in the range **B3:F3** as the labels. Change the chart title to **Venue Revenue Projection** Position the upper left corner of the chart inside the upper left corner of cell **A14**.

8. Click any cell to deselect the chart. Change the **Orientation** to **Landscape**, and then center the worksheet on the page **Horizontally**. Insert a footer with the **File Name** on the left side. Widen the chart so that it displays attractively under the data. Deselect the chart, return to **Normal** view, display the top of the worksheet, and then delete the unused sheets in the workbook.

9. **Save** your workbook, and then examine your worksheet in **Print Preview**. Print or submit electronically as directed. To print formulas, refer to Activity 1.17 in Project 1A.

10. If you printed your formulas, be sure to redisplay the worksheet by pressing Ctrl + `. From the **Office** menu, click **Close**. If you are prompted to save changes, click **No**. **Close** Excel.

End **You have completed Project 2H**

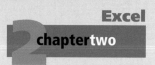

Excel

chaptertwo | **Mastering Excel**

Project 2I — Analysis

In this project, you will apply the skills you practiced from all the Objectives in Projects 2A and 2B.

Objectives: 1. *Create and Save a Workbook from an Existing Workbook;* **2.** *Navigate a Workbook and Rename Worksheets;* **3.** *Enter Dates, Clear Contents, and Clear Formats;* **4.** *Move, Copy, and Paste Cell Contents;* **5.** *Edit and Format Multiple Worksheets at the Same Time;* **6.** *Create a Summary Sheet;* **7.** *Format and Print Multiple Worksheets in a Workbook;* **8.** *Design a Worksheet for What-If Analysis;* **9.** *Perform What-If Analysis;* **10.** *Compare Data with a Line Chart.*

In the following Mastering Excel assessment, you will complete a workbook for the Director of Parks and Recreation, which shows departmental expenses for the three departments reporting to the director. Your resulting worksheet and chart will look similar to Figure 2.52.

For Project 2I, you will need the following file:

e2I_Analysis

**You will save your workbook as
2I_Analysis_Firstname_Lastname**

Figure 2.52

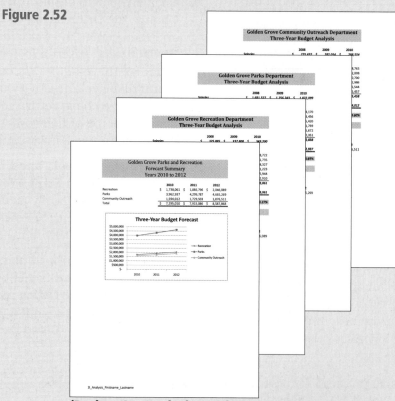

(Project 2I– Analysis continues on the next page)

Content-Based Assessments

(Project 2I–Analysis continued)

1. **Start** Excel, and then from your student files, open the file **e2I_Analysis**. **Rename Sheet1** as **Recreation** and then change the **Tab Color** to **Blue, Accent 1, Lighter 40%**. **Rename Sheet2** as **Parks** and then change the **Tab Color** to **Red, Accent 2, Lighter 40%**. **Rename Sheet3** as **Community Outreach** and then change the **Tab Color** to **Olive Green, Accent 3, Lighter 40%**. **Save** the workbook in your Excel Chapter 2 folder as **2I_Analysis_Firstname_Lastname**

2. Display the **Recreation** worksheet, and then group the three worksheets. Select the range **A1:A2**, change the **Font** to **Cambria**, the **Font Size** to **16**, apply **Bold**, and then apply a **Fill Color** of **Aqua, Accent 5, Lighter 40%**. **Merge and Center** the two worksheet titles across the ranges **A1:D1** and **A2:D2**. Select the years in the range **B4:D4** and apply **Bold**, and **Center** alignment. Select the **Salaries** data in the range **B5:D5**, apply **Accounting Number Format** with **zero decimal places**, and then select the range **A5:D5** and apply **Bold** and **Italic**. Use **Format Painter** to copy the formatting from cell **A5** to cell **A7** and to cell **A14**.

3. Verify that the worksheets are still grouped, and then in **row 14**, sum each year's data for *Expenses*. Apply **Bold** and **Italic** to the totals. Beginning with **Comma Style** and using **zero decimal places**, apply appropriate financial formatting to the *Expenses* data, *without* a Top and Double Bottom Border. Instead, to the range **B14:D14**, apply only a **Top Border**.

4. Ungroup the worksheets and verify that the formatting and editing changes that you made in Steps 2 and 3 were applied to all three worksheets. On the **Recreation** worksheet, **Copy** the text in cell **A16**, and

then **Paste** it to the same location in the **Parks** worksheet and **Community Outreach** worksheet.

5. Display the **Recreation** worksheet and press Esc to cancel the moving border. Group the three worksheets. In cell **B16**, construct a formula that adds the *2008 Salaries* in cell **B5** and the *2008 Total Expenses* in cell **B14**. Fill the formula across the remaining two years, and then with the range **B16:D16** still selected, apply a **Bottom Double Border**. Select the range **A16:D16**, and then apply **Bold** and **Italic**.

6. With the worksheets still grouped, in cell **A18** type **Total Departmental Increase** In cell **C18**, construct a formula that calculates the percent increase of the *Total Departmental Increase* for *2009* from *2008*. Your result is *0.003307521*, an increase of less than 1%. Apply **Percent Style** formatting with **two decimal places** for a result of *0.33%*. Copy the formula to the right for the year 2010; in this year, the percentage increase was more significant—*8.27%*. To the range **A18:D18**, apply **Bold**, **Italic**, and a **Fill Color** using **Aqua, Accent 5, Lighter 40%**.

7. With the worksheets still grouped, in cell **A20** type **Projected Budget Years 2010 – 2012** and then use **Format Painter** to copy the format from cell **A1** to cell **A20**. In cell **A22**, type **Forecasted Increase** In cell **A24**, type **Year** and in cell **A25**, type **Forecasted Total Budget** Apply **AutoFit** to **column A**. In the range **B24:D24**, enter a pattern of years from 2010 through 2012, and then **Center** and **Bold** the years. In cell **B22**, type **8.5%** which will display as *8.50%*. To the range **A22:B22**, apply **Bold** and **Italic**.

8. With the worksheets still grouped, in cell **B25** construct a formula that references cell **D16**—the *Total Department* expenses for *2010*. In cell **C25**, construct a formula

(Project 2I–Analysis continues on the next page)

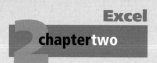

Excel

chaptertwo | **Mastering Excel**

(Project 2I–Analysis continued)

that calculates the *Forecasted Total Budget* for *2011* based on the 8.5% increase in cell **B22**. Be sure to make the reference to cell **B22** absolute. (The result displays as being too wide for the cell.) Copy the formula to cell **D25**, and then use **Format Painter** to copy the formatting from cell **B25** to the range **C25:D25**.

9. **Save** the changes you have made thus far. Insert a new worksheet, rename the worksheet **Summary** and then change the **Tab Color** to **Orange, Accent 6, Lighter 40%**. In cell **A1**, type **Golden Grove Parks and Recreation** In cell **A2**, type **Forecast Summary** In cell **A3**, type **Years 2010 to 2012** In the range **B5:D5**, enter the years **2010** and **2011** and **2012 Bold** and **Center** the years. In the range **A6:A9**, enter the row titles **Recreation** and **Parks** and **Community Outreach** and **Total** Apply **AutoFit** to **column A** and widen columns **B:D** to **95 pixels**.

10. **Merge and Center** each of the three worksheet titles across columns **A:D**, and then change the **Font** to **Cambria**, the **Font Size** to **16**, and apply a **Fill Color** of **Aqua, Accent 5, Lighter 40%**.

11. In cell **B6**, enter a formula that references the **Forecasted Total Budget** for **2010** from cell **B25** in the **Recreation** worksheet. Fill the formula across through cell **D6**, and then construct similar formulas for the **Forecasted Total Budget** amounts from the **Parks** worksheet and the **Community Outreach** worksheet. Calculate totals for each year in **row 9**. Beginning with **Comma Style**, apply appropriate financial formatting to the data with **zero decimal places**.

12. **Save** your changes. Using the data in the range **A6:D8**, insert a line chart using the **Line with Markers** chart type. Position the upper left corner of the chart inside the upper left corner of cell **A11**, apply **Chart Style 2**, and then edit the data source so that the **Horizontal (Category) Axis** displays the years in the range **B5:D5**. Insert a chart title in the **Above Chart** position with the text **Three-Year Budget Forecast**

13. Click any cell to deselect the chart. Move the **Summary** worksheet to become the first worksheet in the workbook, and then group the worksheets. Center the worksheets in the workbook **Horizontally** on the page. Insert a footer on the left side with the **File Name**. Ungroup the worksheets. Adjust the width of the chart so that it is slightly inside the right boundary of **column D** to display attractively below the data. Return to **Normal** view, deselect the chart, and display the top of the worksheet.

14. **Save** your workbook, and then examine your worksheets in **Print Preview**. Print or submit electronically as directed. If the worksheets are grouped, all the worksheets will print. If the worksheets are not grouped, click **Entire workbook** to print all the sheets. Determine if you are to print formulas for any or all of the worksheets in this workbook. To print formulas, refer to Activity 1.17 in Project 1A.

15. If you printed your formulas, be sure to redisplay the worksheet by pressing [Ctrl] + [`]. From the **Office** menu, click **Close**. If you are prompted to save changes, click **No**. **Close** Excel.

End **You have completed Project 2I**

Content-Based Assessments

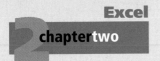

Excel

chaptertwo

Business Running Case

Project 2J—Business Running Case

In this project, you will apply the skills you practiced in Projects 2A and 2B.

From My Computer, navigate to the student files that accompany this textbook. In the folder **03_business_running_case_pg37_86**, locate and open the folder for this chapter. Open and print the instructions for this project, which are provided to you in Adobe PDF format. Follow the instructions and use the skills you have gained thus far to assist Jennifer Nelson in meeting the challenges of owning and running her business.

End You have completed Project 2J ——————————

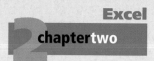

Rubric

The following outcomes-based assessments are *open-ended assessments*. That is, there is no specific correct result; your result will depend on your approach to the information provided. Make *Professional Quality* your goal. Use the following scoring rubric to guide you in *how* to approach the problem and then to evaluate *how well* your approach solves the problem.

The *criteria*—Software Mastery, Content, Format and Layout, and Process—represent the knowledge and skills you have gained that you can apply to solving the problem. The *levels of performance*—Professional Quality, Approaching Professional Quality, or Needs Quality Improvements—help you and your instructor evaluate your result.

	Your completed project is of Professional Quality if you:	Your completed project is Approaching Professional Quality if you:	Your completed project Needs Quality Improvements if you:
1-Software Mastery	Choose and apply the most appropriate skills, tools, and features and identify efficient methods to solve the problem.	Choose and apply some appropriate skills, tools, and features, but not in the most efficient manner.	Choose inappropriate skills, tools, or features, or are inefficient in solving the problem.
2-Content	Construct a solution that is clear and well organized, contains content that is accurate, appropriate to the audience and purpose, and is complete. Provide a solution that contains no errors of spelling, grammar, or style.	Construct a solution in which some components are unclear, poorly organized, inconsistent, or incomplete. Misjudge the needs of the audience. Have some errors in spelling, grammar, or style, but the errors do not detract from comprehension.	Construct a solution that is unclear, incomplete, or poorly organized, containing some inaccurate or inappropriate content; and contains many errors of spelling, grammar, or style. Do not solve the problem.
3-Format and Layout	Format and arrange all elements to communicate information and ideas, clarify function, illustrate relationships, and indicate relative importance.	Apply appropriate format and layout features to some elements, but not others. Overuse features, causing minor distraction.	Apply format and layout that does not communicate information or ideas clearly. Do not use format and layout features to clarify function, illustrate relationships, or indicate relative importance. Use available features excessively, causing distraction.
4-Process	Use an organized approach that integrates planning, development, self-assessment, revision, and reflection.	Demonstrate an organized approach in some areas, but not others; or, use an insufficient process of organization throughout.	Do not use an organized approach to solve the problem.

Excel

chaptertwo

Problem Solving

Project 2K — Fire Stations

In this project, you will construct a solution by applying any combination of the skills you practiced in the Objectives covered in Projects 2A and 2B.

For Project 2K, you will need the following file:

New blank Excel workbook

You will save your workbook as
2K_Fire_Stations_Firstname_Lastname

The City of Golden Grove has approved a bond measure for the construction of three new fire stations. Using the information provided, create a workbook that the City Controller can present to the City Council that details construction costs covered by the bond measure. Design your workbook so that the data for each fire station is on a separate worksheet. First, group the sheets to apply formatting and type the row and column titles that will be the same across all sheets; this will help you avoid unnecessary typing and formatting. Then, ungroup the sheets, include the fire station location at the top of each worksheet, and type the costs into each sheet. To type the costs, it may be helpful to select the range first so that the movement of the insertion point is confined to the range.

Grand Avenue Fire Station	Land Costs	Design Costs	Construction Costs
Phase 1	13840320	343900	2209384
Phase 2	1102984	230098	3384950
Phase 3	1920384	119739	6937409
South Edison Fire Station	Land Costs	Design Costs	Construction Costs
Phase 1	1866428	459320	1938400
Phase 2	293040	664739	6790474
Phase 3	288730	193804	8498502
Hill Street Fire Station	Land Costs	Design Costs	Construction Costs
Phase 1	394058	484927	1849023
Phase 2	1293846	559680	7593084
Phase 3	129800	583920	5890503

For all of the worksheets, calculate totals for each Phase (rows) and for each type of cost (columns). Insert a worksheet that summarizes, for each fire station, the total costs by type of cost (Land, Design, and Construction). Sum the columns. On each worksheet, use borders, fill colors, and font styles and sizes to create a professional worksheet. Add a footer to each worksheet that includes the file name and center the worksheets on the page. Save the workbook as **2K_Fire_Stations_Firstname_Lastname** and submit as directed.

End You have completed Project 2K

Outcomes-Based Assessments

chapter two

Excel

Problem Solving

Project 2L — Water Usage

In this project, you will construct a solution by applying any combination of the skills you practiced in the Objectives covered in Projects 2A and 2B.

> ### For Project 2L, you will need the following file:
>
> New blank Excel workbook

You will save your workbook as
2L_Water_Usage_Firstname_Lastname

Golden Grove is a growing community and the City Council has requested an analysis of future water needs. In this project, you will create a worksheet for the Department of Water and Power that contains data regarding past residential water usage and that forecasts water usage in the future. Create a worksheet with the following data:

Year	2002	2004	2006	2008	2010
Water Use in Acre Feet	62500	68903	73905	76044	80342

Calculate the percent increase in water usage from 2002 to 2004, and then for 2006, 2008, and 2010. Using Project 2B as a guide, add a section to the worksheet to calculate the projected water usage for the years 2010 to 2018 in two-year increments. The 2010 amount is 80,342. Add a comparison of estimates section to the worksheet with three forecasted increases: 4%, 6%, and 9%. Include a worksheet title and use formatting and editing techniques that you practiced in this chapter so that the worksheet looks attractive and professional. Add the file name to the footer. Save the workbook as **2L_Water_Usage_Firstname_Lastname** and submit as directed.

End **You have completed Project 2L** ───────

Excel

chapter two

Problem Solving

Project 2M — Schools

In this project, you will construct a solution by applying any combination of the skills you practiced in the Objectives in Projects 2A and 2B.

For Project 2M, you will need the following file:

New blank Excel workbook

You will save your workbook as
2M_Schools_Firstname_Lastname

As the city of Golden Grove grows, the school district must plan for additional students that will enroll in the elementary, middle, and high schools. In this project, you will create a workbook that contains enrollment projections for the next four years. First, create three worksheets containing the following information:

Elementary Schools	2008	2009	2010	2011	2012
Projected Increase		2%	3.5%	7%	5%
Wyndham	1350				
Warm Creek	956				
Los Serranos	1175				
Hidden Canyon	1465				
Butterfield	854				

Middle Schools	2008	2009	2010	2011	2012
Projected Increase		4.5%	5.75%	3%	3.5%
Townsend	1194				
Canyon Hills	1575				
Golden Springs	1392				

High Schools	2008	2009	2010	2011	2012
Projected Increase		6%	7.5%	4%	2.75%
Poppy Hills	2276				
Diamond Ranch	3150				

On each sheet, create formulas in the 2009 column that increases the 2008 enrollment by the Projected Increase percent. Create similar formulas for each year, increasing the previous year's enrollment by the Projected Increase percent. Calculate totals by year. Insert a line chart on each sheet with the years on the category horizontal axis. Create a summary sheet that includes the total enrollment by year for each *type* of school—Elementary Schools, Middle Schools, and High Schools—and then calculate totals for each year. Use formatting and editing techniques that you practiced in this chapter so that the workbook looks attractive and professional. Add the file name to the footer. Save the workbook as **2M_Schools_Firstname_Lastname** and submit as directed.

End You have completed Project 2M

Excel
chaptertwo

Problem Solving

Project 2N — Park Acreage

In this project, you will construct a solution by applying any combination of the skills you practiced in the Objectives covered in Projects 2A and 2B.

> **For Project 2N, you will need the following file:**
>
> New blank Excel workbook
>
> **You will save your workbook as**
> **2N_Park_Acreage_Firstname_Lastname**

The city of Golden Grove wants to maintain a high ratio of parkland to residents and has established a goal of maintaining a minimum of 50 parkland acres per 1,000 residents. The following table contains the park acreage and the population, in thousands, since 1970. Enter the data in a worksheet, and then calculate the *Acres per 1,000 residents* by dividing the *Park acreage* by the *Population in thousands*. Create a line chart that displays the Acres per 1,000 residents for each year in the table. Use formatting and editing techniques that you practiced in this chapter so that the worksheet looks attractive and professional. On your worksheet, apply yellow fill color to any year in which the goal of a minimum of 50 parkland acres per 1,000 residents was not achieved. Add the filename to the footer. Save the workbook as **2N_Park_Acreage_Firstname_Lastname** and submit as directed.

	1970	1980	1990	2000	2010
Population in thousands	116.3	145.4	180.2	225.3	304.5
Park acreage	5,800	7,250	10,050	11,250	12,240
Acres per 1,000 residents					

 End You have completed Project 2N

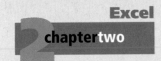

Problem Solving

Project 20 — Transportation

In this project, you will construct a solution by applying any combination of the skills you practiced in the Objectives covered in Projects 2A and 2B.

For Project 20, you will need the following file:

New blank Excel workbook

You will save your workbook as
20_Transportation_Firstname_Lastname

The Public Transportation Director for the city of Golden Grove would like to compare the sources of funding for public transportation in the current year (2009) and the forecasted amounts for 2010, 2011, and 2012. The 2009 sources of funding are:

	2009
Passenger fares	1,524,630
City appropriation	2,358,796
State appropriation	1,857,942
Federal grants	1,564,894
Other funding sources	978,623

The projected increase for 2010 is 5% for passenger fares and 2% for all other categories. The projected increase from the 2010 forecast for 2011 is 3.5% for passenger fares and 1.5% for all other categories. The projected increase from the 2011 forecast for 2012 is 6% for passenger fares and 3% for all other categories. Create a worksheet with formulas that calculate the forecasted funding amounts and that totals each year and each funding source. Then, insert a line chart that illustrates the total funding for each year. Use formatting and editing techniques that you practiced in this chapter so that the worksheet and chart look attractive and professional. Add the filename to the footer and save the workbook as **20_Transportation_Firstname_Lastname** and submit it as directed.

End **You have completed Project 20** _____

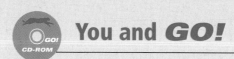

Excel

chaptertwo

You and *GO!*

Project 2P — You and *GO!*

In this project, you will construct a solution by applying any combination of the skills you practiced in the Objectives covered in Projects 2A and 2B.

From My Computer, navigate to the student files that accompany this textbook. In the folder **04_you_and_go_pg87_102**, locate and open the folder for this chapter. Open and print the instructions for this project, which are provided to you in Adobe PDF format. Follow the instructions to create a budget for yourself over a three-month period.

End **You have completed Project 2P** ————————

GO! with Help

Project 2Q — *GO!* with Help

In this chapter, you inserted line charts with markers that identified the data points for each data series. You can add data labels to a line chart so that the value of each data point displays adjacent to the data marker. In this exercise, you will use Help to find out how to add data labels to a chart.

1 **Start** Excel. At the far right end of the Ribbon, click the **Microsoft Office Excel Help** button . Click the **Search arrow**, and then under **Content from this computer**, click **Excel Help**.

2 In the **Search** box, type **insert data labels** and then press Enter. Click **Edit titles or data labels in a chart** and then click **Add or remove data labels in a chart**.

3 Read the information under **Add data labels to a chart**, print the information if you want to do so, close the Help window, and then close Excel.

End **You have completed Project 2Q** ————————

Outcomes-Based Assessments

Group Business Running Case

Project 2R — Group Business Running Case

In this project, you will apply the skills you practiced from the Objectives in Projects 2A and 2B.

Your instructor may assign this group case project to your class. If your instructor assigns this project, he or she will provide you with information and instructions to work as part of a group. The group will apply the skills gained thus far to help the Bell Orchid Hotel Group achieve its business goals.

End You have Completed Project 2R

3

chapterthree

Using Functions and Tables

OBJECTIVES

At the end of this chapter you will be able to:

OUTCOMES

Mastering these objectives will enable you to:

1. Use SUM, AVERAGE, MEDIAN, MIN, and MAX Functions
2. Use COUNTIF and IF Functions, and Apply Conditional Formatting
3. Use a Date Function
4. Freeze Panes and Create an Excel Table
5. Format and Print a Large Worksheet

PROJECT 3A
Track Inventory by Using Math, Logical, and Statistical Functions and by Creating an Excel Table

6. Use Financial Functions
7. Use Goal Seek
8. Create a Data Table

PROJECT 3B
Make Financial Decisions by Using Financial Functions and What-If Analysis

Adamantine Jewelry, Inc.

Adamantine Jewelry is based in Milan, Italy, one of the world's leading centers for fashion and design. The company's designers take inspiration from nature, cultural artifacts, and antiquities to produce affordable, fashionable jewelry that is sold through major retailers around the world. With a 40-year history, the company is well respected among its retail customers and has recently expanded to online and television retailers. In addition to women's bracelets, necklaces, rings, and earrings, the company also produces sport and fashion watches for men and women.

Using Functions and Tables

In this chapter, you will design worksheets that use the library of formulas and procedures provided with Excel to perform specific functions. You will also use more What-If Analysis tools. Using these tools will make your worksheets valuable tools for analyzing data and making financial decisions.

Project 3A Milan Inventory

In Activities 3.1 through 3.13, you will edit a worksheet for Rose Elleni, Vice President of Production, detailing the current inventory of two product types at the Milan production facility. Your completed worksheet will look similar to Figure 3.1.

For Project 3A, you will need the following file:

e3A_Milan_Inventory

You will save your workbook as
3A_Milan_Inventory_Firstname_Lastname

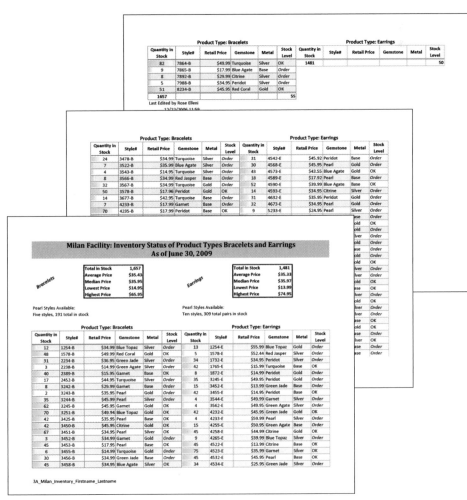

Figure 3.1
Project 3A—Milan Inventory

Objective 1
Use SUM, AVERAGE, MEDIAN, MIN, and MAX Functions

A *function* is a predefined formula—a formula that Excel has already built for you—that performs calculations by using specific values in a particular order or structure.

Activity 3.1 Using the SUM, AVERAGE, and MEDIAN Functions

Rose has a worksheet with information about the inventory of two product types—Bracelets and Earrings—currently in stock at the Milan facility. In this activity, you will use the SUM and AVERAGE functions to gather information about the product inventory.

1 **Start** Excel. From the student files that accompany this text, locate and open **e3A_Milan_Inventory**. From the **Office** menu, display the **Save As** dialog box, click the **Save in arrow**, and then navigate to the location where you are storing your projects for this chapter. Click the **Create New Folder** button, name the folder **Excel Chapter 3** and then press Enter to make your new folder the active folder. In the **File name** box, type **3A_Milan_Inventory_Firstname_Lastname** and then click **Save** or press Enter.

2 Take a moment to scroll down the worksheet to become familiar with the data. Notice that the worksheet contains data related to two product types—*Bracelets* and *Earrings*—and then for each product type, information regarding the *Quantity in Stock*, *Style#*, *Retail Price*, *Gemstone*, and *Metal* is included.

3 In cell **A1**, type **Milan Facility: Inventory Status of Product Types Bracelets and Earrings** and in cell **A2** type **As of June 30, 2009** **Merge and Center** each worksheet title across the columns **A:L**. Format both titles with **Bold**, change the **Font** Calibri to **Cambria**, change the **Font Size** 11 to **16**, and then apply a **Fill Color** of **Dark Blue, Text 2, Lighter 60%**.

4 In cell **A4**, type **Total in Stock** In cell **A5**, type **Average Price** In cell **A6**, type **Median Price** Click cell **B4**. Click the **Formulas tab**, and then in the **Function Library group**, click the **AutoSum** button. Compare your screen with Figure 3.2.

The *SUM function* that you have used is a predefined formula that adds all the numbers in a selected range of cells. You can also insert the SUM function from the Math & Trig button.

Figure 3.2

AutoSum button   Formulas tab selected   Worksheet titles formatted

Function Library group

SUM function started in cell

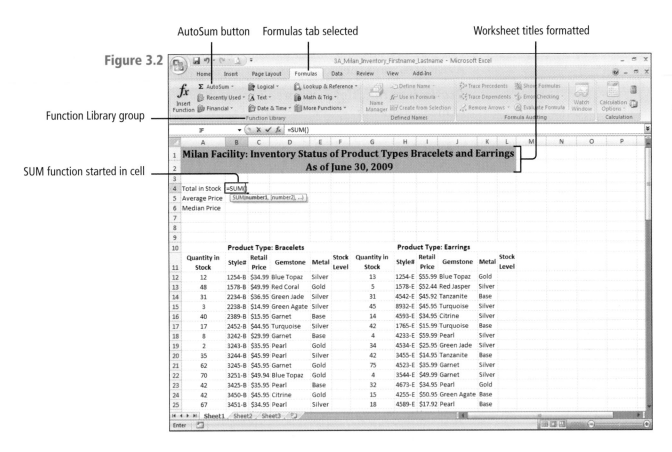

5 With the insertion point blinking in the function, select the range **A12:A66**, dragging downward as necessary, and then press Enter. Scroll up to view the top of your worksheet, and notice your result in cell **B4**, *1657*. Click cell **B4**, look at the **Formula Bar**, and compare your screen with Figure 3.3.

The values in parentheses are the **arguments**—the values that an Excel function uses to perform calculations or operations. In this instance, the argument consists of the values in the range A12:A66.

Argument in parentheses

Figure 3.3

SUM function in Formula Bar

Number of Bracelets in stock

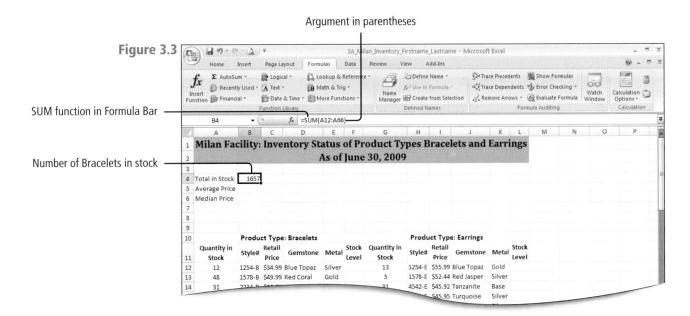

6 Click cell **B5**. In the **Function Library group**, click the **More Functions** button, point to **Statistical**, in the displayed list, point to **AVERAGE**, and then compare your screen with Figure 3.4.

Statistical functions are pre-written formulas that analyze a group of measurements.

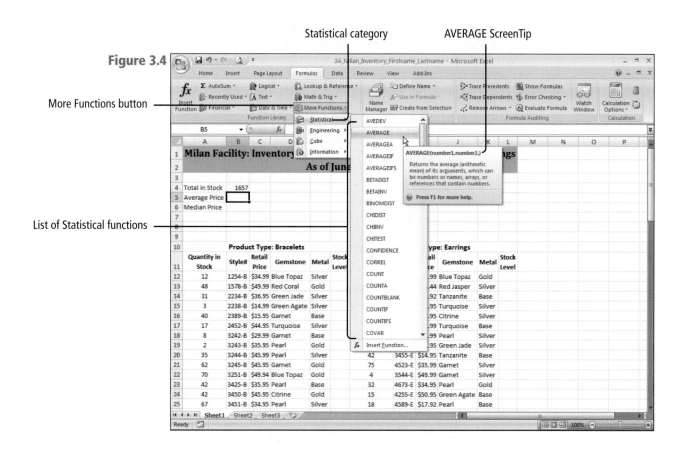

Figure 3.4

More Functions button

List of Statistical functions

Statistical category

AVERAGE ScreenTip

7 Click **AVERAGE**, and then if necessary, drag the title bar of the **Function Arguments** dialog box down and to the right so you can view the **Formula Bar** and cell **B5**.

The Function Arguments dialog box for the AVERAGE function displays. The *AVERAGE function* is a formula that adds a group of values, and then divides the result by the number of values in the group.

In the cell, the Formula Bar, and the dialog box, Excel proposes to average the value in cell B4. Recall that Excel functions will propose a range if data is above or to the left of a selected cell. Because you want to average the values in the range C12:C66—and *not* cell B4— you must edit the proposed range.

8 In the **Function Arguments** dialog box, click in the **Number1** box to display the insertion point. Delete the existing text, type **c12:c66** and then compare your screen with Figure 3.5.

The result displays in the dialog box.

Figure 3.5

Formula Bar displays function and argument

Range of cells to average

Function Arguments dialog box for AVERAGE function

Result displays

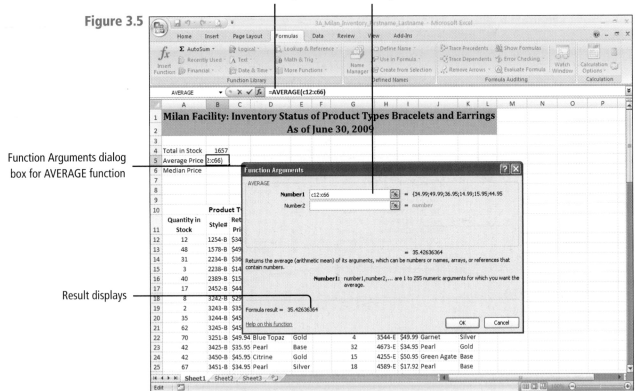

9 In the **Function Arguments** dialog box, click **OK**.

The result indicates that the average Retail Price of all Bracelets is $35.43.

10 Click cell **B6**. In the **Function Library group**, click the **More Functions** button, display the list of **Statistical** functions, scroll down as necessary, and then click **MEDIAN**.

The **MEDIAN function** is a statistical function commonly used to describe a group of data—you have likely seen it used to describe the price of houses in a particular geographical area. The MEDIAN function finds the *middle value* that has as many values *above* it in the group as are *below* it. It differs from AVERAGE in that the result is not affected as much by a single value that is greatly different from the others.

11 In the displayed **Function Arguments** dialog box, to the right of the **Number1** box, click the **Collapse Dialog** button —the square with the red arrow.

The dialog box collapses to a small size containing only space for the first argument. With the dialog box collapsed, you can see more of your worksheet data.

12 Select the range **C12:C66**, and then compare your screen with Figure 3.6.

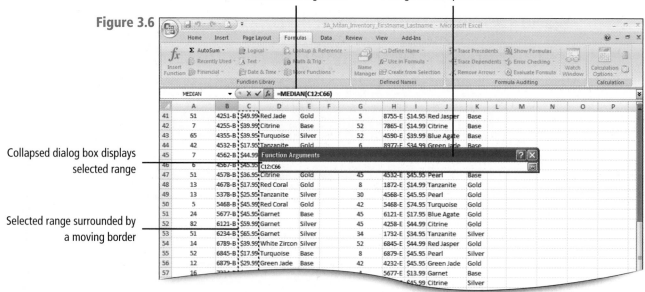

Formula Bar displays
function and argument

Dialog box collapsed to a small size

Figure 3.6

Collapsed dialog box displays
selected range

Selected range surrounded by
a moving border

13 Press Enter.

The dialog box expands to its original size and the selected range displays as the argument in the Number1 box. When entering arguments into a Function Arguments dialog box, you can either select the range of cells in this manner, or type the range into the argument box.

14 In the lower right corner of the **Function Arguments** dialog box, click **OK**. **Save** your workbook.

Your result is *$35.95*—in the range of prices, $35.95 is the middle value. Half of all Bracelet products are priced *above* $35.95 and half are priced *below* $35.95.

15 Select the range **A4:A6**, right-click over the selection, and then from the displayed shortcut menu, click **Copy**. Point to cell **G4**, right-click, and then click **Paste**. Press Esc to cancel the moving border.

16 Scroll to the bottom of your worksheet and notice that the **Earrings** product type ends in **row 61**. Then, in cell **H4**, use the technique you just practiced to **SUM** the total number of **Earrings** in stock. In cell **H5**, use the **AVERAGE** function to display the average **Retail Price** of the **Earrings** product type. In cell **H6**, use the **MEDIAN** function to display the median value of the **Retail Price** for **Earrings**.

17 Select cells **B4** and **H4**, apply **Comma Style** with **zero decimal places**, click any cell to deselect, and then compare your screen with Figure 3.7.

Figure 3.7

Comma style applied

Functions used to calculate
Earrings product information

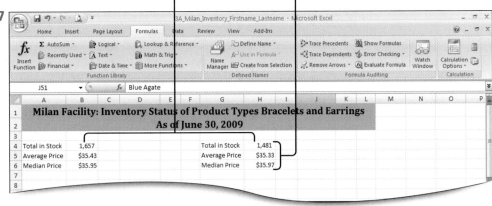

18 Save 🖫 your workbook.

Activity 3.2 Using the MIN and MAX Functions

The **MIN function** determines the smallest value in a selected range of values. The **MAX function** determines the largest value in a selected range of values.

1 In cell **A7**, type **Lowest Price** and then in cell **A8**, type **Highest Price**

2 Click cell **B7**. On the **Formulas tab**, in the **Function Library group**, click the **More Functions** button, display the list of **Statistical** functions, scroll as necessary, and then click **MIN**. At the right end of the **Number1** box, click the **Collapse Dialog** button �️, select the range **C12:C66**, and then press Enter. Click **OK**.

The lowest retail price in the Bracelets product group is *$14.95*.

3 In cell **B8**, using a similar technique, insert the **MAX** function to determine the highest **Retail Price** in the **Bracelets** product type.

The highest Retail Price in the Bracelets product type is *$65.95*.

4 Copy the range **A7:A8** and paste it in cell **G7**. Then in cells **H7** and **H8**, use the **MIN** and **MAX** functions to calculate the lowest and highest **Retail Price** for products in the **Earrings** product type. Compare your screen with Figure 3.8.

Figure 3.8

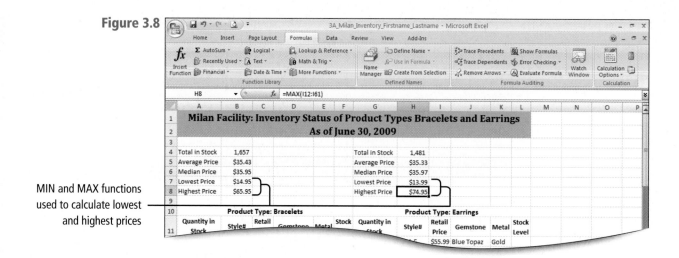

MIN and MAX functions
used to calculate lowest
and highest prices

5 **Save** the changes you have made to your workbook.

Another Way ── **To Insert a Function**

There are several ways to begin a function in Excel. Because the functions are grouped into categories such as *Financial*, *Logical* and so on, it is efficient to locate and insert functions from the Function Library. You can also click the Insert Function button ƒx on the Formula Bar; or, type = in the cell, type the first letter of the function, and then select the function from the list that displays. This feature is called *Formula AutoComplete*. You can also copy a similar function from another cell and edit the arguments within the cell or on the Formula Bar. Finally, you can access the Insert Function dialog box by selecting Insert Function from any of the displayed menus in the Function Library group or by pressing Shift + F3 .

Activity 3.3 Moving Data, Adding Borders, and Rotating Text

Recall that you can select and move a range of cells containing formulas or functions (prewritten formulas). Use borders to emphasize a range of cells—bordered data draws the reader's eye to a specific portion of a worksheet. Similarly, use rotated text to draw attention to data on your worksheet.

1 Select the range **A4:B8**. Point to the right edge of the selected range to display the pointer, and then compare your screen with Figure 3.9.

Figure 3.9

Move pointer

Selected range

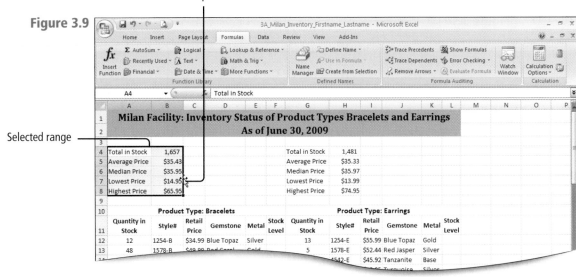

2 Drag the selected range to the right until the ScreenTip displays *C4:D8*, and then release the mouse button. Select **columns C:D**, and then apply **AutoFit** to adjust the column widths. Then, use the same technique to move the range **G4:H8** to the range **I4:J8**. Select **columns I:J**, and then apply **AutoFit**.

3 Select the nonadjacent ranges **C4:D8** and **I4:J8**, right-click to display the Mini toolbar, and then apply **Bold** **B** and a **Thick Box Border** ⊞▾.

4 In cell **A6**, type **Bracelets** Select the range **A5:A7**, right-click over the selection, and then from the shortcut menu, click **Format Cells**. In the displayed **Format Cells** dialog box, click the **Alignment tab**. Under **Text control**, select the **Merge cells** check box.

5 In the upper right portion of the dialog box, under **Orientation**, point to the **red diamond**, and then drag the diamond upward until the **Degrees** box indicates **30**. Alternatively, type the number of degrees directly into the Degrees box. Compare your screen with Figure 3.10.

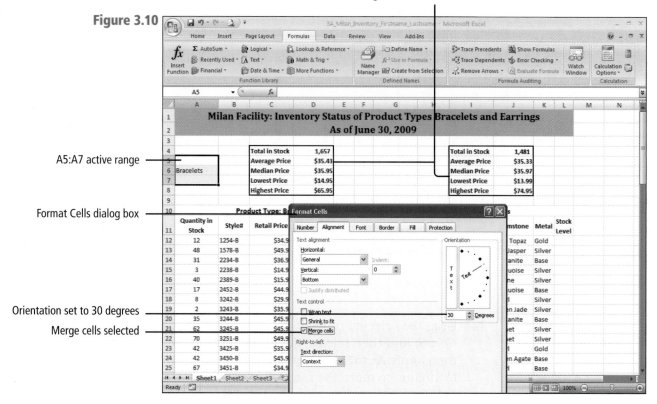

Range of cells moved and formatted

Figure 3.10

A5:A7 active range

Format Cells dialog box

Orientation set to 30 degrees

Merge cells selected

6 In the lower right corner of the **Format Cells** dialog box, click **OK**. With the merged cell still selected, display the Mini toolbar, change the **Font Size** 11 ▾ to **12**, and then apply **Bold** **B** and **Italic** **I**. On the **Home tab**, in the **Alignment group**, apply **Center** ☰ alignment and **Middle Align** ☰.

7 In cell **G5** type **Earrings** Point to the merged cell **A5** and right-click. On the Mini toolbar, click the **Format Painter** button ✍, and then click cell **G5** to copy the formatting. Compare your screen with Figure 3.11.

Text rotated and formatted

Figure 3.11

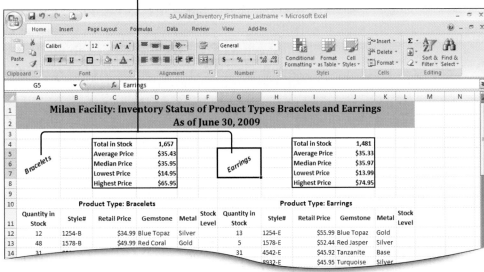

8 **Save** 💾 your workbook.

Objective 2
Use COUNTIF and IF Functions, and Apply Conditional Formatting

Recall that statistical functions analyze a group of measurements. Another group of Excel functions, referred to as **logical functions**, test for specific conditions. Logical functions typically use conditional tests to determine whether specified conditions—called **criteria**—are true or false.

Activity 3.4 Using the COUNTIF Function

The **COUNTIF function** counts the number of cells within a range that meet the given condition—the criteria that you provide. The COUNTIF function has two arguments—the range of cells to check and the criteria.

Rose has learned that Adamantine's pearl bracelets and earrings will be featured on an upcoming segment of a TV shopping channel in Italy. In this activity, you will use the COUNTIF function to determine the number of pearl styles currently available in inventory.

1 From the **row heading area**, point to **row 10**, and then right-click. From the shortcut menu, click **Insert**. Press F4 two times to repeat the last action and thus insert three blank rows. Click cell **D4**, look at the **Formula Bar**, and then notice that the arguments of the **SUM** function adjusted and refer to **rows 15:69**.

The referenced range updates to A15:A69 after you insert the three new rows. In this manner, Excel adjusts the cell references in a formula relative to their new locations.

2 In cell **A10**, type **Pearl Styles Available:** and then press Enter. Copy cell **A10**, and then paste it to cell **G10**. Press Esc to cancel the moving border.

3 Click cell **A11**. On the **Formulas tab**, in the **Function Library group**, click the **More Functions** button, and then display the list of **Statistical** functions. Click **COUNTIF**.

Recall that the COUNTIF function counts the number of cells within a range that meet the given condition.

4 In the **Range** box, click the **Collapse Dialog** button [icon], select the range **D15:D69**, and then press Enter. Click in the **Criteria** box, type **Pearl** and then compare your screen with Figure 3.12.

Function displays
in Formula Bar   Range indicated as *D15:D69*

Figure 3.12

Function Arguments dialog box

Criteria indicated as *Pearl*

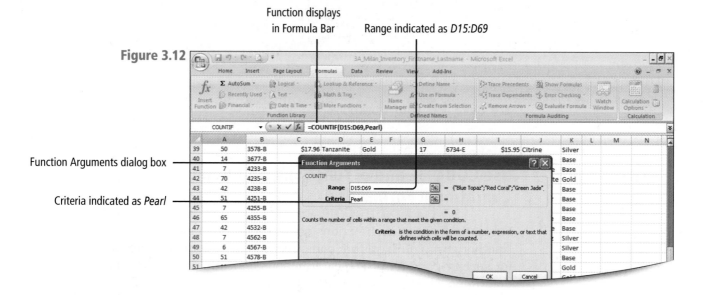

5 In the lower right corner of the **Function Arguments** dialog box, click **OK**.

Five different styles of Pearl bracelets are available to feature on the TV show.

6 Using the technique you just practiced, in cell **G11**, count the number of **Pearl** styles available in the **Earrings** product type.

Ten different styles of Pearl earrings are available to feature on the TV show.

7 Select cells **A11** and **G11**, and then on the **Home tab**, in the **Alignment group**, click the **Align Text Left** button [icon].

8 **Save** [icon] your workbook.

Activity 3.5 Using the IF Function and Applying Conditional Formatting

A **logical test** is any value or expression that can be evaluated as being true or false. The **IF function** uses a logical test to check whether a condition is met, and then returns one value if true, and another value if false. For example, *C8=100* is an expression that can be evaluated as true or false. If the value in cell C8 is equal to 100, the expression is true. If the value in cell C8 is not 100, the expression is false.

In this activity, you will use the IF function to determine the inventory stock levels and determine if more products should be ordered.

1 Click cell **F15**. On the **Formulas tab**, in the **Function Library group**, click the **Logical** button, and then in the displayed list, click **IF**. If necessary, drag the title bar of the displayed **Function Arguments** dialog box up so that you can view **row 15** on your screen.

2 With the insertion point in the **Logical_test** box, click cell **A15**, and then type **<40**

This logical test will look at the value in cell A15, the value of which is *12*, and then determine if the number is less than 40. The expression *<40* includes the *<* **comparison operator**, which means *less than*. Comparison operators compare values.

3 Take a moment to examine the table in Figure 3.13 for a list of comparison operator symbols and their definitions.

Comparison Operators

Comparison Operator Symbol	Definition
=	Equal to
>	Greater than
<	Less than
>=	Greater than or equal to
<=	Less than or equal to
<>	Not equal to

Figure 3.13

4 Press [Tab] to move the insertion point to the **Value_if_true** box, and then type **Order**

If the result of the logical test is true—the Quantity in Stock is less than 40—the cell will display the text *Order* indicating that additional product must be ordered.

5 Press [Tab] to move the insertion point to the **Value_if_false** box, type **OK** and then compare your dialog box with Figure 3.14.

If the result of the logical test is false—the Quantity in Stock is *not* less than 40—then Excel will display *OK* in the cell.

Value if true (less than 40) will indicate *Order*

Figure 3.14

Logical test will determine if
value in A15 is less than 40

Value if false (40 or more)
will indicate *OK*

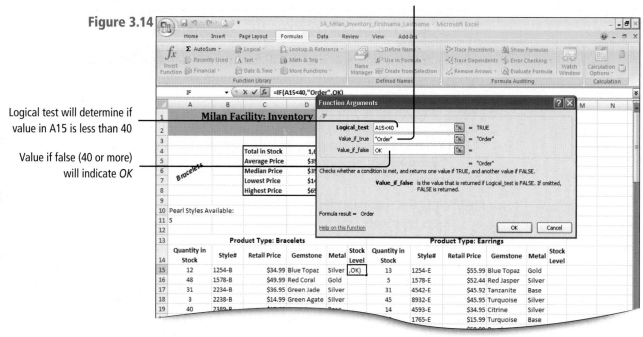

6 Click **OK** to display the result *Order* in cell **F15**. Then, using the fill handle, copy the function down through cell **F69**. Look at cell **A19**, and then look at cell **F19** and notice that the **Stock Level** is indicated as *OK*.

The comparison operator indicated <40 (less than 40) and thus a value of *exactly* 40 is indicated as OK.

7 Click cell **L15**, and then using the technique you just practiced and a quantity *less than* 40, conduct a logical test on the quantities of **Earrings** in stock. Then, scroll to the upper portion of your worksheet, click cell **L15**, look at the **Formula Bar**, and then compare your screen with Figure 3.15.

Note

You can also copy the function in cell F15 to cell L15 and the cell references will adjust accordingly.

Figure 3.15

Formula Bar displays formula

Stock Level status indicated for Earrings

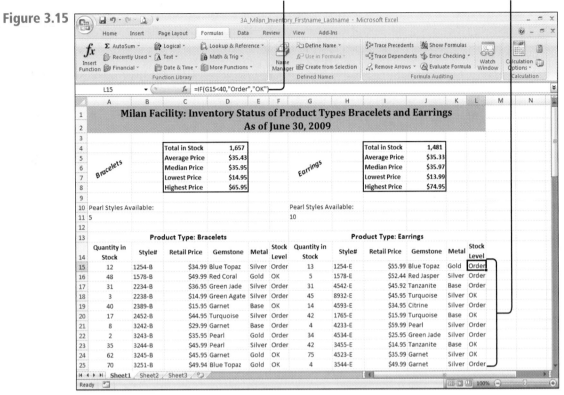

8 **Save** your workbook.

Activity 3.6 Applying Conditional Formatting Using Custom Formats and Data Bars

A *conditional format* changes the appearance of a cell range based on a condition—a criteria. If the condition is true, the cell range is formatted based on that condition; if the condition is false, the cell range is *not* formatted based on the condition. In this activity, you will use conditional formatting as another way to draw attention to the Stock Level of products.

1 Select the range **F15:F69**. On the **Home tab**, in the **Styles group**, click the **Conditional Formatting** button. In the displayed list, point to **Highlight Cells Rules**, and then click **Text that Contains**. In the **Text That Contains** dialog box, with the insertion point blinking in the first box, type **Order** In the second box, click the arrow, and then in the displayed list, click **Custom Format**.

The Format Cells dialog box displays. Here you can select any combination of formats to apply to the cell if the condition is true. The custom format that you specify will be applied to any cell in the selected range if it contains the specific text *Order*.

2 In the displayed **Format Cells** dialog box, on the **Font tab**, under **Font style**, click **Bold Italic**. Click the **Color arrow**, and then under **Theme Colors**, click **Dark Blue, Text 2, Darker 25%**. In the lower right corner of the **Format Cells** dialog box, click **OK**. Compare your screen with Figure 3.16.

Within the selected range, if the cell meets the condition of containing *Order*, the font color will change to Bold Italic, Dark Blue, Text 2 Darker 25%.

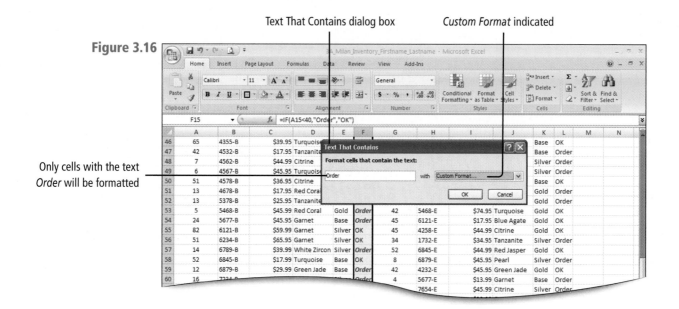

Text That Contains dialog box   *Custom Format* indicated

Figure 3.16

Only cells with the text *Order* will be formatted

3 In the **Text That Contains** dialog box, click **OK** to apply the conditional formatting.

4 Select the range **A15:A69**. In the **Styles group**, click the **Conditional Formatting** button. In the displayed list, point to **Data Bars**, and then in the displayed gallery, click **Orange Data Bar**.

A ***data bar*** provides a visual cue to the reader about the value of a cell relative to other cells. The length of the data bar represents the value in the cell. A longer bar represents a higher value and a shorter bar represents a lower value. Data bars are useful to quickly identify higher and lower numbers within a large group of data, such as very high or very low levels of inventory.

5 Using the techniques you just practiced, apply the same conditional formatting to the *Stock Level* column for the **Earrings** product type, and then apply the same data bars to indicate the *Quantity of Stock* in inventory. Press Ctrl + Home to make cell **A1** the active cell, and then compare your screen with Figure 3.17.

Figure 3.17

Conditional font formatting applied to *Order*

Data bars applied to stock quantities

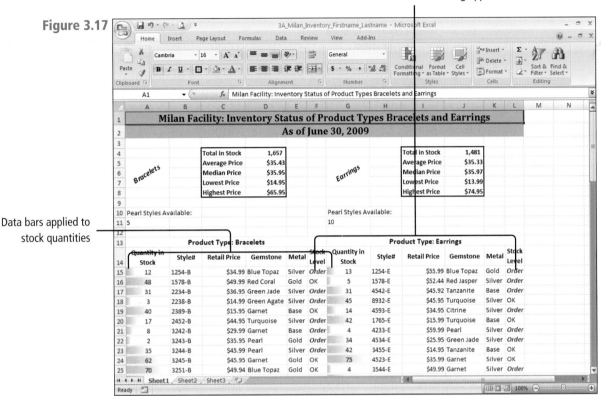

◻ **Save** 💾 your workbook.

More Knowledge

Use Format Painter to Copy Conditional Formatting

You can also use Format Painter to apply the same conditional formatting from one range of cells to another.

Activity 3.7 Using Find and Replace

The **Find and Replace** feature searches the cells in a worksheet—or in a selected range—for matches, and then replaces each match with a replacement value of your choice.

Rose was just informed that because a quality grade of Tanzanite was not readily available for manufacturing, the pieces listed as having a gemstone of Tanzanite were actually set with Peridot. In this activity, you will replace all occurrences of *Tanzanite* with *Peridot*.

◻ To the left of the **Formula Bar**, click in the **Name Box**, type **d15:d69,j15:j64** and then press Enter. Alternatively, select the nonadjacent ranges of Gemstones with your mouse pointer.

The range of cells that contains the gemstone names for both product types is selected. Restrict the find and replace operation to a specific range if there is a possibility that the name occurs elsewhere in the worksheet.

2 On the **Home tab**, in the **Editing group**, click the **Find & Select** button, and then click **Replace**.

3 In the displayed **Find and Replace** dialog box, in the **Find what** box, type **Tanzanite** In the **Replace with** box type **Peridot** and then compare your screen with Figure 3.18.

Find *Tanzanite*

Find & Select button in the Editing group

Figure 3.18

Replace with *Peridot*

Replace All button

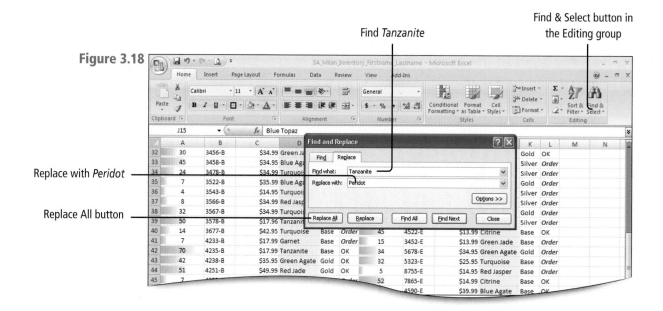

4 Click the **Replace All** button. In the displayed message box, notice that *12 replacements* were made, and then click **OK**. In the lower right corner of the **Find and Replace** dialog box, click the **Close** button. Click any cell to deselect the ranges.

5 **Save** 🖫 your workbook.

Objective 3
Use a Date Function

Excel can obtain the date and time from the computer's calendar and clock and display this information on your worksheet.

Activity 3.8 Using the NOW Function

The **NOW function** retrieves the date and time from your computer's calendar and clock and inserts the information into the selected cell. The result is formatted as a date and time, rather than in the sequential number that Excel uses for dates. This feature is useful to date stamp a worksheet to record when it was last edited.

1 Scroll down to view **row 71**. Click cell **A71**, type **Last Edited by Rose Elleni** and then press Enter.

2 With cell **A72** as the active cell, on the **Formulas tab**, in the **Function Library group**, click the **Date & Time** button. In the displayed list of functions, click **NOW**. Compare your screen with Figure 3.19.

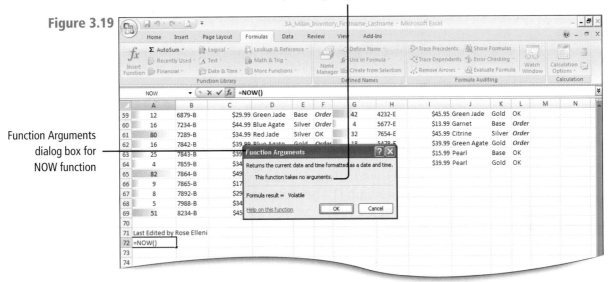

No specific arguments for this function

Figure 3.19

Function Arguments dialog box for NOW function

3 Take a moment to read the description in the displayed **Function Arguments** dialog box, and notice that this result is *Volatile*.

The Function Arguments dialog box displays a message indicating that this function does not require an argument. It also states that this function is **volatile**, meaning the date and time will not remain as entered, but rather the date and time will be updated each time you open this workbook.

4 In the **Function Arguments** dialog box, click **OK** to close the dialog box to display the current date and time in cell **A72**.

5 **Save** your workbook.

Note — NOW Function Recalculates When the Workbook Opens

The NOW function places a sequential number in the cell that corresponds to the date and time at the moment. The NOW function updates this number each time the workbook is opened. If you open a workbook with the NOW function in it and then close the workbook, you will see a message that asks if you want to save the changes. The change to which this message refers is the new date that has been inserted by the NOW function. With the workbook open, you can force the NOW function to update by pressing F9, for example, to update the time.

Objective 4
Freeze Panes and Create an Excel Table

By freezing or splitting panes, you can view two areas of a worksheet and lock rows and columns in one area. When you freeze panes, you select the specific rows or columns that you want to remain visible when scrolling in your worksheet.

To analyze a group of related data, you can convert a range of cells to an **Excel table**. An Excel table is a series of rows and columns that contains related data that is managed independently from the data in other rows and columns in the worksheet.

Activity 3.9 Freezing and Unfreezing Panes

In a large worksheet, if you scroll down more than 25 rows or scroll beyond column O (the exact row number and column letter varies, depending on your screen resolution), you will no longer see the top rows of your worksheet where identifying information about the data is usually placed. You will likely find it easier to work with your data if you can always view the identifying row or column titles.

The **Freeze Panes** command enables you to select one or more rows or columns and freeze (lock) them into place. The locked rows and columns become separate panes. A **pane** is a portion of a worksheet window bounded by and separated from other portions by vertical or horizontal bars.

1 Press Ctrl + Home to make cell **A1** the active cell. Scroll down until **row 40** displays at the top of your screen, and notice that all of the identifying information in the column titles is out of view.

2 Press Ctrl + Home again, and then select **row 15**. Click the **View tab**, and then in the **Window group**, click the **Freeze Panes** button. In the displayed list, click **Freeze Panes**. Click any cell to deselect, and then notice that a line displays along the upper border of **row 15**.

By selecting row 15, the rows above—rows 1–14—are frozen (locked) in place and will not move as you scroll down the worksheet.

3 Watch the row numbers below **row 14**, and then begin to scroll down to bring **row 40** into view again. Compare your screen with Figure 3.20.

Rows 1:14 remain frozen in place and the remaining rows of data continue to scroll. Use this feature when you have long or wide worksheets.

Freeze Panes button in Window group

Figure 3.20

Freeze Panes command
freezes rows 1-14

Row 40 in view

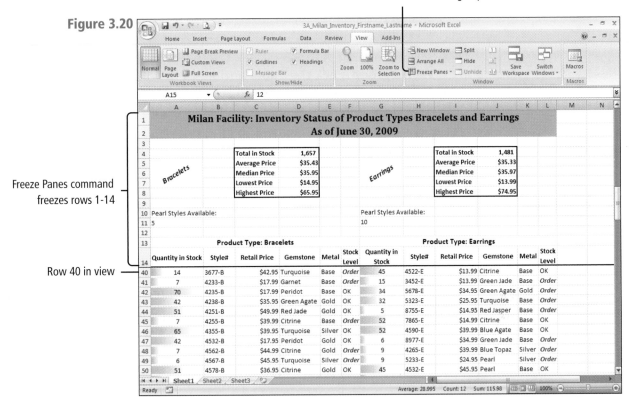

4 In the **Window group**, click the **Freeze Panes** button, and then click **Unfreeze Panes** to unlock all rows and columns.

5 **Save** your workbook.

More Knowledge

Freeze Columns or Freeze both Rows and Columns

You can freeze columns that you want to remain in view on the left. Select the column to the right of the column(s) that you want to remain in view while scrolling to the left, and then click the Freeze Panes Command. You can also use the command to freeze both rows and columns; click a *cell* to freeze the rows *above* the cell and the columns to the *left* of the cell.

Activity 3.10 Sorting and Filtering In an Excel Table

Recall that an Excel table is a series of rows and columns with related data that can be managed independently from the data in other rows and columns. For example, in your 3A_Milan_Inventory workbook, you have data for two product types—*Bracelets* and *Earrings*.

To manage several groups of data, you can insert more than one table in the same worksheet. In Activities 3.10 and 3.11, you will create an Excel table for each of the two product types, and then work with each set of data independently of the other.

1 Press (Ctrl) + (Home) to make cell **A1** the active cell. Be sure that you have applied the Unfreeze Panes command—no rows on your worksheet are locked.

2 Select the range **A14:F69**. Click the **Insert tab**, and then in the **Tables group**, click the **Table** button. In the displayed **Create Table** dialog box, if necessary, click to select the **My table has headers** check box, and then compare your screen with Figure 3.21.

The column titles in row 14 will form the table headers.

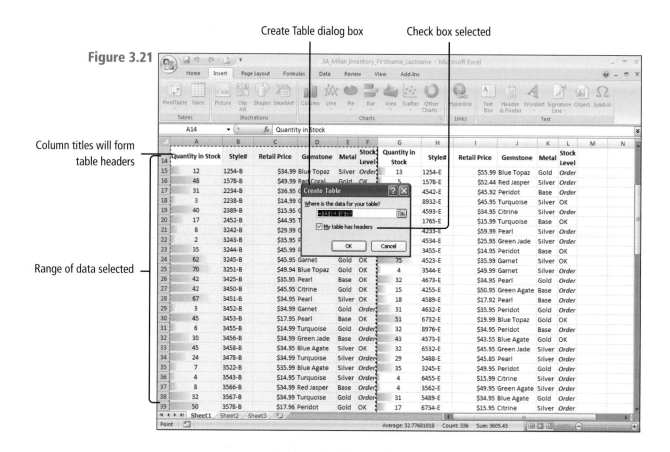

Create Table dialog box   Check box selected

Figure 3.21

Column titles will form table headers

Range of data selected

3 In the **Create Table** dialog box, click **OK**. With the range still selected, on the Ribbon notice that the **Table Tools** are active. On

the **Design tab**, in the **Table Styles group**, click the **More** button ⬇, and then under **Light**, locate and click **Table Style Light 16**. Press (Ctrl) + (Home) to make cell **A1** the active cell and to cancel the selection, and then compare your screen with Figure 3.22.

Sorting and filtering arrows display in the table's header row. You can sort tables in ascending or descending order or by color. You can filter tables to show only the data that meets the criteria that you specify, or you can filter by color.

Figure 3.22

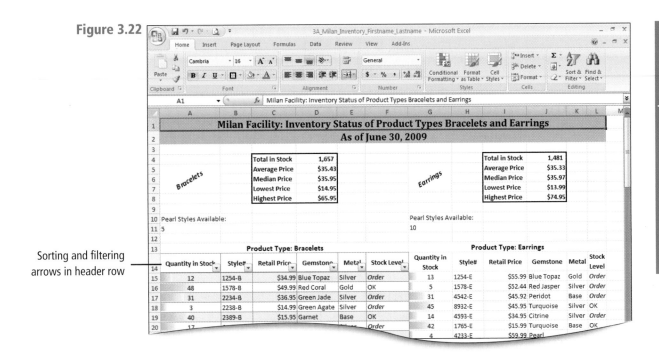

Sorting and filtering
arrows in header row

4 In the header row of the table, click the **Retail Price arrow**, and
then from the displayed menu, click **Sort Smallest to Largest**. Next
to the arrow, notice the small **up arrow** indicating the sort.

The rows in the table, which includes only columns A:F, are sorted
from the lowest retail price to highest retail price. Cells in the same
rows in columns G:L are not affected by the sort because the table
feature isolates the table cells and treats them independently of
other cells outside of the table.

5 In the header row of the table, click the **Gemstone arrow**. From the
displayed menu, click **Sort A to Z**. Next to the arrow, notice the
small **up arrow** indicating an ascending (A to Z) sort.

The rows in the table are sorted alphabetically by Gemstone.

6 Click the **Gemstone arrow** again, and then sort from **Z to A**.

The rows in the table are sorted in reverse alphabetic order by
Gemstone name, and the small arrow points downward, indicating a
descending (Z to A) sort.

7 Click the **Gemstone arrow** again. On the displayed menu, click the
(Select All) check box to clear all the check boxes. Click to select
only the **Pearl** check box, and then click **OK**. Compare your screen
with Figure 3.23.

Only the rows containing *Pearl* in the Gemstone column display, and
the remaining rows are hidden from view. A small funnel in the
Gemstone arrow indicates that a filter is applied to the data in the
table. Additionally, the row numbers display in blue to indicate that
some rows are hidden from view. A filter hides the entire row in the
worksheet.

Only bracelets that have *Pearl* as the gemstone display

Figure 3.23

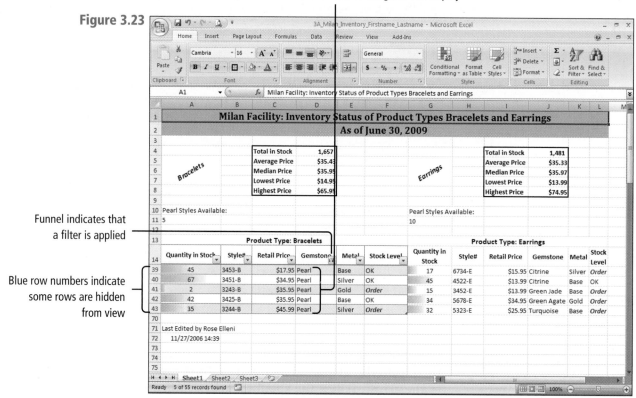

Funnel indicates that a filter is applied

Blue row numbers indicate some rows are hidden from view

---

8 Click any cell in the table so that the table is selected. On the Ribbon, click the **Design tab**, and then in the **Table Style Options group**, click to select the **Total Row** check box.

Total displays in cell A70, and in cell F70, the number *5* indicates that five rows are currently displayed.

9 Click cell **A70**, click the arrow that displays to the right of cell A70, and then in the displayed list, click **Sum**.

Excel sums only the visible rows in Column A, and indicates that *191* bracelets containing the Gemstone *Pearl* are in stock. In this manner, you can use an Excel table to quickly find information about a group of data.

10 Click cell **A11**, type **Five styles, 191 total in stock** and then press Enter.

11 In the table header row, click the **Gemstone arrow**, and then in the displayed menu, click **Clear Filter From "Gemstone"**.

All the rows in the table redisplay. The Z to A sort on Gemstone remains in effect.

12 Click the **Metal arrow**, click the **(Select All)** check box to clear all the check boxes, and then click to select the **Gold** check box. Click **OK**. Click the **Gemstone arrow**, click the **(Select All)** check box to clear all the check boxes, and then click the **Red Coral** check box. Click **OK**, and then compare your screen with Figure 3.24.

By applying multiple filters, Rose can quickly determine that among the Bracelets product type, four styles have a Red Coral gemstone in a Gold setting and there are 117 total in stock.

Four bracelet styles have *Red Coral* as *Gemstone* and *Gold* as *Metal*

Figure 3.24

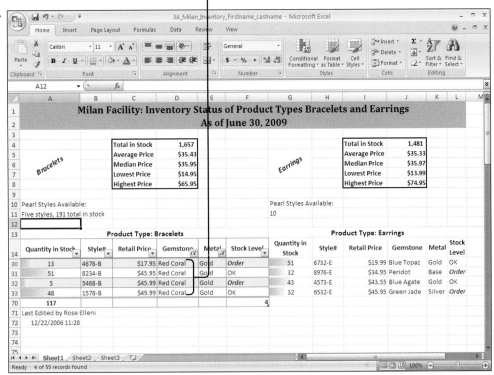

13 Click the **Gemstone arrow**, and then click **Clear Filter from "Gemstone"**. Use the same technique to remove the filter from the **Metal** column.

14 In the table header row, click the **Style# arrow**, and then click **Sort A to Z**, which will apply an ascending sort to the *Style#* column.

15 **Save** the changes to your workbook.

Activity 3.11 Inserting a Second Table in a Worksheet

In this activity, you will format the product information for *Earrings* as a table.

1 Select the range **G14:L64**. On the **Insert tab**, in the **Tables group**, click the **Table** button. Be sure the **My table has headers** check box is selected, and then click **OK**. In the **Table Styles group**, click the

More button , and then under **Light**, click **Table Style Light 18**. Press Ctrl + Home, and then compare your screen with Figure 3.25.

Figure 3.25

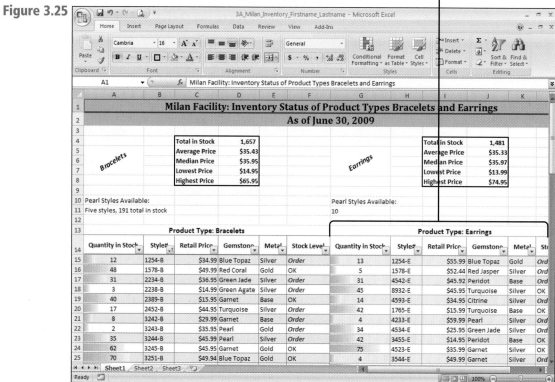

2 In the **Earrings** table, in cell **J14**, click the **Gemstone arrow**, click the **(Select All)** check box to clear all the check boxes, and then click the **Pearl** check box. Click **OK**. Scroll down and to the right as necessary so that you can view the table on your screen.

In the worksheet, rows within the Earrings table that do not contain *Pearl* as the gemstone are hidden.

3 Click any cell in the **Earrings** table to select the table, click the **Design tab**, and then in the **Table Style Options group**, click to select the **Total Row** check box.

Total displays in cell G65, and in cell L65, the number *10* indicates that ten rows are currently displayed.

4 Click cell **G65**, click the arrow that displays to the right of cell G65, and then in the displayed list, click **Sum**. Compare your screen with Figure 3.26.

Excel sums only the visible rows in Column G, and indicates that *309* earrings containing the Gemstone *Pearl* are in stock. Recall that in this manner, you can use an Excel table to quickly find information about a group of data.

Figure 3.26

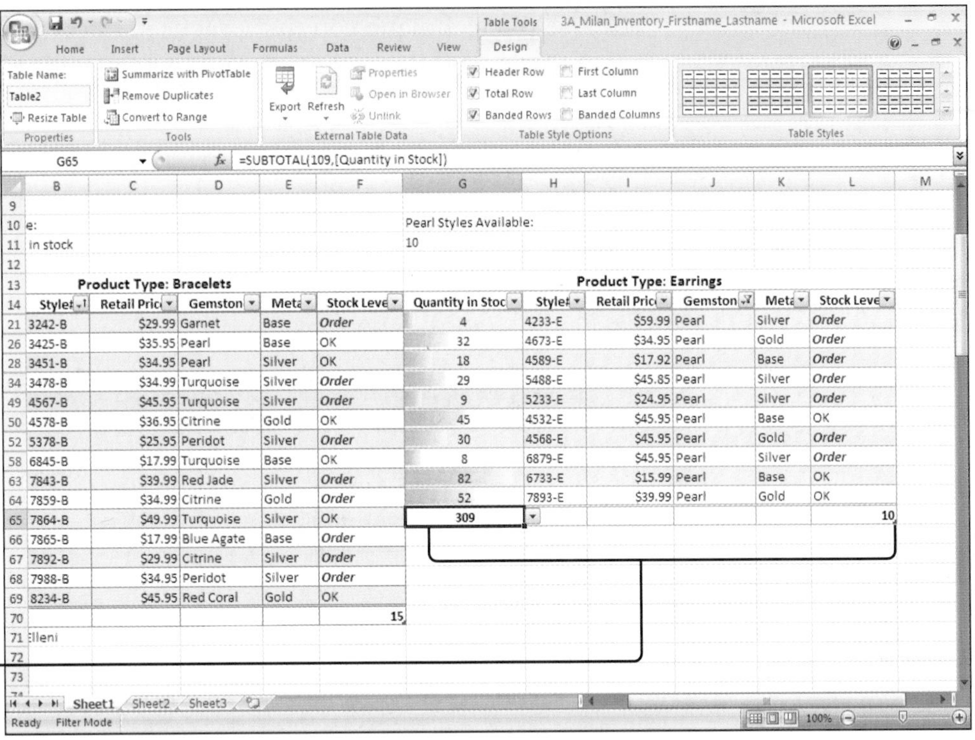

309 total Pearl earrings
in stock; 10 Pearl styles

5 Click cell **G11**, type **Ten styles, 309 total pairs in stock** and then press Enter.

6 In the table header row, click the **Gemstone arrow**, and then in the displayed menu, click **Clear Filter From "Gemstone"** to redisplay all the rows in the table.

7 In the table header row of the **Earrings** table, click the **Style# arrow**, and then click **Sort A to Z**, which will apply an ascending sort to the **Style#** column.

8 **Save** the changes to your workbook.

Activity 3.12 Converting a Table to a Range of Data

When you are finished answering questions about the data in a table by sorting, filtering, and totaling, you no longer need the table. You can remove a table by converting it back to a normal range.

1 Click anywhere in the **Bracelets** table to activate the table and display the **Table Tools** on the Ribbon.

2 On the **Design tab**, in the **Tools group**, click the **Convert to Range** button. In the displayed message box, click **Yes**.

The list arrows are removed from the column titles; the color and shading formats applied from the table style remain.

3 Use the technique you just practiced to convert the **Earrings** table to a range, and then compare your screen with Figure 3.27.

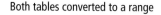
Both tables converted to a range

Figure 3.27

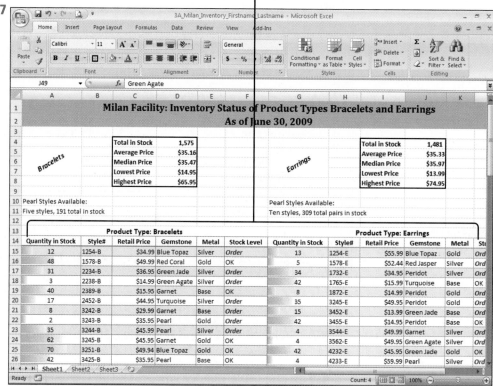

4 **Save** your workbook.

More Knowledge

To Remove Shading Formats from a Table

If you do not want to retain the shading and other formats applied from a table style, apply the *None* table style before converting back to a range.

Objective 5
Format and Print a Large Worksheet

A large worksheet will be too wide, too long—or both—to print on a single page. To make reading multiple printed pages easier, Excel features let you print row and column headings on each page of a worksheet.

Activity 3.13 Printing Large Worksheets

In this activity, you will adjust the columns widths, change the Page Layout so that column titles display on every page, and print the worksheet.

1 Hold down Ctrl, select the nonadjacent **columns C** and **I**, and then set their width to **90 pixels**. Select **column A**, hold down Ctrl and select columns **D**, **G**, and **J**, and then set their width to **80 pixels**. Select **column B**, hold down Ctrl and select **column H**, and then set their width to **70 pixels**.

2 Select **columns E**, **F**, **K**, and **L** and set their width to **55 pixels**. Select the range **A72:B72**, right-click, click **Format Cells**, and then on the **Alignment tab** of the **Format Cells** dialog box, under **Text control**, select the **Merge cells** check box. Click **OK**.

The merged cell is widened so that it can display the result of the NOW function that it contains.

3 Select the column titles in **Row 14**, and then on the **Home tab,** in the **Alignment group**, click the **Wrap Text** button ⊟. Look at the column titles in Row 14 and either verify that the the full column titles display in each cell, or if necessary, click the **Wrap Text** button again so that the full titles display.

4 Press Ctrl + Home to display the top of your worksheet.

5 On the **Insert tab**, in the **Text group**, click **Header & Footer** to switch to **Page Layout view**. In the **Navigation group**, click the **Go to Footer** button, click just above the word *Footer*, and then in the **Header & Footer Elements group**, click the **File Name** button. Click a cell just above the footer to deselect the **Footer area** and view your file name.

6 Click the **Page Layout tab**. In the **Page Setup group**, click the **Orientation** button, and then click **Landscape**. In the same group, click the **Print Titles** button. Under **Print titles**, click in the **Rows to repeat at top** box, and then at the right, click the **Collapse Dialog** button ⊞. From the **row heading area**, select **rows 13:14**, and then compare your screen with Figure 3.28.

Collapsed dialog box displays
the row numbers as an absolute reference

Figure 3.28

Rows 13 and 14 selected;
surrounded by moving border

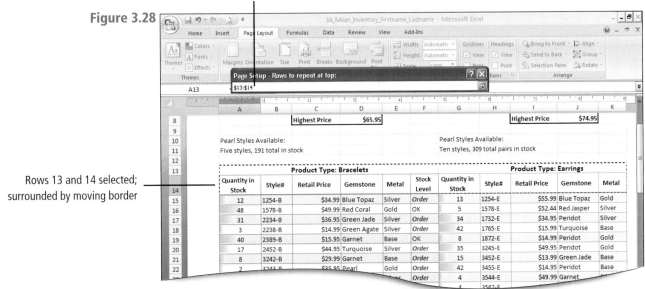

7 Press Enter, and then in the displayed **Page Setup** dialog box, click the **Margins tab**. Under **Center on page**, select the **Horizontally** check box, and then click **OK**. Delete the unused sheets **Sheet2** and **Sheet3**. On the right edge of the status bar, click the **Normal** button ▦, and then press Ctrl + Home to display the top of your worksheet.

8 From the **Office** menu 🗔, point to **Print**, and then click **Print Preview**. Notice that the *Earrings Stock Level* column does not display. In the **Preview Group**, click **Next Page** several times and notice that the *Stock Level column* displays on separate pages. Close the **Print Preview**.

9 On the **Page Layout tab**, in the **Scale to Fit group**, click the **Width button arrow**, and then click **1 page**.

Excel will make the necessary adjustments to fit the worksheet columns to one page.

10 **Save** 🖫 your workbook. To submit electronically, follow the instructions provided by your instructor. To print, from the **Office** menu 🗔, point to the **Print** button, and then click **Print Preview**. In the **Preview group**, click the **Next Page** and **Previous Page** buttons as necessary to view and check each page. Be sure the two header rows and the footer display on each page, and then click the **Print** button. In the displayed **Print** dialog box, under **Print range**, be sure that **All** is selected, and then click **OK**. If you are directed to submit printed formulas, refer to Activity 1.17 to do so.

11 If you printed your formulas, be sure to redisplay the worksheet by pressing Ctrl + `. From the **Office** menu, click **Close**. If the dialog box displays asking if you want to save changes, click **No** so that you do *not* save the changes you made for printing formulas. **Close** Excel.

More Knowledge

Adjust Scaling for Data That is Slightly Larger Than the Printed Page

If your data is just a little too large to fit on a printed page, you can scale the worksheet to make it fit. Scaling reduces the horizontal and vertical size of the printed data to a percentage of its original size or by the number of pages that you specify. To adjust the printed output to a percentage of its actual size, for example to 80%, on the Page Layout tab, in the Scale to Fit group, click the Scale arrows to select a percentage.

End You have completed Project 3A ————

Project 3B **Loan Payment**

In Activities 3.14 through 3.19, you will create a worksheet for Wattana Dithasaro, International Sales Director, that details the loan information to purchase furniture and fixtures for a new Adamantine Jewelry store in Mexico City. Wattana plans to borrow money to pay for the new store furniture and fixtures, and then pay off the loan in monthly payments. She must decide how to arrange the loan to buy the furniture and fixtures she needs and still keep the monthly payment within her budget for new store openings. You will create a worksheet containing payments for combinations of time periods and interest rates so Wattana can identify what range of rates and time periods will meet her requirements. The worksheets of your workbook will look similar to Figure 3.29.

For Project 3B, you will need the following file:

New blank Excel workbook

You will save your workbook as
3B_New_Store_Loan_Firstname_Lastname

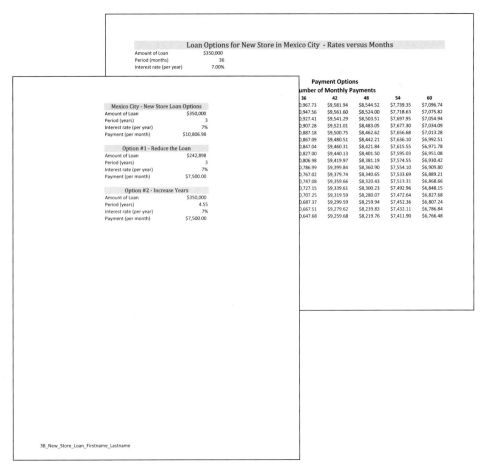

Figure 3.29
Project 3B—Loan Payment

Objective 6
Use Financial Functions

Financial functions perform common business calculations such as calculating a loan payment on a vehicle or calculating how much to save each month to buy something. Financial functions commonly involve a period of time such as months or years.

Activity 3.14 Designing a Loan Worksheet

1 **Start** Excel and display a new blank workbook. From the **Office** menu ⊞, display the **Save As** dialog box, navigate to your **Excel Chapter 3** folder, and then in the **File name** box, name the file **3B_New_Store_Loan_Firstname_Lastname**

2 Widen **column A** to **180 pixels** and **column B** to **100 pixels**. In the range **A2:B5**, enter the following row titles and data. Recall that you can format the numbers as you type by typing them with their symbols as shown:

Amount of Loan	$350,000
Period (years)	3
Interest rate (per year)	7%
Payment (per month)	

3 In cell **A1**, type **Mexico City - New Store Loan Options** Merge and Center ⊞ ▾ the title in the range **A1:B1**, add a **Fill Color** of **Olive Green, Accent 3, Lighter 60%**, change the **Font** Calibri ▾ to **Cambria**, and then change the **Font Size** 11 ▾ to **12**. Rename the worksheet tab **New Store Loan** and then **Save** 🖫 your workbook. Compare your screen with Figure 3.30.

Worksheet title centered with fill color

Figure 3.30

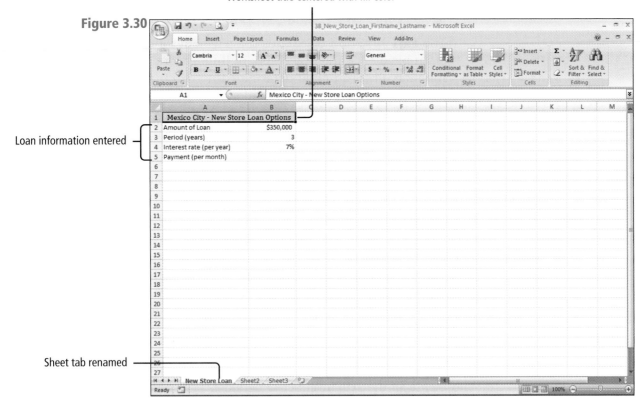

Loan information entered

Sheet tab renamed

Activity 3.15 Inserting the PMT Financial Function

When you borrow money from a bank or a similar lending institution, the amount charged to you for your use of the borrowed money is called *interest*. Loans are typically made for a period of years, and the interest that must be paid is a percentage of the loan amount that is still owed. In Excel, this percentage is called the *rate*. The initial amount of the loan is called the *Present value (Pv)*, which is the total amount that a series of future payments is worth now, and is also known as the *principal*. When you borrow money, the loan amount is the *present value* to the lender. The number of time periods—number of payments—is abbreviated *nper*. The value at the end of the time periods is the *Future value (Fv)*—the cash balance you want to attain after the last payment is made. The future value is usually zero for loans.

In this activity, you will calculate the monthly payments that Adamantine Jewelry will have to make to finance the purchase of the furniture and fixtures for the new store in Mexico City, the total cost of which is $350,000. You will calculate the monthly payments, including interest, for a three-year loan at an annual interest rate of 7.0%. To stay within Wattana's budget, the monthly payment must be approximately $7,500.

1 Click cell **B5**. On the **Formulas tab**, in the **Function Library group**, click the **Financial** button. In the displayed list, scroll down as necessary, and then click **PMT**.

The Function Arguments dialog box displays. Recall that arguments are the values that an Excel function uses to perform calculations or operations.

2 If necessary, drag the **Function Arguments** dialog box to the right side of your screen so you can view **columns A:B**.

The *PMT function* calculates the payment for a loan based on constant payments and at a constant interest rate. To complete the PMT function, first you must determine the total number of loan payment periods (months), which is 12 months × 3 years, or 36 months.

3 With your insertion point positioned in the **Rate** box, type **b4/12** Alternatively, click cell B4 and then type **/12**.

Excel will divide the annual interest rate of 7%, which is 0.070 in decimal notation, located in cell B4 by 12 (months), which will result in a *monthly* interest rate.

When borrowing money, the interest rate and number of periods are quoted in years. The payments on a loan, however, are usually made monthly. Therefore, the number of periods, which is stated in years, and the *annual* interest rate, must be changed to a monthly equivalent in order to calculate the monthly payment amount. You can see that calculations like these can be made as part of the argument in a function.

4 Press [Tab] to move the insertion point to the **Nper** box. In the lower portion of the dialog box, notice that *Nper is the total number of payments for the loan* (number of periods). Type **b3*12** to have Excel convert the number of years in the loan (3) to the total number of months.

Recall that the PMT function calculates a *monthly* payment. Thus, all values in the function must be expressed in months.

5 Press [Tab] to move to the **Pv** box, and then type **b2**

Pv represents the present value—the amount of the loan before any payments are made—in this instance $350,000.

6 In cell **B5** and on the **Formula Bar**, notice that the arguments that comprise the PMT function are separated by commas. Notice also, in the **Function Arguments** dialog box, that the value of each argument displays to the right of the argument box. Compare your screen with Figure 3.31.

Figure 3.31

Cell references entered for PMT function   Argument values

Formula displayed in
Formula Bar; arguments
separated by commas

Optional arguments

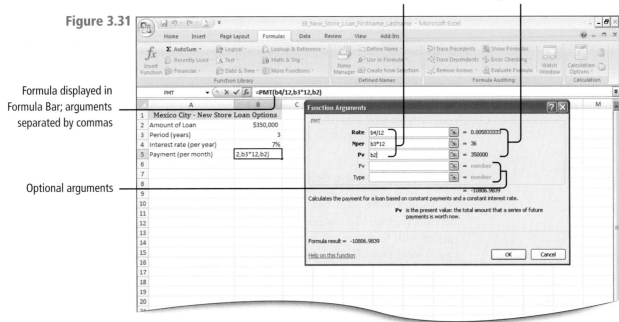

Note — Optional Arguments

The PMT function has two arguments not indicated by bold; these are optional. The Future value (Fv) argument assumes that the unpaid portion of the loan should be zero at the end of the last period. The *Type argument* assumes that the payment will be made at the end of each period. These default values are typical of most loans and may be left blank.

7 In the displayed dialog box, click **OK**.

The monthly payment amount, ($10,806.98), displays in cell B5. The amount displays in red and in parentheses to show that it is a negative number, a number that will be *paid out*. This monthly payment of $10,806.98 is over the budget of $7,500 per month that Wattana has in mind.

8 Click in the **Formula Bar**, and then use the arrow keys on the keyboard as necessary to position the insertion point between the equal sign and *PMT*. Type – (minus sign) to insert a minus sign into the formula, and then press Enter. **Save** your workbook.

By placing a minus sign in the formula, the monthly payment amount, $10,806.98, displays in cell B5 as a *positive* number, which is more familiar and less distracting to work with.

Objective 7
Use Goal Seek

Goal Seek is a method to find a specific value for a cell by adjusting the value of one other cell. With Goal Seek, you can work backward from the desired outcome to find the input necessary to achieve your goal. If you have a result in mind, you can try different numbers in one of the cells used as an argument in the function until you get close to the answer you want. Goal Seek is one of Excel's What-If Analysis tools.

Activity 3.16 Using Goal Seek to Produce the Desired Result

Wattana knows that her budget cannot exceed $7,500 per month for the new store loan. The amount of $350,000 is necessary to purchase the furniture and fixtures to open the new store. Now she has two options—borrow less money and reduce the amount or quality of the furniture and fixtures in the store, or extend the time to repay the loan. To find out how much she can borrow for three years to stay within the budget, or how much to increase the repayment period, you will use the Goal Seek tool.

1 Click cell **B5**. On the **Data tab**, in the **Data Tools group**, click the **What-If Analysis** button, and then in the displayed list, click **Goal Seek**. In the displayed **Goal Seek** dialog box, in the **Set cell** box, confirm that *B5* displays.

The cell address in this box is the cell that displays the desired result.

2 Press Tab. In the **To value** box, type the payment goal of **7500.00** and press Tab. In the **By changing cell** box, type **b2** which is the amount of the loan, and then compare your dialog box with Figure 3.32. Alternatively, you can click cell B2.

In the By changing cell box, if you click cell B2, Excel will make the cell reference absolute.

Desired value is 7500.00

Figure 3.32

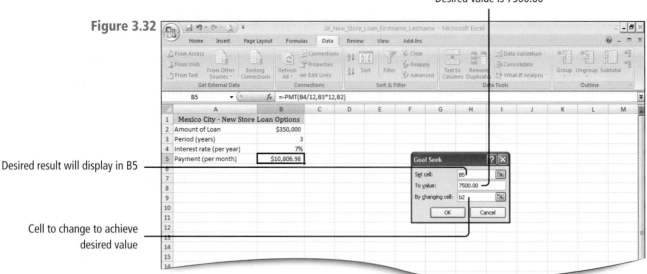

Desired result will display in B5

Cell to change to achieve desired value

3 In the displayed **Goal Seek** dialog box, click **OK**. In the displayed **Goal Seek Status** dialog box, click **OK**.

Excel's calculations indicate that to achieve a monthly payment of $7,500.00 using a 3-year loan, Wattana can borrow only *$242,898*—not $350,000.

4 Click cell **A7**. Type **Option #1 - Reduce the Loan** and press [Enter]. Right-click cell **A7**. On the Mini toolbar, apply a **Fill Color** of **Olive Green, Accent 3, Lighter 60%**, change the **Font** `Calibri` to **Cambria** and the **Font Size** `11` to **12**. **Merge and Center** the title across the range **A7:B7**.

5 Select the range **A2:B5**, right-click, and then click **Copy**. Click cell **A8**, right-click, and then from the shortcut menu, click **Paste Special**. In the **Paste Special** dialog box, under **Paste**, click the **Values and number formats** option button, and then click **OK**.

Press [Esc] to cancel the moving border. **Save** your workbook, click anywhere to deselect, and then compare your worksheet with Figure 3.33.

Recall that with the Paste Special command, you can copy the *value* in a cell, rather than the formula, and the cell formats are retained—cell B5 contains the PMT function formula, and here you need only the value that *results* from that formula.

Values and formats pasted

Figure 3.33

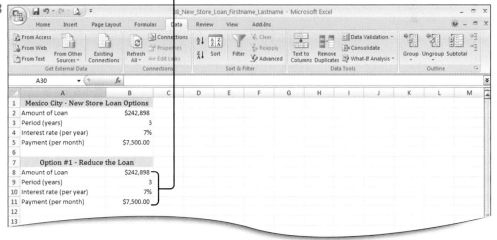

Savings Accounts—Using the Future Value Function

Another commonly used financial function, similar to the PMT function, is the Future Value function. The function has three required arguments: Rate, Nper, and Pmt. The Rate argument is the interest rate paid to you by the financial institution; the Nper is the number of periods; and Pmt is the amount you deposit into the account each period. The function also has two optional arguments—Pv and Type. The Pv argument is the amount you start with in the account. Excel assumes this is zero if you do not provide a starting amount. The Type argument assumes that the payment is made at the beginning of the time period.

For example, in the FV Function Arguments dialog box, enter a rate of 6%/12 (6% annually divided by 12 months), enter 60 (5 years or 60 months) as the number of periods, enter 100 ($100) as the monthly deposit you will make, and enter a present value of 1500 ($1,500 opening deposit in the account). Excel will calculate that at the end of 5 years, you will have $9,000.28 in your savings account.

Activity 3.17 Using Goal Seek To Find an Increased Period

For Wattana's purchase of furniture and fixtures for the new store in Mexico City, an alternative to borrowing less money—which would mean buying fewer items or items of lesser quality—would be to increase the number of years of payments.

1 In cell **B2**, type **350000** and then press Enter to restore the original loan amount. Click cell **B5**. On the **Data tab**, in the **Data Tools group**, click the **What-If Analysis** button, and then click **Goal Seek**.

2 In the **Set cell** box, confirm that **B5** displays. Press Tab. In the **To value** box, type **7500.00** Press Tab. In the **By changing cell** box, type **b3** which is the number of years for the loan. Compare your dialog box with Figure 3.34.

Value of $350,000 restored

Cell with the number of payment periods indicated as the *change* cell

Figure 3.34

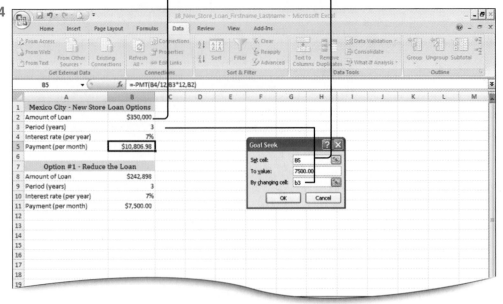

3 Click **OK** two times to close the two dialog boxes.

Excel's calculations indicate that by making payments for 4.5 years—4.552648969—a monthly payment of $7,500.00 is achieved.

4 Click **A13**. Type **Option #2 - Increase Years** and then press Enter. Right-click click cell **A7**, on the Mini toolbar, click the **Format Painter** button , and then click cell **A13** to copy the formats.

5 Select the range **A2:B5,** and then right-click. From the displayed shortcut menu, click **Copy** , and then click cell **A14**. Right-click, click **Paste Special**, and then paste the **Values and number formats**. Press Esc to cancel the moving border.

6 Click cell **B15**, right-click to display the Mini toolbar, and then click the **Decrease Decimal** button until the number of decimal places is two. Click cell **B3.** Type **3** and then press Enter to restore the original value. Compare your worksheet with Figure 3.35.

Figure 3.35

Option 1: Reduce the amount of the loan

Option 2: Increase the number of years to pay off the loan

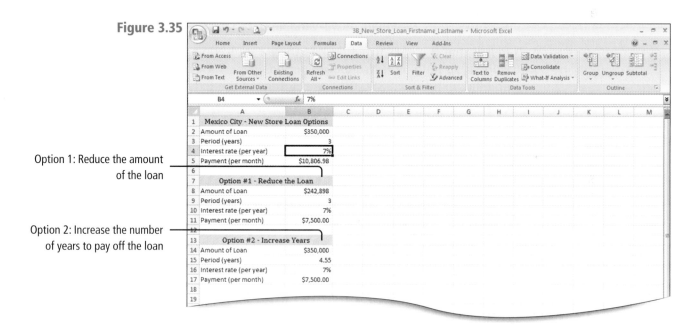

7 Click the **Insert tab**, and then in the **Text group**, click the **Header & Footer** button to switch to **Page Layout View** and open the **Header area**. In the **Navigation group**, click the **Go to Footer** button, click just above the word *Footer*, and then in the **Header & Footer Elements group**, click the **File Name** button. Click in a cell just above the footer to exit the **Footer area** and view your file name.

8 Click the **Page Layout tab**. In the **Page Setup group**, click the **Margins** button, and then at the bottom of the **Margins gallery**, click **Custom Margins**. In the displayed **Page Setup** dialog box, under **Center on page**, select the **Horizontally** check box. Click **OK**, and then on the status bar, click the **Normal** button . Press Ctrl + Home to move to the top of the worksheet.

9 **Save** your workbook.

Objective 8
Create a Data Table

A *data table* is a range of cells that shows how changing certain values in your formulas affects the results of those formulas. Data tables make it easy to calculate multiple versions in one operation, and then to view and compare the results of all the different variations.

For example, banks may offer loans at different rates for different periods of time, which require different payments. Using a data table, you can calculate the possible values for each argument.

A *one-variable data table* changes the value in only one cell. For example, use a one-variable data table if you want to see how different interest rates affect a monthly payment. A *two-variable data table* changes the values in two cells—for example, you can see how both different interest rates *and* different payment periods will affect a monthly payment.

Activity 3.18 Designing a Two-Variable Data Table

Recall that the PMT function has three required arguments: Present value (Pv), Rate, and Number of periods (Nper). Because Wattana would still like to borrow $350,000 and purchase the fixtures and furniture that she has selected for the new store in Mexico City, in this data table the present value will not change. The two values that will change are the Rate and Number of periods. Possible periods will range from 24 months (2 years) to 60 months (5 years) and the Rate will vary from 8% to 6%.

1 Double-click the **Sheet2 tab**, rename it **Payment Table** and then press Enter. Right-click the **Sheet3 tab**, and then from the shortcut menu, click **Delete**.

2 With the **Payment Table** worksheet active, widen **column A to 165 pixels**. Widen **column B to 80 pixels**. Select **columns C:I**, and then widen them to **85 pixels**.

3 In the range **A2:B4**, enter the following row titles and data. Recall that you format numbers as you type by typing them with their symbols as shown:

Amount of Loan	$350,000
Period (months)	36
Interest rate (per year)	7.00%

4 Click cell **C8**. Type **24** and then press Tab. Type **30** and then press Tab. Select the range **C8:D8**. Point to the fill handle, and then drag to the right through cell **I8** to fill in a pattern of months from 24 to 60 in increments of six months.

5 In cell **B9**, type **8.000%** and then press Enter. Type **7.875%** and then press Enter.

The display of both values is rounded to two decimal places.

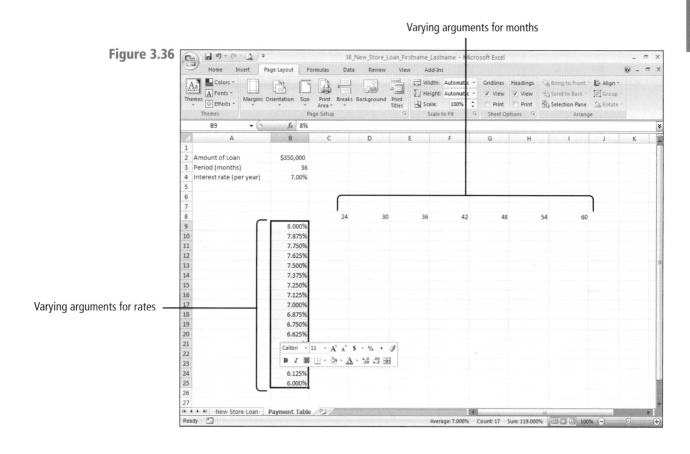

6 Select the range **B9:B10**. Point to the fill handle, and then drag down through cell **B25** to fill in a pattern of interest rates in increments of .125 from 8.00% down to 6.00%. With the range **B9:B25** still selected, right-click anywhere over the range, and then on the Mini toolbar, click the **Increase Decimal** button one time. Compare your screen with Figure 3.36.

Row 8 represents the number of monthly payments, and column B represents a range of possible annual interest rates. These two arguments will be used to calculate varying payment arrangements for a loan of $350,000.

Figure 3.36

Varying arguments for months

Varying arguments for rates

7 Click cell **A1**. Type **Loan Options for New Store in Mexico City - Rates versus Months** and then press Enter. **Merge and Center** this title across the range **A1:I1**. Change the **Font** Calibri to **Cambria**, the **Font Size** 11 to **16**, and then apply a **Fill Color** of **Olive Green, Accent 3, Lighter 60%**.

8 Click cell **C6**. Type **Payment Options** and then press Enter. **Merge and Center** this title across the range **C6:I6**. Change the **Font Size** 11 to **14**, and then apply **Bold** B.

9 Click cell **C7**. Type **Number of Monthly Payments** and then use the **Format Painter** to apply the format of cell **C6** to cell **C7**.

10 Click cell **A9**, type **Rates** and then press Enter. Select the range **A9:A25**. On the **Home tab**, in the **Alignment group**, click the **Merge and Center** button 🔲 ▾, click the **Align Text Right** button 🔲, and then click the **Middle Align** button 🔲. Change the **Font Size** 11 ▾ to **14**, and then apply **Bold** **B**. Compare your screen with Figure 3.37.

Figure 3.37

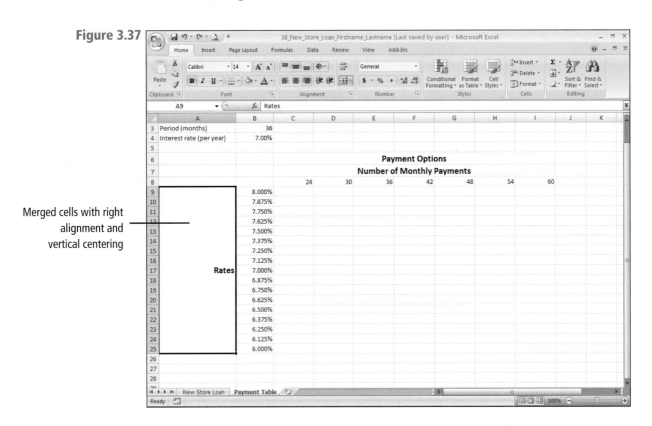

Merged cells with right alignment and vertical centering

11 **Save** 💾 the changes you have made to your workbook.

Activity 3.19 Using a Data Table To Calculate Options

Recall that a data table is a range of cells that shows how changing certain values in your formulas affects the results of those formulas. In this activity, you will create a table of payments for every combination of payment periods, which are represented by the column titles under *Number of Monthly Payments*, and interest rates, which are represented by the row titles to the right of *Rates*. From the resulting table, Wattana can find a combination of payment periods and interest rates that will enable her to go forward with her plan to borrow $350,000 to purchase the necessary furniture and fixtures for the new store in Mexico City.

1 Click cell **B8**, type **=** and notice that in the upper left corner of your screen, in the **Name Box**, *PMT* displays indicating the most recently used function. Click in the **Name Box** to open the **Function Arguments** dialog box for the **PMT** function. Alternatively, use one of the other methods you have practiced to insert the PMT function.

The PMT function is entered in the upper left corner of your range of data, so that when the data table is completed, the months in row 8 and the rates in column B will be substituted into each cell's formula to fill the table with the range of months and interest rate options that are displayed.

2 In the **Rate** box, type **b4/12** to divide the interest rate per year by 12 and convert it to a monthly interest rate.

3 Press Tab to move the insertion point to the **Nper** box. Type **b3** and then press Tab.

The periods in cell B3 are already stated in months and need not be changed.

4 In the **Pv** box, type **-b2** and then click **OK**.

The payment—$10,806.98—is calculated for the values in cells B2, B3, and B4. This is the same payment that you calculated on the first worksheet. Now it displays as a positive number because you entered the loan amount in cell B2 as a negative number.

5 Select the range **B8:I25**. On the **Data tab**, in the **Data Tools group**, click the **What-If Analysis** button, and then in the displayed list, click **Data Table**. In the **Data Table** dialog box, in the **Row input cell** box, type **b3** and then press Tab. In the **Column input cell** box, type **b4** and then compare your screen with Figure 3.38.

The row of months will be substituted for the value in cell B3, and the column of interest rates will be substituted for the value in cell B4.

Column values substituted for interest rates

Figure 3.38

Row values substituted for months

Selected area indicates data table range

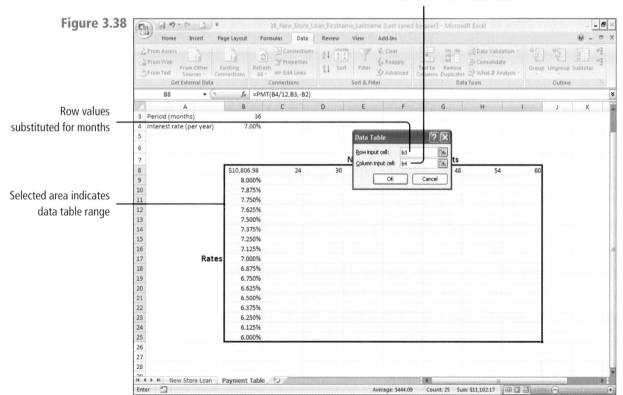

6 In the **Data Table** dialog box, click **OK**. Click cell **H21**, and then examine the formula in the **Formula Bar**. Compare your screen with Figure 3.39.

The table is filled with payment options that use the month and interest rate corresponding to the position in the table. Thus, if Wattana chooses a combination of 54 months at an interest rate of 6.5%, the monthly payment will be $7,492.96.

The data table is one of a group of Excel's What-If Analysis tools.

Period of 54 months, at 6.500% interest, results in $7,492.96 payment

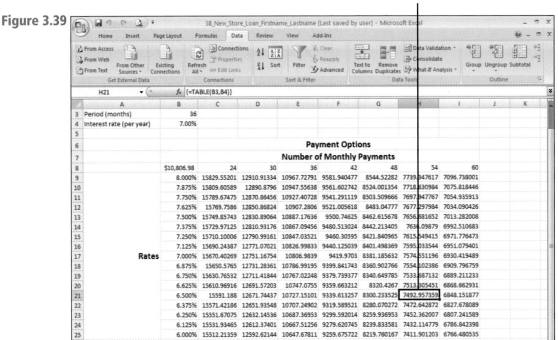

Figure 3.39

7 Right-click cell **B8**, and then on the Mini toolbar, click the **Format Painter** button. Select the range **C9:I25** to apply the same format. Use [Ctrl] to select the non-adjacent ranges **B9:B25** and **C8:I8**. Right-click over the selection, and then on the Mini toolbar, apply **Bold** [B] and **Center**. Click anywhere to deselect the range, and then compare your worksheet with Figure 3.40.

By using a data table of payment options, you can see that Wattana must get a loan for at least 54 months (4.5 years) for any of the interest rates between 6.500% and 6.000% in order to purchase the furniture and fixtures she wants and still keep the monthly payment at approximately $7,500.

For a 54-month period, loan options in this range will be within the budget

Figure 3.40

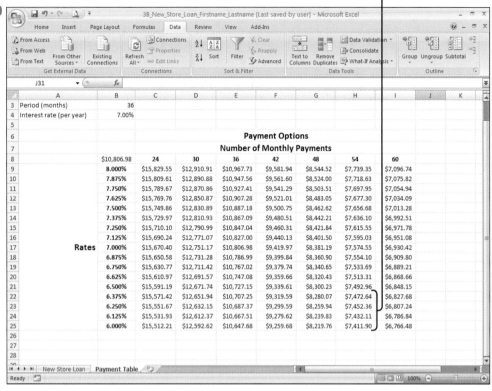

	A	B	C	D	E	F	G	H	I	J	K
3	Period (months)	36									
4	Interest rate (per year)	7.00%									
5											
6						Payment Options					
7						Number of Monthly Payments					
8		$10,806.98	24	30	36	42	48	54	60		
9		8.000%	$15,829.55	$12,910.91	$10,967.73	$9,581.94	$8,544.52	$7,739.35	$7,096.74		
10		7.875%	$15,809.61	$12,890.88	$10,947.56	$9,561.60	$8,524.00	$7,718.63	$7,075.82		
11		7.750%	$15,789.67	$12,870.86	$10,927.41	$9,541.29	$8,503.51	$7,697.95	$7,054.94		
12		7.625%	$15,769.76	$12,850.87	$10,907.28	$9,521.01	$8,483.05	$7,677.30	$7,034.09		
13		7.500%	$15,749.86	$12,830.89	$10,887.18	$9,500.75	$8,462.62	$7,656.68	$7,013.28		
14		7.375%	$15,729.97	$12,810.93	$10,867.09	$9,480.51	$8,442.21	$7,636.10	$6,992.51		
15		7.250%	$15,710.10	$12,790.99	$10,847.04	$9,460.31	$8,421.84	$7,615.55	$6,971.78		
16		7.125%	$15,690.24	$12,771.07	$10,827.00	$9,440.13	$8,401.50	$7,595.03	$6,951.08		
17	Rates	7.000%	$15,670.40	$12,751.17	$10,806.98	$9,419.97	$8,381.19	$7,574.55	$6,930.42		
18		6.875%	$15,650.58	$12,731.28	$10,786.99	$9,399.84	$8,360.90	$7,554.10	$6,909.80		
19		6.750%	$15,630.77	$12,711.42	$10,767.02	$9,379.74	$8,340.65	$7,533.69	$6,889.21		
20		6.625%	$15,610.97	$12,691.57	$10,747.08	$9,359.66	$8,320.43	$7,513.31	$6,868.66		
21		6.500%	$15,591.19	$12,671.74	$10,727.15	$9,339.61	$8,300.23	$7,492.96	$6,848.15		
22		6.375%	$15,571.42	$12,651.94	$10,707.25	$9,319.59	$8,280.07	$7,472.64	$6,827.68		
23		6.250%	$15,551.67	$12,632.15	$10,687.37	$9,299.59	$8,259.94	$7,452.36	$6,807.24		
24		6.125%	$15,531.93	$12,612.37	$10,667.51	$9,279.62	$8,239.83	$7,432.11	$6,786.84		
25		6.000%	$15,512.21	$12,592.62	$10,647.68	$9,259.68	$8,219.76	$7,411.90	$6,766.48		
26											
27											
28											

New Store Loan Payment Table

8 Click the **Insert tab**, and then in the **Text group**, click the **Header & Footer** button to switch to **Page Layout View** and open the **Header area**. In the **Navigation group**, click the **Go to Footer** button, click just above the word *Footer*, then in the **Header & Footer Elements group**, click the **File Name** button. Click in a cell just above the footer to exit the **Footer area** and view your file name.

9 Click the **Page Layout tab**. In the **Page Setup group**, click the **Orientation** button, and then click **Landscape**. Click the **Margins** button, and then at the bottom of the **Margins gallery**, click **Custom Margins**. In the displayed **Page Setup** dialog box, under **Center on page**, select the **Horizontally** check box. Click **OK**, and then on the status bar, click the **Normal** button. Press Ctrl + Home to move to the top of the worksheet.

10 Save your workbook. Press Ctrl + F2 to display the worksheet in **Print Preview**. To print, in the **Print group**, click the **Print** button, under **Print what**, click the **Entire workbook** option button, and then click **OK**. To submit electronically, follow your instructor's directions. Determine if you are to print formulas for any or all of the worksheets in this workbook. To print formulas, refer to Activity 1.17 in Project 1A.

11 If you printed your formulas, be sure to redisplay the worksheet by pressing Ctrl + `. From the **Office** menu, click **Close**. If you are prompted to save changes, click **No**. **Close** Excel.

End **You have completed Project 3B**

There's More You Can Do!

From My Computer, navigate to the student files that accompany this textbook. In the folder **02_theres_more_you_can_do_pg1_36**, locate and open the folder for this chapter. Open and print the instructions for this project, which are provided to you in Adobe PDF format.

Try IT! 1—Apply Conditional Formats by Using Color Scales, Icon Sets, and Top/Bottom Rules

In this Try IT! exercise, you will use Color Scales, Icon Sets, and Top/Bottom rules to help you visualize data distribution and variation.

Content-Based Assessments

Summary

Predefined formulas, referred to as functions, are available in Excel in various categories including Statistical, Logical, Date & Time, and Financial. Such functions enable you to make complex calculations without having to build the formulas yourself. Conditional formatting enables you to highlight interesting cells based on criteria, emphasize unusual values, and visualize data using Data Bars. The DATE function adds the current date to a workbook. Financial functions, along with the Goal Seek tool and data tables, are useful when making choices among various financing options.

Key Terms

Matching

Match each term in the second column with its correct definition in the first column by writing the letter of the term on the blank line in front of the correct definition.

D **1.** A predefined formula—a formula that Excel has already built for you—that performs calculations by using specific values in a particular order.

A **2.** The values that an Excel function uses to perform calculations or operations.

B **3.** A statistical function that adds a group of values, and then divides the result by the number of values in the group.

K **4.** A statistical function that determines the smallest value in a group of values.

G **5.** An Excel feature which, after typing an = (equal sign) and the beginning letter or letters of a function name, displays a list of function names that match the typed letter(s), and from which you can insert the function by pointing to its name, and then pressing the Tab key or double-clicking.

**6.** Conditions that you specify in a logical function.

H **7.** Any value or expression that can be evaluated as being *true* or *false*.

J

C **8.** The symbols < (less than), > (greater than), and = (equal) that evaluate each field value to determine if it is the same, greater than, less than, or in between a range of values as specified by the criteria.

E **9.** A cell format consisting of a shaded bar that provides a visual cue to the reader about the value of a cell relative to other cells; the length of the bar represents the value in the cell—a longer bar represents a higher value and a shorter bar represents a lower value.

L **10.** A function within the *Date & Time* category that retrieves the date and time from your computer's calendar and clock and inserts the information into the selected cell.

E **11.** A series of rows and columns in a worksheet that contains related data, and that is managed independently from the data in other rows and columns in the worksheet.

M **12.** A portion of a worksheet window bounded by and separated from other portions by vertical and horizontal bars.

I **13.** The amount charged for the use of borrowed money.

O **14.** The total amount that a series of future payments is worth now; also known as the principal.

N **15.** An Excel function that calculates the payment for a loan based on constant payments and at a constant rate of interest.

A Arguments

B AVERAGE

C Comparison operators

D Criteria

E Data Bar

F Excel table

G Formula AutoComplete

H Function

I Interest

J Logical test

K MIN

L NOW

M Pane

N PMT

O Present value

Content-Based Assessments

Fill in the Blank

Write the correct answer in the space provided.

1. The Excel function that adds all the numbers in a selected range of cells is the _Sum_ function.

2. Prewritten formulas that analyze a group of measurements are _Statistical_ functions.

3. A statistical function commonly used to describe a group of data, and which finds the middle value in a group of values that has as many values above it in the group as are below it is the _Median_ function.

4. The MAX function determines the _largest_ value in a selected range of values.

5. Prewritten formulas that test for specific conditions, and which typically use conditional tests to determine whether specified conditions, referred to as criteria, are true or false, are _logical_ functions.

6. To count the number of cells within a range that meets the given condition, use the _CountIF_ function.

7. The IF function uses a logical test to check whether a condition is met, and then returns one value if true, and another value if _False_.

8. A format that changes the appearance of a cell range—for example by adding cell shading or font color—based on a condition is a _Conditional_ format.

9. The command that searches the cells in a worksheet—or in a selected range—for matches, and then replaces each match with a replacement value of your choice is called _Find & Replace_.

10. The term used to describe an Excel function that is subject to change each time the workbook is reopened; for example, when the NOW function updates itself to the current date and time each time the workbook is opened, is _Volatile_.

11. The command that enables you to select one or more rows or columns and freeze (lock) them into place as separate panes is _Freeze panes_

12. The group of functions in Excel that performs common business calculations, such as calculating a loan payment on a vehicle, and that

Fill in the Blank

commonly involves a period of time such as months or years, are called ~~financial~~ functions.

13. The value at the end of the time periods in an Excel function is known as the ~~Future Value~~

14. One of Excel's What-If Analysis tools, which provides a method to find a specific value for a cell by adjusting the value of one other cell, is ~~Goal Seek~~

15. A range of cells that shows how changing certain values in your formulas affects the results of those formulas, and that makes it easy to calculate multiple versions in one operation, is a _____

~~DATA TABLE~~

Content-Based Assessments

Project 3C—Pendants

In this project, you will apply the skills you practiced from the Objectives in Project 3A.

Objectives: 1. *Use SUM, AVERAGE, MEDIAN, MIN, and MAX Functions;* **2.** *Use COUNTIF and IF Functions, and Apply Conditional Formatting;* **3.** *Use a Date Function;* **4.** *Freeze Panes and Create an Excel Table;* **5.** *Format and Print a Large Worksheet.*

Adamantine Jewelry creates castings, which it sells to other jewelry makers. In the following Skills Review, you will edit a worksheet for Rose Elleni, Vice President of Production, detailing the current inventory of pendant castings at the Milan production facility. Your completed worksheet will look similar to the one shown in Figure 3.41.

For Project 3C, you will need the following file:

e3C_Pendants

You will save your workbook as 3C_Pendants_Firstname_Lastname

Figure 3.41

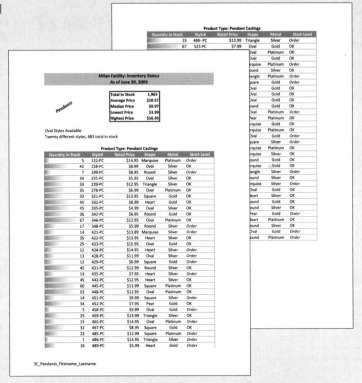

(Project 3C–Pendants continues on the next page)

(Project 3C–Pendants continued)

1. **Start** Excel. From the student files that accompany this text, locate and open **e3C_Pendants**. From the **Office** menu, display the **Save As** dialog box, click the **Save in arrow**, and then navigate to your **Excel Chapter 3** folder. In the **File name** box, type **3C_Pendants_Firstname_ Lastname** and then click **Save** or press Enter.

2. Click cell **B4**. Click the **Formulas tab**, and then in the **Function Library group**, click the **AutoSum** button. Select the range **A12:A77**, dragging downward as necessary, and then press Enter. Right-click cell **B4**, and then apply **Comma Style** with zero decimal places.

3. Click cell **B5**. In the **Function Library group**, click the **More Functions** button, and then point to **Statistical**. Click **AVERAGE**, and then if necessary, drag the title bar of the **Function Arguments** dialog box down and to the right so you can view the **Formula Bar** and cell **B5**. In the **Function Arguments** dialog box, in the **Number1** box, delete the existing text, and then type **c12:c77** Click **OK** to calculate the average product price.

4. Click cell **B6**. In the **Function Library group**, click the **More Functions** button, display the list of **Statistical** functions, scroll down as necessary, and then click **MEDIAN**. In the displayed **Function Arguments** dialog box, to the right of the **Number1** box, click the **Collapse Dialog** button. Select the range **C12:C77**, and then press Enter. Click **OK** to calculate the median product price.

5. Using either of the techniques that you practiced in Steps 3 and 4, in cell **B7**, insert the **MIN** function for the range **C12:C77**. In cell **B8** insert the **MAX** function for the range **C12:C77**.

6. Select the range **A4:B8**. Point to the right edge of the selected range to display the ⌖ pointer. Drag the selected range to the right until the ScreenTip displays *C4:D8*, and then release the mouse button. Select **columns C:D**, and then apply **AutoFit** to adjust the column widths. Select the range **C4:D8**, and then apply **Bold** and a **Thick Box Border**.

7. In cell **A6**, type **Pendants** Select the range **A5:A7**, right-click over the selection, and then from the shortcut menu, click **Format Cells**. In the displayed **Format Cells** dialog box, click the **Alignment tab**. Under **Text control**, select the **Merge cells** check box. In the upper right portion of the dialog box, under **Orientation**, point to the **red diamond**, and then drag the diamond upward until the **Degrees** box indicates *30*. Click **OK**.

8. With the cell still selected, click the **Home tab**, change the **Font Size** to **12**, and then apply **Bold** and **Italic**. In the **Alignment group**, apply **Center** alignment and **Middle Align**.

9. From the **row heading area**, point to **row 10** and right-click. From the shortcut menu, click **Insert**. Press F4 two times to insert two more rows. In cell **A10** type **Oval Styles Available:** and press Enter.

10. With cell **A11** active, on the **Formulas tab**, in the **Function Library group**, click the **More Functions** button, and then display the list of **Statistical** functions. Click **COUNTIF**. In the **Range** box, click the **Collapse Dialog** button, select the range **D15:D80**, and then press Enter. Click in the **Criteria** box, type **Oval** and then click **OK** to calculate the number of Oval pendant castings that Adamantine Jewelry has in stock.

(Project 3C–Pendants continues on the next page)

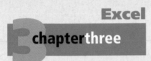

(Project 3C–Pendants continued)

11. Click cell **F15**. On the **Formulas tab**, in the **Function Library group**, click the **Logical** button, and then in the displayed list, click **IF**. With the insertion point in the **Logical_test** box, click cell **A15**, and then type **<25** Press Tab to move the insertion point to the **Value_if_true** box, and then type **Order** Press Tab to move the insertion point to the **Value_if_false** box, and then type **OK** Click **OK** to display the result *Order* in cell **F15**. Then, using the fill handle, copy the function down through cell **F80** to indicate the order status for each Style#.

12. Be sure the range **F15:F80** is selected. On the **Home tab**, in the **Styles group**, click the **Conditional Formatting** button. In the displayed list, point to **Highlight Cells Rules**, and then click **Text that Contains**. In the **Text That Contains** dialog box, with the insertion point blinking in the first box, type **Order** In the second box, click the arrow, and then in the displayed list, click **Custom Format**. On the **Font tab**, under **Font style**, click **Bold Italic**. Click the **Color arrow**, and then under **Theme Colors**, click **Dark Blue, Text 2, Darker 25%.** Click **OK**, and then click **OK** again to apply the formatting to the items that need to be ordered.

13. Select the range **A15:A80**. In the **Styles group**, click the **Conditional Formatting** button. In the displayed list, point to **Data Bars**, and then in the displayed gallery, click **Blue Data Bar** to visually indicate the quantity in stock for each item.

14. To the left of the **Formula Bar**, in the **Name Box**, type **e15:e80** and then press Enter. On the **Home tab**, in the **Editing group**, click the **Find & Select** button. From the displayed menu, click **Replace** to display the **Find and Replace** dialog box. In the **Find what** box, type **Base** In the

Replace with box type **Platinum** Click the **Replace All** button, and then click **OK** to replace 16 occurrences of *Base* with *Platinum*. **Close** the **Find and Replace** dialog box.

15. Scroll down to view **row 81**. Click cell **A81**, type **Last Edited by Rose Elleni** and then press Enter. With cell **A82** as the active cell, on the **Formulas tab**, in the **Function Library group**, click the **Date & Time** button. In the displayed list of functions, click **NOW**. In the **Function Arguments** dialog box, click **OK** to close the dialog box. Adjust the width of **column A** to **110 pixels** to display the current date and time. Apply **Align Text Left** to cell **A82**.

16. **Save** your changes up to this point. Press Ctrl + Home to make cell **A1** the active cell. Select the range **A14:F80**. Click the **Insert tab**, and then in the **Tables group**, click the **Table** button. In the displayed **Create Table** dialog box, if necessary, click to select the **My table has headers** check box. Click **OK** to create the table.

17. On the **Design tab**, in the **Table Styles group**, click the **More** button, and then under **Light**, locate and click **Table Style Light 9**.

18. In the header row of the table, click the **Retail Price arrow**, and then from the displayed menu, click **Sort Smallest to Largest** to rearrange the data so that the products display in ascending order with the lowest price item first and the highest price item last.

19. In the header row of the table, click the **Shape arrow**. From the displayed menu, click **Sort A to Z**. Click the **Shape arrow** again. On the displayed menu, click the **(Select All)** check box to clear all the check boxes. Then, click to select only the

(Project 3C–Pendants continues on the next page)

Content-Based Assessments

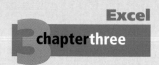
(Project 3C–Pendants continued)

Oval check box, and then click **OK** to display only the **Oval** products.

20. Click any cell in the table so that the table is selected. On the Ribbon, click the **Design tab**, and then in the **Table Style Options group**, click to select the **Total Row** check box. Click cell **A81**, click the arrow that displays, and then in the displayed list, click **Sum** to display *683*—the total number of oval shaped pendant castings in stock. Click cell **A11**, type **Twenty different styles, 683 total in stock** and then press Enter.

21. Click any cell in the table. On the Ribbon, click the **Design tab**, and then in the **Table Style Options group**, click the **Total Row** check box to clear it and remove the Total row from the bottom of the table. In the table header row, click the **Shape arrow**, and then in the displayed menu, click **Clear Filter From "Shape"** to redisplay all of the products.

22. In the table header row, click the **Style# arrow**, and then click **Sort A to Z**, which will apply an ascending sort to the **Style#** column. In the **Tools group**, click the **Convert to Range** button. In the displayed message box, click **Yes**.

23. Press Ctrl + Home to display the top of your worksheet. On the **Insert tab**, in the **Text group**, click **Header & Footer** to switch to **Page Layout view**. In the **Navigation group**, click the **Go to Footer** button, click just above the word *Footer*, and then in the **Header & Footer Elements group**, click the **File Name** button. Click a cell just above the footer to deselect the **Footer area** and view your file name.

24. Press Ctrl + Home to display the top of your worksheet. On the **Page Layout tab**, in the **Page Setup group**, click the **Print Titles** button. Under **Print titles**, click in the **Rows to repeat at top** box, and then at the right, click the **Collapse Dialog** button. From the **row heading area**, select **rows 13:14**. Press Enter, and then in the displayed **Page Setup** dialog box, click the **Margins tab**. Under **Center on page**, click the **Horizontally** check box, and then click **OK**. Delete the unused sheets **Sheet2** and **Sheet3**. On the right edge of the status bar, click the **Normal** button.

25. **Save** your workbook. To submit electronically, follow the instructions provided by your instructor. To print, from the **Office** menu, point to the **Print** button, and then click **Print Preview**. In the **Preview group**, click the **Next Page** and **Previous Page** buttons as necessary to view and check each page. Be sure the two header rows and the footer display on each page, and then click the **Print** button. In the displayed **Print** dialog box, under **Print range**, be sure that **All** is selected, and then click **OK**. If you are directed to submit printed formulas, refer to Activity 1.17 to do so.

26. If you printed your formulas, be sure to redisplay the worksheet by pressing Ctrl + `. From the **Office** menu, click **Close**. If the dialog box displays asking if you want to save changes, click **No** so that you do *not* save the changes you made for printing formulas. **Close** Excel.

End **You have completed Project 3C**

Content-Based Assessments

Skills Review

Project 3D — Auto Loan

In this project, you will apply the skills you practiced from the Objectives in Project 3B.

Objectives: 6. *Use Financial Functions;* **7.** *Use Goal Seek;* **8.** *Create a Data Table.*

In the following Skills Review, you will create a worksheet for Jennifer Bernard, U.S. Sales Director, that details loan information for purchasing eight automobiles for Adamantine Jewelry sales representatives. The monthly payment for the eight automobiles cannot exceed $3,000. The two worksheets in your workbook will look similar to Figure 3.42.

> **For Project 3D, you will need the following file:**
>
> New blank Excel workbook

You will save your workbook as
3D_Auto_Loan_Firstname_Lastname

Figure 3.42

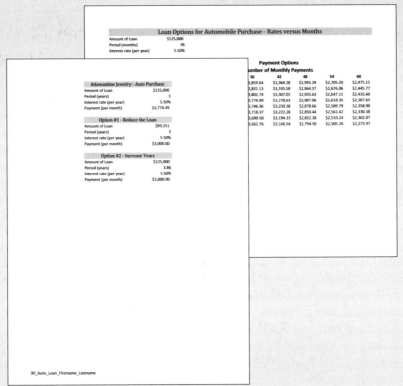

(Project 3D–Auto Loan continues on the next page)

Content-Based Assessments

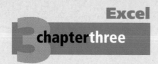 chapter **three** | Excel

Skills Review

(Project 3D–Auto Loan continued)

1. **Start** Excel and display a new blank workbook. From the **Office** menu, display the **Save As** dialog box, navigate to your **Excel Chapter 3** folder, and then in the **File name** box, type 3D_Auto_Loan_Firstname_ Lastname Click **Save** or press Enter.

2. Widen **column A** to **180 pixels** and **column B** to **100 pixels**. In cell **A1**, type Adamantine Jewelry – Auto Purchase **Merge and Center** the worksheet title in the range **A1:B1**, change the **Font** to **Cambria**, the **Font Size** to **12**, and then add a **Fill Color** of **Orange, Accent 6, Lighter 40%**. Rename the worksheet tab as **Auto Loan** In the range **A2:B5**, enter the following row titles and data.

Amount of Loan	$125,000
Period (years)	3
Interest rate (per year)	5.5%
Payment (per month)	

3. Click cell **B5**. On the **Formulas tab**, in the **Function Library group**, click the **Financial** button, and then click **PMT**. Drag the **Function Arguments** dialog box to the right side of your screen so you can view **columns A:B**.

4. In the **Rate** box, type **b4/12** to convert the annual interest rate to a monthly interest rate. Press Tab, and then in the **Nper** box, type **b3*12** to have Excel convert the number of years in the loan (3) to the total number of months. Press Tab, and then in the **Pv** box, type **b2** to enter the present value of the loan. Click **OK** to create the function. In the **Formula Bar**, between the equal sign and *PMT*, type – (minus sign) to insert a minus sign into the formula, and then press Enter to display the loan payment as a positive number.

5. The result of *$3,774.49* is higher than the monthly payment of $3,000 that Jennifer wants. One option is to reduce the amount of money that she is going to borrow; she can determine the maximum amount that she can borrow and still keep the payment at $3,000 by using Goal Seek. Click cell **B5**. On the **Data tab**, in the **Data Tools group**, click the **What-If Analysis** button, and then in the displayed list, click **Goal Seek**. In the displayed **Goal Seek** dialog box, in the **Set cell** box, confirm that *B5* displays.

6. Press Tab. In the **To value** box, type the payment goal of **3000** and then press Tab. In the **By changing cell** box, type **b2** which is the amount of the loan. Click **OK** two times. For three years at 5.5%, Jennifer can borrow only $99,351 if she maintains a monthly payment of $3,000.

7. Click cell **A7**. Type **Option #1 - Reduce the Loan** and then press Enter. Right-click cell **A1**, on the Mini toolbar, click the **Format Painter** button, and then click cell **A7** to copy the formats.

8. Select the range **A2:B5**, right-click, and then click **Copy**. Click cell **A8**, right-click, and then from the shortcut menu, click **Paste Special**. In the **Paste Special** dialog box, under **Paste**, click the **Values and number formats** option button, and then click **OK**. Press Esc to cancel the moving border.

9. In cell **B2**, type **125000** and then press Enter to restore the original loan amount. Another option that Jennifer can explore with Goal Seek is to increase the number of years over which she finances the automobiles. Click cell **B5**. On the **Data tab**, in the **Data Tools group**, click the **What-If Analysis** button, and then click **Goal Seek**.

(Project 3D–Auto Loan continues on the next page)

Content-Based Assessments

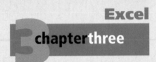
(Project 3D–Auto Loan continued)

10. In the **Set cell** box, confirm that **B5** displays. Press Tab. In the **To value** box, type **3000** Press Tab. In the **By changing cell** box, type **b3** which is the number of years for the loan. Click **OK** two times. Extending the loan over 3.86 years will maintain a monthly payment of $3,000 at the current interest rate.

11. Click **A13**. Type **Option #2 - Increase Years** and then press Enter. Use the **Format Painter** to copy the formats from cell **A7** to cell **A13**. Select the range **A2:B5**, right-click, click **Copy**, and then click cell **A14**. Right-click, click **Paste Special**, and then paste the **Values and number formats**. Press Esc to cancel the moving border.

12. Click cell **B15**, right-click to display the Mini toolbar, and then click the **Decrease Decimal** button until the number of decimal places is two. Click cell **B3**. Type **3** and then press Enter to restore the original value.

13. Click the **Insert tab**, and then in the **Text group**, click **Header & Footer** to switch to **Page Layout View** and open the **Header area**. In the **Navigation group**, click the **Go to Footer** button, click just above the word *Footer*, then in the **Header & Footer Elements group**, click the **File Name** button. Click in a cell just above the footer to exit the **Footer area** and view your file name.

14. Click the **Page Layout tab**. In the **Page Setup group**, click the **Margins** button, and then at the bottom of the **Margins gallery**, click **Custom Margins**. In the displayed **Page Setup** dialog box, under **Center on page**, select the **Horizontally** check box. Click **OK**, and then on the status bar, click the **Normal** button. Press Ctrl + Home to move to the top of the worksheet.

15. **Save** the changes you have made thus far. To determine how variable interest rates and a varying number of payments affect the payment amount, Jennifer will set up a two-variable data table. Double-click the **Sheet2 tab**, rename it **Payment Table** and then press Enter. In cell **A1** type **Loan Options for Automobile Purchase - Rates versus Months** and then press Enter. **Merge and Center** this title across the range **A1:I1**. Change the **Font** to **Cambria**, the **Font Size** to **16**, and apply a **Fill Color** of **Orange, Accent 6, Lighter 40%**.

16. Widen **column A** to **165 pixels**. Widen **column B** to **80 pixels**. Select **columns C:I** and widen them to **85 pixels**. In the range **A2:B4**, enter the following row titles and data.

Amount of Loan	$125,000
Period (months)	36
Interest rate (per year)	5.5%

17. Click cell **C8**. Type **24** and then press Tab. Type **30** and then press Tab. Select the range **C8:D8**. Drag the fill handle to the right through cell **I8** to fill a pattern of months from 24 to 60 in increments of six months.

18. In cell **B9**, type **7.0%** and press Enter. Type **6.5%** and press Enter. Select the range **B9:B10**, and then drag the fill handle down through cell **B16** to fill a pattern of interest rates in increments of .5% from 7.00% down to 3.50%.

19. Click cell **C6**. Type **Payment Options** and then press Enter. **Merge and Center** this title across the range **C6:I6**. Change the **Font Size** to **14** and apply **Bold**. Click cell **C7**. Type **Number of Monthly Payments** and then use the **Format Painter** to apply the format of cell **C6** to cell **C7**.

(Project 3D–Auto Loan continues on the next page)

(Project 3D–Auto Loan continued)

20. Click cell **A9**, type **Rates** and then press Enter. Select the range **A9:A16**. On the **Home tab**, in the **Alignment group**, click the **Merge and Center** button, click the **Align Text Right** button, and then click the **Middle Align** button. Change the **Font Size** to **14** and apply **Bold**.

21. Click cell **B8**. On the **Formulas tab**, in the **Function Library group**, click the **Financial** button, and then click **PMT**. In the **Rate** box, type **b4/12** to divide the interest rate per year by 12 to convert it to a monthly interest rate. Press Tab, and then in the **Nper** box, type **b3** Press Tab. In the **Pv** box, type **-b2** and then click **OK**.

22. Select the range **B8:I16**. On the **Data tab**, in the **Data Tools group**, click the **What-If Analysis** button, and then in the displayed list, click **Data Table**. In the **Data Table** dialog box, in the **Row input cell** box, type **b3** and then press Tab. In the **Column input cell** box, type **b4** In the **Data Table** dialog box, click **OK** to create the data table.

23. Click cell **B8**, and then right-click to display the Mini toolbar. Click the **Format Painter** button. Select the range **C9:I16** to apply the same format. Select the ranges **B9:B16** and **C8:I8** and apply **Bold** and **Center**. Notice that in cell **G9**, the payment is *$2,993.28*, which is close to Jennifer's goal of a monthly payment of $3,000. At any of the interest rates, she will have to extend the loan over at least 48 months to stay within her goal of $3,000 per month.

24. Click the **Insert tab**, and then in the **Text group**, click **Header & Footer** to switch to **Page Layout View** and open the **Header area**. In the **Navigation group**, click the **Go to Footer** button, click just above the word *Footer*, then in the **Header & Footer Elements group**, click the **File Name** button. Click in a cell just above the footer to exit the **Footer area** and view your file name.

25. Click the **Page Layout tab**. In the **Page Setup group**, change the **Orientation** to **Landscape**. Click the **Margins** button, and then at the bottom of the **Margins gallery**, click **Custom Margins**. In the displayed **Page Setup** dialog box, under **Center on page**, select the **Horizontally** check box. Click **OK**, and then on the status bar, click the **Normal** button. Press Ctrl + Home to move to the top of the worksheet. Delete **Sheet3** from the workbook.

26. **Save** your workbook. Press Ctrl + F2 to display the worksheet in **Print Preview**. To print, in the **Print group**, click the **Print** button, under **Print what**, click the **Entire workbook** option button, and then click **OK**. To submit electronically, follow your instructor's directions. Determine if you are to print formulas for any or all of the worksheets in this workbook. To print formulas, refer to Activity 1.17 in Project 1A.

27. If you printed your formulas, be sure to redisplay the worksheet by pressing Ctrl + `. From the **Office** menu, click **Close**. If you are prompted to save changes, click **No**. **Close** Excel.

End **You have completed Project 3D**

Content-Based Assessments

Mastering Excel

Project 3E — Castings

In this project, you will apply the skills you practiced from the Objectives in Project 3A.

Objectives: 1. *Use SUM, AVERAGE, MEDIAN, MIN, and MAX Functions;* **2.** *Use COUNTIF and IF Functions, and Apply Conditional Formatting;* **3.** *Use a Date Function;* **4.** *Freeze Panes and Create an Excel Table;* **5.** *Format and Print a Large Worksheet.*

Adamantine Jewelry manufactures castings, which it sells to other jewelry makers. In the following Skills Review, you will edit a worksheet for Rose Elleni, Vice President of Production, detailing the current inventory of ring and earring castings at the Milan production facility. Your completed worksheet will look similar to the one shown in Figure 3.43.

For Project 3E, you will need the following file:

e3E_Castings

You will save your workbook as 3E_Castings_Firstname_Lastname

Figure 3.43

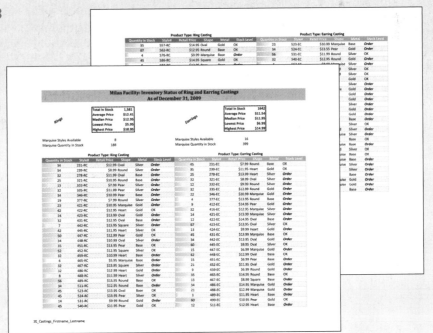

(Project 3E–Castings continues on the next page)

Content-Based Assessments

(Project 3E–Castings continued)

1. **Start** Excel. From the student files that accompany this text, locate and open **e3E_Castings**. In your **Excel Chapter 3** folder, save the file as **3E_Castings_Firstname_Lastname**

2. In cell **B4**, enter a function that sums the range **A12:A70**, and then apply **Comma Style** with zero decimal places. In cell **B5**, enter a function to calculate the average ring casting price in the range **C12:C70**. In cells **B6**, **B7**, and **B8**, use statistical functions to calculate the median ring casting price, the lowest ring casting price, and the highest ring casting price.

3. In the range **H4:H8** and by using the **Earring Casting** data, insert functions to make calculations similar to those you created in Step 2. The *Total in Stock* data is located in **column G** and the *Price* data is located in **column I**.

4. Move the range **A4:B8** to the range **C4:D8**, and then apply **Bold** and a **Thick Box Border** to the range. **AutoFit columns C:D**. In cell **A6**, type **Rings** Select the range **A5:A7**, merge the cells, and then change the **Orientation** to **30 Degrees**. Change the **Font Size** to **12**, and then apply **Bold** and **Italic**. **Center** and **Middle Align** the text.

5. Move the range **G4:H8** to the range **I4:J8**, and then apply **Bold** and a **Thick Box Border** to the range. **AutoFit columns I:J**. In cell **G5**, type **Earrings** and then use **Format Painter** to format in the same manner as cell **A5**.

6. Insert 3 rows above **row 10**. In cell **A10**, type **Marquise Styles Available** and then in cell **A11**, type **Marquise Quantity in Stock** Copy the two cells that you just typed, and then paste to the range **G10:G11**. In cell **C10**, enter a **COUNTIF** function that

counts **Marquise** items in the range **D15:D73**, and then create a similar formula in cell **I10** to count the **Marquise** items in the range **J15:J73**.

7. In cell **F15**, insert an **IF** function, and then test whether the value in cell **A15** is less than **35**. If true, display **Order** and if false, display **OK** Copy the function down through cell **F73**. Insert a similar **IF** function in **L15** to test whether the value in cell **G15** is less than **35**. If true, display **Order** and if false, display **OK** Copy the function down through cell **L73**.

8. To the range **F15:F73**, apply **Conditional Formatting** consisting of **Bold Italic** to any text that displays *Order*. Then, use the same **Conditional Formatting** rules to format the range **L15:L73**. Use **Conditional Formatting** to apply an **Orange Data Bar** to all of the quantities in stock for both **Ring Castings** and **Earring Castings**. **Save** the changes you have made to your workbook.

9. For both **Ring Castings** and **Earring Castings**, replace all occurrences of **Triangle** with **Pear** In cell **A74**, type **Last Edited by Rose Elleni** In cell **A75**, insert the **NOW** function. Adjust the width of **column A** to **110 pixels** so that the date and time display fully.

10. Select the range of data that comprises the **Ring Casting** data, insert a **Table** with a header row, and then apply **Table Style Medium 5**. **Sort** the table on the **Retail Price** from **Smallest to Largest**. Then filter the table by displaying only the **Marquise** shapes.

11. Click any cell in the table so that the table is selected, and then modify the **Table Style Options** to include a **Total Row**. In cell

(Project 3E–Castings continues on the next page)

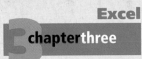

(Project 3E–Castings continued)

A74, calculate the **Sum** for the *Quantity in Stock* column. In cell **C11**, type the value that displays in cell **A74**. Clear the **Total Row** from the table, and then clear the filter from the **Shape** column. **Sort** the table from **A to Z** on the **Style#** column, and then convert the table to a range.

12. Select the range of data that comprises the **Earring Casting** data, insert a **Table** with a header row, and then apply **Table Style Medium 4**. **Sort** the table on the **Retail Price** from **Smallest to Largest**. Then filter the table by displaying only the **Marquise** shapes.

13. Modify the **Table Style Options** to include the **Total Row**, and then in cell **G74**, calculate the **Sum** for the *Quantity in Stock* column. In cell **I11**, type the value that displays in cell **G74**. Clear the **Total Row** from the table, and then clear the filter from the **Shape** column. **Sort** the table from **A to Z** on the **Style#** column, and then convert the table to a range.

14. Insert a **Footer** with the **File Name** in the left section. On the **Page Layout tab**, change the **Orientation** to **Landscape**. Change the **Print Titles** option by repeating rows **13:14** at the top of each page, and then **Center** the worksheet **Horizontally**. On the **Page Layout tab**, in the **Scale to Fit group**, click the **down Scale arrow** several times to display **80%**. Delete the unused worksheets, and then return to **Normal** view.

15. **Save** 💾 your workbook. **Print** the worksheet, or submit electronically. If you are directed to submit printed formulas, refer to Activity 9.17 to do so.

16. If you printed your formulas, be sure to redisplay the worksheet by pressing Ctrl + `. From the **Office** menu, click **Close**. If the dialog box displays asking if you want to save changes, click **No** so that you do *not* save the changes you made for printing formulas. **Close** Excel.

End **You have completed Project 3E**

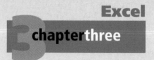

Excel
chapterthree

Mastering Excel

Project 3F — Studio

In this project, you will apply the skills you practiced from the Objectives in Project 3B.

Objectives: 6. *Use Financial Functions;* **7.** *Use Goal Seek;* **8.** *Create a Data Table.*

In the following Mastering Excel project, you will create a worksheet for Marco Canaperi, President of Adamantine Jewelry, that analyzes loan options for a house in Maine that the company is considering purchasing and converting to a design studio. Marco wants to establish a design facility in the United States, but would like to keep the monthly loan payment below $6,000. The worksheets of your workbook will look similar to Figure 3.44.

For Project 3F, you will need the following file:

New blank Excel workbook

You will save your workbook as
3F_Studio_Loan_Firstname_Lastname

Figure 3.44

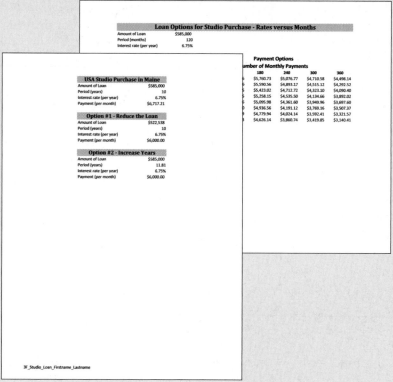

(Project 3F–Studio continues on the next page)

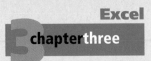

(Project 3F–Studio continued)

1. **Start** Excel and display a new blank workbook. **Save** the workbook in your **Excel Chapter 3** folder as 3F_Studio_Loan_ Firstname_Lastname Widen **column A** to **185 pixels** and **column B** to **100 pixels**. In cell **A1**, type USA Studio Purchase in Maine **Merge and Center** the title in the range **A1:B1**, change the **Font** to **Cambria**, change the **Font Size** to **14**, apply **Bold**, and then add a **Fill Color** of **Blue, Accent 1, Lighter 40%**. Rename the worksheet tab as **Studio Purchase** In the range **A2:B5**, enter the following row titles and data.

Amount of Loan	$585,000
Period (years)	10
Interest rate (per year)	6.75%
Payment (per month)	

2. In cell **B5**, insert the **PMT** function using the data from the range **A2:B5**. Be sure that you divide the interest rate by 12 and multiply the years by 12, and that the payment displays as a positive number. The result is *$6,717.21*. Recall that Marco would prefer to keep the monthly payment below $6,000. Use **Goal Seek** to reduce the loan amount so that the payment does not exceed $6,000.

3. In **A7**, type **Option #1 - Reduce the Loan** Copy the format from cell **A1** to cell **A7**. Copy the range **A2:B5**, and then paste the **Values and number formats** to cell **A8**.

4. In cell **B2**, type **585000** to restore the original loan amount. Then use **Goal Seek** to increase the number of years in which to finance the studio so that the payment does not exceed $6,000. In **A13**, type **Option #2 - Increase Years** Format the cell the same as cell **A7**. Copy the range **A2:B5**, and then paste the **Values and number formats** to cell **A14**. Display the

value in **B15** with two decimal places, and then in cell **B3**, type **10** to restore the original value. Insert a footer with the **File Name** in the left section, and then **Center** the worksheet **Horizontally** on the page.

5. **Save** your workbook and return to **Normal** view. To determine how changes in interest rates and number of payments affect the payment amount, Marco will set up a two-variable data table. Rename the **Sheet2 tab** to **Studio Payment Table**

6. In the new worksheet, widen **column A** to **165 pixels**. Widen **column B** to **80 pixels**. In cell **A1**, type **Loan Options for Studio Purchase - Rates versus Months Merge and Center** this title across the range **A1:H1**. Change the **Font** to **Cambria**, the **Font Size** to **16**, apply **Bold**, and then apply a **Fill Color** of **Blue, Accent 1, Lighter 40%**.

7. Widen **columns C:H** to **85 pixels**. In the range **A2:B4**, enter the following row titles and data.

Amount of Loan	$585,000
Period (months)	120
Interest rate (per year)	6.75%

8. The lender with whom Adamantine Jewelry is financing the studio purchase has loan programs based on 5-, 10-, 15-, 20-, 25-, and 30-year terms. In cell **C8**, type **60**—the number of months in a 5-year loan. In **D8**, type **120**—the number of months in a 10-year loan. Then, fill the series across for the remaining four terms. **Center** and **Bold** the series information.

9. Beginning in cell **B9**, enter varying interest rates in increments of .5% beginning with **8.5%** and ending with **5%**. Format all the interest rates with two decimal places, and then **Center** and **Bold** the rates. In cell **C6**, type **Payment Options** and then **Merge**

(Project 3F–Studio continues on the next page)

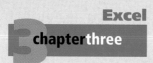

(Project 3F–Studio continued)

and Center the title across the range **C6:H6**. Change the **Font Size** to **14**, and then apply **Bold**. In cell **C7**, type **Number of Monthly Payments** and then copy the format of cell **C6** to cell **C7**.

10. In cell **B8**, enter a **PMT** function using the information in cells **B2:B4**. Be sure that you convert the interest rate to a monthly rate and that the result displays as a positive number. Create a **Data Table** in the range **B8:H16** using the information in cells **B2:B4** in which the **Row input cell** is the **Period** and the **Column input cell** is the **Interest rate**. Copy the format from **B8** to the results in the data table. Insert a

footer with the **File Name** in the left section. Change the **Orientation** to **Landscape**, and then **Center** the worksheet **Horizontally** on the page. Delete **Sheet3** from the workbook, and then return to **Normal** view.

11. **Save** your workbook. **Print** the **Entire workbook**, or, submit electronically. If you are directed to submit printed formulas, refer to Activity 1.17 to do so.

12. If you printed your formulas, be sure to redisplay the worksheet by pressing Ctrl + `'`. From the **Office** menu, click **Close**. If you are prompted to save changes, click **No**. **Close** Excel.

End **You have completed Project 3F**

Content-Based Assessments

Excel

chapterthree

Mastering Excel

Project 3G — Sales

In this project, you will apply the skills you practiced from the Objectives in Project 3A and 3B.

Objectives: 1. *Use SUM, AVERAGE, MEDIAN, MIN, and MAX Functions;* **2.** *Use COUNTIF and IF Functions, and Apply Conditional Formatting;* **3.** *Use a Date Function;* **4.** *Freeze Panes and Create an Excel Table;* **5.** *Format and Print a Large Worksheet;* **7.** *Use Goal Seek.*

In the following Mastering Excel assessment, you will edit a worksheet for Jennifer Bernard, U.S. Sales Director for Adamantine Jewelry, that calculates the October sales commission and bonuses for the U.S. sales representatives. The sales representatives earn 15% commission and those whose sales exceed $20,000 per month earn a bonus of $750. The worksheet will also provide sales statistics for the month of October and will detail November sales goals. The worksheets of your workbook will look similar to Figure 3.45.

For Project 3G, you will need the following file:

e3G_Sales

You will save your workbook as
3G_Sales_Firstname_Lastname

Figure 3.45

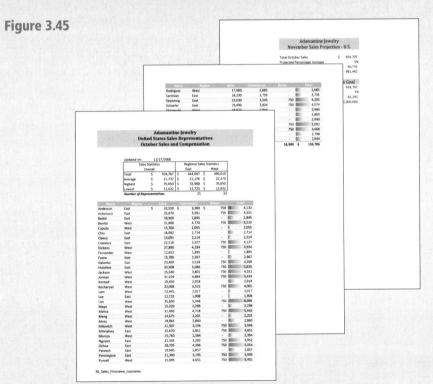

(Project 3G–Sales continues on the next page)

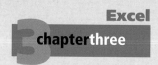

Mastering Excel

(Project 3G–Sales continued)

1. **Start** Excel, locate and open the file **e3G_Sales**, and then save the file in your **Excel Chapter 3** folder as 3G_Sales_ Firstname_Lastname Rename **Sheet1** as **Sales Data** In cell **C6**, enter the **NOW** function, and then on the **Home tab**, in the **Number group**, click the **Number Format arrow** and apply the **Short Date** format to the date. In cell **C9**, enter a function that sums the total sales in the range **C16:C58**. In cells **C10**, **C11**, and **C12**, use statistical functions to calculate the average sales, the highest sales, and the lowest sales.

2. In cell **D16**, construct a formula to calculate the commission on sales earned by **Anderson** by using a commission formula of *Sales times 15%*. Format the result with **Comma Style** and **zero decimal places**. Copy the formula down for each sales representative. In cell **E16**, enter an **IF** function and test whether the sales value in cell **C16** is greater than **20000**. If true, display **750** and if false, display **0** Format the result as **Comma Style**, with **zero decimal places**, and then fill the formula down for each sales representative. Those representatives who receive no bonus will display – in the cell.

3. In cell **F16**, construct a formula to calculate the total compensation by adding the **Commission** and **Bonus** amounts for **Anderson**. The format of Comma Style and zero decimal places will be applied based on the reference to cell D16. Fill the formula down for each sales representative. With the range **F16:F58** still selected, apply **Light Blue Data Bar Conditional Formatting** to the **Total** column. In cell **D13**, enter a **COUNTIF** function to count the number of sales representatives in the **East** region. Enter a similar function in cell **E13** for the **West** region.

4. Select the range **A15:F58** and then **Insert** a **Table** with headers. Apply **Table Style**

(Project 3G–Sales continues on the next page)

Medium 7. In the **Name** column, **Sort** the table **A to Z**. Change the **Table Style Options** to display the **Total Row**.

5. If necessary, scroll up so that you can view **rows 1:18** on your screen. Then, select **row 16**, click the **View tab**, in the **Window group**, click the **Freeze Panes** button, and then click **Freeze Panes**. Scroll to bring the **Total row** at the bottom of the table closer to **row 15**—it is OK to leave three or four rows visible for visual reference. Recall that you can freeze panes in this manner to keep row titles visible while scrolling down through a large amount of data.

6. Filter the table to display only the sales representatives in the **East** region—the table will be filtered even though not all rows are in view. Click cell **C59**, and then by using the functions available from the **Total row arrow** in the **Sales** column, **Sum** the **Sales** for the **East** region. Right-click over the result, **Copy** the result, right-click over cell **D9**, click **Paste Special**, and then **Paste** its **value and number format** to cell **D9**. Using the same technique, and by using the **Total row arrow** in the **Sales** column, calculate the **Average** for the **East** region, and then copy and paste the **value and number format** to cell **D10**. By using the **Total row arrow** in the **Sales** column, calculate the highest and lowest sales amount for the **East** region, and paste the **values and number formats** to cells **D11** and **D12**. You can see that by freezing panes and using the shortcut menus, you can easily copy and paste values from one section of your worksheet to another without unnecessary scrolling.

7. Filter the **Sales** data for the **West** region, scroll to view the data and notice that the Freeze Panes command is still in effect. Position the **Total row** close to **row 15**. Then, by using the **Total row arrow** in the

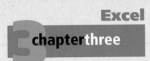

(Project 3G–Sales continued)

Sales column in the manner you did in the previous step, make similar calculations and then copy and paste the **values and number formats** into the range **E9:E12**.

8. Clear the filter to redisplay all of the data in the table, and then in the **Total** row, **Sum** the **Sales**, **Commission**, **Bonus**, and **Total** columns. Select the four totals, right-click, and then apply **Accounting Number Format** with **zero decimal places**. Click the **View tab**, in the **Window group**, click the **Freeze Panes** button, and then click **Unfreeze Panes**. Click inside the table, and then on the **Design tab**, convert the table to a range. To the ranges **C9:E12** and **C16:F16**, apply **Accounting Number Format** with **zero decimal places**.

9. Insert a **Footer** with the **File Name** in the left section, and then **Center** the worksheet **Horizontally**. Click the **Print Titles** button and repeat **row 15** at the top of each page. Return to **Normal** view and display the top of your worksheet.

10. **Save** your work up to this point. **Rename Sheet2** as **November Sales Goal** In cell **A1**, type **Adamantine Jewelry** and then adjust the column width of **column A** to **220 pixels**. **Merge and Center** the title across **A1:B1**. Change the **Font** to **Cambria**, change the **Font Size** to **14**, and then add a **Fill Color** of **Orange, Accent 6, Lighter 40%**. In cell **A2**, type **November Sales Projection – U.S.** Copy the format from cell **A1** to cell **A2**. In the range **A4:B7**, enter the following data.

Total October Sales	
Projected Percentage Increase	5%
Projected November Increase	
Sales Projection November 2010	

11. Click cell **B4**, type = to begin a formula, click the **Sales Data worksheet** to make it the active sheet, click cell **C9**, and then press Enter to return to the **November Sales Goal** worksheet and reference the **Total October Sales** in cell **B4**. Format the result with **Accounting Number Format** with **zero decimal places**.

12. In cell **B6**, construct a formula to multiply the **Total October Sales** times the **Projected Percentage Increase**, and then format the result the same as cell **B4**. In cell **B7**, construct a formula to add the **Total October Sales** and the **Projected November Increase**.

13. Jennifer's sales goal for the U.S. sales representatives is $1,000,000. Use **Goal Seek** to determine the **Projected Percentage Increase** if the **Sales Projection November 2010** value is **1,000,000**. In cell **A9**, type **Increase Needed to Reach Sales Goal** and then format the cell the same as cell **A1**. **Copy** the range **A4:B7**, and then paste the **Values and number formats** to cell **A10**. In cell **B5**, reset the original value to **5%** and press Enter.

14. Insert a **Footer** in the left section with the **File Name**, and then **Center** the worksheet **Horizontally** on the page. Return to **Normal** view and display the top of the worksheet. Delete **Sheet3** from the workbook.

15. **Save** your workbook. **Print** the **Entire workbook** or submit electronically as directed. If you are directed to submit printed formulas, refer to Activity 9.17 to do so. If you printed your formulas, be sure to redisplay the worksheet by pressing Ctrl + ˋ. From the **Office** menu, click **Close**. If you are prompted to save changes, click **No**. **Close** Excel.

End You have completed Project 3G

Content-Based Assessments

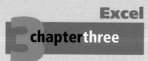
Project 3H — Retirement

In this project, you will apply the skills you practiced from the Objectives in Projects 3A and Project 3B.

Objectives: 3. *Use a Date Function;* **6.** *Use Financial Functions;* **8.** *Create a Data Table.*

In the following Mastering Excel project, you will create a data table for Rosetta Caputo, the Chief Financial Officer for Adamantine Jewelry, that she will use to consider investment alternatives for the employee benefits retirement fund. Your workbook will look similar to Figure 3.46.

For Project 3H, you will need the following file:

New blank Excel workbook

**You will save your workbook as
3H_Retirement_Firstname_Lastname**

Figure 3.46

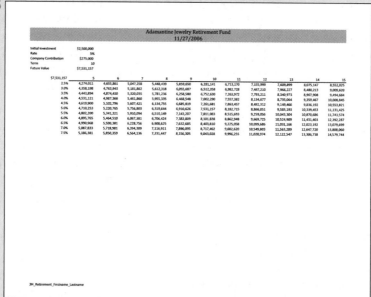

(Project 3H–Retirement continues on the next page)

(Project 3H—Retirement continued)

1. **Start** Excel and display a new blank workbook. In your **Excel Chapter 3** folder, **Save** the file as 3H_Retirement_Firstname_Lastname In cell **A1**, type **Adamantine Jewelry Retirement Fund** and then **Merge and Center** the text across **A1:L1**. Change the **Font** to **Cambria**, change the **Font Size** to **16**, and then apply a **Fill Color** of **Red, Accent 2, Lighter 40%**.

2. Copy the formatting from cell **A1** to cell **A2**. Then, in cell **A2**, enter the **NOW** function. On the **Home tab**, in the **Number group**, click the **Number Format arrow**, and then apply the **Short Date** format. In the range **A4:B8**, enter the following row titles and data and then **AutoFit column A.**

Initial Investment	$2,500,000
Rate	5%
Company Contribution	$275,000
Term	10
Future Value	

3. Click cell **B8**. Click the **Formulas tab**, and then insert the **Financial** function **FV** to calculate the future value of the retirement fund based on the data that you entered in Step 2. Complete the arguments as follows: the **Rate** is the value in cell **B5**, and **Nper** is the value in cell **B7**. **Pmt** is the amount of the **Company contribution** in cell **B6**, and **Pv** is the **Initial Investment** in cell **B4**. Click **OK**, and then edit the formula in the **Formula Bar** so that the result displays as a positive number. Format the **Future Value** with **zero decimal places**. Based on the calculations, at the end of ten years, the fund will have a value of $7,531,157.

4. In the range **B10:L10**, in 1-year increments, use **AutoFill** to enter a series of years from **5** to **15**, indicating the term of the retirement fund. Apply a **Thick Bottom Border** to the range. Beginning in cell **A11**, enter the possible interest rates for the fund beginning with **2.5%** and increasing in increments of .5% up to 7.5%. Format the interest rates with **one decimal place**.

5. In cell **A10** type **=b8** to enter a formula that references cell **B8**. Select the range **A10:L21**, and then create a **Data Table** with a **Row input cell** that references cell **B7** and a **Column input cell** that references **B5**. Format the results in the data table with **Comma Style, zero decimal places**. You can see by the resulting data table, that the higher the interest rate that can be obtained for the investment, the higher the value of the fund will be in future years.

6. Insert a footer in the left section with the **File Name**, exit the **Footer area**, display the **Page Layout tab**, and then **Center** the worksheet **Horizontally** on the page. Change the **Orientation** to **Landscape**. In the **Scale to Fit group**, set the **Width** to **1 page** and the **Height** to **1 page** (or scale to 70%). Return to **Normal** view, display the top of the worksheet, and then delete the extra worksheets from the workbook.

7. **Save** your workbook. **Print** the worksheet, or submit electronically as directed. If you are directed to submit printed formulas, refer to Activity 9.17 to do so.

8. If you printed your formulas, be sure to redisplay the worksheet by pressing Ctrl + `. From the **Office** menu, click **Close**. If you are prompted to save changes, click **No**. **Close** Excel.

End **You have completed Project 3H** ─────────

Content-Based Assessments

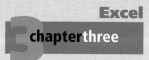

Excel

chapterthree Mastering Excel

Project 3I — Opals

In this project, you will apply the skills you practiced from all of the Objectives in Projects 3A and 3B.

Objectives: 1. *Use SUM, AVERAGE, MEDIAN, MIN, and MAX Functions;* **2.** *Use COUNTIF and IF Functions, and Apply Conditional Formatting;* **3.** *Use a Date Function;* **4.** *Freeze Panes and Create an Excel Table;* **5.** *Format and Print a Large Worksheet;* **6.** *Use Financial Functions;* **7.** *Use Goal Seek;* **8.** *Create a Data Table.*

In the following Mastering Excel assessment, you will edit a worksheet for Adamantine Jewelry's Chief Financial Officer, Rosetta Caputo. Adamantine Jewelry is considering the purchase of Opal Industries—a large distributor of elegant and expensive opal jewelry. The purchase includes the entire current inventory held by Opal Industries. Rosetta wants to compute the value of the Opal Industries inventory and determine which items are still in production and which items are in a warehouse. She must also explore alternatives for financing the purchase. Your completed workbook will look similar to Figure 3.47.

For Project 3I, you will need the following file:

e3I_Opals

You will save your workbook as
3I_Opals_Firstname_Lastname

Figure 3.47

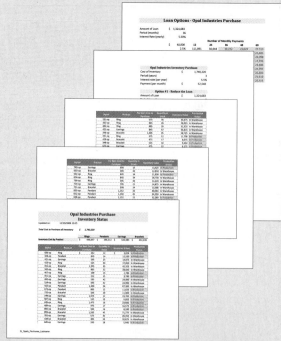

(Project 3I–Opals continues on the next page)

Content-Based Assessments

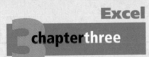

Mastering Excel

(Project 3I–Opals continued)

1. **Start** Excel. From the student files that accompany this text, locate and open the file **e3I_Opals**, and then save it in your **Excel Chapter 3** folder as 3I_Opals_ Firstname_Lastname

2. In cell **B3**, insert the **NOW** function. In cell **E11**, construct a formula to calculate the **Inventory Value** of the first Style# by multiplying the **Per Item Cost to Purchase** times the **Quantity in Stock**, and then copy the formula down through **row 76**. Format the selected range with **Comma Style** and **zero decimal places**.

3. Opal Industries moves stock from the production facility to the warehouse after 20 items are produced. In cell **F11**, enter an **IF** function to test whether the **Quantity in Stock** value in cell **D11** is **greater than or equal to 20**. If true, display In Warehouse and if false, display In Production Copy the formula down through **row 76**. With the range still selected, use the **Text that Contains** conditional formatting to apply **Green Fill with Dark Green Text** to cells that contain In Production

4. Select the range **A10:F76**, and then **Insert** a **Table** with headers. Apply **Table Style Light 9**. Change the **Table Style Options** to display the **Total Row**. Press Ctrl + Home to deselect the table and view **row 1** on your screen. Select **row 11**, click the **View tab**, in the **Window group**, click the **Freeze Panes** button, and then click **Freeze Panes**.

5. Filter the table to display only the **Ring** products, and then scroll so that the **Total row** is closer to the column titles in **row 14**. In the **Total row**, calculate the **Sum** for the **Inventory Value** of Rings, right-click over the result, click **Copy**, right-

click over cell **C8**, right-click, click **Paste Special**, and then click **Values and number formats**. Even though some rows are out of view, the calculation is made on the appropriate rows. Recall that by freezing panes and using shortcut menus in this manner, you minimize the amount of scrolling necessary to perform actions.

6. Repeat Step 5 for the **Pendant**, **Earrings**, and **Bracelet** products in the appropriate cells. Then clear any filters to display all of the data in the table. Click any table cell, click the **Design tab**, remove the **Total Row** from the table, and then convert the table to a range. In cell **C5**, enter a function to calculate the cost to purchase the total inventory, which is the sum of the range **C8:F8**. Your result is 1,740,220. On the **View tab**, in the **Window group**, click the **Freeze Panes** button, and then click **Unfreeze Panes**. Hold down Ctrl and select cell **C11**, cell **E11**, cell **C5**, and the range **C8:F8**. To the selected cells, apply **Accounting Number Format** with **zero decimal places**. Set **columns C:F** to **100 pixels**.

7. Insert a footer with the **File Name** in the left section, and then **Center** the sheet **Horizontally**. Set the **Print Titles** option to repeat **row 10** at the top of each page. Change the **Orientation** to **Landscape**, return to **Normal** view, and then display the top of your worksheet. **Save** your workbook.

8. **Copy** cell **C5**, display the **Goal** sheet, and then use **Paste Special** to paste the **Values and number formats** to cell **B2** in the **Goal** sheet. In cell **B5**, insert the **PMT** function using the data from the range **B2:B4**. Be sure that you convert the interest rate and period to reflect monthly payments by dividing the interest rate by 12

(Project 3I–Opals continues on the next page)

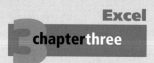
(Project 3I–Opals continued)

and multiplying the years by 12. Display the result as a positive number. Apply the **Accounting Number Format** with **zero decimal places** to cell **B5**—your result is *$52,548.*

9. Rosetta prefers that the monthly payment not exceed $40,000. Use **Goal Seek** to determine the amount of money that Adamantine Jewelry can finance to keep the payment at $40,000. The interest rate and period will not change. The result is *$1,324.683.07.*

10. **Copy** the range **B2:B5**, and then paste the **Values and number formats** to cell **B8**. In cell **B2** type **1740220** to restore the original amount.

11. Insert a footer in the left section with the **File Name**, and then **Center** the sheet **Horizontally** on the page. Display the sheet in **Normal** view, and then **Save** your workbook.

12. **Copy** cell **B8**, display the **Financing** sheet, and then in cell **B3**, paste the value and number format; this will reference the amount that Rosetta has decided to finance as the **Amount of Loan**. In cell **B7**, enter a **PMT** function using the data in the range **B3:B5**. The period is already expressed in months, but the rate is not. Be sure that the result displays as a positive number. To determine how changes in interest rates and number of payments affect the payment amount, Rosetta will set up a two-variable data table. Rosetta is exploring loan programs from 12 to 60 months in duration and at rates of 2.5% to 6.5%.

13. Select the range **B7:G16**, and then create a **Data Table** using the information in cells **B3:B5** in which the **Row input cell** is the **Period** and the **Column input cell** is the **Interest rate**. Format the data with **Comma Style** and **zero decimal** places. Format cell **B7** with **Accounting Number Format** and **zero decimal places**.

14. Select the data table results—the range **C8:G16**. Recall that Rosetta prefers a monthly payment that does not exceed $40,000. Apply **Conditional Formatting** using the **Highlight Cells Rules Less Than** option. In the **Format cells that are LESS THAN** box, type **40000** and use **Light Red Fill with Dark Red Text**. Click any cell to deselect. Rosetta can clearly see which financing rates and terms are acceptable.

15. Insert a footer in the left section with the **File Name**, and then **Center** the sheet **Horizontally** on the page. Display the sheet in **Normal** view and press Ctrl + Home to display the top of the worksheet.

16. **Save** your workbook. **Print** the **Entire workbook**, or submit electronically as directed. If you are directed to submit printed formulas, refer to Activity 9.17 to do so.

17. If you printed your formulas, be sure to redisplay the sheet by pressing Ctrl + `. From the **Office** menu, click **Close**. If you are prompted to save changes, click **No**. **Close** Excel.

End **You have completed Project 3I**

Content-Based Assessments

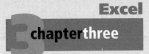

Project 3J—Business Running Case

In this project, you will apply the skills you practiced in Projects 3A and 3B.

From My Computer, navigate to the student files that accompany this textbook. In the folder **03_business_running_case_pg37_86**, locate and open the folder for this chapter. Open and print the instructions for this project, which are provided to you in Adobe PDF format. Follow the instructions and use the skills you have gained thus far to assist Jennifer Nelson in meeting the challenges of owning and running her business.

 End You have completed Project 3J _____

Outcomes-Based Assessments

Excel
chapterthree

Rubric

The following outcomes-based assessments are *open-ended assessments*. That is, there is no specific correct result; your result will depend on your approach to the information provided. Make *Professional Quality* your goal. Use the following scoring rubric to guide you in *how* to approach the problem, and then to evaluate *how well* your approach solves the problem.

The *criteria*—Software Mastery, Content, Format and Layout, and Process—represent the knowledge and skills you have gained that you can apply to solving the problem. The *levels of performance*—Professional Quality, Approaching Professional Quality, or Needs Quality Improvements—help you and your instructor evaluate your result.

	Your completed project is of Professional Quality if you:	Your completed project is Approaching Professional Quality if you:	Your completed project Needs Quality Improvements if you:
1-Software Mastery	Choose and apply the most appropriate skills, tools, and features and identify efficient methods to solve the problem.	Choose and apply some appropriate skills, tools, and features, but not in the most efficient manner.	Choose inappropriate skills, tools, or features, or are inefficient in solving the problem.
2-Content	Construct a solution that is clear and well organized, contains content that is accurate, appropriate to the audience and purpose, and is complete. Provide a solution that contains no errors of spelling, grammar, or style.	Construct a solution in which some components are unclear, poorly organized, inconsistent, or incomplete. Misjudge the needs of the audience. Have some errors in spelling, grammar, or style, but the errors do not detract from comprehension.	Construct a solution that is unclear, incomplete, or poorly organized, containing some inaccurate or inappropriate content; and contains many errors of spelling, grammar, or style. Do not solve the problem.
3-Format and Layout	Format and arrange all elements to communicate information and ideas, clarify function, illustrate relationships, and indicate relative importance.	Apply appropriate format and layout features to some elements, but not others. Overuse features, causing minor distraction.	Apply format and layout that does not communicate information or ideas clearly. Do not use format and layout features to clarify function, illustrate relationships, or indicate relative importance. Use available features excessively, causing distraction.
4-Process	Use an organized approach that integrates planning, development, self-assessment, revision, and reflection.	Demonstrate an organized approach in some areas, but not others; or, use an insufficient process of organization throughout.	Do not use an organized approach to solve the problem.

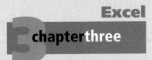

Problem Solving

Project 3K — Capital Equipment

In this project, you will construct a solution by applying any combination of the skills you practiced from the Objectives in Projects 3A and 3B.

For Project 3K, you will need the following file:

New blank Excel workbook

You will save your workbook as
3K_Capital_Equipment_Firstname_Lastname

Adamantine Jewelry plans to renovate the Milan production facility. The renovation consists primarily of the purchase and installation of new capital equipment used in the production of earrings and pendants. The renovation and equipment will cost $1,500,000. Rosetta Caputo, Chief Financial Officer, is exploring financing options for the purchase of the equipment. Create a workbook with two worksheets that Rosetta can use to analyze loan payment information. In the first worksheet, enter a title in cell A1. In A2:A5 enter the following row titles: Amount of Loan, Period (years), Interest Rate (per year), and Payment (per month). In B2:B4 enter the loan amount, $1,500,000; the Period, 10 years; and the Interest rate, 6.5%. Adjust the column widths as necessary. In B5 use the preceding data to construct a PMT function to calculate the monthly loan payment, converting the interest rate and the period to reflect monthly payments.

Marco Canaperi, the company president, has asked Rosetta to keep the loan payments below $15,000. Use Goal Seek to explore two options for reducing the loan payment, either by reducing the loan or by increasing the number of years. Arrange the worksheet so that the two loan options display similar to Project 3B in the chapter.

In the second worksheet, using your work in Project 3B as a guide, create a data table to calculate payments over 10, 15, 20, and 25 years with varying interest rates from 3.5% to 8.5% in .5% increments. In A2:B4 enter the row titles and the loan information. In C6:C7 enter titles that describe the data table. In C8:F8 enter the yearly increments. In B9:B19 enter the interest rates in .5% increments. In B8 construct the PMT function, and then create the data table. On each worksheet, apply appropriate number formatting, use borders, fill colors, and font styles and sizes to create a professional worksheet. Add a footer to each worksheet that includes the file name, center the worksheets on the page, and delete unused sheets. Save the workbook as **3K_Capital_Equipment_Firstname_Lastname** and submit as directed.

End You have completed Project 3K ⸻⸻

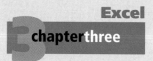

Problem Solving

Project 3L—Commission

In this project, you will construct a solution by applying any combination of the skills you practiced from the Objectives in Projects 3A and 3B.

For Project 3L, you will need the following file:

e3L_Commission

**You will save your workbook as
3L_Commission_Firstname_Lastname**

The U.S. Sales Director for Adamantine Jewelry, Jennifer Bernard, wants a report on the December sales and compensation for the U.S. sales representatives. From your student files, open e11L_Commissions. Calculate the Commission (Commission Rate times Sales) for each sales representative, using absolute cell references as necessary. Sales representatives whose sales exceed $20,000 receive a bonus of $750. In the Bonus column, use an IF function to calculate bonuses—the value_if_true is 750 and the value_if_false is 0. Then calculate the total Compensation (Commission + Bonus) for each sales representative. Use Conditional Formatting to apply Data Bars to the Total Compensation column. In the range B8:C12, enter functions to calculate the total sales and commission, the average sales and commission, the median sales and commission, and the highest and lowest sales and commission.

Insert a table using the range of data A16:F59. Sort the table from A to Z on the Name column. Add a Total Row to the table, freeze panes if you want to do so, and then Filter the table for each region. Calculate the total Sales and Commissions for each region and enter the amounts in cells F8:G11 being sure to paste the value and number format. Then, total the Sales and Commissions in F12:G12. Convert the table to a range and unfreeze panes if necessary. Use the NOW function to enter the current date in cell B5 and apply the Short Date format. Add the file name to the footer, delete unused sheets, set up for printing appropriately, including printing the table header row on each page. Save the workbook as **3L_Commission_Firstname_Lastname** and submit it as directed.

End You have completed Project 3L _____

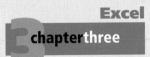

Problem Solving

Project 3M — Truck Purchase

In this project, you will construct a solution by applying any combination of the skills you practiced from the Objectives in Projects 3A and 3B.

For Project 3M, you will need the following file:

New blank Excel workbook

**You will save your workbook as
3M_Truck_Purchase_Firstname_Lastname**

Rosetta Caputo, Chief Financial Officer for Adamantine Jewelry, is exploring financing options for the purchase of five new delivery trucks for the Milan production facility. The cost of the five trucks is $150,000.

Rosetta wants to look at various loan arrangements by creating a data table. In A1 enter an appropriate title for the worksheet. In A2:A4 enter the following row titles: Amount of Loan, Period (months), Interest Rate (per year). In B2:B4 enter the financing data: $150,000; 36; 4.5%. In C6 fill the payment periods in six-month increments beginning with 24 and concluding with 60. In the column beginning in cell B7, create a list of varying interest rates from 4.5% to 8% in .5% increments. In B6 construct a PMT function using the data in cells B2:B4, then create the data table. Use formatting and editing techniques that you practiced in this chapter so that the workbook looks professional and is easy to read. Add the file name to the footer, delete unused sheets, and then arrange for attractive printing. Save the workbook as **3M_Truck_Purchase_Firstname_Lastname** and submit it as directed.

End You have completed Project 3M ——————

Excel

chapterthree

Problem Solving

Project 3N—Watches

In this project, you will construct a solution by applying any combination of the skills you practiced from the Objectives in Projects 3A and 3B.

For Project 3N, you will need the following file:

e3N_Watches

**You will save your workbook as
3N_Watches_Firstname_Lastname**

Rose Elleni, Vice President of Production, has requested a worksheet detailing the current inventory of watches at the Milan production facility. She wants the worksheet to include quantities, styles, prices, product descriptions, and stock levels. Open e3N_Watches and complete the worksheet as follows: In the Stock Level column, enter an IF function that tests the Quantity in Stock. Items with less than 35 in stock must be ordered. If the items do not need to be ordered, the Stock Level is OK. Use Conditional Formatting to apply bold and italic to the items in the Stock Level column designated as Order. In B5 use a function to sum the Quantity in Stock column. In B6:B9 use functions to calculate the Average, Median, Lowest, and Highest values in the Retail Price column.

Insert a table using the range A12:F65. Sort the table from Smallest to Largest on Style# and then use filters to display and calculate the Quantity in Stock for each type of Band and enter the values and number formats in F6:F8. In F9, construct a formula to calculate the total Quantity in Stock. Convert the table to a range. Add the file name to the footer, delete unused pages, print the table headers and use the Print Titles option so that row 12 prints at the top of every page. Save the workbook as **3N_Watches_Firstname_Lastname** and submit it as directed.

End **You have completed Project 3N** ⎯⎯⎯⎯⎯⎯⎯⎯

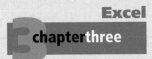
Project 3O—Sales Directors

In this project, you will construct a solution by applying any combination of the skills you practiced from the Objectives in Projects 3A and 3B.

For Project 3O, you will need the following file:

e3O_Sales_Directors

You will save your workbook as
3O_Sales_Directors_Firstname_Lastname

The U.S. Regional Directors for Adamantine Jewelry are responsible for maximizing profits at several retail locations. Jennifer Bernard, the U.S. Sales Director, has requested an annual profit analysis. Open the file e3O_Sales_Directors, which contains summary information about the sales, expenses, and profits in the Eastern Region. Apply Data Bars to the Profit column. Insert a table and then sort the table from A to Z on the City column. Sort again from Smallest to Largest on the Sales Director column. Filter the table by each region and then calculate the total profit by region and enter the results in the range C5:C8. Convert the table to a range and if necessary wrap the text in row 10. Use formatting and editing techniques that you learned in this chapter so that the worksheet is attractive and easy to read. Add the file name to the footer and save the workbook as **3O_Sales_Directors_Firstname_Lastname** and submit it as directed.

End **You have completed Project 3O** _____

Outcomes-Based Assessments

You and *GO!*

Project 3P — You and *GO!*

In this project, you will construct a solution by applying any combination of the Objectives found in Projects 3A and 3B.

From My Computer, navigate to the student files that accompany this textbook. In the folder **04_you_and_go_pg87_102**, locate and open the folder for this chapter. Open and print the instructions for this project, which are provided to you in Adobe PDF format. Follow the instructions to create a data table to compare vehicle loan terms.

End **You have completed Project 3P** ———————

GO! with Help

Project 3Q — *GO!* with Help

In this chapter, you practiced using statistical, logical, and financial functions. Sometimes a single function is not sufficient to complete a calculation. For example, when you create an IF function, you must specify the value_if_true and the value_if_false. Either of these values may require that you sum a range of cells. You can nest (combine) the functions by making the sum function a part of the IF function argument. In this exercise, you will use Help to find out how to nest functions.

1 **Start** Excel. At the far right end of the Ribbon, click the **Microsoft Office Excel Help** button .

2 Click the **Search arrow**, and then under **Content from this computer**, click **Excel Help**. In the search box, type **IF Function** and then press Enter. Click the link for **Nest a function within a function**.

3 Read the information that displays. When you are finished, close the Help window, and then **Close** Excel.

End **You have completed Project 3Q** ———————

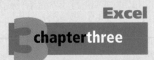

Excel

chapterthree

Group Business Running Case

Project 3R — Group Business Running Case

In this project, you will apply all the Objectives found in Projects 3A and 3B.

Your instructor may assign this group case project to your class. If your instructor assigns this project, he or she will provide you with information and instructions to work as part of a group. The group will apply the skills gained thus far to help the Bell Orchid Hotel Group achieve its business goals.

End **You have completed Project 3R** ——————————————

Glossary

Absolute cell reference A cell reference that refers to cells by their fixed position in a worksheet; an absolute cell reference remains the same when the formula is copied.

Accounting Number format The Excel number format that applies a thousand comma separator where appropriate, inserts a fixed U.S. dollar sign aligned at the left edge of the cell, applies two decimal places, and leaves a small amount of space at the right edge of the cell to accommodate a parenthesis for negative numbers.

Active cell The cell, surrounded by a black border, ready to receive data or be affected by the next Excel command.

Adjacent ranges Cell ranges that are next to each other.

Arguments The values that an Excel function uses to perform calculations or operations.

Arithmetic operator The symbols +, −, *, /, %, and ^ used to denote addition, subtraction (negation), multiplication, division, percentage, and exponentiation in an Excel formula.

Auto fill An Excel feature that extends values into adjacent cells based on the values of selected cells.

AutoComplete An Excel feature that speeds your typing and lessens the likelihood of errors; if the first few characters you type in a cell match an existing entry in the column, Excel fills in the remaining characters for you.

AutoCorrect An Excel feature that assists in your typing by automatically correcting and formatting some text as you type; for example Excel compares your typing to a list of commonly mistyped words and when it finds a match, it substitutes the correct word.

AutoSum Another term for the Sum function.

AVERAGE function A pre-written formula that adds a group of values and then divides the result by the number of values in the group.

Base The starting point when you divide the amount of increase by it to calculate the rate of increase.

Category axis The area along the bottom of a chart that identifies the categories of data; also referred to as the x-axis.

Category labels The labels that display along the bottom of a chart to identify the categories of data; Excel uses the row titles as the category names.

Cell In an Excel worksheet, the small box formed by the intersection of a column and a row.

Cell address Another name for a cell reference.

Cell content Anything typed into a cell.

Cell reference The identification of a specific cell by its intersecting column letter and row number.

Chart A graphic representation of data in a worksheet; data presented as a chart is usually easier to understand than a table of numbers.

Chart layout The combination of chart elements that can be displayed in a chart such as a title, legend, labels for the columns, and the table of charted cells.

Chart layouts gallery A group of predesigned chart layouts that you can apply to an Excel chart.

Chart sheet A workbook sheet that contains only a chart and is useful when you want to view a chart separately from the worksheet data.

Chart style The overall visual look of a chart in terms of its graphic effects, colors, and backgrounds; for example, you can have flat or beveled columns, colors that are solid or transparent, and backgrounds that are dark or light.

Chart styles gallery A group of predesigned chart styles that you can apply to an Excel chart.

Chart types Various chart formats used in a way that is meaningful to the reader; common examples are column charts, pie charts, and line charts.

Color scales Visual guides that help you understand data distribution and variation.

Column A vertical group of cells in a worksheet.

Column chart A chart in which the data is arranged in columns and which is useful for showing data changes over a period of time or for illustrating comparisons among items.

Column heading The letter that displays at the top of a vertical group of cells in a worksheet; beginning with the first letter of the alphabet, a unique letter or combination of letters identifies each column.

Comma style The Excel number format that inserts thousand comma separators where appropriate, applies two decimal places, and leaves space at the right to accommodate a parenthesis for negative numbers.

Comparison operators The symbols < (less than), > (greater than), and = (equal) that evaluate each field value to determine if it is the same, greater than, less than, or in between a range of values as specified by the criteria.

Conditional format A format that changes the appearance of a cell range—for example by adding cell shading or font color—based on a condition; if the condition is true the cell range is formatted based on that condition, and if the condition is false the cell range is *not* formatted based on the condition.

Constant value Numbers, text, dates, or times of day that you type into a cell.

Context sensitive Information or commands related to the current task.

Contextual tabs Tabs that are added to the Ribbon when a specific object, such as a chart, is selected, and that contain commands relevant to the selected object.

Contextual tools Sets of commands added to the Ribbon when a specific object is selected and which enable you to perform specific commands related to the selected object; contextual tools display only when needed and no longer display after the object is deselected.

COUNTIF function A statistical function that counts the number of cells within a range that meet the given condition—the criteria that you provide.

Criteria Conditions that you specify in a logical function.

Data Text or numbers in a cell.

Data bar A cell format consisting of a shaded bar that provides a visual cue to the reader about the value of a cell relative to other cells; the length of the bar represents the value in the cell—a longer bar represents a higher value and a shorter bar represents a lower value.

Data marker A column, bar, area, dot, pie slice, or other symbol in a chart that represents a single data point; related data points form a data series.

Data point A value that originates in a worksheet cell and that is represented in a chart by a data marker.

Data series Related data points represented by data markers; each data series has a unique color or pattern represented in the chart legend.

Data table A range of cells that shows how changing certain values in your formulas affects the results of those formulas, and which makes it easy to calculate multiple versions in one operation.

Detail worksheet Within a workbook of multiple worksheets, a worksheet that contains the details of information summarized on a summary worksheet.

Dialog Box Launcher A small icon that displays to the right of some group names on the Ribbon, and which opens a related dialog box or task pane providing additional options and commands related to that group.

Displayed value The data that displays in a cell.

Double-click The action of clicking the left mouse button twice in rapid succession while keeping the mouse still.

Drag The action of moving something from one location on the screen to another; the action of dragging includes releasing the mouse button at the desired time or location.

Drag and drop A method of moving or copying the content of selected cells in which you point to the selection and then drag it to a new location.

Edit The action of making changes in a worksheet or workbook.

Embedded chart A chart that displays as an object within a worksheet.

Excel table A series of rows and columns in a worksheet that contains related data, and that is managed independently from the data in other rows and columns in the worksheet.

Expand Formula Bar button An Excel window element with which you can increases the height of the Formula Bar for the purpose of displaying lengthy cell content.

Expand horizontal scroll bar button A button with which you can increase the width of the horizontal scroll bar.

Fill color The background color a cell.

Fill handle The small black square in the lower right corner of a selected cell.

Financial functions Prewritten formulas that perform common business calculations such as calculating a loan payment on a vehicle or calculating how much to save each month to buy something; financial functions commonly involve a period of time such as months or years.

Find and Replace A command that searches the cells in a worksheet—or in a selected range—for matches and then replaces each match with a replacement value of your choice.

Font A set of characters with the same design, size, and shape; the default font in Excel is Calibri.

Font size The size of characters in a font measured in points; there are 72 points in an inch, with 10 or 11 points being a typical font size in Excel.

Font style Formatting emphasis such as bold, italic, and underline.

Footers Text, graphics, or page numbers that print at the bottom of every page of a worksheet.

Format as you type The Excel feature by which a cell takes on the formatting of the number typed into the cell.

Format Painter An Excel feature with which you can copy the formatting of a specific cell to other cells.

Formatting The process of specifying the appearance of cells and the overall layout of a worksheet; accomplished through various commands on the Ribbon, many of which are also available using shortcut menus or keyboard shortcuts.

Formula An equation that performs mathematical calculations on values in a worksheet.

Formula AutoComplete An Excel feature which, after typing an = (equal sign) and the beginning letter or letters of a function name, displays a list of function names that match the typed letter(s), and from which you can insert the function by pointing to its name and pressing the Tab key or double-clicking.

Formula Bar An element in the Excel window that displays the value or formula contained in the active cell; here you can also enter or edit values or formulas.

Freeze Panes A command that enables you to select one or more rows or columns and freeze (lock) them into place; the locked rows and columns become separate panes.

Function A predefined formula—a formula that Excel has already built for you—that performs calculations by using specific values in a particular order.

Future value The value at the end of time periods in an Excel function; the cash balance you want to attain after the last payment is made—usually zero for loans.

Fv The abbreviation for *future value* in various Excel functions.

Gallery An Office 2007 feature that displays a list of potential results; it shows the results of commands rather than just the command name.

General format The default format that Excel applies to numbers; the general format has no specific characteristics—whatever you type in the cell will display, with the exception that trailing zeros to the right of a decimal point will not display.

Goal Seek One of Excel's What-If Analysis tools that provides a method to find a specific value for a cell by adjusting the value of one other cell.

Headers Text, graphics, or page numbers that print at the top of every page of a worksheet.

Help button A button at the far right of the Ribbon tabs that you click to display the program's Help window.

Horizontal window split box A small box with which you can splits the document into two horizontal views of the same document.

Icon set A collection of icons such as arrows, flags, bars, or circles that annotate and classify data into three to five categories separated by a threshold value. Each icon, for example a colored flag, represents a range of values. In the 3 Flags icon set, the red flag represents lower values, the yellow flag represents middle values, and the green flag represents higher values.

IF function A logical function that uses a logical test to check whether a condition is met, and then returns one value if true, and another value if false.

Insert Worksheet button Located on the row of sheet tabs, a sheet tab that inserts an additional worksheet into the workbook.

Interest The amount charged for the use of borrowed money.

Keyboard shortcut An individual keystroke or a combination of keys pressed simultaneously that can either access an Excel command or navigate to another location on your screen.

Landscape orientation A page orientation in which the printed page is wider than it is tall.

Left aligned The cell format in which characters align at the left edge of the cell; this is the default for text entries and is an example of formatting information stored in a cell.

Legend In a chart, an explanation of the patterns or colors that are assigned to a data series that represents a category.

Line chart A chart type that displays trends over time; time displays along the bottom axis and the data point values are connect with a line.

Live Preview A technology that shows the result of applying an editing or formatting change as you move your pointer over the results presented in a gallery.

Logical functions Pre-written formulas that test for specific conditions, and which typically use conditional tests to determine whether specified conditions, referred to as criteria, are true or false.

Logical test Any value or expression that can be evaluated as being true or false.

MAX function A statistical function that determines the largest value in a group of values.

MEDIAN function A statistical function commonly used to describe a group of data, and which finds the middle value in a group of values that has as many values above it in the group as are below it.

MIN function A statistical function that determines the smallest value in a group of values.

Mini toolbar A small toolbar containing frequently used formatting commands and which displays as a result of right-clicking or selecting cells; the toolbar fades when you move the mouse away and dismisses itself when you click outside of the toolbar.

Name Box An element of the Excel window that displays the name of the selected cell, table, chart, or object.

Navigate To move within a document or workbook.

Nonadjacent ranges Cell ranges that are not next to each other.

Normal view A screen view that maximizes the number of cells visible on your screen and keeps the column letters and row numbers close to the columns and rows.

NOW function A function within the *Date & Time* category that retrieves the date and time from your computer's calendar and clock and inserts the information into the selected cell.

Nper The abbreviation for *number of time periods* in various Excel functions.

Number format A specific way in which Excel displays numbers in a cell.

Office button The large button to the left of the Quick Access Toolbar that displays a list of commands related to things you can do *with* a workbook, such as opening, saving, printing, or sharing.

Office Clipboard A temporary storage area maintained by your Windows operating system.

One-variable data table A data table that changes the value in only one cell.

Operators The symbols with which you can specify the type of calculation you want to perform in an Excel formula.

Order of operations The mathematical rules for performing multiple calculations within a formula.

Page Layout view A screen view in which you can use the rulers to measure the width and height of data, set margins for printing, hide or display the numbered row headings and the lettered column headings, and change the page orientation; this view is useful for preparing your worksheet for printing.

Page orientation The position of your printed worksheet on paper—either portrait or landscape.

Pane A portion of a worksheet window bounded by and separated from other portions by vertical and horizontal bars.

Paste The action of placing cell contents that have been copied or moved to the Office Clipboard to another location.

Paste area The target destination for data that has been cut or copied using the Office Clipboard.

Paste Options button A button that displays in the lower right corner of a pasted selection and that displays a list of options that lets you determine how the information is pasted into your worksheet; the list varies depending on the type of content you are pasting and the program you are pasting from.

Paste Special A dialog box that offers various options for the manner in which you can paste the contents of the Office Clipboard into one or more cells; for example, you can paste the calculated result of a formula rather than the actual formula.

Percent for new value = base percent + percent of increase Formula for calculating a percentage by which a value increases by adding the base percentage—usually 100%—to the percent increase.

Percent rate of increase The percent by which one number increases over another.

Picture element A point of light measured in dots per square inch on a screen; sixty-four pixels equals 8.43 characters, which is the average number of digits that will fit in a cell using the default font.

Pie chart A type of chart that shows the relationship of each part to a whole.

Pixel An abbreviated name for picture element.

PMT function An Excel function that calculates the payment for a loan based on constant payments and at a constant rate of interest.

Point The action of moving the mouse pointer over something on the screen.

Point and click method The technique of constructing a formula by pointing to and then clicking cells; this method is convenient when the referenced cells are not adjacent to one another.

Points The unit of measure for font size; one point is equal to 1/72 of an inch.

Portrait orientation A page orientation in which the printed page is taller than it is wide.

Present value The total amount that a series of future payments is worth now; also known as the principal.

Principal Another term for present value.

Program-level buttons Buttons at the far right of the title bar that minimize, restore, or close the program.

Pt. An abbreviation for point.

Pv The abbreviation for *present value* in various Excel functions.

Quick Access Toolbar A small toolbar in the upper left corner of the program window that displays buttons to perform frequently used commands with a single click.

Range Two or more selected cells on a worksheet that are adjacent or nonadjacent; because the range is treated as a single unit, you can make the same change, or combination of changes, to more than one cell at a time.

Range finder An Excel feature that outlines cells in color to indicate which cells are used in a formula; useful for verifying which cells are referenced in a formula or for quickly positioning the insertion point within the cell to perform editing directly in the cell.

Rate In the Excel PMT function, the term used to indicate the interest rate for a loan.

Rate = amount of increase/base The mathematical formula to calculate a rate of increase.

Relative cell reference In a formula, the address of a cell based on the relative position of the cell that contains the formula and the cell referred to.

Ribbon The user interface in Office 2007 that groups the commands for performing related tasks on tabs across the upper portion of the program window.

Right-click The action of clicking the right mouse button.

Rounding A procedure in which you determine which digit at the right of the number will be the last digit displayed and then increase it by one if the next digit to its right is 5, 6, 7, 8, or 9.

Row A horizontal group of cells in a worksheet.

Row headings The numbers along the left side of an Excel worksheet that designate the row numbers.

ScreenTip A small box that displays useful information when you perform various mouse actions such as pointing to screen elements or dragging.

Scroll box The box in the vertical and horizontal scroll bars that can be dragged to reposition the worksheet on the screen. The size of the scroll box also indicates the relative size of the worksheet and provides a visual indication of your location in a worksheet.

Select Highlighting, by clicking or dragging with your mouse, one or more cells so that the selected cells can be edited, formatted, copied, or moved; selected cells are indicated by a dark border.

Select All box A box in the upper left corner of the worksheet grid that selects all the cells in a worksheet.

Series A group of things that come one after another in succession; for example, January, February, March, and so on.

Serif A font design that includes small line extensions on the ends of the letters to guide the eye in reading from left to right.

Sheet tab The labels along the lower border of the worksheet window that identify each worksheet.

Sheet tab scrolling buttons Buttons to the left of the sheet tabs used to display Excel sheet tabs that are not in view; used when there are more sheet tabs than will display in the space provided.

Shortcut menu A menu that displays a quick way to activate the most commonly used commands for a selected area.

Spin box A small box with an upward- and downward-pointing arrow that lets you move rapidly through a set of values by clicking.

Spreadsheet Another name for a worksheet.

Statistical functions Pre-written formulas that analyze a group of measurements.

Status bar The area along the lower edge of the program window that displays, on the left side, the current mode, page number, and document information, and on the right side, displays buttons to control how the window looks.

Sum An Excel function (prewritten formula) that sums the numbers in a selected range of cells.

SUM function A predefined formula that adds all the numbers in a selected range of cells.

Theme A predefined set of colors, fonts, lines, and fill effects that look good together and that can be applied to your entire workbook or to specific items—for example to a chart or table.

Three-color scale Compares a range of cells by using a gradation of three colors; the shades represent higher, middle, or lower values. For example, in a green, yellow, and red color scale, you can specify higher value cells with the green color, middle value cells with the yellow color, and lower value cells with the red color.

Title bar The bar at the top edge of the program window that indicates the name of the current workbook and the program name.

Toggle buttons Features in which clicking one time turns the feature on and clicking again turns the feature off.

Top/Bottom Rules Enable you to apply conditional formatting to the highest and lowest values in a range of cells. For example, you can identify the top 5 selling products or the top 25 salaries in a personnel analysis.

Two-color scale Compares a range of cells by using a gradation of two colors. The shade of the color represents higher or lower values. For example, in a green and red color scale, you can specify one color to show higher value cells and the other color to specify lower value cells.

Two-variable data table A data table that changes the values in two cells.

Type argument An optional argument in the PMT function that assumes that the payment will be made at the end of each time period.

Underlying formula The formula entered in a cell and visible only on the Formula Bar.

Underlying value The data that displays in the Formula Bar.

Value Another name for constant value.

Value after increase = base × percent for new value Formula for calculating the value after an increase by multiplying the original value—the base—by the percent for new value (see the *Percent for new value* formula).

Value axis A numerical scale on the left side of a chart that shows the range of numbers for the data points; also referred to as the Y-axis.

Vertical window split box A small box on the vertical scroll bar with which you can split the window into two vertical views of the same document.

View options Buttons on the right side of the status bar for viewing in normal, page layout view, or page break preview; also displays controls for zoom out and zoom in.

Volatile A term used to describe an Excel function that is subject to change each time the workbook is reopened; for example, the NOW function updates itself to the current date and time each time the workbook is opened.

What-if analysis The process of changing the values in cells to see how those changes affect the outcome of formulas in your worksheet.

Workbook An Excel file that contains one or more worksheets.

Workbook-level buttons Buttons at the far right of the Ribbon tabs used to minimize or restore a displayed workbook.

Worksheet The primary document that you use in Excel to store and work with data, and which is formatted as a pattern of uniformly spaced horizontal and vertical lines.

Worksheet grid The area of the Excel window that displays the columns and rows that intersect to form the cells of the worksheet.

X-axis Another name for the category axis.

Y-axis Another name for the value axis.

Index

The CD symbol represents Index entries found on the CD (See CD file name for page numbers).

SINGLE PC LICENSE AGREEMENT AND LIMITED WARRANTY

READ THIS LICENSE CAREFULLY BEFORE OPENING THIS PACKAGE. BY OPENING THIS PACKAGE, YOU ARE AGREEING TO THE TERMS AND CONDITIONS OF THIS LICENSE. IF YOU DO NOT AGREE, DO NOT OPEN THE PACKAGE. PROMPTLY RETURN THE UNOPENED PACKAGE AND ALL ACCOMPANYING ITEMS TO THE PLACE YOU OBTAINED THEM. *THESE TERMS APPLY TO ALL LICENSED SOFTWARE ON THE DISK EXCEPT THAT THE TERMS FOR USE OF ANY SHAREWARE OR FREEWARE ON THE DISKETTES ARE AS SET FORTH IN THE ELECTRONIC LICENSE LOCATED ON THE DISK:*

1. GRANT OF LICENSE and OWNERSHIP: The enclosed computer programs ("Software") are licensed, not sold, to you by Prentice-Hall, Inc. ("We" or the "Company") and in consideration of your purchase or adoption of the accompanying Company textbooks and/or other materials, and your agreement to these terms. We reserve any rights not granted to you. You own only the disk(s) but we and/or our licensors own the Software itself. This license allows you to use and display your copy of the Software on a single computer (i.e., with a single CPU) at a single location for academic use only, so long as you comply with the terms of this Agreement. You may make one copy for back up, or transfer your copy to another CPU, provided that the Software is usable on only one computer.

2. RESTRICTIONS: You may not transfer or distribute the Software or documentation to anyone else. Except for backup, you may not copy the documentation or the Software. You may not network the Software or otherwise use it on more than one computer or computer terminal at the same time. You may not reverse engineer, disassemble, decompile, modify, adapt, translate, or create derivative works based on the Software or the Documentation. You may be held legally responsible for any copying or copyright infringement which is caused by your failure to abide by the terms of these restrictions.

3. TERMINATION: This license is effective until terminated. This license will terminate automatically without notice from the Company if you fail to comply with any provisions or limitations of this license. Upon termination, you shall destroy the Documentation and all copies of the Software. All provisions of this Agreement as to limitation and disclaimer of warranties, limitation of liability, remedies or damages, and our ownership rights shall survive termination.

4. DISCLAIMER OF WARRANTY: THE COMPANY AND ITS LICENSORS MAKE NO WARRANTIES ABOUT THE SOFTWARE, WHICH IS PROVIDED "AS-IS." IF THE DISK IS DEFECTIVE IN MATERIALS OR WORKMANSHIP, YOUR ONLY REMEDY IS TO RETURN IT TO THE COMPANY WITHIN 30 DAYS FOR REPLACEMENT UNLESS THE COMPANY DETERMINES IN GOOD FAITH THAT THE DISK HAS BEEN MISUSED OR IMPROPERLY INSTALLED, REPAIRED, ALTERED OR DAMAGED. THE COMPANY DISCLAIMS ALL WARRANTIES, EXPRESS OR IMPLIED, INCLUDING WITHOUT LIMITATION, THE IMPLIED WARRANTIES OF MERCHANTABILITY AND FITNESS FOR A PARTICULAR PURPOSE. THE COMPANY DOES NOT WARRANT, GUARANTEE OR MAKE ANY REPRESENTATION REGARDING THE ACCURACY, RELIABILITY, CURRENTNESS, USE, OR RESULTS OF USE, OF THE SOFTWARE.

5. LIMITATION OF REMEDIES AND DAMAGES: IN NO EVENT, SHALL THE COMPANY OR ITS EMPLOYEES, AGENTS, LICENSORS OR CONTRACTORS BE LIABLE FOR ANY INCIDENTAL, INDIRECT, SPECIAL OR CONSEQUENTIAL DAMAGES ARISING OUT OF OR IN CONNECTION WITH THIS LICENSE OR THE SOFTWARE, INCLUDING, WITHOUT LIMITATION, LOSS OF USE, LOSS OF DATA, LOSS OF INCOME OR PROFIT, OR OTHER LOSSES SUSTAINED AS A RESULT OF INJURY TO ANY PERSON, OR LOSS OF OR DAMAGE TO PROPERTY, OR CLAIMS OF THIRD PARTIES, EVEN IF THE COMPANY OR AN AUTHORIZED REPRESENTATIVE OF THE COMPANY HAS BEEN ADVISED OF THE POSSIBILITY OF SUCH DAMAGES. SOME JURISDICTIONS DO NOT ALLOW THE LIMITATION OF DAMAGES IN CERTAIN CIRCUMSTANCES, SO THE ABOVE LIMITATIONS MAY NOT ALWAYS APPLY.

6. GENERAL: THIS AGREEMENT SHALL BE CONSTRUED IN ACCORDANCE WITH THE LAWS OF THE UNITED STATES OF AMERICA AND THE STATE OF NEW YORK, APPLICABLE TO CONTRACTS MADE IN NEW YORK, AND SHALL BENEFIT THE COMPANY, ITS AFFILIATES AND ASSIGNEES. This Agreement is the complete and exclusive statement of the agreement between you and the Company and supersedes all proposals, prior agreements, oral or written, and any other communications between you and the company or any of its representatives relating to the subject matter. If you are a U.S. Government user, this Software is licensed with "restricted rights" as set forth in subparagraphs (a)-(d) of the Commercial Computer-Restricted Rights clause at FAR 52.227-19 or in subparagraphs (c)(1)(ii) of the Rights in Technical Data and Computer Software clause at DFARS 252.227-7013, and similar clauses, as applicable.

Should you have any questions concerning this agreement or if you wish to contact the Company for any reason, please contact in writing:

Multimedia Production
Higher Education Division
Prentice-Hall, Inc.
1 Lake Street
Upper Saddle River NJ 07458